Connecting JavaBeans™ with InfoBus™

Reaz Hoque

WILEY COMPUTER PUBLISHING

John Wiley & Sons, Inc.

New York • Chichester • Weinheim • Brisbane • Singapore • Toronto

Publisher: Robert Ipsen
Editor: Theresa Hudson
Assistant Editor: Kathryn A. Malm
Managing Editor: Marnie Wielage
Electronic Products, Associate Editor: Mike Sosa
Text Design & Composition: Benchmark Productions, Inc.

Designations used by companies to distinguish their products are often claimed as trademarks. In all instances where John Wiley & Sons, Inc., is aware of a claim, the product names appear in initial capital or ALL CAPITAL LETTERS. Readers, however, should contact the appropriate companies for more complete information regarding trademarks and registration.

This book is printed on acid-free paper. ⊗

This publication is designed to provide accurate and authoritative information in regard to the subject matter covered. It is sold with the understanding that the publisher is not engaged in professional services. If professional advice or other expert assistance is required, the services of a competent professional person should be sought.

Library of Congress Cataloging-in-Publication Data
Hoque, Reaz.
    Connecting JavaBeans with InfoBus / Reaz Hoque.
      p. cm.
    "Wiley Computer Publishing."
    Includes index.
    ISBN 0-471-29652-X (paper/CD-ROM)
    1. Application program interfaces (Computer software)
  2. JavaBeans. 3. InfoBus (Computer file) 4. Java (Computer program language) I. Title.

QA76.76.A65H67 1998
005.13'3--dc21   98-30224
                                                                  CIP

Printed in the United States of America.

10 9 8 7 6 5 4 3 2 1

There are many smart people who cannot contribute to this world because of a lack of opportunities. I dedicate this book to those who are fighting every day to survive, and who wait for that break of their lives. I salute those especially in countries like Bangladesh and Somalia who must worry each day about what will happen tomorrow. God bless you!

Contents

Preface

If you are an enterprise developer, you know very well that the industry is embracing Java more than ever. Now the question is not "When do we adopt Java?" but rather "How quickly can we adapt Java?" Among Sun Microsystems' many Java specs and tools, an interesting technology has emerged—JavaBeans. JavaBeans are components that let developers write applications easily. Imagine if you were in charge of decorating a living room. If you had to build every piece of furniture from scratch using raw materials, you would drive yourself crazy. Instead, you want to get the chairs, tables, TV, and everything else to put together a nice setup for the room. JavaBeans work the same way. Beans, or components, are prewritten and you write supporting code to put together the application with these components. Using this process means that you write less code (you can usually reuse a lot of components written by others) and have more time to customize the application for your own needs.

While you create JavaBeans to independently perform specific tasks such as spell check, search, and so forth, InfoBus allows JavaBeans to communicate among each other. Say you create a word processor and have all of these Beans that can perform particular tasks (e.g., create a template, cut and paste, etc.), you still need to write a certain amount of code to ensure that all Beans work together without any conflict. This is where InfoBus comes into the picture. InfoBus helps Beans exchange dynamic data. Because the InfoBus article is simple yet powerful, it's equipped to handle real workflow for multiple components in a web application. The best part of InfoBus is that with this technology it's possible to pass large amounts of data of various types between JavaBeans. For example, one database can have multiple types of data that originate from various databases and this data can all be dynamic. They can be generated depending on the database specifications by the developer. Instead of manually connecting Beans with scripts, today with InfoBus, corporate developers can use this client-side technology to create mission-critical applications faster.

WHAT TO EXPECT FROM THIS BOOK

This book is for those programmers and developers who are not familiar with InfoBus and know only a little bit about JavaBeans. We start with a chapter on JavaBeans (Chapter 1) and show you how to create Beans from scratch. Next we give an introduction to the InfoBus technology. We tell you what it is and provide an overview of the whole architecture. We cover the business prospective and the potential of the technology.

In Chapters 3 through 5, we cover all the details about InfoBus. We talk about InfoBus members, event hierarchy, and data items. We also supply code snippets to make sure that you understand everything you need to write component-based applications using InfoBus. The code snippets are mostly for conceptual purposes; therefore, we have tried to keep them as simple as possible.

The last four chapters, Chapters 6 through 9, are dedicated to developing industry-standard applications with InfoBus. We provide step-by-step descriptions for each example in the book. To make sure that we cover some practical scenarios, we show you how to use InfoBus with CORBA, RMI, and JDBC. These applications are useful for serious corporate developers who use these cutting-edge technologies regularly.

WHO SHOULD READ THIS BOOK?

The book assumes prior knowledge about object orientation, C++, or Java. If you are not familiar with these technologies, you should pick up a copy of a C++ or Java book before you dive into this one. The chapters on RMI, JDBC, and CORBA assume that you are familiar with relational databases and distributed technologies.

This book is for you if you are:

- An intranet/Internet/extranet application developer who wants to create mission-critical, cross-platform, component-based applications.
- Learning how distributed objects work.
- A software developer who wants to learn how to work with RMI, JDBC, and CORBA together with InfoBus.
- A student or researcher who wants to keep up with cutting-edge object technology.

CONVENTIONS USED IN THE BOOK

There are two simple conventions used to get your attention throughout the text. They are:

NOTES that are used to point out something of importance or where you should take extra care.

TIPS that provide suggestions on certain topics. They are used to ensure that you can perform a task easily if you follow the TIP's suggestion.

The authors of this book have done their best to present the InfoBus technology in an-easy-to-understand fashion. We hope that the book will help you to create practical enterprise applications that are scaleable and user friendly.

Lastly, many of us are public speakers who speak at the major industry conferences. Please feel free to give us your comments about the book if you see us. Happy coding . . .

Acknowledgments

First of all, I would like to thank my publisher, who has done a great job of making this book a success. I especially thank my editor, Terri Hudson, and her assistant, Gerrie Cho, for their constant help and feedback.

Peter Rive and I spent hours creating a table of contents that would make this book an interesting read. Although Peter couldn't help me write the actual book, I thank him for his help on this project and wish him all the best. I am sure we will be able to work together on another book someday soon.

Next I would like to thank the team I have worked with during the long process. Without Vishal Anand, Sukanta Ganguly, John Baum (let's go hang out sometime now that we are done!), Mark Colan, Jim Alateras, and Darren Govoni's help this book would not be possible. They took the project very seriously and did their very best to help make it a success.

I would like to extend my thanks to those who gave me permission to include software for the accompanying CD-ROM: IBM's Sheila Richardson, Bill Reichle, and Terry McElroy were all a great help. Thanks also to Iona's Sarah Lima for helping me get the OrbixWeb and Orbix 2 software.

Thanks to my family and friends who were my constant support. As always, my parents, Faisal Hoque and his wife Christine, will always have a special place in my heart. Thanks to my friends and colleagues

Rahat Wahid, Reshma and Tarun Sharma, Adel Khan, Azzama, Ed Zhang, Erik Krock, John Small, and many others who have always wished me well.

I know that I am very fortunate to be able to do all of the things that I do today. I understand that they happen because of God's mercy. Thanks to the Almighty one for all the good things that have happened to my life lately.

About the Author

REAZ HOQUE

Reaz Hoque is an author, consultant, and a technology evangelist who specializes in the latest Internet technologies. At the time of this writing, he was working as a technical engineer for an e-commerce company called EcCubed. Prior to joining EcCubed, Reaz worked as a technology evangelist for Netscape Communications Corporation where he wrote sample code and technical articles on Netscape Technologies. In 1996, Reaz was involved in creating one of the first online e-commerce web applications for General Electronics' startup company called FGIC Public Sourcing Services. With his many years of Internet experience, he has developed a number of web applications and has worked with some of the hottest development tools today. Reaz has presented at many conferences including Netscape's DevCon, Software Development '97, Web Design '97, Object Expo '98, Internet World, and Web '98.

Reaz contributes web-related articles for online and print magazines around the world. Some of his articles have been seen in Netscape's *DevEdge Site* (www.developer.netscape.com), *ZD Internet Magazine*, *Web Techniques*, *Internet World*, and *NetscapeWorld*. His other books include *Practical JavaScript Programming* (IDG Books, 1997), *Programming Web Components* (McGraw-Hill, 1998), *CORBA 3* (IDG Books, 1998), *JavaBeans 1.1 Handbook* (McGraw-Hill, 1998), and *CORBA for Real Programmers* (AP Professional, 1998).

ABOUT THE CONTRIBUTING AUTHORS

Vishal Anand

Vishal Anand is a software engineer and object-oriented design consultant who specializes in NT and C++ programming. He maintains a developer's forum on the Internet where he answers questions on C++, MFC/SDK, and NT-related issues. He also does consulting on web technologies and is often found helping friends and foes develop web sites. Anand graduated with a bachelor of engineering degree in computer science from Delhi Institute of Technology. He enjoys reading humor and going for long drives with his wife Priya.

Sukanta Ganguly

Sukanta Ganguly has been in the computing profession for the past eight years, and has been involved with distributed computing for the past three years. Among his passions are compilers, interpreters, and programming languages. He has spent many long hours studying the different types of distributed development environments and platforms and also possesses a strong attraction to operating systems and databases. He is lucky enough to have a strong and supportive wife and the blessings of his parents.

John Baum

John Baum is a project manager with Cambridge Technology Partners (CTP). His primary technical focus is in CORBA, Java, and distributed objects, and he has lead a number of projects delivering enterprise systems based on the technology. When not running a project with an insane deadline, he can be found motorcycling on a winding mountain road or dropping into "some steeps" on the ski slopes. John currently lives in San Francisco with his wonderful wife Alice and his daughter Stephanie.

Darren Govoni

Darren Govoni, a Virginia Tech graduate, is currently a senior software engineer specializing in distributed application technologies using Java. His research efforts focus on distributed architectures and large, scalable framework designs that utilize object persistence and mobile agent technologies. He has contributed to various online and print publications and is currently working on his next book project.

CHAPTER 1

JavaBeans and Java Applets

Welcome to the world of Java! Well, the welcoming statement was sooth-ing enough, but what is the world of Java and, more importantly, why does everybody talk about it? Good questions indeed, and obviously I have even more exhilarating answers to them. Java is virtually every-where in this world; look around and you will see the proof. It is being used in most of the prominent aspects of computer science. People are using Java to write applets to put up on their web pages. Java is being used to write portable applications that run on multiple platforms. Embedded Java processors are being discussed and worked on for ded-icated devices. We even hear talk about JavaOS. Java is being used for writing applications ranging from very simple applets doing ordinary animation to complex system like compilers, huge data processing appli-cations, operating systems, and more. It is a good example of a *"write once, run many"* type of application. We all know by experience that such systems are in great demand. Many of us have spent countless hours writing applications on one platform and then porting them to another. Most of the operating environments support Java today, and almost all web browsers are Java aware.

Today, Java is not just a programming language, it also supports distributed architectures and hence is being used in those types of work. Java embraced web technology and has made the lives of many web-based programmers easy. This chapter discusses some of its features, provides a simple explanation of Java, and then takes a detour and focuses on Java applets and JavaBeans. If you are already familiar with Java and JavaBeans, we suggest that you go right to Chapter 2, "Say Hello to InfoBus." If you are not very familiar with Java, this chapter is a good start, but you should also consider purchasing other Java- and JavaBeans-specific books to master the two technologies.

This chapter covers the following topics:

- A Little about Java
- What Are Java Applets?
- What Are JavaBeans?
- Where Is Java Heading Today?

A LITTLE ABOUT JAVA

Java is an object-oriented programming language. It is also a programming environment of its own. It is generic in nature and can be used for multiple purposes. The Java environment incorporates a *virtual machine*, which is needed to run a Java executable. The virtual machine is an intermediate layer that interprets the code during runtime and lets the execution happen. The Java Virtual Machine (JVM), just like actual machine architecture, has a well-defined architecture, instruction set, operating registers, and address space. It controls the execution of the Java executable. The virtual machine itself is a systems program that executes on an operating system. This is exactly how Java manages to have portability among different operating systems.

Java has something called *bytecodes*. Every Java program compiled with the Java compiler is converted into bytecodes. Bytecodes are platform independent and are executed by the JVM. The JVM is present nowadays in most popular operating systems, and Java programs can work on them. Java also has an interface for native calls, which can be used if absolutely necessary. This, however, is not encouraged as it defies the whole purpose of program portability. If a Java application is written on Windows NT and makes Windows-specific calls using the native interface, it is impossible to make this Java application execute on a Solaris machine without modifying the source code.

The Java environment supports two types of executable: the *application* and the *applet*. There are some differences between them and the way in which they are organized. They also differ in their execution strategy. A Java application can be executed from the command line. Every Java application has an entry point called *main*, which indicates the starting point of program execution. This is identical to applications written in *C* or *C++*, where *main* is the point at which execution begins. The Java application has to first be compiled with the *javac* compiler provided in the Java Development Kit (JDK). To run a Java application, we have to use the tool (also provided in the JDK) called *java*. Since Java needs the virtual machine to execute, the virtual machine must be loaded so the execution can start. The JVM is a fairly compact program and does not have a huge memory footprint; hence, it is being used in many dedicated devices. Such devices have the JVM programmed within the programmable read-only memory. The small footprint of the virtual machine acts as a boon to these types of working environments. There is a lot to discuss about developing applications in Java, but in this chapter we concentrate on Java applets. Let's take a look at them now.

WHAT IS A JAVA APPLET?

The use of applets in web programming has become one of the most popular uses of Java and has greatly simplified what was once a lengthy and sometimes tedious task. Applets were introduced with the idea of having them executed from within web browsers. Web browsers understand HTML; hence, in order to make applets work with web browsers they need to be embedded within the web documents (which are HTML files). This led to the creation of a new tag that was introduced in HTML. The JDK also comes with a tool called *applet viewer* that could be used to execute an applet.

The applet is a very good way of making web pages on web servers much more active. It helps in data transfers from the client machines to the remote servers, and vice versa. The methodology followed during the process is safe and secure. With the help of applets, vendors can put the active components on their web pages, allowing them to perform business transactions relatively easily in the absence of a human being. Java applets adhere to the Java security rules, and clients can rely on the integrity of the programs. They can rest assured that no malicious code has been downloaded from a remote site, which may corrupt their systems.

Unlike the Java applications, an applet does not have a specific entry point. It does not need a *"main"* method. The source code, written in Java, is compiled with the Java compiler to produce the bytecode. The compiled version of the applet has to have an extension of .*class* (e.g., if *foo.java* is the name of your source file, then after compilation the output obtained would be named *foo.class*). This class file has to be embedded within an HTML document to be executed by the web browser. Once the applet is ready, it is embedded within the web page using the *applet* and */applet* HTML tag.

Java, being object oriented, has classes. New classes can be created by extending the previously existing classes. Every Java applet starts by extending the java.applet.Applet class, which needs to be the base class of all the applets because it provides the base functionality. If you are familiar with C++ you know that in C++ we create class definition and generally place it in the header file. The header file stores the class prototype. The implementation of the class is generally present within a C++ source file. The header file and the C++ source file together become the complete class definition. In Java, there is no such thing as a header file. The classes are defined and implemented at the same source file.

A Primer on Creating a Java Applet

Listing 1.1 is the source for our very first Java applet. In about three to four pages of the chapter we already have our first applet ready (that is because this book is right to the point; it doesn't patronize a fast learner like you!). Isn't it exciting?

LISTING 1.1   A Simple Java Applet's Source Code

```
/*
A basic extension of the java.applet.Applet class
*/

import java.awt.*;
import java.applet.*;

import symantec.itools.multimedia.Firework;

public class Ex1 extends Applet
{
public void init()
{
   symantec.itools.lang.Context.setApplet(this);

   setLayout(null);
```

LISTING 1.1 *Continued*

```
    setSize(307,176);

    setBackground(new Color(12632256));

    label1 =
    new java.awt.Label("Welcome to the World of Java Applets");


    label1.setBounds(48,72,216,34);

    add(label1);

    firework1 = new symantec.itools.multimedia.Firework();

    firework1.setBounds(84,12,87,29);

    add(firework1);
}

    java.awt.Label label1;

    symantec.itools.multimedia.Firework firework1;
}
```

The first three lines in the source file are import statements. They are a way of informing the system what classes are to be used within this file. From these lines of code, the system knows that these classes are not defined here in the listing, but are imported from other class files. In the program, instances of those classes are used and their methods are called. The first two imports are standard classes shipped with the JDK, and the third import statement is for a Symantec multimedia object class. We know by now that all Java applets start by extending the java.applet.Applet class, which is exactly how we start our Applet class Ex1. The Applet class has many methods. In this example, we are overriding the *init* method (the initialization method). The browser calls this method of the applet (the applet does not call it). When the browser first loads the applet it calls the *init* method. If the applet has overridden the *init* method (as in our case), then the applet-specific initialization is performed. Most of the applets will override the *init* method to perform their custom initialization.

TIP We have used Symantec's VisualCafé for the development of the example in Listing 1.1. If you haven't used this tool, you should know that the integrated development environment is very handy and assists in the development of Java-based applications as well as applets. Such tools have all the development procedures nicely planned. For instance, most of the integrated development environments have the compilers available from within the tool, and the developer can write the source in the provided editor and start building them instantly. The debugger is also provided from within the tool. Most such tool vendors also provide their own custom class libraries, which can be used in the development process, thereby eliminating the need to develop the classes from scratch. In our first example we notice that one of Symantec's multimedia classes has been used. For more information on the software, visit Symantec's Web site at www.symantec.com.

NOTE Every method in the Applet class has a default implementation. If a particular method of the Applet class is not overridden, the default implementation is used. We will see some other methods of the Applet class later in the chapter.

Inside our *init* method we set the layout and the size of the applet. The size of the applet is the size of the applet window on the screen. We also set the background color of the applet. We used Symantec's class to set the applet with the *this* pointer, which sets the language context for the applet. At the bottom of the source code you see that two objects are declared. The first object is called label1, which is of type java.awt.Label, and the second object is called firework1, which is of type symantec.itools.multimedia.Firework. The label object is used to display the string "Welcome to the World of Java Applets" and is constructed using the string parameter. This object displays a static text. The second object is used to display the fireworks display on the screen. It is a multimedia object. We use the *new* keyword to create an instance of these objects.

Every object within the applet has to be assigned a position on the screen, within the bounds of the applet. Once the position and all required attributes of the object are set we add it to the applet. The addition of the objects to the applet is accomplished using the *add* method. These objects are created within our *init* method for custom initialization. There are other methods that we can override, but we haven't gotten to that level of complexity in our first example. We are not finished yet! We have just completed our applet coding. Now we have to compile our applet using the Java compiler. The output generated is called Ex1.class. We then have an HTML file wherein we embed our class file. Let's call the HTML file Ex1.html. Without going into the details of explaining the HTML syntax, we look into the syntax that is applicable for our Java applet. Within the HTML file we see a line with the applet tag.

```
<APPLET CODE = Ex1.class WIDTH=307 HEIGHT=176></APPLET>
```

This line tells the web browser that the applet code is called Ex1.class and has a specified width and height. The width and the height parameters are expressed in pixels and tell the browser the amount of space to be left unused around the applet. We then execute the HTML file using the appletviewer. Get ready to see your first new applet. Behold your eyes, ladies and gentlemen, here it comes. Isn't it great?

Since java.applet.Applet is the heart of all applets in the world it would be smart on our part to dissect this class and understand it well. This will give us an insight to the basics of the applets. Take a look at Listing 1.2.

LISTING 1.2   java.applet.Applet

```
public class Applet extends Panel
{

transient private AppletStub stub;

public final void setStub(AppletStub stub)
{                                                    Continues
```

LISTING 1.2   java.applet.Applet *(Continued)*

```
    this.stub = (AppletStub)stub;
  }

  public boolean isActive()
  {
    if (stub != null)
    {
      return stub.isActive();
    }
    else
    {
      return false;
    }
  }

  public URL getDocumentBase()
  {
    return stub.getDocumentBase();
  }

  public URL getCodeBase()
  {
    return stub.getCodeBase();
  }

  public String getParameter(String name)
  {
    return stub.getParameter(name);
  }

  public AppletContext getAppletContext()
  {
    return stub.getAppletContext();
  }

  public void resize(int width, int height)
  {
    Dimension d = size();
    if ((d.width != width) || (d.height != height))
    {
```

LISTING 1.2 *Continued*

```java
      super.resize(width, height);
      if (stub != null)
      {
        stub.appletResize(width, height);
      }
    }
  }

public void resize(Dimension d)
{
  resize(d.width, d.height);
}

public void showStatus(String msg)
{
  getAppletContext().showStatus(msg);
}

public Image getImage(URL url)
{
  return getAppletContext().getImage(url);
}

public Image getImage(URL url, String name)
{
  try
  {
    return getImage(new URL(url, name));
  }
  catch (MalformedURLException e)
  {
    return null;
  }
}

public AudioClip getAudioClip(URL url)
{
  return getAppletContext().getAudioClip(url);
}
```

Continues

LISTING 1.2   java.applet.Applet *(Continued)*

```
public AudioClip getAudioClip(URL url, String name)
{
  try
  {
    return getAudioClip(new URL(url, name));
  }
  catch (MalformedURLException e)
  {
    return null;
    }
}

public String getAppletInfo()
{
  return null;
}

public Locale getLocale()
{
  Locale locale = super.getLocale();
  if (locale == null)
  {
    return Locale.getDefault();
  }
  return locale;
}

public String[][] getParameterInfo()
{
  return null;
}

public void play(URL url)
{
  AudioClip clip = getAudioClip(url);
  if (clip != null)
  {
    clip.play();
  }
}
```

LISTING 1.2 *Continued*

```
public void play(URL url, String name)
{
  AudioClip clip = getAudioClip(url, name);
  if (clip != null)
  {
    clip.play();
  }
}

public void init()
{
}

public void start()
{
}

public void stop()
{
}

public void destroy()
{
}
}
```

The preceding code is picked up from the Applet.java class supplied by the JDK. When we start writing our applets, we extend the Applet.java class. It is a very good idea to familiarize ourselves with the methods available in the class as we will need them for writing other applets. The first thing we observe within the class is the private data member called the *stub*. It is of type AppletStub class and is transient. The AppletStub class maintains an interface of the applet with its environment. This can be a browser or an applet viewer. The interface is used to manage the state of the applet, whether active or inactive. As we will find out later, there are methods within the Applet class that are called from the operating environment to activate and deactivate them. The setStub does the linking and is called automatically. The isActive method informs the caller whether the applet is in active state or not. If the stub data member is not initialized it causes an error condition, implying a proper initialization is not performed and the system cannot be relied upon. The check for the state of the applet is passed onto it as the AppletStub manages the interface. The AppletStub class maintains the relationship between the applet and the environment on which it is functioning.

Because an applet is loaded via an HTML page, it has a base URL associated with it. The getDocumentBase method returns the base URL associated with the applet. The getCodeBase method returns the *codebase* of the applet. A codebase is a URL of the Applet class. This is one of the attributes of the <applet></applet> HTML tag. We have seen in our first example that CODE=Ex1.class tells the browser the name of the class file, but the class file can be located at a different site than the current directory. It can either be in another subdirectory on the machine or somewhere on the Internet or the local intranet. In such cases we would want to provide the right URL of the class file. The CODEBASE construct is used for this purpose. The getParameter method returns the parameters passed to the applet via the HTML file. The getAppletContext method returns the context of the applet. The context of the applet comprises with the environment on which it is executing. It also consists of the document in which the applet is present. This document may also have other applets embedded in it. AppletContext is an interface class of its own. All this information is originally made available to the browser with the help of the HTML file. The browser provides this information to the AppletStub class linked to the applet object.

Next, we arrive at some applet resizing methods. Actually, the *resize* method is polymorphic and has two forms depending on the way the parameters are passed while invoking them. The first form takes the width and the height as separate parameters, and the second form takes a dimension that has the width and the height embedded in it. Both of them directly or indirectly call the appletResize method from the stub interface. The *showStatus* method returns the applet's current status. This can be used to display on the status window. While the applet is performing a particular operation, it is a good idea to indicate the status to the user.

The *getImage* method is also polymorphic and has two forms. It returns the image object specified by the URL, which is passed as an input parameter. This does not download the image object immediately.

The image is downloaded only when the painting of the image begins on the screen. The downloading of the image is done in an incremental fashion. The first form of the *getImage* method takes in the absolute URL for the image to be activated. The second form of the *getImage* method takes in two parameters, the first being just the URL of the site that contains the image and the second being the name of the image file. Basically, the second form of the *getImage* method generates the absolute URL object consisting of the complete address and the image filename.

The *getAudioClip* method is somewhat similar to the *getImage* method. It has two forms and returns the audio clip object. It does not start playing the clip immediately. The clip has to be played separately with the help of the *AudioClip* method. The actual audio clip is downloaded when it starts playing it or when the audio clip is activated. The *getAppletInfo* method returns the information about the applet. This method needs to be overridden by the developer of the applet to return the applet-specific information. For instance, this is a perfect place for the author of the applet to specify the details about the applet, its version, any copyright messages, or any marketing talks about the developers, the developing company, and so on. This information in this area is totally at the discretion of the developing parties.

The *getLocale* method returns the locale information for the applet from the super class if it is set. If the locale is not set then it returns the default available locale. The *getParameterInfo* method has a default implementation, which returns a null. The applet needs to override this method to provide a list of parameters and their descriptions that are understood by the applet. This is like the Help command available in command-line utilities. When the user does not remember the types of parameters and their formats, the Help command on the utilities lists all the parameters and their acceptable ranges. The return value of *getParameterInfo* returns an array of strings. Each element of the array contains the name of the parameter, the type of the parameter, and its description. The next two methods are polymorphic in nature and are called *play*. They take the URL of the audio clip to be played. There are two forms of the method. The first form takes in the absolute URL of the audio clip and calls the *play* method of the *AudioClip* interface class. The second form does a similar job, except that it takes in two parameters. The first parameter is the URL, which does not have the audio clip object name in it, and the second parameter is the audio clip object name found relative to the URL. The second method generates the absolute audio clip URL from the two passed-in parameters and calls the play method of the *AudioClip* interface class.

Now we come to the most important part of the Applet class. The methods already discussed are important to know but are basic in nature. They help in the ancillary functionality. The next four methods are very important and have to be thoroughly understood in order to write good Java applets. The first among them is the *init* method, which we previewed in our first example. The executing environment always calls the *init* method, which can be either a web browser or the applet viewer. This method is called the first time the applet is loaded or when the applet is reloaded. This is the place where construction-related tasks can be performed. One thing to keep in mind is that the *init* should not have any time-consuming code. All types of initialization, which can be done very quickly, can be placed here. For instance, *getImage* call or *getAudioClip* can be placed here. Applets generally do not have constructors because they do not have the entire environment until the *init* method is called, so even if someone has a constructor for an applet it would not serve any good purpose. All one-time initialization should be done in the *init* method.

The next method is called the *start* method. Many developers get confused between what to do in the *start* method versus the *init* method. Let's look at the *start* method first. *Start* is called from outside, from either the browser or the applet viewer, whenever the browser visits the page. The *start* method is a good place to perform tasks that would make sense while the page is active. For example, say a page has an animation applet. In this case, keeping the applet active when the page is not active does not make sense; hence, the *start* is a good place to continue with the execution of the applet when the page is brought into focus. The *start* method is also an appropriate place to create execution threads, which are active within the applet. Since the *start* method is called every time the page is activated, work that needs to be performed on the active page should be present in it. The *init* method, however, is called only once. Therefore, construction types of tasks need to be performed in it.

The third important method we need to talk about is the *stop* method. The *stop* method is just the opposite of the *start* method. A *stop* method is called whenever a page is deactivated or when the browser leaves the page. It is always called from the environment like the browser or the applet viewer. All the work that has been started in the *start* method needs to be undone in the *stop*; for example, stopping the execution of the threads, halting the animation within the applet, and so on.

The last method you should note within the Applet class is the *destroy* method. The browser or the applet viewer calls this method when the applet needs to be reclaimed. This can be viewed as analogous to a destructor of the class, though it actually is not. However, in the applet's world it does function like a destructor. All the creations done in the applet (e.g., resource allocations) must be freed in this method.

All of these four methods are called from outside, and the applet programmer does not need to call them from within the applet. Also, all four methods have a default implementation, which does nothing; hence, if the applet writer needs to do something in them he or she needs to override them. Let's walk through an example that shows all the four important methods occurring.

Figure 1.1 depicts a Java applet being loaded by the web browser. The top left-hand corner shows a page loaded by a web browser. The Java applet is embedded within the page. Since this is the first time the web page is loaded, the web browser calls the *init* method first. It then immediately calls the *start* method. Going to the next image at the top right-

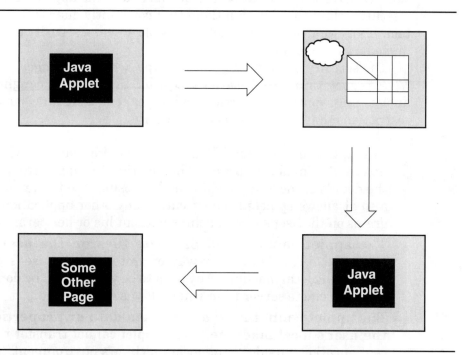

FIGURE 1.1   The applet invocation process.

hand corner we see that the web browser goes to another link within the web page; hence, the web browser calls the *stop* method. Going to the third image in the bottom right-hand corner we see that the web browser comes back to the web page having the Java applet; hence, a *start* method is called again. Next, going to the bottom left-hand corner we see that the Java applet is reclaimed and therefore the *stop* method is called followed by the *destroy* method. The applet gets activated just before the *start* method is called and gets deactivated just after the *stop* method.

Applets are entities that can be downloaded from a remote site via the browser. Since the code is being written by somebody else, there needs to be some kind of a trust element so that the user can allow the applet to download and execute on the local system. If no such security was provided, then you and I would never allow any applet to run on our local machines. So, obviously, security is a very important aspect. Companies pay huge sums of money to protect their private data. Even we as individuals have much private and personal information that we store in our computers and do not want anyone to access it without our permission. To correct this situation the browsers and the applet viewers have a security class object within them that constantly guards the local system. If any kind of security violation is observed, a security exception is immediately generated.

The security manager object is of type *SecurityManager*. The *SecurityManager* throws a *SecurityException* that can be caught by the applet, and appropriate action can be taken. Here are some of the restrictions that an applet needs to observe:

> **The applet cannot load libraries or make use of native methods on the local machine.**   This restricts the applet from querying the details of the local machine and exposing it to the remote site. It also disallows applets from executing any other applications or programs on the user's local machine without his or her permission.

> **The applet cannot read or write files on the user's local machine.**   This is another way of protecting the user's personal data on the local machine. Any data to be written can be done on the applet's remote server from where it was downloaded.

> **The applet cannot read any system data or properties from the user's local machine.**   The applet cannot transfer the user's configuration outside of the local machine's environment. The user can rest assured that all personal data is intact.

The applet cannot make network connection to some other machine on the network other than the server from which it is downloaded.   This stops the applet from performing any malicious act by connecting to the user's local network or tampering with the user's network connection tables.

These are some minor precautions, but most of them help in stopping security breaches in such a distributed environment. In the future, perhaps more precautionary measures will be identified and implemented to make the environment safe and sound to work with.

The Applet's Role on the Web

Applets are a way of expressing Java in a practical world. The applet architecture was created keeping in mind that it would be used with the Web very closely. Right from the days of its discovery at CERN, the European Laboratory for Particle Physics, located at Geneva, Switzerland, the Web was consistently researched by the computing community to derive the best usage out of it. The commercial usage of the Web was a pending question to the world of computers for quite a long time. With the invention of Java, maybe we have an answer.

Applets make the Web an even more interesting area. The Web is already a very interesting area for everybody. It is an ocean of wealth in itself. There is much that every one of us can learn from it, provided we have the proper tools with which to acquire the information desired. That has been one of the main issues surrounding web technology. We have this immense knowledge mine that needs to be explored by many, but either the tools available for this purpose are too complex for the masses to make use of or they are not yet available. Proper tools can make the job very easy; unavailability of such tools can make the task impossible. More work has yet to be done in this area so that everyone, regardless of level of experience, can make proper use of the Web without getting lost in the hunt. Intelligent guides are required, and developers and creators of such information need to provide a path by which the information may find its browser. It is more of a two-sided approach: The information travel activity needs to be initiated from both sides, the producer and the right consumer.

None of the previous statements expunges any credits from the Web architecture or questions its existence at all. We, as intellectual creations of this universe, are constantly searching for knowledge. We keep looking for answers to many questions we have and strive to obtain more information on them. We, as researchers of the computing community, always try to make the lives of the information consumer easy. At least we try to do so, and the Java applet architecture is a very good example of our efforts. It not only provides a good way in which to distribute information actively as a unit, but also provides a common understanding platform that can help users digest the distributed information in a simple form. The process is built upon the premise that every channel it passes through is active and intelligent, which helps it to move forward along the right path. If it works out the way we are planning it to be, the information will never be lost. Awareness will increase. Applets are not merely tools with which to demonstrate tiny little animation objects moving on our Web pages. They can be and should be used to perform much more valuable tasks. Applets spread technology harmony, which is sorely needed in the chaos of our computing world. To some extent it is a great success and continues to be ubiquitous in nature.

The Web works on HTTP (HyperText Transfer Protocol), and though it has been extensively used, it has limitations. HTTP is stateless; therefore, trying to integrate this protocol to work with distributed applications is a very difficult task. Every application that has tried to do so has inherently devised its own ways of attaching state and semantic to the process. This makes the system far less portable and reduces the distribution capacity; therefore, instead of creating solutions for the problem, we created much more difficult problems to solve. Applets make writing programs for the Web very easy. They reduce the difficulties that one would have otherwise faced if he or she had to write applications that could distribute themselves on the Web and maintain their integrity. The Java language is well equipped to handle the task and has many rich capabilities, which make it the language of choice. The Web has been a passive information repository system similar to a library, where information is in abundance but the user does not know how and where to begin looking for it. With applets, we can make it a much more active system. Instead of the user trying to pull information from the Web, the intelligence introduced into it with applets can be a suggestive guide for the information browser, helping to build the bridge of intelligence and information encapsulation on the Web. The flexible nature by which the system acknowledges information transfer is good, and there is much room for improvement in the process. One of the good parts to this story is that the innovations have not stopped. The folks responsible for the development (namely, Sun) are constantly coming up with newer, innovative ways of modularizing systems.

The applets developed in Java make use of the web communication protocol "underneath the covers"; in other words, they are not exposed to the developers necessarily, but if the developer wants to tinker with it then he or she can. The applet architecture relieves the developer of the communication protocol involvement. It links the application-level protocol with the communication system underneath and does not portray any type of impedance mismatch between the two. The developer can then concentrate on retrieving the resources that are needed to make his or her applets work correctly. How these are retrieved is left up to the base-operating environment, which in this case is the Java framework. Applets make use of the higher-level interfaces. The developer only needs to write an applet in such a manner that the right address is given to the Java system to work on. All these are also true for Java applications. Since both of them work on the same base framework they share the benefits offered by the system with equal ease.

With all that said, now let's look at a real-life applet. This example will show you how to build an applet step by step and also provide the you with a starting point from which to work. The example is a very small email client tool written as a Java applet. There are many improvements that can be made by the readers on this applet. It provides a basic platform that can be extended as desired.

Creating an Advanced Applet

An email tool is the most widely used application in the world of networks. Communication of data between users is done via mail. Analogous to the postal mail system it provides a way for information to be transferred from the sender to the receiver, only much faster. Mail system is used in the Internet environment as well as the intranet-aware environment. The scope of the users provides the differentiation between them.

Our Java applet is designed to be an email client. It has a few networking features that provide the capability of data transfer from one terminal to another. The goal of the example is not to make users proficient network programmers; therefore, the system is kept very simple. The focus is on Java, and we will limit the depth of our discussion to it.

However, it is important to understand the basics of the email client workings so a simplified version of the explanation is provided next.

Every email is routed through a mail domain server. It is the server to which the registered users send the information to be routed to the receiver, either directly or indirectly. Imagine this situation to be similar to the mailboxes we have in our offices. When we intend to send somebody a postal mail from our office, we drop the mail at a particular location. Everybody drops his or her mail at this location. The mailman picks up the mail from this location and delivers it to the receiver via the post office. The mail domain server is a similar thing. Every registered user sends the mail to the mail domain server. Encoded within the mail message is the address of the receiver. The header of the mail has this information. The mail domain server decodes the address of the recipient and performs its task of mail delivery. To learn more about this technology, refer to RFC (Request For Comments) 821. There are more RFCs that deal with SMTP (Simple Mail Transfer Protocol), but RFC 821 is the first in the row.

Figure 1.2 illustrates the mail flow path from the sender to the receiver. It shows the mail domain servers that act as delivery agents. The clients are registered to the local mail domain servers. The mail domain servers talk to each other via the Internet protocol. The base communication is done via TCP/IP.

Now let's look at the first four lines of our Java applet source code, which results in our own simple email client tool.

```
import java.awt.*;
import java.applet.*;
import java.net.*;
import java.io.*;
```

We have imported *java.awt.** for the windowing functions present in our applet. We will see later on in the code that we have used some visual controls, which are used to accept input from the users and display results of our operation. The AWT (Abstract Windowing Toolkit) is used for the purpose. Since we have written an applet we need to have the *java.applet.** package. It has all the applet-related methods. Next we see the *java.net.** package. The *java.net.** package is used for the networking constructs that we have used in our applet. Later we will see where they are needed in the code. Last, but not least, is the *java.io.**

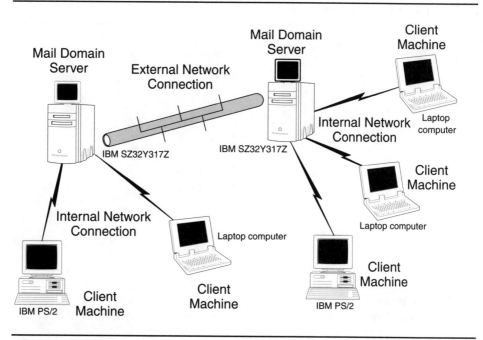

FIGURE 1.2   The mail flow path.

package. This is used for the input/output operations that are performed within the applet.

```
public class JavaMailClient extends Applet
```

Next we create a class called *JavaMailClient*, which extends Applet. *JavaMailClient* is our class. Here is a riddle for you. What would be the name of our Java source file? Think hard! Yes, our Java source file would be called *JavaMailClient.java,* and when we compile it with the Java compiler the output file would be called *JavaMailClient.class*. Since this is an applet it needs to be embedded within an HTML file.

We have overridden the *init* method in our applet and performed some custom initialization. We need to create some visual controls and have them at the appropriate location. Then we need to add them to the applet. Some of the visual controls also have to be initialized. That is exactly what our *init* method does. The routine may appear pretty big, but do not be intimidated by the size of it. The work itself is pretty simple, as shown in Listing 1.3.

LISTING 1.3   The Init() Method

```
public void init()
{
  setLayout(null);
  setSize(645,496);
  setBackground(new Color(12632256));
  To_Label = new java.awt.Label("To :");
  To_Label.setBounds(12,96,24,24);
  add(To_Label);
  To_text = new java.awt.TextField();
  To_text.setBounds(156,96,348,24);
  add(To_text);
  textArea1 = new java.awt.TextArea();
  textArea1.setBounds(48,252,468,108);
  add(textArea1);
  textField1 = new java.awt.TextField();
  textField1.setBounds(72,168,504,24);
  add(textField1);
  sub_label = new java.awt.Label("Subject :");
  sub_label.setBounds(12,168,48,24);
  add(sub_label);
  msg_label = new java.awt.Label("Message");
  msg_label.setBounds(48,216,60,24);
  add(msg_label);
  send_btn = new java.awt.Button();
  send_btn.setActionCommand("button");
  send_btn.setLabel("Send");
  send_btn.setBounds(564,340,60,40);
  send_btn.setBackground(new Color(12632256));
  add(send_btn);
  mailsrvr_label = new java.awt.Label("Mail Server Name");
  mailsrvr_label.setBounds(12,12,108,24);
  add(mailsrvr_label);
  mailsrvr_text = new java.awt.TextField();
  mailsrvr_text.setBounds(156,12,348,24);
  add(mailsrvr_text);
  snrd_label = new java.awt.Label("Senders Email address");
  sndr_label.setBounds(12,48,132,24);
  add(sndr_label);
  sndr_text = new java.awt.TextField();
  sndr_text.setBounds(156,48,348,24);
```

LISTING 1.3 *Continued*

```
      add(sndr_text);
      Reply = new java.awt.TextArea();
      Reply.setBounds(48,400,470,60);
      Reply.setEditable(false);
      add(Reply);

      Action react = new Action();
      send_btn.addActionListener( react );
}
```

The last two lines in our *init* method are worth mentioning. The next to the last line of the code creates a variable called *react*, which is of type *Action*. You have a lingering question in your mind as to why this is done and what is the need for such an operation. Well, the applet performs some task based on some interaction from the user. The user of the applet initiates this interaction when he or she enters all the relevant data for the tool to function properly. In our case, when the user has finished entering the data to be mailed to the specified receiver via the mentioned mail domain server, he or she starts the mail-sending process by clicking on the *Send* button, initiating an action. Later on in the code we will see what kind of job is performed after the click. The last line of the *init* method code adds the *react* variable to the *Send* button. This adds the *Send* button as the listener to the action. When the mouse is clicked within the applet's bound, the action channel built will send events to all the listener objects registered in a likewise fashion. The object, which represents the *Send* button in the applet, is called *send_btn*. This is just the driver of the action. We will see later on how the processor of the action processes the action message.

Following is the code that creates the *Action* class that we have used in our *init* method to create the *react* object.

```
class Action implements java.awt.event.ActionListener
{
public void actionPerformed(java.awt.event.ActionEvent event)
{
  Object object = event.getSource();
  if (object == send_btn)
```

```
        StartEmailProcess();
    }
}
```

The *Action* class implements the *java.awt.event.ActionListener* interface. This interface is used to generate events from the AWT controls and process them. In our applet we have many AWT controls, the most relevant of them being the *Send* button, which would need to process the user's mouse click and react to it. Within this class we see one method called *actionPerformed*. This method has an input parameter, which turns out to be the event. The *event* object has the information about the source where the event was generated and some more information related to the event. In our applet we are concerned only with the source of the event; hence, we retrieve the source of the event. Then the code checks to see if the source is the *Send* button. We need to start the mail process only if the *Send* button is clicked; no other click is important to us. If the source of the event is the *Send* button, we then call the *StartEmailProcess* method.

Following is the section of code that does the object declaration:

```
java.awt.Label To_Label;
java.awt.TextField To_text;
java.awt.TextArea textArea1;
java.awt.TextField textField1;
java.awt.Label sub_label;
java.awt.Label msg_label;
java.awt.Button send_btn;
java.awt.Label mailsrvr_label;
java.awt.TextField mailsrvr_text;
java.awt.Label sndr_label;
java.awt.TextField sndr_text;
java.awt.TextArea Reply;
```

Each object used in the program needs to be declared along with its type. For instance, *To_Label* is an object that is used in the applet and is of type *java.awt.Label*. Notice that all the objects are visual controls, and hence *java.awt.** was imported.

Now let's take a look at the *StartEmailProcess* method shown in Listing 1.4.

LISTING 1.4   The StartEmailProcess() Method

```java
void StartEmailProcess()
{
  Reply.setText("");
  try
  {
    Socket dataport = new Socket(mailsrvr_text.getText(),
                          25, true);

    PrintStream ps = new PrintStream(
                            dataport.getOutputStream());

    ps.println("HELO " + mailsrvr_text.getText());
    Reply.appendText(PortResponse(dataport) + "\n");

    ps.println("MAIL FROM: " + sndr_text.getText());
    Reply.appendText(PortResponse(dataport) + "\n");

    ps.println("RCPT TO: " + To_text.getText());
    Reply.appendText(PortResponse(dataport) + "\n");

    ps.println("DATA");
    Reply.appendText(PortResponse(dataport) + "\n");

    ps.println("Subject: "+textField1.getText()+
        "\n"+textArea1.getText());
    Reply.appendText(PortResponse(dataport) + "\n");

    ps.println("\n" + "." + "\n");
    Reply.appendText(PortResponse(dataport) + "\n");

    ps.println("QUIT");
    Reply.appendText(PortResponse(dataport) + "\n");
    ps.close();
    dataport.close();
  }
  catch( IOException Ex )
  {
    System.out.println(Ex.getMessage());
  }
}
```

This method performs the entire communication part of the applet. We see the networking of the code within this method. We are using the *Socket* object in this routine to perform our network communication. There are certain things that need to be done before the applet actually starts to send email across the Internet. The user should have a live TCP/IP stack available that the *Socket* routines can make use of it, so either you dial into your Internet Service Provider (ISP) so that an IP stack is available to you or you connect via your company's network that has Internet connectivity. Notice that there is a *java.awt.TextArea* called *Reply*. This is the bottom-most multiline text control. This is a noneditable control. We have used it to display the messages obtained when each individual request is sent to our mail domain server at the specified port.

```
Reply.setEditable(false);
```

The preceding code makes this control noneditable and is present in the *init* method. A response is sent to every request sent to the communication port on the mail domain server. This response informs us whether the request was successful or not. We read the response from the data port and append it to our *Reply* display control. The entire communication logic is enclosed within the *try* and *catch* blocks. If any of the calls throws an exception within the *try* block, the *catch* block will capture it. Only input/output exceptions are caught and the error message is displayed. This is how standard exception handling is done. Since data is input to the communication port and the resultant data is obtained as an output at the communication port, we need to catch the input/output exception only.

First we create an object called *dataport* that is of type *Socket*. (This is the reason we have imported *java.net.*.*) Port 25 is used for the data input/output on the mail domain server. This information can be located within the RFC for SMTP. The mail domain server acts as our host. If you notice within the applet, it asks for the user to enter the mail domain server name. The mail domain server name is obtained from *mailsrvr_text* object. A stream is needed to perform an input/output operation. The stream is linked to the appropriate channel to make the communication happen during its creation phase. We create a *PrintStream* object called *ps*. Linking it with our communication port's output stream creates this object. Once we have created the port and a stream with it, we can start our input/output operations.

We first send the *HELO* command to the mail domain server to initiate the conversation. These commands are discussed in RFC 821, and we advise you to refer to it for detailed explanation. After the server receives the command, the host server responds back. The response is in terms of an error string and an error code. Please note that although we refer to the response as error string and error code, they may not actually be errors. It could be a successful operation, in which case we see the success code and the return message indicating just that. The response from the server is read by the *PortResponse* method. After the port initialization we send the *MAIL FROM:* command. This tells the host server the email address of the sender. This is needed, as the server sends this to the receiver. The response from the operation is immediately read and displayed within the *Reply* control. We then send the *RCPT TO:* command, which informs the server of the recipient's email address. This is the location to which the server sends the email.

The email address consists of two parts: the user identifier and the domain address. The user identifier is the string just before the @ sign. Following the @ sign is the domain address. The host server selects the domain address from the recipient's address and starts looking for the domain within the network. Once the recipient's domain is located, the host server sends the email to it. The recipient's domain server then resolves the user identifier from the address and forwards it to the appropriate user. Until now we sent the header information to the host server. Now we have to send the data associated with the email, and the *DATA* command informs the server exactly that. Anything following the *DATA* command should be the email content. We send the subject matter and the actual email body. The email message is terminated by the . on a line by itself. This acts as the terminator signal to the server. We then send the *QUIT* command to the host server port informing it of our intention of terminating the communication. We then close the *PrintStream* and the *Socket*.

Now we have the *PortResponse* method as shown here:

```
String PortResponse(Socket incoming)
{
  try
  {
    DataInputStream myDIS = new
    java.io.DataInputStream(incoming.getInputStream());
    return myDIS.readLine();
  }
```

```
catch (java.io.IOException Ex)
{
  return Ex.getMessage();
}
}
```

This method has the input parameter as the *Socket* on which the communication is initiated. The data port associated with email sends a response on the same port address. Some communication ports have a different input and output address. In such cases, the input is sent to one port and the response is sent on the other. In our case, it is the same port. We have a *try* and *catch* block in our communication code to catch any exception thrown within the process. The exception that we are interested in is the input/output exception of the type *java.io.IOException*. In case of the exception we just return the message associated with the exception to the calling routine. Since we are interested in reading the output from the port we create a *DataInputStream* object. This input stream object is linked to our communication-input stream. We read the response from the port and return a string to the caller. There is one issue with this code; can you guess what it is? Yes, you guessed right. The *PortResponse* method returns a string to the caller. The caller would never know whether there was an error generated or not unless the returned string is interpreted. Well, it is up to the reader to resolve the issue, but the point made is very clear.

This is great, we have already developed our first email client tool in Java. The reader can use this applet as a launching pad. There can be many enhancements made to it. The applet can be refined to give it a professional look and feel. For instance, you can provide checkpoints at the code to confirm that the user has entered all the data that is needed for the system to function. One of the important checks is to see that the user has entered the address of the mail domain server and the recipient's email address before the *Send* button is clicked. The tool can also be improved by allowing multiple recipients. You can also enhance the tool to provide a carbon-copy feature and a blind-copy feature.

WHAT ARE JAVABEANS?

JavaBeans are components. They are not any ordinary types of components; in fact, they have a different attribute that makes them very useful. Beans are active, reusable components. The term *reusable* is a very strong attribute. The formal definition of JavaBeans is as follows (as defined by JavaSoft): "A JavaBean is a reusable software component that can be manipulated visually in a builder tool." In the world of GUI (Graphical User Interface), we are sure that everyone has used at least one graphical development environment, all of which seem to present an object-oriented approach in the development tools. Many classify themselves as rapid application development environments and rightfully so. The past few years have seen many such tools appear in the industry. Every one of them concentrates on one aspect of development: Some focus on object-oriented development, others concentrate on rapid development through extensive class libraries and drag-and-drop facilities, and some focus their efforts on developing components that can be plugged in to programs to make development easier.

JavaBeans also focuses on something, and that is *component reusability*. It is not code reusability as in having generic classes and others derive or inherit from the generic class and keep on building on top of them. This is more in terms of reusing the executable entity. Not much fussing with source code is required; as a matter of fact, the concept tries its best to avoid any mucking around with source code. Source code inheritance is kept to the minimum and as transparent to the developers as possible. An active development idea is shown with Beans. The Beans are always kept active when they are used or reused. Bean objects are queried when they are live, and relationships are built upon the current active states.

Let's look at JavaBeans in detail. JavaBeans come with some key elements that need to be discussed. They are the Introspection class, the Core Reflection application programming interface, and the BeanInfo object. The Introspection class allows the environment to retrieve information on a particular Bean, and every JavaBean can be queried to get its relevant information. Any JavaBean-aware program builder tool could query the Bean and get the information required for it to work with the Bean. The Introspection class uses the Core Reflection application-programming interface for this information retrieval process. The Core Reflection API is a very strong interface and very intimate with the Beans. It can be used to retrieve any type of internal data of the Bean.

Every JavaBean supports a BeanInfo object. The BeanInfo object is created from the BeanInfo interface class. The Introspection class fills up the BeanInfo object with the relevant class-related data. The Bean-Info object can be queried for the information about the Bean. The object contains data that can be used by the builder tool or any Bean-aware development tool to expose the data of the Bean. The data could be the set of properties of the object, the methods used to get the data property and set them, the events supported by the Bean, and so on.

JavaBeans are self-confined units that can exist on their own; they do not have to work in conjunction with any builder tool at all. Using components with other working entities like the platform on which it operates, or any other component, is just one way of using them. Currently, that seems to be the most common usage, but it is not limited in any fashion. It makes Beans easily deployable and also keeps the upgrade procedures simple. Deploying a newer version of the Bean can be simply performed by shipping just the new version of the Bean to the customers, who can download it onto their application framework and start using it.

For example, consider a scenario in which you are developing a report writing tool. It does all the fancy reporting in multiple formats and provides the user with good graphics and attractive reporting mechanisms. This tool does the front-end work. The reporting tool needs to talk to some kind of a data store. It needs the data store to retrieve the information and report it to the user. This may seem like a simple task, but in actuality it is not. The tool needs to know the location of the data store in the correct format so that it can understand. It also needs to understand the details of the data store so that it can accept a proper kind of query from the user. It takes the query and converts it to the appropriate format so that the data store engine understands it. It can then feed in the query to the data store engine and wait for the engine to return the result set. The result set is later shown to the user in the requested format. This can be done in a number of ways, and every way has its own advantages and disadvantages. The front end can be a Java application, which does the user interface and performs the tasks of input and output. Based on the type of data store requested it can query the appropriate Bean, which can then be activated. The Bean sets up the environment for that specific data store and starts the job.

Figure 1.3 shows an example of the Java application talking to the data stores directly. We see in the figure that a Java application is communicating with three different data stores: D1, D2, and D3. In this case, since the application talks directly to the data stores, it would need to have specific code for each data store understood by the application within the application itself. This is too much unwanted code that is being carried around by the application itself. Furthermore, whenever a new data store support is to be added to the Java application, it

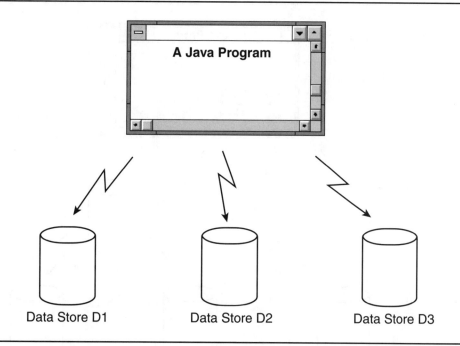

FIGURE 1.3 Java application and the data stores.

becomes difficult for the developer to upgrade the existing systems being used at different customer sites—the entire application has to be rebuilt and deployed to each customer's site. It has been a very normal behavior of the application users to not disturb the existing setup if it works well within the existing environment. They do not like the uncertainty involved in uprooting and shaking up the existing working setup in order to try a newer version that is questionable to them. A smooth migration path is needed for such circumstances. Our deployable Beans strategy comes in very handy in such a situation.

Figure 1.4 shows another configuration of a similar situation. In this figure we notice that the application is talking to the Bean repository. The application logs itself to the Bean repository, which consists of multiple Beans that can talk to different types of data stores. Each Bean has a one-to-one relationship with the data stores. When the reporting tool gets the information on the type of data store it needs to work with, it searches the Bean repository to see if it has the Bean that can do the job. If it can find an appropriate Bean it activates it. The active Bean then starts its communication with the appropriate repository. It performs

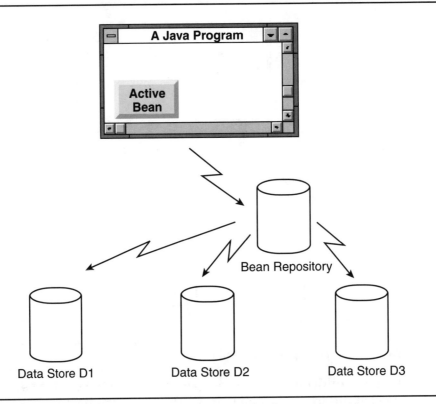

FIGURE 1.4   JavaBeans with the application and the data stores.

the task on behalf of the Java application. The benefits with this type of a working configuration are tremendous.

One thing to notice in Figure 1.4 is the entity called Active Bean. It does not have to be a visible Bean; it could be invisible. In our case, it is probably invisible; the entity is shown as a visible unit only for the sake of explanation. Returning to our explanation, the configuration is much cleaner and more modular in nature because the application does not talk to any specific data store. It does not have to carry data store-specific code and make itself nonportable. The appropriate Bean takes care of business. Also, in such a configuration, when a new Bean is to be shipped for supporting a new type of data store, it does not have to be a disruptive process. The upgrade procedure is simple and clean. A customer can either download the Bean from the company Web site or FTP site, or the software can be shipped to the customer. When the customer receives the software he or she can run the executable, which has a self-registering module. The self-registration process searches the system for the existing installation and registers itself. This way, the existing installation is not damaged and the new addition becomes usable by the client. Beans help simplify the software upgrade procedure and make the lives of developers much easier.

Java somehow projects a view that it is very similar to the GUI. This perception is becoming very strong, and it is not known as to how it started. Nowhere in the Java manual is it mentioned that way. The general feeling is that since everybody has some animation going in their Java applets on their web pages, it must be good only for that. This is not entirely true. Java is good for animation-related applications and/or applets; however, it is equally good for applications and/or applets that do not perform animation at all. It is a strong distributive environment with an extraordinarily strong language supporting it. The environment is growing stronger and stronger with new features being added that are needed for a ubiquitous development set. As far as a Bean is concerned, it does not have to derive itself from any specific class. If the Bean needs to be visible then it has to inherit java.awt.Component class. This allows the Bean to be visually added into the visual containers. Beans can also be invisible, which was the case in our Data Store Bean example, and they do not need to inherit the java.awt.Component class.

Let's take a moment to discuss a matter that has been noted by the creators of Java and JavaBeans and some work that has been initiated to provide a solution. Java exhibits a single inheritance model. This means every Java class can extend only one other Java class. In Java, the key word relating to inheritance is *extends*. There is some goodness derived from it, and some limitations are observed in it. In other programming languages like C++, multiple inheritance is used. Many times developers may feel a need for the application to inherit the behavior of multiple classes. A Java developer may be no different. This urge has grown even stronger with Beans, which, being a reusable component, makes these ideas much more relevant. Since Beans introduce the idea of creating and designing Java objects during runtime, such a solution is more and more desirable. This becomes relatively easy in programming languages like C++ because the language allows this kind of a behavior. In Java, however, it is not possible. Hence, the developers of Java and JavaBeans have begun to address the matter. A consequence of this would lead to the application and/or applet developers to view the object as a different type. Therefore, they came up with a concept of *type view*. Type view allows the same Bean to be viewed as an instance of a different type. It would help the developer to view the type of the same JavaBean as a different cast. In JavaBeans 1.0 all type views of the same Bean simply represent different casts of the same object to different Java types. The future releases of JavaBeans are planned for a revolution in this area. They intend to have an implementation that different type views of the JavaBean could be implemented as different Java objects. In essence, this would result in having multiple inheritance in an indirect sense. Since different type views of the same Bean object could be implemented as different objects, the Java object would have multiple derivations in it.

If we have an *abc_bean* of type *ABC* and we want to generate a view of this object of type *java.awt.Component*, then the following should be performed:

```
java.awt.Component abc_new_view =
   (java.awt.Component)Beans.getInstanceOf(
   abc_bean, java.awt.Component.class);
```

The preceding code snippet is just for the sake of explanation. *java.awt.Component* is a valid Java class, but *ABC* is fictitious. The source interprets that *abc_new_view* is an instance of *java.awt.Component* and created as a view of *abc_bean*. Since *abc_bean* is of a different type, in other words, *ABC*, it needs to tell the system that the resultant should be of type *java.awt.Component*. The Bean developers during such an operation should note a few points. They are stated here:

- They should never use Java *instanceof* or Java cast to navigate between different views of the Bean.
- They should never assume that the result object of the *Beans.getInstanceOf* call is the same object as the input object.
- They should never assume that the result object of the *Beans.getInstanceOf* call supports the same properties, events, or methods supported by the original type view.

So what tool should we use for JavaBeans development? The Java-Beans development environment comes with the Bean Development Kit (BDK). The BDK is available for free to be downloaded from the Java-Soft site (www.javasoft.com/beans). The BDK comes with many different tools to aid developers in creating JavaBeans. One tool worth mentioning here that is very handy during the Bean development phase is called the BeanBox. If you remember, we started our discussion of JavaBeans as being components. The components are entities that need a framework or a platform to work on. Also, they need to be queried, and data needs to be sent to them to let them perform their tasks. They need to be activated by some outside live entity. The BeanBox tool provided with the BDK is a basic Bean container. With BeanBox, developers can develop their Beans and load them into the tool and work with them. Does that mean that the Beans can be used only with the BeanBox? If that's the case, then shouldn't we stop reading about JavaBeans and start looking around from some other component development environment? Don't worry. That's not the case at all.

The BeanBox is a simplistic view of the application having the Bean containment awareness. An application that you may develop in the future could have the capabilities of host JavaBeans within its frame. That would imply the application could be in the position to read custom Beans brought from some other site and start activating them. If such capabilities are to be provided by your system then it should have the introspection capabilities. The BeanBox demonstrates such capability in a very simple form. It has three main parts to it. The first portion is the ToolBox, which is the list of all Beans that the BeanBox can show you. When you get into the details of writing JavaBeans you will learn how JAR (Java archive) files are generated. The developer can generate a JAR file, which has the Beans in it. The JAR file can then be registered with the BeanBox. The BeanBox decodes the JAR file and registers the Beans with the Tool-Box. The ToolBox displays a menu of all the Beans registered with it. The third portion of the BeanBox is the Property Sheet window. When a Bean is selected from the ToolBox for introspection, the BeanBox shows the properties of the Bean in the Property Sheet window. The BeanBox make use of the introspection to retrieve the properties of the Bean.

Now you have an understanding of the BeanBox tool and its usage. As you use it more and more you will find that the tool is pretty nifty. Bean-Box is a very healthy little tool that not only helps the user to develop JavaBeans but also provides a source of inspiration for creating applications that can act as robust Bean containers. We have noticed this kind of a technology spread previously with web browsers. With the advent of Mosaic from the University of Illinois, Urbana Champaign, web browsers became a very popular tool for browsing the Internet. Immediately we saw that everybody started having web browsing capabilities in their application. Any application that had a graphical user interface tried to provide some way for the end user to browse the Web with it. We envision the same thing happening with the Bean containers. Very soon we will see most of the applications being Java aware and having some interfaces that can provide the Bean container ability. It is time, and we should also jump on the bandwagon for obvious reasons.

An Example of a JavaBean

Let's start looking into our first JavaBean example. The Bean that we will be developing is a simple Bean. We will be using an applet on which the Bean will be placed. Also, we will see how our applet communicates with the Bean. The example is very simple, but it will demonstrate the basic Bean building technique. We will go step by step explaining and understanding the logic behind the application. The goal of this chapter is not to make everyone an expert in developing JavaBeans, but to create a feeling of interest. Once the basic understanding is available, anyone can then spend more time trying fancier things with it.

The example consists of three files. The first Java file contains the source related to creating the applet. Our applet will host the Bean, so we start our discussion with the applet source code.

```
import java.awt.*;
import java.applet.*;
import java.awt.event.*;
import JavaBean;
```

The preceding code shows the *import* statements. These are used in our applet and thus need to be declared. The first three *import* statements are not unusual, but the fourth line is importing the JavaBean object, which we will be creating in our example. The name of the Bean in our example is JavaBean, so do not confuse this with JavaBean as a technology.

```
public class BeanApp extends Applet
```

Our applet in this example is called *BeanApp* and, as expected, it extends the *Applet* class. *BeanApp* is a public class. Nothing very interesting as of yet, but the fun will begin very soon.

```
JavaBean bean;
```

Before we start our *init* method we notice an interesting thing. As mentioned earlier, our Bean object in this example is called *JavaBean*, and we see the preceding code declaring an instance of our Bean. The name of the instance is *bean*. So we notice that we have declared an instance of our Bean object within our applet that will be instantiated later on in the *init* method. (Things are heating up!)

LISTING 1.5   The init() Method for the JavaBean Example

```
public void init()
{
  super.init();
  setLayout(null);
  setSize(389,228);
  Move_btn = new java.awt.Button();
  Move_btn.setActionCommand("button");
  Move_btn.setLabel("Move");
  Move_btn.setBounds(156,180,60,40);
  Move_btn.setForeground(new Color(0));
  Move_btn.setBackground(new Color(12632256));
  add(Move_btn);

  bean = new JavaBean();
  add(bean);

  SymAction lSymAction = new SymAction();
  Move_btn.addActionListener(lSymAction);
}
```

As you see in Listing 1.5, the *init* method does our custom initialization of the code. The first line of our initialization method calls the super class's *init* method. Then we set the layout of the applet, which happens to be null in this case. We also set the size of our applet. Next we create a new button object called *Move_btn*. This object is of the type *java.awt.Button*. We then make a call to the setActionCommand method, which is a method of the *java.awt.Button* class. It sets the command name of the action event fired by this button. The default value is the label of the button. We will see why we have used this method later on in the code. We next change the label of the button to *Move*. We set the bounds of the button and the foreground and background colors of the button. Once the button is initialized, we add it to the applet.

Now we create our Bean object called *bean* and add it to our applet. After adding the Bean object to our applet, we create an instance of the *SymAction* class. *SymAction* is a class created within the applet whose job is to implement the *ActionListener*. We have a button object in our applet, which we will be using for informing the Bean to do certain things. The button object will generate events that need to be processed. The *ActionListener* object does this processing. We have created a relationship between the event generation and the handler by registering the *ActionListener* with the button. Therefore, any event generated by the button object will go through the processing class called *SymAction*. Later on in the code we will find the *SymAction* class definition and the method associated with processing of the event request by the button. It is very important that we understand the relationship completely, as these are basic development tactics. These concepts of event generation by components and processing them are fairly generic in nature and are used in all client/server development environments. Other development tools may add their flavors to the technique, but the basic functionality remains the same.

The following code fragment shows the class that was created to implement the *java.awt.event.ActionListener* interface.

```
class SymAction implements java.awt.event.ActionListener
{
  public void actionPerformed(java.awt.event.ActionEvent)
  {
    Object object = event.getSource();
    if (object == Move_btn)
      MoveBtn_Action(event);
  }
}
```

The class is called *SymAction*. The *SymAction* class implements the events generated by the AWT objects. Also, as seen in the preceding code, we need to register the AWT objects whose events are to be processed. The *SymAction* class has one method called *actionPerformed* that takes the *java.awt.event.ActionEvent* as the input parameter. Within the *actionPerformed* method we see that the source of the event is located. If the source is the *Move_btn* object, then we need to process it. Remember that we added the *Move_btn* object as the listener to the event. We call a MoveBtn_Action method in response to the clicking of the button object.

The generated event is passed as an input parameter to this method. Next we will see what is done in the *MoveBtn_Action* method.

```
void MoveBtn_Action(java.awt.event.ActionEvent event)
{
  Rectangle rect = bean.getBounds();
  Dimension dim = getSize();
  if( rect.x < ( dim.width - rect.width ) )
    rect.x = rect.x + 10;
  else
    rect.x = 0;
  bean.setBounds(rect);
}
```

The *MoveBtn_Action* method provides the logic behind the movement of our Bean object. The method checks the current location of the Bean on the applet. If it is found that the bean can be moved horizontally on the applet and still keep it visible, then we move it. If goes to the extreme right end of the applet and any more movement to the right would take it out of view, we bring it back to the leftmost end of the applet. Note that movement is kept confined to the horizontal axis; no vertical movement is performed. If you desire, you can add those capabilities to it. The *getBounds* method returns the bounds of the Bean object. The *getSize* method is used to get the dimension of the applet on the screen. These two values are used to generate the movement logic. It is very simple but does give us an idea of how to animate objects on an applet. In our case, the object happens to be a Bean object.

The next file we will discuss is the actual Bean source code. The name of the source file is *JavaBean.java*. What is this Bean all about and what does it do? Our Bean object is a simple circle that responds to a mouse click. A mouse click has two events associated with it. First is the mouse press, which will generate the mouse press event, and next is the mouse release, which will generate a mouse release event. When the user places the mouse on top of the circle and presses it, the color of the circle changes to black. On releasing the mouse the color changes back to red. This is a very simple Bean. Now let's look at the source code associated with this Bean.

```
import java.awt.*;
import java.awt.event.*;
import java.beans.*;
```

Since we are writing a Bean, you will notice that we import *java.beans.**. This class provides all the Bean control methods that are needed to write a Bean. Our Bean is an object, and hence it would have its constructor. The initialization of the Bean should be done in the constructor.

```
public class JavaBean extends Canvas implements
```

```
java.io.Serializable
```

The preceding statement shows the name of our Bean object, *Java-Bean*. Notice that it extends the *Canvas* class and implements the *java.io.Serializable* interface. Every JavaBean must implement the *java.io.Serializable* interface. Every JavaBean has the capability to serialize and deserialize itself, a requirement for a JavaBean. The Java-Bean specification talks about it. The interface tells that the object is serializable. It does not have any methods associated with it. Any class that does not implement this interface cannot have its state serialized or deserialized. Our Bean also extends the *Canvas* class. This is a generic component that needs to be subclassed in order to provide any kind of functionality. Take a look at the following code, which shows the constructor of our JavaBean class.

```
public JavaBean()
{
  super();
  setSize(40,40);
  enableEvents(MouseEvent.MOUSE_EVENT_MASK);
}
```

The code calls the constructor of the super class and sets the size of the Bean. It then enables the mouse events for the Bean. Now check out the paint method, as shown in the following code:

```
public void paint(Graphics context)
{
  if (down)
  {
    context.setColor(pressedColor);
```

```
  }
  else
  {
    context.setColor(releasedColor);
  }
  context.fillArc(5,5,getSize().width-10,
          getSize().height-10,0,360);

}
```

This method is called to paint the Bean control. If the Bean control needs some custom painting, it has to do it in the paint method. The paint method receives the graphics context. The canvas background can be painted using the graphics context. The *Graphics class* is an abstract base class. The Graphics *object* encapsulates the state information needed for the various rendering operations that Java supports. It has various methods required for drawing and painting the component. In our code, based on whether the mouse is pressed or released, we change the color of the component. The *fillArc* method paints the arc with the set color.

```
protected void processMouseEvent (MouseEvent e)
{
  switch(e.getID())
  {
    case MouseEvent.MOUSE_PRESSED:
      down = true;
      repaint();
      break;
    case MouseEvent.MOUSE_RELEASED:
      down = false;
      repaint();
      break;
  }
  super.processMouseEvent(e);
}
```

The preceding method has code associated with the processing of mouse events. This method is defined in *java.awt.Component*. We are overriding this method to provide an implementation related to our component. The method has *MouseEvent* as the input parameter. This method helps in processing the mouse event occurring in the component. The event is dispatched to all the *MouseListener* objects. In our example, the Bean is listening to the mouse events. It has registered itself as the valid listener by making a call to the *enableEvents* method and passing it the *MouseEvent.MOUSE_EVENT_MASK*. In the method we have a *switch* statement, which checks for the type of mouse event generated. If the event is a *MouseEvent.MOUSE_PRESSED*, it sets the *down* variable to *true* and requests that a paint message be generated. This request is initiated by the repaint method. If a *MouseEvent.MOUSE_RELEASED* message is generated, the down variable is turned false and the paint message is requested. After doing all this we call the super class's *processMouseEvent* method. If we do not call the super class's *processMouseEvent*, the objects of the super class would not be in the position to process the mouse event. In doing this, we delegate the event upwards.

LISTING 1.6   The Four Properties of the Bean

```
public synchronized Color getReleasedColor()
{
   return releasedColor;
}

public void setReleasedColor (Color newColor)
{
   treleasedColor = newColor;
   repaint();
}

public synchronized Color getPressedColor()
{
   return pressedColor;
}

public void setPressedColor (Color newColor)
{
   pressedColor = newColor;
   repaint();
}
```

The four methods shown in Listing 1.6, which do the Getter and Setter operations on the private variables, are the properties of the Bean.

The Getter and Setter methods help us to verify the values of the properties and change them if desired. There are two variables that we have in our Bean; one is *pressedColor* and the other is *releasedColor*. Notice that after we set a particular color we ask for a paint message to be generated. A synchronized method acquires a lock before the method is called. This does not allow the data to be corrupted by being called from multiple threads.

Next we see three variables defined and initialized.

```
private Color pressedColor = Color.black;
private Color releasedColor = Color.red;
transient boolean down = false;
```

Notice that *down* is a *boolean* variable, which is also qualified by the keyword *transient*. Do you know why it is transient? As you know, a JavaBean has the capability of persisting its state. That means a JavaBean can store itself and save the current state onto an output stream or device. Earlier we saw that our Bean implements the *java.io.Serializable* interface. If that is the case, and we assume that the Bean needs to store its state, then don't you think storing the *down* variable would be useless? It would serve no purpose. The *down* variable is used for temporary needs and has to have persistent value. In cases like this in which we do not like to store a particular data related to the JavaBean we declare it *transient*.

The third file in this example is *JavaBeanBeanInfo.java*. As mentioned before, JavaBeans are reusable components. Any Bean container can use the Bean via the introspection mechanisms. Also, every Bean has a capability of providing an instance of the *BeanInfo* interface, providing information about the Bean to the outside world. Anyone interested in getting to know the Bean would make use of the information provided by the *BeanInfo* interface implementation. The provision of information about the Bean is based on the discretion of the developer. It is up to him or her as to how much information is exposed in this manner. If the information seeker is interested in learning more about the Bean, then he or she can make use of the low-level reflection of the Bean class method and also use the design patterns to understand the properties of the Bean. The BDK also provides a class called *SimpleBeanInfo*. This class provides a *noop* information about the base class. Any information that the user wishes to provide can be included. This serves two purposes. First, it allows a user to protect the information that he or she does not desire to expose by offering the *noop*. Second, when the information seeker sees a *noop* then he or she understands that the user did not intend to expose any information. Also, it helps the seeker to start with the introspection methods and apply the design patterns to decode the information.

```
import java.beans.*;

public class JavaBeanBeanInfo extends SimpleBeanInfo
```

The first line of the preceding code shows that only *java.beans.** is imported in this file. The next line shows the creation of our class called *JavaBeanBeanInfo*. It extends the *SimpleBeanInfo* class. As discussed earlier, we have not implemented the *BeanInfo* interface because we did not intend to have an implementation of all the methods of the *BeanInfo* interface. We would be selectively exposing the information about our class. In this example our class does not have too much information to protect; however, it does show a way of protecting information when we need to do so. This is an excellent technique. It provides the flexibility as well as maintains the strictness of the system.

The following method, called *getAdditionalBeanInfo*, tries to retrieve the information about the Bean.

```
public BeanInfo[] getAdditionalBeanInfo()
{
  try
  {
    BeanInfo[] bi = new BeanInfo[1];

    bi[0] = Introspector.getBeanInfo(
                       beanClass.getSuperclass());

    return bi;
  }
  catch( IntrospectionException e )
  {
    throw new Error(e.toString());
  }
}
```

It makes use of the introspection methods. The entire code is present within the *try* and *catch* blocks. If the introspection methods throw an exception it will be of type *IntrospectionException* and will be caught in the *catch* block. The catch block retrieves the string associated with the exception and creates an instance of *java.lang.Error* class, which is a subclass of *java.lang.Throwable*. Hence, we see a *throw* keyword in front of the *Error* instance creation. These types of errors are serious and should not be caught by normal applications. They are generally abnormal errors and not much mending can be done when generated.

In the *try* block we see that an array of *BeanInfo* object is created. It is called bi, and there happens to be just one element within the array. We see the usage of the *java.beans.Introspector* class. This class provides a way for tools or Bean containers to learn about the Bean's properties, methods, and events. The introspector can be used to build a complete list of information about the Bean. The next line of code does exactly the same. The *getBeanInfo* is a method of the Introspector class, which gets all the information that it can retrieve about the specified class. This information will encompass the events, methods, and its properties. The parameter of the *getBeanInfo* method retrieves the super class of our JavaBean class. We will see that later in the code *beanClass* is defined as a *Class* variable. It is initialized to the name of our JavaBean component class file. In this example it happens to be *JavaBean.class*. This is a very simple example of using introspection, but it is very important to learn it. Most sophisticated Bean container applications deep down in their heart of operation are doing the same.

Now let's talk about returning the icon associated with our Bean. The method is called *getIcon*. Listing 1.7 shows the code.

LISTING 1.7   The getIcon() Method

```
public java.awt.Image getIcon(int iconKind)
{
  if (iconKind == BeanInfo.ICON_COLOR_16x16 ||
    iconKind == BeanInfo.ICON_MONO_16x16)
  {
    java.awt.Image img = loadImage("JavaBeanIcon16.gif");
    return img;
  }

  if (iconKind == BeanInfo.ICON_COLOR_32x32 ||
```
Continues

LISTING 1.7   The getIcon() Method *(Continued)*

```
    iconKind == BeanInfo.ICON_MONO_32x32)
  {
    java.awt.Image img = loadImage("JavaBeanIcon32.gif");
    return img;
  }
  return null;
}
```

Based on the type of the icon present it would either return the icon with the dimensions of 32×32 or the icon with the dimensions of 16×16. Note that the return value of the method is of type *java.awt.Image* and thus, as seen in the source, the *loadImage* method is called to load the icon file. The icon is in GIF format.

The getPropertyDescriptors method is shown in Listing 1.8.

This method returns the properties associated with the Bean. Every property object of a Bean has a method to get it and another method to set it. These are usually called the Getter and the Setter methods. All the *PropertyDescriptor* methods have the capability of throwing an exception of the type *IntrospectionException*; hence, the entire code is present within the *try* and *catch* blocks. Notice that the *catch* block follows the same policy of generating the error object as seen earlier.

The *try* block has the code associated with creating the *PropertyDescriptor* objects. First it creates *PropertyDescriptor* objects called *releasedColor* and *pressedColor*. The constructor takes in the property name and the class filename. After the creation of the two objects we notice that the *setBound* method is called on both the objects. The parameter passed to this method is true. This sets a *PropertyChange* event to be fired as soon as the property of the object is changed, which causes the property of the object to be updated with the new value. To understand this, take a look at the next line of code. The immediate next line of code is a call to the method *setDisplayName*. This method changes the display name of the object. This causes a change in the property value, and the *setBound* method causes the *PropertyChange* event to be fired, which will update the property of the Bean. After changing the display names of both the properties we create an array of the *PropertyDescriptor* object called *rv*. It has two elements in the array. This is then returned by the method. Note that the return type is an array of *PropertyDescriptor* objects.

LISTING 1.8   The getPropertyDescriptors() Method

```
public PropertyDescriptor[] getPropertyDescriptors()
{
  try
  {
    PropertyDescriptor releasedColor = new
    PropertyDescriptor("releasedColor", beanClass);

    PropertyDescriptor pressedColor = new
    PropertyDescriptor("pressedColor", beanClass);

    releasedColor.setBound(true);
    releasedColor.setDisplayName("Released Color");
    pressedColor.setBound(true);
    pressedColor.setDisplayName("Pressed Color");

    PropertyDescriptor rv[] = {releasedColor, pressedColor};
    return rv;
  }
  catch (IntrospectionException e)
  {
    throw new Error(e.toString());
  }
}
```

This ends the discussion of our JavaBean example. It is interesting to see how all the parts of the components were used to make the application a Bean. Also, we had an applet on which the Bean was placed. The applet could make the Bean animate with the help of basic movement techniques. Although this was a simple example, it was very involved and detailed many of the parts of an applet and a JavaBean. It showed how a JavaBean is structured and how the *SimpleBeanInfo* class could be used for the benefit of the developer and the user. The explanation delved into the workings of the introspection. We used the introspection to query the Bean and toggle with its property value. JavaBeans is a much more involved topic, and all of it cannot be covered in one chapter. There are many books on the market that deal with JavaBeans in detail. This chapter was designed to provide a feel of the technology and generate an interest in the minds of the readers.

WHERE IS JAVA HEADING TODAY?

This is a very interesting time for Java developers and Java lovers. We do not know whether the heading for this topic is appropriate or not. The suspicion that we have is, should we be asking it as a question or should it be an exclamation, which gives an impression of the amazing things Java is going through. The exclamation is a better way of putting it as it indeed is impressive. Java is expanding its wings and soaring very high. It has absorbed the distributive component technology by the Remote Method Invocation (RMI) technology. It absorbed the Web technology with the Applet invention. Now there are Servlets (Java entities that can be executed on the server). Java has already proven that it is a perfect choice for embedded software and dedicated devices. It started with a common execution environment and proved to be tremendously strong. Database technology was something that Java did not touch for a while, but very soon it turned around to come up with a standard for databases: JDBC (Java Database Connectivity). JDBC is a standard interface for communicating with databases. Any Java application making use of the database can safely write to this common set of interfaces and rest assured that the application will work on most existing databases. No database-specific custom routine needs to be written, nor does the code need to be altered for different databases. This is possible only if the database supports the JDBC interface. But guess what! The majority of databases today do support JDBC.

Recently we have seen some effort by the developers of Java and related tools to address mail technology. They are working on the Java Mail technology, a Java-dependent mail specification. The database market has seen the two different sectors it is getting split up with. The database market is not actually splitting, but the separation is becoming more and more prevalent. The industry has realized that along with the relational database technology the object database technology has also found applications. More and more users realize this and are converting themselves to use it. The application demands the flexibility of an object environment and a less-entangled architecture. In order to address this market Java is working on a relational-to-object mapping system known as Java Blend. You can find more detailed specifications of this on JavaSoft's web site. It would certainly take many pages to introduce Java Blend, and we will not go into the details of it here. This effort is being co-worked with another company. The effort is directly targeted at the database market. Many existing large database users would not completely agree to convert their applications and data into a new environment. This resistance may not be due to ignorance but simply because these could be mission-critical data and no risk should be assumed in the process. Furthermore, the migration effort may demand serious resource commitments that the company is not ready to make. In such a scenario the Java Blend technology is a great solution. The approach provides the user the best of both worlds. For a change, it is possible to have your cake and eat it too.

These are just some of the efforts of the creators of Java. There certainly will be more to come, and we will have to wait and see what is next. But by observing the trend, it is clear to see that they appear to approach every bit and piece of technology and provide a solution to it with Java. It is a very interesting and well-rounded approach, as many of these approaches are joint efforts with other development companies. This does not keep any bias in the solution. The solution is something that the users can actually make good use of and benefit from. The open standard approach has given many of us great freedom in not only being a part of the beneficiaries but also a part of the creators. There is great satisfaction in being known as a creator of technology used by the masses. Every creator basks in the glory of appreciation. This is a technology with so much open architecture that it can be molded to serve many needs. Java is trying the same. They are willing to entertain each and every possibility and work on them to find a better solution. This is just the beginning of a new Java era. By the time this book goes to print there very well may be such technologies announced by the creators of Java.

CONCLUSION

This chapter has taken a big ride. We started out with explaining Java applet technology. Then we created our first Java applet. We then learned some more intriguing facts about applet technology. It was an important step, as it will help you in writing better applets. We then moved on to JavaBeans, one of the hottest technologies in town. People knowing JavaBeans have tremendous opportunity in the industry. They are paid much higher salaries and, best of all, everyone wants a Java-Beans guru. This chapter explained what JavaBeans is all about. It then mentioned the attributes of JavaBeans. It talked about the benefits of JavaBeans and how to make use of them. We then developed our first Bean and also made it integrate with an applet. We studied the details about the operation and learned about introspection. We saw some introspection code and studied its workings.

The goal of the chapter was to let you get your feet wet with the technology. We all agree that everything cannot be learned about something without actually getting your hands dirty. So our suggestion is, go and start coding in Java. Writing some more applets and Beans will certainly provide the kind of information that you desire. To learn more about Java and JavaBeans, you should check out www.javasoft.com and www.rhoque.com/javabeans.

CHAPTER 2

Say Hello to InfoBus

The world of technology is changing constantly. The creation process is on and keeps churning out new technology. This is good for the users of the technology as it keeps providing us with better solutions to everyday computing problems. As developers of products we can really appreciate the effort as it enables us in creating better and much sophisticated products. After all, we all love creativity don't we? Nonetheless, it always keeps us busy. We have to keep on learning new things, and it is a never-ending process. The process of creation of newer technology generally has a basis of its creation and a proper justification to its existence. If the creator cannot defend the creation then it will fade out very fast. We all abide by this rule of thumb and walk our paths in the technology world. The changing technology is driving the next wave of growth in this industry sector. To profit from the system we need to apply not only the new technology but also the thinking process that was applicable in the creation of the new technology.

As you know, Sun Microsystems caused a tremendous change in the world of computing with the creation of Java. Along with the creation of Java came a bunch of newer deductive solutions in the industry. The world started looking at many solutions with Java glasses on. Many initiatives have been undertaken to attempt to solve various computer science tasks using Java. Such triumphant efforts have not met with any major disappointment. After testing the technology over time, the industry overall has committed significant resources in terms of man hours and dollars to using Java. It has undauntedly become the technology that will take us to the next generation. Java is actively pursued as a development environment in all corners of the world, in both academia and the commercial technology industry. Many related technologies have been born since then that serve a good purpose for technology lovers and product developers.

We developers tend to thrive in difficult and challenging areas. Something just starts our creative juices flowing. Let's ponder some matters that will help us paint the right kind of picture within the canvas. Data is an important ingredient of computer science. Data has various attributes and has different definitions at different locations. Some entity that is viewed as data at one phase tends to be an operational unit at the other phase. Hence the term *data* is loosely applied and is greatly overused. The importance of data increases when it has relevance for the interpreter. Data becomes information and is valued at some point when the data is used for some tangible or intangible value it brings with it. The developer community tries to make the information valuable to the user. The user of the program has specific needs and requirements that the program needs to fulfill. The developer of the program works on the data and presents it to the user, on request, in a format that satisfies him or her. The data, which is used to drive applications, is handled in multiple ways. The data is converted from one form to another, shared among different modules for different types of applicability, and so forth. Sharing of data is an important factor in application development.

To understand the use of data in a real-world application, let's look at a particular scenario. The discussion pertains to a business application suite that is used by an organization having offices at different geographical sites. The entire system is linked via a fault-tolerant networking system. Since the organization has business needs at most of its office sites, the business data needs to flow from any originating site to any destination site without having a bias in the operational path. This finally ends up being a properly distributed site with a transparent storage involved. Assume a condition in which site A generates a business proposal. The proposal is in its initial stages and consists only of discussion that introduces the business. This business is being jointly performed with site B, which also needs to insert its input into the system. The final version of the proposal ends up having the introduction of the business model and the business logic involved in it. It also encompasses the percentage of involvement of the concerned sites, including the participation responsibilities, the possible outcomes, and the graphical display of the value added to the client and to the business organization. This is a fairly complex example, but it is certainly a useful one.

Such applications are happening in the real world every day, and multimillion-dollar businesses are organized in this manner. The business application needs to store different types of data and needs to migrate them from one site to another based on demand. Since the application ends up having a huge amount of data, they need not be migrated from one site to another at every instantiation of the process. When site B is updating the business proposal, it does not need to download the graphical possible outcomes, as they may not make any sense to site B at that point. Therefore, the business application needs to have this functional intelligence within itself. The system learns this intelligence while the application development is in process. The hints to this data are generated by the developers and are captured by the system.

Another facet that needs to be discussed is the dynamic extrapolation of information from one entity to another for further usage. This is a topic not generally covered in many technical books, and most software packages do not provide stronger interfaces to it. It may very well be the case that while the existing software package interprets a data set for the user in a specific range of accuracy and to some level of understanding, the same set of data can be used by another software package in a very different way. The other software package could provide a different viewpoint and present a very different understanding of it. This idea may seem very unlikely to many of you immediately, but the best way to understand it is to make an analogy with human behavior.

We all interpret the same information in different ways. It is not to say that all the interpretations are accurate, but it might very well be the case that many do interpret the same information in multiple, sensible ways. Also, more than one interpretation ends up being correct due to the way the information is posted to the individuals. Since businesses are part of such information creation and interpretation processes, these outcomes are quite possible. If such possibilities exist, then the software application that is being used for the creation of such business documents and logic should explore them and attempt to provide a solution to them. It is not possible for one set of applications to provide solutions to all existing situations within the domain, but they can certainly provide ways for the users to use the information in a different set of applications and generate different interpretations. This is an era of open standards, and the proprietary methods and logic do not go a long way.

When we talk about open standards and principles we need to identify the options available to explore these features. The information extrapolated from one set of applications needs to be made available to another set of applications. One way of doing so is to make use of the static form, which ends up in decoding the proprietary storage format and retrieving the relevant information. This approach is strenuous and error prone. Furthermore, it never ends up being the right solution as the logic applied by the application is always dependent on the format of the information generator. If the original creator of the information decides to change the format of its persistent storage, the application would fail. The follow process has to be in sync with the creator and can be very difficult at times. Since these issues cannot be policed via some standard approaches, this choice is the lowest in the list of solutions.

The better approach is to have a standard design principle introduced in this process. Since a standards body or a consortium guides the standard, one does not have to worry about the compliance of the others in this area. Anybody who respects the standard design principle can conveniently work in unison with other applications. The effort is diverted in two directions, and both end up being fruitful for the application creators and the application users. The direction of concentration is to develop the best application software in that domain. The company then excels, as the consumers cherish being a customer of the company due to the quality of the software. The second direction of concentration is toward establishing the standard design principles. It helps reduce the chaos in the area of development. It also benefits the industry as every part of the standards body works together. The software application created by the member of the consortium then works with many other participating software applications. The incompatibilities are eliminated, and harmony within the working environment is introduced.

All this being said, how about having an environment that facilitates all this dynamic data access and much more? A good way of doing this is to tap into a flowing stream to get some information diverted in your direction; for example, a phone conference in which anyone interested in participating dials a toll-free number that provides an access code to authenticate that individual as a legitimate participant. Once the legitimacy is verified, the logger then becomes part of the phone conference, listening to the discussion and exchanging information with the other listeners. Does that sound good enough? Well, then let us get to the introduction of InfoBus. This chapter is dedicated to introducing this Java-related technology.

WHAT IS INFOBUS?

By now you're probably wondering, "So what is InfoBus anyway?" Before we answer that, let's start with some background information. As you know, Java provides us with the power of building platform-independent applications. In cases other than Java, the development of an application and its usage had many factors in play for a successful coordination. Apart from the domain the application was targeting, the platform also played a very important role in this relationship. With Java, this unnecessary factor could be isolated. The application could be developed in any platform and executed in any other platform. Java also introduced many other technologies and tools that help create distributed applications. Also, Internet awareness was realized pretty early in the Java environment; hence, the architecture was developed in such a manner that the applications would work on the Internet.

This brought applets into the picture. They were designed to work in an Internet environment. Applets became very popular because of the simplicity involved in their development process. It involved far less time and did a pretty good job, as you gathered from Chapter 1, "Java-Beans and Java Applets." Applets could be used for enhancing web pages and also for business-related projects in their initial phases. Slowly and steadily it was discovered that as the network environment was getting closer and closer to the application development process, the developers lacked the capabilities of having a uniform development environment. Since the network was so integral to our lives, the distinction between applications working on a nonnetworked environment and a networked environment faded away.

Then came the phase of the Internet and the intranet. This made the distinction vanish even faster as now every development and execution environment was at least intranet aware. This congruency is gaining more momentum. Realizing the facts, JavaBeans were introduced. These made available to the developers the flexibility of distributed application development without incurring the extra overhead. JavaBeans provided the distributed, shared, application development environment, which provided appropriate transparencies to the developer with respect to the lower operating environment. JavaBeans greatly simplified the development of reusable components. JavaBeans are a great concept and do a perfect job for the kind of work they are targeted to do. However, there is one more essential component that is not taken care of with JavaBeans. This is related to data exchanges. JavaBeans provide a flexible and uniform reusable component development environment, but you have to understand that applications deal with data. Data needs to flow from one component to another for intelligent processing, and there needs to be a facility provided for it. This is an active data exchange. This is what InfoBus is all about. It deals with an information bus, wherein complying JavaBeans can tap in and acquire the relevant data.

InfoBus offers a solution in terms of providing a small number of interfaces, helping JavaBeans interconnect with each other to perform dynamic data exchanges. The participating Beans need to comply with the specifications by supporting the interfaces stated in the InfoBus. The fundamental building block for data exchange is the *data item*, which is created and used for communication purposes. The data to be communicated has to be converted in the data item form and placed in the information bus (we will talk about it in detail in the paragraphs following). Any Bean implementing the InfoBus interface can register itself into the communication channel. Once it is registered, it can participate in the process by passing data around and reading data from the channel. In general, the bus does not have any master/slave configuration. It works in an asynchronous fashion. It is very open-ended in its configuration. However, it is possible to have the bus operate in a master/slave fashion with a controller. The controlling component acts as the guide or the arbitrator of the information within the bus.

This configuration has its positive side as well as its drawbacks. The positive side of this configuration is that due to the arbitrator's presence the information is controlled. The system does not get overloaded with information of various types. In such a bus architecture many types of information can flow. If the variety of information increases then it becomes difficult for the system to operate and "noise" overloads the system. The controller can moderate the functionality and police the information flow. The drawback imposed with such a configuration is that the bus starts functioning synchronously. The synchrony can degrade the performance of the bus and reduce the usage of the system. Also, the controller is involved more in moderating the channel; hence, the productivity of the controller reduces. Also, it functions in a client/server mode wherein the arbitrator acts as the server and clients passing information to other clients get routed through the arbitrator. However, the point here is that the InfoBus configuration is flexible enough to facilitate any type of usage. The user needs to identify the right usage model and configure the system accordingly.

The InfoBus model supports a producer/consumer model. Within an InfoBus environment, one end acts as the producer of information and the other acts as the consumer. To be InfoBus compliant, the Java component needs to implement the InfoBus interface, which is a small set of Java interfaces. When the InfoBus interface is implemented by a Java component, it becomes an InfoBus component. The first release of InfoBus is called version 1.1 and supports JDK 1.1. The next version of InfoBus is version 1.2, which supports the JDK 1.2 features.

As you know, all Java applications, applets, and Beans are executed over the JVM. The JVM hosts everything in Java. The loader loads all Java executable components within a specified virtual machine. If you recall the functioning of JavaBeans, the loader loads them. Once they are loaded, the reason one Bean can see the properties and events of the other entire Bean component is due to the same presence within the same virtual machine. We make use of the introspection interfaces and the design patterns to retrieve the names of the property methods and events. Once we get a handle on the methods and their parameters, we can start making calls to the Bean and start communicating with it. This is a dynamic approach as the interaction between two different Beans is built up dynamically.

The approach is flexible but has initial delays in the discovery process. With InfoBus it is much more static. The interfaces are implemented by the Java components. No dynamic query and learning are involved. Since the cooperating component has already implemented the interface, direct calls can be made. Though the method and events do not have to be queried by any means in an InfoBus component, there needs to be a way for the data to be understood. The InfoBus components can be created by different sites without having any prior knowledge about the type of data each one produces or receives. A lack of data type recognition can cause misinterpretation of the data flowing through the channel. The solution to this is suggested in the following manner. The semantics of the data flow are based on interpreting the contents of data that flows across the InfoBus interface. Unlike Beans, they do not depend on the names of the methods, parameters, or event types.

As we have just seen, InfoBus can work in a synchronous as well as an asynchronous model. Based on this there exists three different types of InfoBus component: the data producer, the data consumer, and the data controller. Notice that a particular InfoBus component can act as a data producer as well as a data consumer. Data items are the named objects in which data flows between InfoBus components. The data controller, as the name suggests, mediates the rendezvous between the data producers and the data consumers. The version 1.1 specification of InfoBus talks about a few principle requirements. They are listed here:

The InfoBus should support the creation of interactive applications without requiring support of a "builder" application. That is, application designers should be able to assemble these applications using conventional web page editing tools. Further, these applications should run in standard HTML interpreted environments (browsers) without requiring specific extensions or support beyond the basic Java language environment. Note that this does not preclude enhanced capabilities in the presence of the JavaBeans-enabled environment.

The InfoBus must support semantics that allow data to be communicated in a canonical format for consumption by multiple consumers. A canonical format involves both the encoding of data (numbers, strings, etc.) and navigation of data structures (rows, columns, tuples, etc.). Our intent is that mechanisms used to format and recover data be based as closely as possible on mechanisms already available from Java itself and JavaBeans.

The requirements stated by the creators of InfoBus are few and simple. They intend to keep the InfoBus environment as ordinary as possible by avoiding any kind of extensions whatsoever within the operating environment. They do not propose extensions to the Java language of HTML. They want it to be operable by simple web editing tools. This clearly paints the picture of the global market they are targeting. No special requirements keep the backward-compatibility monkey off the back of InfoBus. Also, they make a clear point about supporting the semantics of the data being communicated over the InfoBus interface. The communication needs to be performed in a canonical format. And like many other communication protocols, the data item possesses the data encoded in it, and if any special navigational rules are required to traverse the data structure, they are encoded within it. This tight data semantics relieves the data consumer of any overheads in data browsing and interpreting. All this being said, none of the mechanisms need to be custom built for InfoBus; they intend to make use of the mechanisms built in Java and JavaBeans. In short, InfoBus does not have any special requirements for the system to be operable, apart from the base set of InfoBus interfaces. A pictorial representation of an InfoBus environment is shown in Figure 2.1.

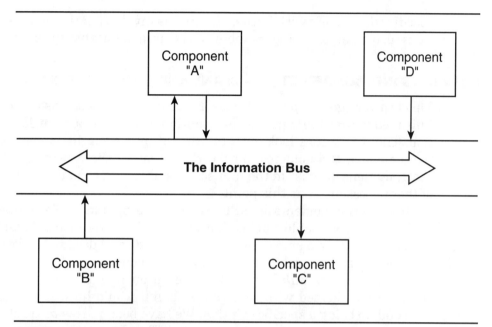

FIGURE 2.1   An InfoBus system.

In Figure 2.1 we see an InfoBus wherein information is flowing in both directions. The direction of information is never limited within an InfoBus environment. Within the image we see four components: A, B, C, and D. The arrows from the InfoBus channel to the components and the ones from the components show the direction of flow of information. As we notice, component A is both a producer as well as a consumer of information. The two arrows depict this, one flowing towards it and the other going away from it. Component B is just an information producer or generator. The arrow clarifies its disposition. Component C is only an information consumer. Component D acts as an information producer. This is a very simplistic model, but most of the practical models are very much like it. This is due to the fact that the InfoBus model is a very simple model to generate applications on. Again, this is only a part of the actual application. The application functionality is not shown within Figure 2.1.

Who invented the InfoBus technology? InfoBus is a result of the joint efforts of a few companies. Douglass Wilson from Lotus created the concept of InfoBus. Douglass wrote the first specification and technical guidance document. Currently, Mark Colan leads the development effort of InfoBus at Lotus. He is the lead architect and editor of the latest specification. Along with Lotus, JavaSoft is involved in the process. Oracle is also a participating member in the area of database access.

HOW DOES INFOBUS AFFECT JAVABEANS AND JAVA APPLETS?

This is a very good topic to discuss. Notice that it is posed as a question. This means that the topic needs attention. InfoBus is a pure Java solution. The way things look with InfoBus, it may seem like a competitor to other Java technologies; however, that is not the case at all. Many contradictions do exist in the industry about it, and good understanding of them is essential at this point.

InfoBus complements JavaBeans and is the right kind of a solution for a distributed, reusable application execution environment. JavaBeans brings into picture a smooth way of reusing code and design. It provides a true meaning to reusability of software components. In the component world, the term *reusability* needs to be an open-ended architecture. If reusability is defined with constraints then it would limit its usage and thus end up being a specific solution. We have been in this mode of usage wherein "If this is true then you can do this" has been buzzing around our ears. Whenever we needed to reuse code blocks or self-contained executable entities, we always had to alter our current state in order to prepare for the reuse. The extra startup requirement not pertaining to the actual solution is the overhead, which the reusable components carry. All this has been shattered with JavaBeans. The concept of reusability has extended into other benefits like ease of deployment. The deployment of JavaBeans is also a very simplified process.

JavaBeans project an architecture wherein one can reuse an existing component dynamically—no questions asked or no requirements waved in your face. With all this dynamism involved in the system, wouldn't it be great to have a dynamic data exchange policy also? That's exactly what InfoBus is all about. It extends JavaBeans by providing the facility and makes the environment impregnable. We haven't yet gotten into the details of the InfoBus data exchange policies, but when we do, you will find out how easy it makes the working environment. Therefore, InfoBus does not compete with JavaBeans in any way. As we have seen, both attack different problem zones and are very closely linked so that each can assist the other.

JavaBeans also provides a rather indirect way to transfer data from one component to the other. Although this technique is available, it is very rough. The types of data that are communicated between the sender and the receiver need to be known in advance by both of them. With

InfoBus, more dynamic data interchange features are provided in the system. Imagine a situation in which the communication within a channel is being driven by the content of data flowing through it. In such a scenario, the nature of data to be expected is pretty much dynamic and can theoretically change between every dialogue. The two technologies combined provide the developers with more choices. The choice of flexibility with a very lose binding architecture or the performance improvements with a closely bound structure complement each other. The matter of tightly binding the interfaces in the InfoBus is not only for performance but also due to the fact that such components fall into a different class of applications. Practically speaking, when multiple components are working within one environment, it is much easier if developers know that particular types of components can exchange data. Also, it is very helpful to know that the receiver can identify the types of data sent by the data producer. It is a matter of ease and simplicity that is provided to the developer community. Finally, the choice lies in the actual usage strategy and is up to the actual programmer to make use of any option suitable to him or her. But it is always nice to know that there is an option available.

Applets in association with InfoBus become a much sweeter composition. As a matter of fact, applets gain a lot more in this association. Applets have the basic behavior of moving from the server to the client to begin execution. Applets are generally written as execution entities, which on invocation from an outside unit begin execution. This implies that unless the client system invokes the applet, it will stay dormant. The process of invocation is also unique, as the client cannot deterministically tell whether the applet was already active or not before it encountered it. When the client hits the web pages in which the applet is embedded, the applet starts loading itself into the client's virtual machine's address space. The loader from the client's virtual machine invokes the activity. The loading process of the applet involves downloading the applet completely. Once downloading is completed, the applet starts its execution. The execution is done within the client's virtual machine space. We refer to it as the client's *address space* for the sake of this explanation, although *address space* is a much grander term.

This process of being downloaded onto the client's address space for execution is great, but what about multiple applets trying to coordinate among each other? That is not defined. This is where the custom solutions come into the picture. Custom solutions create more problems in the long run than trying to solve the original issue. It provides a solution for a scenario that is limited to one type of a problem in that domain. The visibility of the problem is very limited; hence, the solution is limited to the type of cases it can handle. The other big problem with custom solutions is that one company provides it; therefore, the knowledge of the solution is limited to that company. The other software developing companies may not accept the solution, or they may not be in the position to acquire the solution completely from the creators because of internal problem-solving techniques involved with it. Also, due to privacy issues, the creators of the solution may not be in the position to completely oblige the other parties.

Imagine such a situation: You have written an applet, which is provided by the users to submit some information to your organization. It could be any kind of information; for example, survey purposes or customer feedback. If the client machine already has this information made available to some active entity like a JavaBean or a Java application, then the applet could easily acquire the information. The user does not have to enter the data twice—perhaps a little relief in this busy world. The other important factor in this case would be that the other active entity that has the data needs to know that this downloaded applet needs it. How can this communication be performed when both the entities are created by different people and there is no standard interface that provides such semantics? This requires that there is a common understanding between the two entities about the semantics involved in data transfer. It is then up to the discretion of the entity as to whether it wants to share the data.

There are, however, some strong repercussions to this solution. The information may be private to the user and the user may not like to expose it to an outside entity like an applet from another web page; hence, the semantics must be rich enough to provide secure as well as unsecured data exchanges. In these cases it is quite obvious that the user will not allow the information to flow in an unsecured data channel. The protected information will not become unprotected in an InfoBus environment; hence, such issues will not come up at all. The point of the example is to explain the coordination that can exist between an applet and other Java-aware active entities within an InfoBus-compliant environment.

Both JavaBeans and Java applets will gain by using the InfoBus technology. They compliment each other and make each much stronger than they would otherwise be individually. The coordination between these technologies is quite smooth and does not have any impedance mismatch. They add value to each other and end up providing a better-qualified solution to the developers. The software developer who gets access to a better-suited development environment reaps the overall benefits. The combined solution set targets more area and provides a much better synchronized tool set. It does not impose a threat to any one type of technology. To put it plainly, InfoBus would not be as useful as it is today without having JavaBeans and Java applets using it well, and vice versa.

THE DATA EXCHANGE PROCESS

The discussion pertaining to data exchange is very elementary in this chapter. The gory details of the data exchange policy are discussed in Chapter 3, "Inside the InfoBus." The next chapter lists the methods involved in the data exchange process. It explains the data structures in detail and the way the methods react on invocation. This section merely creates a need to the data exchange within the InfoBus application and provides a rather basic explanation of data exchange.

InfoBus provides a dynamic data exchange technique. This is the heart of the topic and deserves a good discussion. There are few steps involved in this process. Let's dig deep into each of them and identify their significance in the process. When we talk of data exchange there are some involved parts to it. The first and foremost one is the information provider. There is at least one entity within this symbiotic relationship that provides the information. The provider is not concerned about whether any other entity is interested in retrieving the information; it acts as the source of a type of information and theoretically publishes many different types. But in the practical world, one does not find many such publishers who publish various types of information. We then come to the information consumer, or the *sink*. The consumer is interested in absorbing information from the provider.

We now come to the functional attribute of the data exchange technique. InfoBus provides a regulated exchange technique called the *membership*. Any Java component interested in participating in the data exchange process needs to obtain a membership. This is a very natural process, and we all do it every now and then in our day-to-day life. For example, many of us have brokerage accounts with stock brokerage companies, which deal with stocks, bonds, mutual funds, futures, and so forth. There are many financial assets to play around with, and many of us are regular participants. We follow the stock and mutual funds market and roll our capital from one asset to another based on the opportunity available. Financial assets like stocks, bonds, and mutual funds are traded in properly organized markets. In order for us to participate in them we need to have some type of membership. We either do it as registered stock brokerage licenses or have accounts with one of these companies that work on our behalf. In either circumstance we extend our participation, directly or indirectly. Membership is the key to it all. Of course, our capital also plays a very important role.

In a similar fashion, InfoBus also follows the membership pattern. Any Java component wishing to participate has to implement the Java interface called InfoBusMember. By implementing this interface the Java component can connect to the InfoBus. It acquires an InfoBus instance by implementing the InfoBusMember interface. The InfoBus object maintains a list of InfoBusMembers that have attached to it.

The image in Figure 2.2 is taken from the InfoBus version 1.1 specification. This figure is very intuitive and is extremely helpful in explaining the concept. It clearly shows the working of the InfoBus architecture, which is why we use it here.

The figure shows the inside of the JVM. InfoBus works on Java; hence, all its functioning is done within the JVM and all its discussion is relevant to it. The InfoBus bus class is the core of the entire InfoBus operation. The InfoBus uses static methods and data members to access the list of active InfoBus instances. This is shown in the diagram with the help of the box, which has the static-text InfoBus data members in it. Inside the box we see a small list containing two elements. Each element has a reference to the active InfoBus instance. With the help of this list the InfoBus class keeps accountability of all the active InfoBus instances. This list can grow much longer. On the right side of the figure we see two dotted boxes. These two boxes represent InfoBus components. One of the components is acting as the data producer and the other is acting as the data consumer.

We have learned that every InfoBus component has to implement the InfoBusMember interface. We notice that the dotted boxes representing the data consumer and data producers each have an InfoBusMember implementation. To join the InfoBus they have to make a call to the *join* method in the InfoBus class. We will look at the complete interface definition of the InfoBus interface and the InfoBusMember interface in the next few paragraphs that follow. Every call to the *join* method of the InfoBus class creates an instance of InfoBus. It also creates an element within the list that keeps a reference to the active InfoBus instance just created. This active instance of InfoBus is the representative of the InfoBus component, which can be either a data consumer or a data pro-

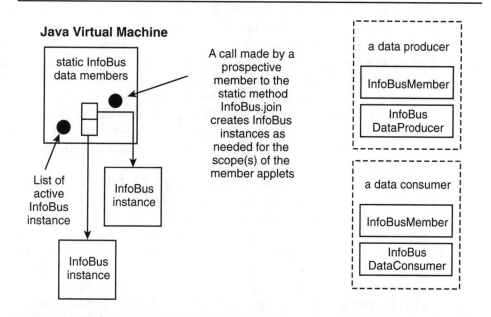

FIGURE 2.2   InfoBus instance management before members have joined.

ducer, to the InfoBus data channel. It is quite possible for one InfoBus component to act as both a data producer and a data consumer.

In the previous paragraph we studied the figure and the activation model of the InfoBus component. Now let's look at the theory behind the operation. The members join an instance of InfoBus, which functions as the connection point of the communication. The default instance of the InfoBus is one that is created by the generic name calculated from the *DOCBASE*. The *DOCBASE* is the document base location. It is the path of the URL. The filename is not included in it. Applets have the *DOCBASE* since they are associated with a URL. Therefore, to locate the default InfoBus instance the component either needs to be an applet or at least have an AWT containment hierarchy in it. The upward traversal of the applet helps to locate the *DOCBASE*. To recollect the applet concept, we know that the applet needs to be invoked by some outside entity, like a web browser.

We also know that when the outside entity invokes the applet it supplies a component context, which the applet needs to function properly. In our case of the InfoBus component, it needs to provide the Component context. As opposed to the default InfoBus instance the application can also provide a name to it, which ends up in creating the named InfoBus instance. It is also possible for classes to not have a Component context and still join the InfoBus by means of a name. This name can be specified by a property of the class. If the environment is facilitated by means of an application builder, or if the system itself works within a builder, then the builder environment can provide the Component context. Builders will have access to the Component context as they work very closely with them and can provide this context needed to join the InfoBus. In essence, the InfoBus can be joined in a number of ways. We have just identified them in this paragraph.

We have learned how to register with the InfoBus, projecting either as a data producer and/or data consumer. The next question we certainly have in mind is, when does the data producer provide the data into the channel and how does a data consumer receive the data? The data producer has the data but there needs to be an opportune time when it is ready to send the data into the channel. First, it has to be ready with the data, and second, the channel must be ready to accept the data. If both are not ready, the data may be lost in the process. Similarly, the data consumer needs to be ready to accept the data. If it is not ready, the data may be lost in the channel. To make these efforts coordinate properly, InfoBus uses the event mechanisms available in Java. When the component implements the *InfoBusMember* interface, it also prepares itself to receive events about the data. Hence, the components must create *event listener* objects for listening to the events generated.

There are two basic event interfaces for the two basic types of InfoBus application. They are the *consumer listener interface* and the *producer listener interface*. The bus generates the events, and therefore the implementation of the listener interfaces has to be added to it. The data consumer InfoBus component implements the consumer listener interface as it is interested in the events generated for the data consumption process. They get the event notification of the availability of data within the channel. Whenever data is made available in the InfoBus channel this event is generated, and any data consumer component that has a registered consumer listener object with the bus is notified. The data producer components implement the producer listener interface as it is interested in the events generated for the data production process. When data is needed in the channel it will issue an event notification for the generation of data to be supplied into the channel. On receiving the event notification, the data producer component can safely assume that the channel is ready for the data and provide the data into the channel.

A component can join more than one InfoBus. The current InfoBus architecture facilitates such a process, but for this to work without any confusion the component must have a separate InfoBusMember object for each InfoBus it wants to join. This means that the component needs a separate copy of the active InfoBus instance for each conversation. This takes the load of sharing information among all off of the InfoBus architecture. The current architecture does not provide a way for multiple InfoBuses to share information or visibility among each other. (This may be something addressed in the next few releases; however, no promises are made by the creators yet.) Although the component needs separate InfoBusMember objects for each InfoBus, it still can work with one event listener object. The event listener object listens to the event generated from within Java. Since there is one instance of the JVM within which all of these take place, it is sufficient to have a single listener object.

Figure 2.3 depicts the instance of a data producer and a data consumer registered to an InfoBus channel. The JVM is shown enclosing the entire InfoBus system. We see that the static InfoBus data members store a reference to an active InfoBus instance that has a data producer and a data consumer registered in it. The active InfoBus instance keeps a list of all the participants in it. The data items generated by the data producer are routed through the bus to the data consumer. If another data consumer or data producer wants to join the InfoBus, it has to make a call to the static *open* method of the InfoBus. The data producer or the consumer intending to join the InfoBus specifies the name of the bus it desires to join. The *open* returns to it the InfoBus reference to be used for all further coordination by the producer or the consumer component. The *open* method first tries to locate the requested InfoBus within the existing ones in the list. If it exists then it returns the reference. If it does not exist, then it creates one for the requester and returns the reference to it.

Next, the component makes a call to the static *join* call to the InfoBus returned by the *open* method. If *join* is successful, meaning no exception is generated, then the component can go along with its act of data production or data consumption. This seems to be a very simple process, but there are a lot of events listener objects created to make it work. The events listeners listen to events, which are generated whenever a component changes states.

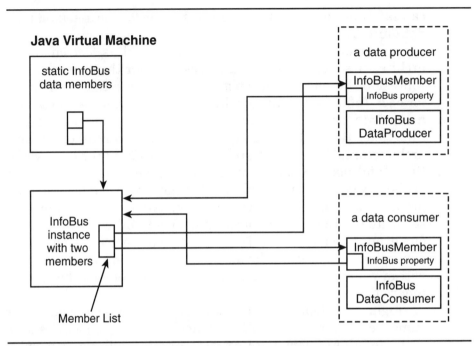

FIGURE 2.3   A producer and consumer as InfoBus members.

We have seen how the active instance of the InfoBus is created, but we haven't explored the clean-up procedure of the InfoBus. Who deletes the InfoBus after it has been used? How does one determine when to clean up the InfoBus not being used? To answer these questions, let's walk through the scenario in detail. When the InfoBus is created and a producer or consumer component joins it, the InfoBus creates a *PropertyChangeListener* object. (The InfoBus implements the *PropertyChangeListener* interface.) The InfoBus adds a listener for each *InfoBusMember* joining it. This helps the InfoBus keep track of the number of members present within it. Whenever a component decides to leave the InfoBus, it sends an event to the InfoBus, which is caught by the listener related to it and maintained by the InfoBus. Upon receiving the notification of the event, the InfoBus decrements its counter and removes the listener object added to it with regards to the component. When the counter's value reaches zero, which implies that the InfoBus does not have any more members, the InfoBus can destroy itself. This is a safe assumption because nobody is referring to it anymore. On the other hand, the component also needs to change its InfoBus property value; it either changes it to a new InfoBus that it has joined or sets it to null.

The clean process is eloquently designed without having any operating overhead. The system takes care of cleaning up any unused InfoBuses. There is not a creator assigned with the InfoBus. This removes the overhead of cleaning up the bus before leaving it that the first visitor of the bus would have encountered. A very good application for the InfoBus technology that comes to mind immediately is the Internet Relay Chat (IRC) applications. Such IRC applications have discussion channels. Every user logging in to the channel is both a data producer as well as the data consumer. The only operating difference between the base design of InfoBus- and IRC-based applications is that in IRC systems the data is broadcast to all the users of the channel. But this can very well be accomplished by sending events to all the data consumers. The consumers without any discretion would accept the data generated by the producer. There are many more applications of the InfoBus system. The business environment is a big customer of such applications. Nowadays, with the concept of satellite offices and dispersed work setups, InfoBus-based applications can work miracles. They can make the distributed work environment highly productive and provide a real-time approach to it.

At this point it is appropriate to discuss the InfoBus class definition. We have been talking about the methods used in performing the operations, but not the type of method or the information the method takes in. Since the InfoBus class is responsible for maintaining the *InfoBusMember* objects we will also be looking into the *InfoBusMember* interface in detail. These two definitions will provide us with more insights into their workings.

Please note that this section of the chapter explains only the InfoBus class. Chapter 3, "Inside the InfoBus," shows examples of code that actually use these methods within InfoBus applications. A good understanding of the InfoBus class is necessary, and the discussion in this section provides an understanding of the methods and how they can be used in an InfoBus application. Chapter 3 takes it to the next level by providing source code snippets that use these methods. This kind of a second helping will expunge the doubts, if any, from the minds of the readers about their actual importance.

```
public class InfoBus extends Object
```

The InfoBus class extends the *Object* class. It keeps a list of the *InfoBusMember* objects that have attached to it. It helps in enabling the communication between them. The attaching members have the capability of throwing an *InfoBusEvent* to the *InfoBus*. The event is sent to the *DataController*. The *DataController* functions as a guide to the communication going on in the InfoBus; hence, the controller knows who to route the event to. If the data controller is not present then the event is sent to all the *InfoBusEventListeners*. This is the order in which events are dispatched.

```
public String getBusName()
```

The InfoBus has a name associated with it, which is unique. This name is set via two methods. The first way of setting this name is via the application defined string. The application can specify the name for the Bus, which is used to represent the Bus uniquely. The second way is via automatic calculation, for which the *DOCBASE* is required. The name is uniquely calculated by walking up the class hierarchy to retrieve the HTML and the Document Base. Either the applet class is required or the AWT container must be present somewhere in the hierarchy. This guarantees that all the InfoBusMembers within the same HTML page have this Document Base InfoBus.

```
public static synchronized InfoBus open(
   Component component)
public static synchronized InfoBus open(
   String busName)
```

These two methods perform the function of opening an InfoBus and returning its reference. Notice that the method is overloaded and has two polymorphic forms. The first form of the method takes the Component object, which is of *type java.awt.Component* class. The second form of the *open* method takes in a string form of the name. Both the methods are static and synchronized. We have talked about most of the methods of the InfoBus class as static. The static call helps in keeping one instance of the originator. Therefore, everyone logs into the same instance and starts the InfoBus process from the similar site. If they were not static then every prospective member of the InfoBus would need to have their own copy of InfoBus, which would create great difficulty in sharing conversation channels among the data producers and data consumers. The *open* method is kept synchronized in order to avoid any problems related to multiple threads making calls at the same time. This keeps the responsibility of call synchronization within the domain of the system. This method is explained in full detail, including a code example, in Chapter 3, "Inside the InfoBus."

```
public sybchronized void join(
   InfobusMember member) throws
   PropertyVetoException, InfoBusMembershipException
```

This method is called on the active InfoBus instance. The input parameter is the *InfoBusMember*, which needs to join the current InfoBus. It helps to join the InfoBusMember to the InfoBus on which this method is called. Notice that this is not a *static* method. Within this method, the InfoBus calls the *setInfoBus* method of the InfoBusMember to set itself as the value for the member's InfoBus property. The InfoBus also registers itself as an *InfoBusListener* to listen to the events related to changes in property in the future.

This method is capable of throwing two exceptions: *PropertyVetoException* and *InfoBusMembershipException*. *PropertyVetoException* is thrown when a change in property occurs and the new value of the property is unacceptable or not within the value range. The *setInfoBus* method of the InfoBusMember object, called *member*, generates this exception if it encounters any violations.

The *InfoBusMembershipException* is thrown when the specified InfoBus is not active or is stale. This may happen if the specified InfoBus was closed for conversation or made inactive in general. This exception will also be thrown if membership is not granted to the new InfoBusMember object. This can happen if the channel is either limited to some specified number of participants and the limit has been reached, or if it is a secured channel and the new member is not authenticated to participate in the discussion. These are all application-specific restrictions.

```
public void register( InfoBusMember member )
```

This method registers the InfoBusMember with the InfoBus. Within this method the InfoBus registers itself as the *PropertyChangeListener* on the InfoBusMember's *InfoBus* property. An InfoBus can have many InfoBusMembers associated with it. These are the participants in the Bus. They are DataControllers, data producers, or data consumers. The instance of the InfoBus keeps track of all the participants and maintains a list of them. The list keeps on growing as new members register themselves with the InfoBus. When they leave, the list is reduced. Once the list becomes empty the InfoBus can lose itself. The resources related to the InfoBus instance are freed up. This is a good technique of resource management by the system itself; otherwise, the creator of the Bus would have to be alive and keep track of the InfoBus instance. The management overhead moves toward the creator, which may limit its performance and productivity.

```
public void propertyChange( PropertyChangeEvent pce )
```

This method is used to propagate the property changes of the InfoBus. It accepts the notification for the change done in terms of the *PropertyChangeEvent* object. The *PropertyChangeEvent* object *pce* is constructed with the string InfoBus as its property name and the InfoBus-Member as its source. The *PropertyChangeEvent* object *pce* contains within itself the *InfoBusMember* having its *InfoBus* property changed. It also has the old value of the property and the new value of the property.

```
public synchronized void leave(
   InfoBusMember member) throws PropertyVetoException
```

The *leave* method allows the InfoBusMember to remove itself from the InfoBus. The InfoBus, on which the *leave* method is called, calls the *setInfoBus* method of the *InfoBusMember* object. The parameter it passes to this method is null. This will inherently set the InfoBus value of the InfoBusMember to NULL. When the register method is called the InfoBus sets itself as the listener to the InfoBusMember object. In the leave method it removes itself from listening to the events from the specified InfoBus-Member.

This method has the capability of throwing the *PropertyVetoException*. If the listener object, which is a *VetoableChangeListener* and is watching the InfoBusMember's InfoBus property object, wants to oppose the change then it throws this exception. The listener object may want to oppose the setting of the InfoBusMember's InfoBus property to null. This opposition arises only if the listener object wants the InfoBus-Member to be a part of the Bus.

```
public synchronized void addDataProducer(
   InfoBusDataProducer producer)
   Throws InfoBusMembershipException
```

This method allows a data producer to register itself as a data producer for the specified InfoBus. A component may want to register itself as a data producer to the InfoBus when it realizes its capabilities of providing data to the Bus. The data consumers of the Bus can use the data. The input parameter is the data producer, which would like to add itself to the InfoBus. This method would set it up in such a way that the data producer receives request notifications from the data consumers in the form of *InfoBusItemRequestedEvents*. The data producer then responds to the events by sending the data into the Bus.

The method has the capability of throwing the *InfoBusMembershipException*. This exception is thrown if the data producer is not offered membership to the InfoBus. There are various reasons for not being offered membership to the Bus. One of the reasons may be that the Bus can accommodate a limited number of participants, and the limit has already been reached. The other reason may be that the InfoBus is secured and only certain specific participants can register with it. The InfoBus may verify credentials of the participants before they are allowed membership.

```
public synchronized void removeDataProducer(
    InfoBusDataProducer producer)
```

This method allows a data producer to remove itself from the InfoBus. This results in the data producer being removed from the distribution list of the *InfoBusItemRequestedEvents*. After this operation the data producer can no longer receive events but can still be a passive participant of the InfoBus. The data producer may want to remove itself from receiving any more events if it has finished producing the data and supplying it to the Bus. The data generation process may have exhausted or completed. The data producer can add itself again when it is ready to produce more data.

```
public synchronized void addDataConsumer(
    InfoBusDataConsumer consumer)
    throws InfoBusMembershipException
```

This method allows an InfoBus component to register itself as a data consumer. The input parameter represents the component interested in adding itself as a data consumer. The operation is performed on the InfoBus in which it is interested in participating as the consumer. The

InfoBus adds the component to the list of data consumers who are supposed to receive the *InfoBusItemAvailableEvents* and the *InfoBus- ItemsRevokedEvents*. After this addition, the data consumer receives notifications to events informing the availability of data in the Bus and the notifications to events announcing the data item's revocation from the Bus. This is a synchronized method, which implies that the method is kept synchronized by the system and multiple threads can safely call the method without performing any external measures.

The method is capable of throwing *InfoBusMembershipException*. This exception is thrown if the data consumer is not provided membership in the InfoBus.

```
public synchronized void removeDataConsumer(
  InfoBusDataConsumer consumer)
```

The *removeDataConsumer* method allows a data consumer already added into the InfoBus to remove itself. This method also removes the data consumer from the distribution list of *InfoBusItemAvailableEvents* and *InfoBusItemsRevokedEvents*. After a call to this method, the data consumer will not receive any of the aforementioned events from the InfoBus; however, it will still be part of the InfoBus. A data consumer component may like to do this when it finishes collecting data from the InfoBus, allowing the consumer application to process the information collected from the InfoBus without being disconnected from it.

```
public synchronized void fireItemAvailable(
  String dataItemName, InfoBusDataProducer source)
```

This method is used to announce the availability of data items in the Bus. The *InfoBusEventListener* object calls this method. It acts on behalf of the data producer. In this method, the InfoBus creates an *InfoBusItemAvailableEvent* and sends it to all the data consumers who have registered with the Bus. Only data consumers who have added themselves to the InfoBus using the *addDataConsumer* call will receive the *InfoBusItemAvailableEvent* event notification. The data consumers interested in getting the data item use the *findDataItem* method to get the data item. This results in the data source's *requestDataItem* being called to retrieve the data. The input parameters for the method are the data item and the data producing source. The data item is of type string, and the data producer is of type *InfoBusDataProducer*.

```
public synchronized void fireItemRevoked(
  String dataItemName, InfoBusDataProducer source)
```

This method is used to inform the InfoBus that the specified data item is revoked. It also informs the InfoBus that the specified data item will never be made available from the specified source. The input parameters are the data item that is revoked from the InfoBus and the data producer or the data source from where the data item was originally generated. Within the method the InfoBus creates an *InfoBusItemRevokedEvent* and dispatches it to all the data consumers who have registered with the InfoBus via the *addDataConsumer* call.

```
public synchronized DataItem findDataItem(
   String dataItemName, InfoBusDataConsumer consumer)
public synchronized DataItem findDataItem(
   String dataItemName, InfoBusDataConsumer consumer,
  InfoBusDataProducer producer)
```

The *findDataItem* is a polymorphic method and has two forms. The first form takes the data item in the string format and the data consumer of type *InfoBusDataConsumer*. The second form takes in the data item in the string format, the data consumer of type *InfoBusDataConsumer*, and the data producer of type *InfoBusDataProducer*. The data consumer gears the method toward locating the data item. The second form of the method is a more specific search. The target location is made specific in the call. The method returns the data item requested by the data consumer.

The data consumer makes a call to this method. Within this method the InfoBus constructs an appropriate *InfoBusItemRequestedEvent* and dispatches it to all active data producers of the InfoBus. The producer who has the requested data item puts the data item in the Event's dataItem field. When the InfoBus gets the data back, it sends it to the caller of the *findDataItem* method. In the first form of the request, where the target is not specified, the InfoBus keeps on dispatching the *InfoBusItemRequestedEvent* to the data producers one at a time. As soon as a response from the data producer is non-null, the InfoBus stops sending more requests to the data producers. The non-null response from the data producer implies that the requested data is returned to the InfoBus, which the InfoBus can in turn send back to the caller. In case of the second form of the *findDataItem* method the target is well known and the *InfoBusItemRequestedEvent* is specifically sent to the target. The InfoBus does not loop through the entire data producer list. Please note that even in the second form of the method call, the response of dispatching the event to the data producer can be null. Most of the time the response will be non-null; since the data producer does have the data item, the possibility cannot be ignored. In such a case the InfoBus will not try the other data producer in the distribution list.

```
public synchronized DataItem[] findMultipleDataItems(
    String dataItemName, InfoBusDataConsumer consumer)
```

This method can be considered a superset of the *findDataItem* method. Here the request is not targeted towards a specific data producer. In this request the InfoBus loops through the entire data producer distribution list and sends the *InfoBusItemRequestedEvent* to each of them. It does not stop sending requests as soon as it gets the first non-null response, as is the case with the *findDataItem* method with the data item and the data consumer as the input parameters. The InfoBus picks up the response from each registered data producer and populates an array of *DataItem*. Once the InfoBus has finished its rounds, it then sends the array back to the data consumer who issued the method call. If no response is obtained from any of the data producers, it returns a null to the caller.

```
public static void setDebugOutput( boolean b )
```

This method is used for debugging purposes. The input parameter to this call is a *boolean* variable, which is used to set the debugging state to on or off. Making a call to this method with the input parameter being true sets the debugging state to on. In such a case, the debugOutput property is set to true and InfoBus logs the bus activity. If the *lotus.util.Debug* window is enabled, the log will be written there. If it is not enabled, then the log output is sent to System.out. The logging process involves creating a record of each event sent to each listener.

```
public static boolean getDebugOutput()
```

This method returns the current value of the *debugOutput* property.

With this we conclude our explanation of the *InfoBus* class description. The InfoBus is the most important class in the InfoBus technology, and understanding the method of the class and its function is very important in order to understand the technology. The next class we will be talking about is the InfoBusMember interface object. The InfoBus class manages the InfoBusMember objects.

```
public interface InfoBusMember extends Object
```

The InfoBusMember interface extends the *Object* class. All InfoBus-Members are required to implement a constrained property called InfoBus. The InfoBusMember interface class guarantees the presence of that property. Every InfoBus component intending to participate in a bus needs to implement the InfoBusMember interface. The property called the InfoBus, maintained by the InfoBusMember interface, is set to the actual bus to which the component registers itself. The bus to which the connection is desired attempts to set it. The attempt may be vetoed if the property is already set by the builder tool.

```
public abstract InfoBus getInfoBus()
```

This method returns the InfoBus, to which the InfoBusMember is logged in. When the InfoBusMember registers itself to an InfoBus, the InfoBus tries to set the InfoBus property of the requesting InfoBus-Member object to itself. This method helps identify the InfoBus to which the InfoBusMember component is currently connected.

```
public abstract void setInfoBus(InfoBus b)
   throws PropertyVetoException
```

The *setInfoBus* method is used to set the InfoBus property of the InfoBusMember component. The input parameter is the new value of the InfoBus property, which the method will attempt to set. The InfoBus itself calls this method. When the InfoBusMember wishes to join the InfoBus by calling the static *join* method of the InfoBus, the InfoBus will attempt to set the value of the property. (This method is explained in more detail in Chapter 3, "Inside the InfoBus.")

```
public abstract void addInfoBusListener(
   VetoableChangeListener l)
```

```
public abstract void addInfoBusListener(
   PropertyChangeListener l)
```

The *addInfoBusListener* method is polymorphic and has two forms. Both the methods are used to add listener objects to the InfoBusMember. The type of event on which they listen, however, differs. The first *addInfoBusListener* method adds the *VetoableChangeListener* object to the InfoBusMember. These listeners are guardian objects that have the capability of vetoing the changes made to the InfoBusMember. The changes in this case are made to the InfoBus property.

The second form of *addInfoBusListener* method adds the *Property-ChangeListener* object. An event is sent to the *PropertyChangeListener* object when the property of the InfoBusMember is changed and the change is allowed. The change is successful. The property that is changed is the InfoBus property.

```
public abstract void removeInfoBusListener(
   VetoableChangeListener l)

public abstract void removeInfoBusListener(
   PropertyChangeListener l)
```

The *removeInfoBusListener* method is also polymorphic and also has two forms. Both the methods remove the listener objects from the InfoBusMember, but they differ in the types of listener they remove. The first *removeInfoBusListener* method removes the *VetoableChange-Listener* object from the InfoBusMember object. The second *removeInfo-BusListener* method removes the *PropertyChangeListener* object from the InfoBusMember object.

With this we end the discussion on the InfoBusMember interface object. The two classes just discussed are extremely important to understand. The entire InfoBus technology revolves around them. This is not to imply that the other InfoBus-related classes are not useful, but in every technology there is a core system on which the entire environment functions.

THE NATURE OF DATA BROKERING

The InfoBus technology is all about data and ways to transfer it from the generator to the requester. Using the InfoBus terminology, it means transferring data from the data producer to the data consumer. Keeping this as the goal, the technology provides ways for this approach to be systematic and scalable. The technology has to be designed in line with the base Java technology, as Java is the operating environment. The data being transferred from one point to another needs to be discussed. The discussion (or the negotiation, to be more appropriate) has a greater importance in the InfoBus technology. This negotiation is referred to as *rendezvous*. The dictionary definition of *rendezvous* is a meeting place or a gathering place. Its emphasis is on the encountering of multiple parties to gather and share. The sharing in this context would be data, which is what we are dealing with for our concerns.

In InfoBus the data just does not move from one site to another without much preparation. As a matter of fact, the process of data transfer requires a lot of initial groundwork. In a classic InfoBus example, the data consumer needing the data generates an event requesting the data. The InfoBus, which acts as the channel of data flow, listens to the event. As soon as the InfoBus gets the event notification, it contacts the right data producer for the data. When the data producer receives the requests, it obliges the bus with the data. This data in turn is sent to the data consumer via the InfoBus. This is more of a *pull* approach for data transfer. The *pull* approach is one in which the data is being pulled from the generator to the consumer. You won't find the *pull* approach specifically mentioned in the InfoBus specification, but this is exactly how it works.

The other scenario is the *push* approach. Again, you may not find the *push* approach in the specifications. This is an analogy that has been applied to make it easier to understand. The *push* approach is one in which the data is pushed by the data producer to the appropriate data consumers. When the data producer has the data ready to be sent into the channel, it does not stuff the channel with the data instantly. It follows the Good Samaritan route of generating an event, informing the listener about the availability of data. The InfoBus is again the listener to these kinds of events. When the bus gets the notification, it contacts the consumer for the data availability. So even though the producer publishes the data, it goes through some well-documented paths before the actual data is moved around.

Since events are so essential in the data transfer task of InfoBus, let's look at the types of events that are generated in this process. The events are sent by the InfoBus to the listeners of each component of the bus. There are three types of events that we deal with: *InfoBusItemAvailableEvent*, *InfoBusItemRevokedEvent*, and *InfoBusItemRequestedEvent*. The first two events, *InfoBusItemAvailableEvent* and *InfoBusItemRevokedEvent*, are broadcast on behalf of the data producers. The *InfoBusItemRequested-*

Event is broadcast on behalf of the data consumers. We have already discussed the creation of the events and their listeners.

An InfoBus component can act as a data producer as well as a data consumer. For the component to do both, it needs to implement *InfoBusDataProducer* and *InfoBusDataConsumer*. *InfoBusDataProducer* is needed for the component to act as a data producer or data source. *InfoBusDataConsumer* is needed for a component to act as a data consumer or a data sink. These types of components can be very useful. A filtering component is a very good example of such a scenario.

To understand this concept, let's discuss a hypothetical scenario of a publisher/subscriber environment; for example, a financial officer in a private financial institution. The responsibility of the officer is to keep her eyes open for all the good opportunities the external business has to offer to the company. She cannot miss any market opportunity to make good and healthy investments for the company. Her responsibility is to keep up to date on the financial condition of the business and to also be aware of the financial market's movements. Since the business is global in nature, she has to be informed about the international business scenes. To accomplish this task she needs to read various types of financial magazines, business reviews, financial newspapers, online articles, and so on. In doing so, she may encounter a lot of information that has no relevance to the business at hand. This data is garbage for her and she does not need to read it to determine its validity. In order to avoid the loss of her time doing such work she has assistants to help. The job of the assistants is to filter the information from all the media and pass along the relevant information to the officer, and each assistant (filter) targets one type of media.

This process helps the officer concentrate on matters relevant to her business. In this example, the individual acting as a filter for the company performs a very significant and responsible task. He collects a lot of information, goes through it to figure out the details, and determines its significance to the particular model. He acts as the data consumer at this point. His second role is providing the relevant information to his supervisor; he then becomes a data producer. (Although the data provided to the supervisor is not his own data, he is still considered the data producer. This is due to the fact that the consumer and the producer are decided between the two parties involved. In this situation, the two involved parties are the person filtering the data and the officer who absorbs the data.)

The preceding is an example of a human being acting as a filter. In a similar manner, many applications and components also act as filters. A good example of an application acting as a filter is the firewalls that most companies have installed to protect the company's private data. The firewalls protect any intruder from outside the firewall from breaking in and retrieving valuable company information. On similar grounds, one can have a publisher/subscriber application environment wherein the publisher keeps on sending various types of information, some of which the consumer may not be interested in. Since these types of information publishing applications target many types of consumers, they cannot limit themselves to the types of information they publish. It then becomes the responsibility of the consumer application to pick and choose the information that is relevant to it. If the consumer application is designed to take in the information and process it, then it has to take in the right kind of information. Processing of the information is its main goal, and it cannot spend resources filtering the information for the source. In such scenarios, a filtering component exists whose only job is to filter the information generated from the source and feed it to the main module for processing. This demands that the filter function as a consumer as well as a producer.

If such a filter is developed in the Java environment using InfoBus, then the component has to implement the *InfoBusDataProducer* as well as the *InfoBusDataConsumer*. When doing so, the component connects to two different buses; this connection is a rather indirect one. The component connects to one bus as the data consumer and to the other as data producer. It acquires information from the bus to which it is connected as the data consumer. After getting hold of the information from this bus, it processes it. It then takes the filtered information to the other bus and announces the data availability. In essence, it is moving the information from one InfoBus to another. No principles are violated in doing so.

In our earlier discussion, we focused on the component implementing both the *InfoBusDataProducer* and the *InfoBusDataConsumer* as filters. In essence, we were type-casting the use of such components as just filters, but that is not necessarily true. Such components can very well act as bridges. Consider two different InfoBuses operating within the same JVM. Each bus has different types of information flowing through it. We have another component that wants to get the information from both buses. What do you think needs to be done in such a case?

Well, we need to build a bridge-like application that allows the information to flow from one InfoBus to another so that the component can make good use of both of them.

Any of the Java component products like the Java applet or the JavaBean can use InfoBus. All they have to do is implement the interfaces required for InfoBus to function properly. The *InfoBusEvent*, when distributed across the InfoBus, contains a reference to the creator of the event. By now we all know that either the *InfoBusDataProducer* or the *InfoBusDataConsumer* can generate the *InfoBusEvent*. The recommendation to that effect for the Java components using InfoBus is to implement the DataProducer and/or DataConsumer interfaces on objects separate from the one implementing the InfoBusMember interface. This is due to the fact that the InfoBus property member of the InfoBusMember interface does not go wild with the getInfoBus and setInfoBus methods associated with the property. The methods are used to retrieve and alter the value of the InfoBus property. The Get/Set of the InfoBus property is distributed with the InfoBusEvents. The *InfoBusDataProducer* and the *InfoBusDataConsumer* are very sensitive of the InfoBus to which they are connected. The process of retrieving and sending data is dependent on the bus. An apparent corruption of the placeholder of the bus results in the data being sent at the wrong InfoBus. Furthermore, the InfoBusMember likes to implement the JDK 1.2 version of the security checks for getting and setting the property.

The rendezvous process of the InfoBus is subject to some security implications. Let's discuss them now in detail. The rendezvous process is subject to two levels of security checks. The levels are defined based on the granularity of the checks. There is the large-grained approach and a fine-grained approach. The large-grained approach deals with the security checks done before permitting the distribution of the InfoBusEvents. The fine-grained approach is involved during the security checks done when the InfoBusEvent is delivered to the producer and/or the consumer.

The large-grained approach makes use of the *InfoBusPolicyHelper* interface. The *InfoBusPolicyHelper* interface helps in centralizing the security-related decisions. The decisions made in this class help implement the permissions and security mechanisms used for all producers, consumers, and data controllers. It encapsulates many security decisions and some default InfoBus name-generation rules. The *InfoBusPolicyHelper* interface is implemented on the assumption that the action is being requested on behalf of the caller, and it may throw a runtime exception if it disapproves. The implementation based on the aforementioned assumption makes it a good candidate for the large-grained security check mechanism. The large-grained security approach works on the principle that the caller checks the access permission of the receiver before it generates the *InfoBusEvent*. Although this approach is at a much higher level, it is useful because it helps to avoid an unwanted event in the bus. Too many events in the bus reduce its performance, and if the events are unwanted, then it is a bad programming strategy. The *InfoBusEvent* has three subtypes, which we have already seen. The *InfoBusPolicyHelper* has matching calls for all three *InfoBusEvent* subtypes. Each call is geared towards distributing that specific type of event. At any point in time, the implementer can make use of the JDK 1.2 security mechanisms.

The fine-grained approach is more involved. This type of security check occurs only in the producer or the consumer. The fine-grained security check is done after the *InfoBusEvent* has already been distributed. The producer and the consumer have to do some extra work to keep track of the validity of the receiver and the requester, respectively. In the case of the producer, it has to create a data access permission class. This permission class is similar to the FilePermission class and is created with the system security policy files. This helps the producer enumerate all the classes to figure out its access permissions. The reason this is needed is as follows: When the producer receives an *InfoBusItemRequestEvent* from the bus, it can call the AccessController's *checkPermission* method to verify that all objects in the call stack have the necessary access permission. The objects in the call stack include the consumer. The goal of this check is to make sure that the consumer who is requesting the data has the required permission to access the data. Once an approval is given by the check routine, the producer is free to provide the data to the requesting consumer.

The consumers, on the other hand, have to do something different to have the fine-grained security check implemented. They need to implement the *javax.infobus.SecureConsumer* interface. This interface is very essential, as the producers of the data essentially work with the SecureConsumer calls. If the consumer does not implement the SecureConsumer interface, the InfoBus does not allow the data to reach the consumer from the producer; it returns the requested data. Also, the producer is never exposed on the call stack on the consumer side; hence, the consumer does not know about the data producer in any way. For the consumers who implement the SecureConsumer interface, the producer inherently calls the *SecureConsumer.setDataItem* method. This call performs two tasks: First, it performs the security check on the consumer of the data. It performs an AccessController *checkPermission* to see whether the consumer has access permission to the data it wishes to receive. The next task is the delivery of the data, if the consumer passes the check successfully.

The current 1.1 compatible version of the DefaultController performs none of the large-grained checks in the rendezvous methods. The next version of InfoBus (version 1.2) will use the 1.2 JDK security checks on the other InfoBus activity. It will still not implement the large-grained security checks before distributing events. This was decided because the default implementation would add in unwanted extra code and overhead in management of system security policies.

The large-grained approach can be classified as more of a pessimistic model and the fine-grained approach as more of an optimistic model. The large-grained approach does not tend to rely on the access privileges of the consumer component. It actually does the check of the permissions before it releases the data to the consumer. The suspicion is blatantly shown in the functionality of the large-grained security model. The fine-grained design is just the opposite. Here the data producer lets the security check fall into the domain of the data acceptor. It lets the receiver check on its access permissions. This is obviously done in an indirect fashion. If the option were left completely open to the consumer, the consumer would never perform any verification. So, in a very loose way, the verification of the access permission is deferred by the producer.

Until now we have been discussing the data transfer mechanisms. Let's now concentrate on the data item itself. The data item is the entity that moves from one component to another via the process defined earlier. The data item has a naming convention, which needs to be followed for the data to be queried and transferred. The data items can be named using the recommended convention of the Uniform Resource Identifier (URI) format. The URI format is just a recommendation; there's no hard-and-fast rule attached to it. The only two requirements suggested by the InfoBus specification are 1) no data item name can begin with the % character, which defines a reserved space for data item names; and 2) if the data item name starts the same as the URI-based convention in the following list (i.e., starts with infobus: or /), it must follow all of the rules of the convention.

The URI-based InfoBus naming convention is shown next.

```
<infobus_uri>      ::= <abs_infobus_uri>  | <rel_infobus_uri>

<abs_infobus_uri> ::= <infobus_schema> ':' <rel_infobus_uri>
<infobus_schema>   ::= 'infobus'

<rel_infobus_uri> ::= '/' <infobus_name>
{ '/' <infobus_producer_class> }
{ <infobus_producer_discriminator> }
'/' <infobus_data_item_name>


<infobus_name> ::= <unreserved>*


<infobus_producer_class> ::= fully qualified Java class name
<infobus_producer_discriminator> ::= <unreserved>*
<unreserved> = ALPHA | DIGIT | safe | extra
<extra>   = '!' | '*' | ''' | '(' | ')' | ','
<safe>    = '$' | '-' | '_' | '.'
```

The naming convention is self-explanatory and we will not spend time discussing it, but it is important to know it. Note that the Internet standards are adhered to wherever possible. (More details on the URI form can be found in the RFC, which can be found at ds.internic.net/rfc/rfc1738.txt.)

Now that we know about the data item naming conventions, it is be appropriate for us to move on to understanding the data items. InfoBus projects the idea that the data producer and the data consumer do not have to know about each other or the type of data that they transfer before they actually start the process. If that is the case, then how does the consumer know what kind of data the producer provides? What is the format of the data? How does the consumer interpret the data? The next few paragraphs clear up this mystery for us. To help solve the data identification problem, InfoBus brings in the concept of DataFlavors. DataFlavors and the mime strings attached to them describe the data item provided in the InfoBus rendezvous.

When the data producer supplies the data it can supply an array of DataFlavors available for the item by way of a parameter on the *InfoBus.fireItemAvailable* method. This parameter is provided for the data producer to specify a way through which the consumer can interpret the data. The consumer of the data, on the other hand, can get the DataFlavors provided by the producer with the help of the *InfoBusItemAvailableEvent.getDataFlavors* method. The consumer of data is not given any lower preferences in the InfoBus system. The consumer can also provide a list of formats of data items. It can do this by providing an array of DataFlavors ordered by its preference. The consumer can do it with the help of *InfoBus.findDataItem* or *InfoBus.findMultipleDataItems* method calls. If the producer has the capability of providing the data to the consumer in different formats, it reads the consumer's preferential DataFlavors list. The producer can get hold of the DataFlavor list of the consumer with the help of the *InfoBusItemRequestedEvent.getDataFlavors* method call.

Specific InfoBus interfaces can be utilized as DataFlavors. They can be specified as strings prefixed with x-InfoBus/. The actual interface name follows the prefix. Such ways of transferring mime strings are very common. The most common use of such a technique is in mail readers, web browsers, and so forth. These specific interfaces are available for both available and requested events.

In case of availability of standard transferable data types, the data producer may implement the Transferable interface on the data item and offer the transferable data types via the *getTransferDataFlavors* method. These standard mime strings may also be specified for items available and requested events. The specification indicates the availability or support for getting data via the *Transferable.getTransferData* method. DataItem also provides a way for specifying the DataFlavors for the DataItem. This is done with the *getDataFlavors* method. This is optional, but the DataFlavors for the DataItem can be retrieved by it; however, caution should be observed in doing so. The DataFlavors specified by the Transferable interface should not be the same as the interfaces available through the DataItem interfaces. They should be different interfaces all together. No mix-and-match is allowed in these two sets of interfaces.

Based on the discussion on DataItems we can conclude that InfoBus has paid special attention to this aspect. Since DataItems are the entity that flows from one component to another they have been well defined and created in such a manner that they come with their own interpretation semantics. They do not burden the communicating components with the extra information that is needed to interpret the data. This is a true use of *encapsulation*. The data encapsulates the complete information about itself with it, such that anybody intending to interpret it can do so. No qualifiers are needed for this process except for the fact that they need to be within the InfoBus environment. We have truly been longing for such an attribute of the information set. There needs to be some minor understanding of the system, which is easily acquired by the component by just being a part of the InfoBus. Just from the design of it, it can be easily interpreted that a great deal of attention was paid in designing the concept of DataItem as being totally separate from the application.

BEANCONNECT, RMI, AND CORBA

In this section we start discussing some other component technologies. Why do we need to talk about them? The answer is actually quite simple. InfoBus is a component technology that helps us build and integrate components geared towards operating on data. The data flows from the producer to the consumer in a well-defined manner. The technologies that we talk about in the next few pages also help us do similar types of work. These are popular industry concepts that have been created to solve the programming difficulties of the developers. The technologies each target different areas. Moreover, even after focusing on different areas they provide us ways and techniques to integrate them. The integration of these technologies will help developers produce a complete application suite that works with synergy in a diverse operating environment and over a highly dispersed domain. Understanding the efforts put into coordinating new technologies will help us profit from their strengths and isolate their weaknesses.

The information about one specific technology helps us identify the specific type of solution that it can provide to that domain. Along with this solution may arise the need for many more related technologies. It helps us see a potential problem that may not have been visible prior to the existence of the current solution. In this manner, the domain becomes rather robust as the amount of research being done in that area to completely solve the problems greatly increases. Such things constantly happen in the computer science industry. History has shown us that the trends are rather cyclical. One specific technology catches the wave, and all of a sudden the entire industry researches it. This goes on for a while, and then all of a sudden the amount of opportunities existing in that area starts diminishing and then the next technology catches on the popularity train and the entire industry is focused on it. The reason I say it is cyclical is that after a certain period of time the same thing repeats, only now the same technology is viewed from a different angle. This creates more options and solutions to be discovered in it.

We do not necessarily need to integrate the solutions provided by new technologies, although that is one of the available options. The idea is to expand our thinking capacity. The imaginary powers that every individual carries within are nourished in a very effective way. It is very difficult for an individual to know all the technologies inside and out at the same time. Let me put it this way: It is humanly impossible. However, the study of these technologies side by side provides us an appreciation that is far more difficult to achieve if the study is done in isolation. We are not going to go into details of explaining the technologies. In the next few pages we will go through the basic concept behind these technologies. These are covered in much more detail in the next few chapters to follow.

In order to use Java components within the HTML documents we use Java applets. The applets are embedded within the HTML page using the *<APPLET>* and *</APPLET>* tags. This is a fine model for certain types of applications. The applets are great if used within a single context. They are used as individual entities and do not offer any kind of shared execution environment. Each applet is restricted to one AWT Frame object. They cannot share multiple frames or different contexts. Furthermore, though they are embedded within the HTML page they cannot interoperate with them more intricately. They cannot participate in HTML form posting. These are some of the limitations that are observed when making use of applets in the dispersed environment with multiple objects floating around. BeanConnect provides an answer to this. It is designed to be a crossware programming model. The alternative approach suggested by BeanConnect does not require any major rewriting of the existing Java code. If the Internet Foundation Class (IFC) components are used, then the BeanConnect can be used with it without any alteration required to the existing code. Also, an applet's lifetime is not controlled by the developer. The applet technology does not provide any facility to control the lifetime. This type of feature is sometimes needed in multiple-object environments. To do this, applications developers have to write external routines that can project the view of controlled Java applets.

The advantages offered by BeanConnect are:

Shared execution space. All Java objects in the program run in the same execution space in the JVM.

Direct communication between Java objects. Embedded Java objects can communicate directly in and across HTML pages without the need for JavaScript or LiveConnect.

Participation in HTML forms and posting. Existing Java components that implement FormElement in netscape.application.FormElement, such as those provided by the IFC, can be used to enhance form appearance and capabilities. Java code can be used to control and validate data entry on the client before posting, and can be used to process form data on posting.

Handling of program logic with Java and JavaScript. All BeanConnect programs are implemented by embedding Java objects in one or more HTML pages. In its simplest incarnation, a BeanConnect program consists of embedded objects that are handled through JavaScript and LiveConnect entirely within the context of the HTML pages where the embedded objects are declared. In a more complex and flexible BeanConnect program, one of the Java objects embedded in each page of the program can be designated as a special program object that handles program logic. The designated program object must be implemented in Java. Finally, program logic can be handled with a combination of Java and JavaScript.

Multipage and multiframe operation within a single execution context in the JVM. A Java program object can be embedded in any number of HTML documents, and from any frames within those documents. Only the first instance of that object that is encountered is instantiated. Subsequent references to the program object are linked to the original instance of the object and run in the program's space, minimizing further allocation of system resources.

Direct control of program objects and their lifetimes. All BeanConnect programs use a special Java control object called an *embedded owner* to manage the startup and lifetime of the Bean-Connect program and its Java components. A program is active as long as any HTML page that contains the reference of the program object is open. When the last page that references the program is flushed from the history list, the program is queried for permission to shut down. Developers can permit or prevent shutdown at this time and can provide alternative shutdown methods or let the program shut down when the JVM shuts down.

The listed advantages offered by BeanConnect are self-explanatory. Within a BeanConnect program model a Java program is implemented in one or more HTML pages by embedding the *<OBJECT>* tag in each page. This is completely different from the applet programming model. Here the program is shared between multiple pages. The *CLASSID* attribute of an object tag indicates whether a Java object is a visual component used by the BeanConnect program (*CLASSID=javabean*) or is a Java program object that is used to start and run the BeanConnect program when a user opens the HTML page (*CLASSID=javaprogram*). There can be one explicit Java object associated with the javaprogram CLASSID in each program, or there can be none. It is not mandatory to have an explicit implementation of a javaprogram for a BeanConnect program.

Most of the issues raised with multiple objects within the web environment are handled quite easily with the BeanConnect architecture. The shared execution space provides a flexible working environment. The isolation of the entities is reduced. Furthermore, the flexibility of one component communicating with the others using JavaScript and LiveConnect also helps greatly. One of the most important gains of using the BeanConnect crossware model is the predictability of the components. The environment brings predictability to the life of Java components, which reduces a lot of extra processing a developer has to do to keep the application under certain execution control. You will find more description of the BeanConnect environment in later chapters. Now let's discuss RMI.

Remote Method Invocation (RMI) is a technique created by the originators of Java. This technique helps Java developers perform the remote method execution within the Java environment. Execution of remote methods has its advantages. Before RMI, there was no way for Java developers to perform such an execution. In a distributed object environment, the participating objects can reside in any physical location. This concept of utilizing the services of objects at dispersed locations was an important phenomenon. It was realized that it was practically impossible to collect all the objects required to complete a development system. The difficulty of performing such a task was twofold. First, it was not possible for all the objects to agree on a particular style of working. The different components participating in the environment are generally created by different developers and vendors. The vendors select the type of business they feel comfortable in and try to gain expertise and build history in that particular area. Second, the lack of distribution reduces the number of competitors within the environment. Lack of competitors is not a good solution at all as it reduces the choices made available to the developers and it compromises the quality of the products. The complexity in going into such a model is unimaginable.

Both the business model and the technology in the industry will be rather compromised. This is a very unhealthy model. Diversification in technology helps the industry to grow. One company cannot let the technology grow in all the areas. For a uniform growth we need more industry to compete within the same area. Competing solutions and strategies help us attain an open design and architecture. The days of proprietary solutions are long gone. The industry does not fall for closed black-box systems anymore. Users want an open architecture that can be discussed in open consortiums to debate the advantages and disadvantages of such systems openly. They also want to have a say in deciding the fate of the technology. The industry wants to guide the flow of the technology such that everyone benefits from it rather than just one or two companies. These efforts in the technology industry make it healthy and permit its growth for the benefit of all.

This is one of the strongest reasons for supporting the distributed model. It helps different vendors concentrate on their individual strengths. The network of distribution and coordination is strengthened by the open-design solution, which caters to the growth of the environment. This is a very organic technique. The setup lets the environment grow and isolate most of its problems. The coordination of all these strong and concentrated solutions provides a network that is diverse and well distributed. The coupling of solutions needs to be strong. The object-oriented environment is a perfect match for the distributed world. The objects tend to keep their dependencies on the environment as minimal as possible. At least, the dependencies are well known.

RMI brings in a standard way of making Java objects perform remote method execution. The execution of the method is done in the address space of the remote machine. Though the execution is initiated from another machine, it is subject to the execution rules of the local machine. This prevents it from violating any of the local machine's operating principles. Moreover, the execution of the method is under the guidance of the local machine. With such architecture, the work can be easily redistributed to multiple machines. RMI provides Java with the capabilities of taking advantage of the uniform distributed environment. It actually helps in extrapolating the tangible value of such a uniform environment. The Java programs making use of RMI do not have to do anything special to make the system work. Some classes' interfaces are defined that need to be incorporated in order to make the Java objects remote. In other words, any Java object can very easily and with very minor changes become an RMI object. It can serve the task of remote execution without overloading the execution environment.

RMI was introduced by JavaSoft with JDK version 1.1. The RMI system needs a central collection within the machine for all the RMI objects. This central collection unit is called the rmiregistry. The registry is responsible for a temporal storage of all the RMI objects. It is temporal because no persistent form of the registry exists, as of yet. If an object needs to serve as an RMI object, it has to register itself with the rmiregistry. The object needs to introduce itself to the registry and provide a way for the registry to locate it when needed. Every JVM has just one registry. If the environment consists of multiple Java machines (i.e., many machines running the Java environment), then the registries can communicate with each other. This is essential as the network of registries can help an application locate a particular RMI object that it is looking for. The registries just keep a reference of each other within the network. They do not expose any internals about the RMI objects registered with them. This is a good feature as the RMI object can be contacted for its service from anywhere within the network without actually exposing its internals to the entire network. This is the core operating principle of RMI. The next few chapters talk about RMI in much more detail.

Next we come to the discussion of extensively flexible, well-developed, distributed object-oriented programming. This environment has been in the industry for quite a while and has been time-tested by many organizations. The technology is called CORBA. The Object Management Group (OMG) started it. The OMG is an industry-open consortium that was established to develop an open object-oriented development environment. It targeted the solution to be very open in nature so that most of the application domains could be addressed by it. The consortium began by defining the basic need of such open platforms. It then went on to design the core system that could be used to base a huge development platform. A lot of time was spent in designing the base system as it was geared to cover many domains. The original members of the consortium had this view in mind that the system would have applicability in all application domains. Also, because it was an industry-open consortium (i.e., any company could become a participating member of the consortium and voice its views), the work was slow. OMG made progress, but it was slow because no decisions were made without having a majority accept them. We all know how difficult that can get in the practical world.

OMG still functions in a very open manner. Whenever there is a problem discussed, they first formulate the requirements for it. This is done by selecting a group. The group can be represented by any member of the consortium, but in practice the group is formed by representatives of the companies that are actually interested in producing solutions in that area. This does not complete the story. Next, the group studies the requirements thoroughly and generates an RFC (Request for Comments). The RFC is kept open for a specific period of time. This time is provided so the interested parties can come up with proposals. The proposals have to satisfy the requirements presented in the RFC and also have to be a working demonstration. They are the two criteria for the proposal to be considered. Also, the consortium needs at least two such proposals from different vendors or groups so that the decision is not biased. Submissions from all the interested parties are thoroughly scrutinized and then the best proposal is accepted as the standard. During the scrutiny period all the members have the right to demand justification and clarification of the suggested design. It is the responsibility of the concerned submitter to satisfy the inquiring party. The design suggested by the winning party then becomes the standard. This process takes a long time to finalize; though the process is slow, it works. Most of the standards defined and selected in such a manner have proven to be fruitful to the industry.

After the consortium has finished defining a strong and scalable core for the CORBA architecture, they begin concentrating on the vertical markets. It has often been found that such industry consortiums are formed and they start solving a particular type of a problem. In doing so, they come to a consensus on a particular architecture that solves the problem at hand. After that design is approved, the consortium stops the work. This gets a little tricky if the problem domain changes a little. Such things happen all the time. Due to a change in the technology, the industry starts demanding a solution to a different type of a problem. At this time, the entire effort has to be repeated all over again. Also, many times just the core of the system is created by the group. Its applicability to other related areas is never discussed.

The OMG has taken a much different attitude. They not only do the work on the core of the system, but also start targeting the vertical markets that can use the technology to solve their problems. The approach is rather neat as the actual developers of the vertical market are within the consortium working on the solution. Since the organizations that are in the vertical sector represent those task groups, they bring in the first-hand knowledge about the problem domain. They bring their industry experience with them. They can be better guides. The consortium has grown in the last few years and now is represented by almost all the business sectors that use the technology for developing products. There are many task forces that are busy working on developing solutions and standards in different horizontal as well as vertical markets.

CORBA at its core is a distributed services environment. The services are exhibited by objects. The objects are present in different places on the network. When the client application logs in to the system, it requests a service offered by one of the objects. The client application has no idea of the location of the service-providing object. It is kept completely transparent. As a matter of fact, the client is unable to distinguish between the services provided by two different objects providing similar types of services. This kind of location and object transparency relieves the client of any assumptions that may make the client component nonportable at any point. The CORBA objects support interfaces, which act as services. They are called *services* from the end-user's point of view. The objects maintain their distance from the outer world with the help of these interfaces. They are the sole means of communication between the CORBA objects and the client components.

The Object Request Broker (ORB) is the base of the system. It helps to connect the service-desiring objects to the service-providing objects. It has certain principles that need to be followed. The entire operation is performed in a client/server mode. The roles may change at any time. Client applications and components make use of the interfaces provided by the server objects to get the job done. When there are interfaces, there needs to be some way in which the interfaces are made available to the clients who would like to use them. These interfaces are developed using the standard Interface Definition Language (IDL). IDL is a standard language that has been used to define interfaces in many environments. It has been time-tested and found to be satisfactory for the job. That is the exact reason why OMG decided to use it.

The interfaces that the server objects expose can be made available to the clients in two ways: the *static* way and the *dynamic* way. The static way of exposing the interface is rather simple. The server objects provide the interface by means of IDL files. The client applications make use of the IDL files to generate the stubs that they can use in their application. This technique is also known as the Static Interface Invocation (SII) mechanism. The next technique is a much more dynamic one. Here the server object allows the client to query for the interfaces. The client can retrieve the relevant interface by searching for it. After getting the right interface it can issue calls that do the task for the client. This is also known as the Dynamic Interface Invocation (DII) mechanism. The DII involves some more code, but it's worth it. The flexibility offered by this technique is unparalleled. With these two techniques of building the applications, CORBA developers have the freedom of opting for either performance or flexibility in their applications. The SII brings in the tight-binding idea, which precludes that the application already knows what type of object it is connecting to and what specific interfaces it will be using from the object. With the DII they bring out a different perspective. Here the application developer does not want to be bound to any specific type of an object or its interface. The application wants to do the job of selecting the object during runtime based on certain criteria. It will also make use of the interfaces that best satisfy its needs at that time.

The dynamic approach may seem a lot of work, but it is not very slow in its processing. As a matter of fact, most of the custom applications in the industry use the DII because of the ease it offers users with which to customize the ready-made system based on their specific requirements.

The CORBA environment supports various standard services, which have been defined and established based on their use. Along with the core system, CORBA has the horizontal services and the services defined to the vertical markets. Among them there exists the trader services. These are very important services that help clients locate the actual service object, which they need to get their jobs done. This is like the standard yellow-pages service that we use in our day-to-day lives. It makes perfect sense to have such a facility in a program development environment as the practical use of such services is very useful to us. The trader services are a highly used service within CORBA. The entire CORBA application development environment is huge. It is difficult for one company to have an entire set of services. (Many companies do have the entire service sets, but this is not very common. For example, any programming language development company needs to provide its compiler, debugger, linker, libraries, header files, and set of utilities that are essential for the development within that programming language. This is essential for the company. They cannot rely on just providing the compiler and leave the rest for the developers to find out. They have to provide some support to that extent. A good thing about CORBA application development is that many companies can do a part of the services set. The client can purchase such tools from different vendors and put them together to set up a uniform development environment for the company. This makes the technology even more desired in the industry as many vendors develop the product parts and they all fit together.

Like the trader services there are many other services. Another worth mentioning is the Interface Repository (IR). This entity helps the third-party CORBA-compliant applications retrieve the right kind of interface for the use of the application. When the CORBA object registers itself for rendering services to other client applications, it needs to register its interfaces that the client application can use. This registration process is well defined. The process involves the application to register the service with some type of semantics associated with the interface. The semantics of the interface help the objects express its views about the service. The client applications can make use of the semantics to understand the service and select it. The semantics are also useful to perform a static migration of the service from one interface repository to another. A CORBA environment can have many interface repositories. Ideally, every CORBA machine would have an interface repository that contains the interfaces of all the CORBA server objects present within that physical machine. It is not a hard-and-fast rule to have such a configuration. Remote interfaces can also be registered with the interface repository. We do not intend to get into the details of the services. There is a much more detailed discussion on CORBA later in this book.

LIMITATIONS

No technology is perfect; with every new solution comes its shortcomings. The discussion on the limitations is an interesting topic for the writer. The author starts by explaining the technology that he or she is writing about. The author after explaining the workings of the technology presents examples and projects in his or her view of why the technology is good and how it addresses problems in certain domains. Then at the end, the same author talks about the limitations of the technology. The limitations in no way take away any credit from the technology or the creators, but it is present within the chapter to enlighten readers and developers about the pitfalls they may encounter. This awareness is important. If limitations are not clearly explained, the developers may end up spending unwanted time going down a route that leads nowhere.

InfoBus has some limitations. The working of InfoBus is extremely dependent on the event mechanisms in Java. Events are resources, and they come with some cost associated with them. The cost of using the events is unnoticeable when a small amount of events flow through the system; however, with extensive use of events the amount of resources consumed will be high. This is especially the case when a particular bus has many data producers and data consumers participating in it. There may be either two or three events associated with every data item. Imagine a situation in which a bus has 40 data consumers and 5 data producers. We're talking about a lot if events here that slow down the process. The performance of the system is degraded. Using it for minor applications is acceptable, but complex applications with huge data traffic needs may find the system lacking. To put it more accurately, the system needs to be studied well for large participants within the same bus. Some benchmarking needs to be done to find out how the system reacts in such a situation. This technology is fairly new and not used extensively. As the technology matures we will have a much better idea of this issue. Currently, it is just based on speculation.

The entire working of InfoBus is limited to a single JVM, and InfoBus does not provide a way for applications to share information from within multiple JVMs. This capability would increase the usage of InfoBus to a great extent. One InfoBus application does not have any means of finding out other buses from the other JVMs, especially when Java provides a uniform approach for Java applications whether they are being executed in one JVM or distributed among many. The InfoBus specification talks about this feature being studied for the next release of InfoBus. Originators have realized that this is an important requirement and needs to be implemented to provide the true distributed application development feel.

InfoBus applications have information routing done explicitly via the bus to which they connect. This kind of technique is desirable and should be supported. However, another type of facility should also be provided: trusted communication channel. It is my feeling that InfoBus should provide an alternative way for applications to communicate once they have accepted this mode. This mode of communication is especially important for applications that need to transfer data among each other at a much faster rate. There are many types of applications that generate and process data in a real-time mode, and InfoBus needs to cater to those applications in a different manner. This mode demands that the data producer and the data consumer have a trusted mode of communication. Once the data consumer authenticates to the data producer, the data flow should take place between these two components without any outside interference; not even the InfoBus should be allowed to interfere. When the two components are finished with their data transfer they can inform the bus about closing the resources associated with the open instance of the InfoBus. The clean-up process would be performed by the InfoBus. This type of feature adds to the flexibility made available by the technique.

CONCLUSION

No technology comes out of nowhere. The developer knows why he or she is creating the solution. He or she must have found something lacking, which will be addressed by the solution. It is critical that the technology be thoroughly defined and explained for users. The terminology used must be well defined and explained as well; it is an essential part of understanding the technology. After all, it is the terminology developers use in their day-to-day communication. If it is not defined and explained thoroughly, the ensuing confusion is never-ending. With that in mind, we tried to keep this chapter as simple and explanatory as possible by providing just an introduction to the topic. Anything essential for the readers to understand the topic was discussed here. While this book is being written, the seasons are changing. Winter is raging its final wrath upon us and we can smell the freshness of spring. The morning sun fills me up with the spirit of excitement and happiness. We have crossed our initial hurdle.

CHAPTER 3

Inside the InfoBus

In Chapter 2, "Say Hello to InfoBus," we introduced InfoBus. In this chapter, we walk you through the details behind the major InfoBus components and provide an overview for how these components operate together through the use and implementation of standard interfaces. Topics introduced in the previous chapter are now covered in depth, and the technical relationships within the InfoBus system are revealed in greater detail. The primary components of InfoBus include members, consumers, producers, and data items. There are, however, various support and utility objects and access interfaces within the system that we discuss as well. As you will soon see, InfoBus components are designed with the JavaBeans model in mind and follow its conventions wherever possible. This provides for maximum interoperability with future Java products and APIs.

Let's begin our discussion with an overview of the central operating component in InfoBus.

THE INFOBUS CLASS

The *InfoBus class* creates and manages all active InfoBus instances within a single JVM. Because InfoBus is a final class, it cannot be extended and is typically not directly instantiated in applets or applications. Instead, static class methods are used to obtain or create an active InfoBus instance. If you run a Java applet, InfoBus provides a default instance termed the *Applet default InfoBus*, whose name is based on the common document base of the applet. In order for the Applet default InfoBus to exist, an applet context must be present. Therefore, applications typically don't initialize with a default InfoBus activated. There is a very good reason why a default InfoBus is useful. Beans or applets within a single web page should attempt to join the default InfoBus when they initialize. Following this guideline ensures future operability between your components and someone else's. Since this is not known until runtime, the InfoBus class maintains the default InfoBus instance for applets requesting it specifically.

In addition to providing the default InfoBus instance, this class services requests for *named* InfoBus instances. In the situation where a potential member sends a static message to the InfoBus class requesting an InfoBus by name, the InfoBus class returns the respectively named instance. If the requested InfoBus instance does not exist, it is created and added to an internally managed list of active InfoBus instances. Future requests for the named InfoBus simply return the appropriate InfoBus instance from the list. Let's take a look at the code segment that shows the acquisition of a default InfoBus instance.

```
public class MyApplet extends Applet {
  ...
  public void init()
  {
    ...
// Acquire the default InfoBus for the current web
// page.
    InfoBus defaultInfoBus = InfoBus.get(this);
    ...
  }
  ...
}
```

Notice in the code segment that we pass the this reference that means the current instance of Applet. Because this parameter is of type Component, InfoBus automatically determines the default InfoBus instance name by resolving the applet context from this component and examining the document base. Similarly, acquiring a named InfoBus would look like this:

```
public class MyApplet extends Applet {
  ...
  public void init()
  {
```

```
    ...
    // Acquire the InfoBus named MyInfoBus or create it.
    InfoBus myInfoBus = InfoBus.get("MyInfoBus");
    ...
  }
  ...
}
```

This code example returns the active InfoBus instance with the name MyInfoBus, creating it if necessary. The following two method variants are used for obtaining an active InfoBus instance:

```
public static synchronized InfoBus get(Component component)

public static synchronized InfoBus get(String infoBusName)
throws InfoBusMembershipException
```

Using the named InfoBus convention is applicable in a variety of circumstances such as builder environments in which a Bean exposes a String property like infoBusName to be the InfoBus to which it joins. In other cases, the BeanContext may provide the InfoBus instance internally and enforce it upon its Bean components through their setInfoBus() method. Alternatively, applications that want to restrict or protect certain information use specific InfoBus names to segregate event notifications between multiple InfoBus instances. Once we have successfully obtained an InfoBus instance, we can link members to it by calling InfoBus.join().

```
// Get the InfoBus
InfoBus dataBus = InfoBus.get("MyInfoBus");
dataBus.join(infoBusMember);
dataBus.release();
```

The InfoBus.join() method is defined as:

```
public synchronized void join(InfoBusMember member)
throws PropertyVetoException, InfoBusMembershipException
```

When an InfoBusMember joins an InfoBus in this manner, the following actions take place:

1. A check is made to determine if the InfoBus instance joined is stale. When all members depart an InfoBus instance and all event listeners have been removed, the InfoBus class removes that InfoBus instance and previous references to it become stale. If an InfoBusMember attempts to join a stale InfoBus instance, a StaleInfoBusException is thrown. To avoid this problem, join the InfoBuses soon after acquiring their reference.

2. The InfoBusMember's setInfoBus() method is called, passing in the currently invoked InfoBus instance. If the InfoBusMember contains the InfoBus instance as a property with registered VetoablePropertyChange listeners, the setInfoBus() method can fail and the InfoBusMember will not join the InfoBus instance. If this situation occurs, a PropertyVetoException is thrown.

3. The indicated InfoBusMember joins the InfoBus and is added to the list of active members for that InfoBus instance.

4. The InfoBus joined is added to the InfoBusMember's list of PropertyChangeListeners. This allows the InfoBus instance to be notified when a member changes its InfoBus property and updates its internal list of active members.

Figure 3.1 shows the simple relationship between the InfoBus instance and its members.

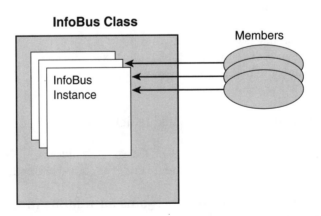

FIGURE 3.1 Relationship diagram that shows InfoBus instances and members.

Similarly, to leave an InfoBus instance you will have an InfoBus-Member that calls an InfoBus.leave() method like this:

```
// Get the InfoBus
InfoBus dataBus = InfoBus.get("MyInfoBus");
dataBus.join(infoBusMember);
dataBus.release();
...
// Leave the dataBus InfoBus.
// We do not use the direct reference in this call,
// because it may prove stale.
getInfoBus().leave(infoBusMember);
...
```

When an InfoBusMember calls InfoBus.leave(), notice that the following actions take place inside the InfoBus instance:

1. It removes its InfoBus property change listener from the InfoBus-Member.
2. It removes the InfoBusMember from its internal list of active members.
3. If this is the last member that leaves the InfoBus, the InfoBus instance is removed from the list of active InfoBus instances in the class.

Further details on the InfoBus class are covered in Chapter 4, "Advanced InfoBus Concepts."

MEMBERS

An InfoBus member is an object that manages an InfoBus property through which it can be joined and removed from active InfoBus instances. It is responsible for following the JavaBean event model by notifying appropriate listeners on its property about subsequent changes or attempted changes. The methods required by InfoBus members are contained in the InfoBusMember interface.

The InfoBusMember Interface

Now let's talk about the *InfoBusMember Interface*. Before a Java object can become a member of an InfoBus, it must implement the InfoBus-Member interface. This essentially binds implementers of the interface to the InfoBus contract and enables them to send and receive event notifications and data references through an InfoBus instance. The interface allows object implementers to join InfoBus instances. InfoBusMembers can implement the required functionality of the interface themselves or delegate to a default support implementation that we discuss shortly. When an InfoBusMember is supplied in the call to InfoBus.join(), its InfoBusMember.setInfoBus() method is called with the InfoBus instance as a parameter.

```
public void setInfoBus(InfoBus newInfoBus)
throws PropertyVetoException
```

This method is called from the InfoBus instance that the member is attempting to join. It can also be invoked from other sources as well. When implementing this method, you must keep these guidelines in mind:

- The method must broadcast PropertyChangeEvent to both its VetoableChangeListeners and PropertyChangeListeners.
- The PropertyName of the event must be InfoBus. This is in concordance with the introspection/reflection API coding standards and allows inspectors of the event to retrieve the property value through the appropriate Getter/Setter methods.
- The InfoBusMember that originates the event must set itself as the Event source.
- The InfoBusMember must invoke InfoBus.register(member), passing itself as member.

If you decide to manage the InfoBus property in your InfoBusMember, you must do so as a *bound* property. Bound properties are properties with listeners that oversee changes to them. The InfoBusMember interface defines methods to support the addition and removal of two types of property listeners: *PropertyChangeListener* and *VetoableChangeListener*. Objects that wish to receive notification about changes to the InfoBus property and possibly veto those changes would add and remove VetoableChangeListeners with the following methods, respectively.

```
public void
addInfoBusVetoableListener(VetoableChangeListener listener)
public void
removeInfoBusVetoableListener(VetoableChangeListener listener)
```

TIP   You can add VetoableChangeListeners to your InfoBusMember to transform your InfoBus property to a bound property as defined by the JavaBeans event model. This is useful in Bean builder environments in which a number of other components can approve or disapprove the setting of this property in your InfoBusMember. These connections can be made visually in a builder environment and maintained during application execution. Consider the following example:

A security Bean component is registered as a VetoableChangeListener for many different InfoBusMembers in a system. These associations can be made in a visual Bean builder and persist upon application execution. When an entity attempts to alter the InfoBus a member is currently joined to, the Security Bean receives a VetoableChangeEvent and either allows or restricts the new setting based on some predefined permissions within the Security Bean. If the Security Bean prohibits the new setting, a PropertyVetoException is thrown and received by the object attempting to set the member's InfoBus property through InfoBusMember.setInfoBus().

If you have objects that you want to simply receive notification of changes to the InfoBus property—for example, to keep current—you have to register the objects as a PropertyChangeListener using the following methods (see Figure 3.2):

```
public void
addInfoBusPropertyListener(PropertyChangeListener listener)
public void
removeInfoBusPropertyListener(PropertyChangeListener listener)
```

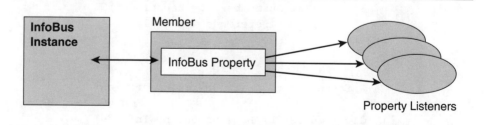

FIGURE 3.2   Relationship diagram that shows property listeners and members.

Now let's take a look at a complete listing. Listing 3.1 shows a sample implementation of the InfoBusMember interface.

LISTING 3.1 **A Sample Implementation of the InfoBusMember Interface**

```
import javax.infobus.*;
import java.beans.*;
import java.util.*;

public class IBMember implements InfoBusMember {

  // Bound property, set to null
  private InfoBus infoBus = null;

  // We are required to provide implementation
  // that manages the appropriate change listeners.

  // List of VetoableChangeListeners
  Vector vetoListeners = new Vector(10,10);

  // List of PropertyChangeListeners
  Vector propertyListeners = new Vector(10,10);


  public IBMember()
  {
  }

  public void joinInfoBus(InfoBus infoBus)
  throws PropertyVetoException
  {
    try {
       infoBus.join(this);
    } catch (InfoBusMembershipException e) {
       // infoBus reference was stale
    }
  }

  // InfoBusMember interface implementation

  public void setInfoBus(InfoBus newInfoBus)
  throws PropertyVetoException
```

LISTING 3.1   *Continued*

```
        {
          int i = 0;

          PropertyChangeEvent event = new
        PropertyChangeEvent(this,"InfoBus",infoBus,newInfoBus);

          // Cycle through listeners and send a
          // PropertyChangeEvent with newInfoBus as the
          // new property and infoBus as the old. Any
          // exceptions will not be caught, but passed up
          // and the setting will not take place.
          for(i=0;i<vetoListeners.size();i++) {
            VetoableChangeListener listener =
          (VetoableChangeListener)vetoListeners.elementAt(i);
            listener.vetoableChange(event);
          }

   // Since we have not been vetoed,
   // we can now notify our non-veto
   // change listeners

          for(i=0;i<propertyListeners.size();i++) {
            PropertyChangeListener listener =
        (PropertyChangeListener)propertyListeners.elementAt(i);
            listener.propertyChange(event);
          }
          // Leave the old InfoBus
          infoBus.leave(this);

          // Register and set the new property.
          newInfoBus.register(this);
          infoBus = newInfoBus;
        }

      public InfoBus getInfoBus()
      {
        return infoBus;
      }

   public void
```

Continues

LISTING 3.1   A Sample Implementation of the InfoBusMember Interface *(Continued)*

```
        addInfoBusVetoableListener(VetoableChangeListener vcl)
        {
          vetoListeners.addElement(vcl);
        }

    public void
        removeInfoBusVetoableListener(VetoableChangeListener vcl)
        {
          vetoListeners.removeElement(vcl);
        }

    public void
        addInfoBusPropertyListener(PropertyChangeListener pcl)
        {
          propertyListeners.addElement(pcl);
        }

        public void
        removeInfoBusPropertyListener(PropertyChangeListener pcl)
        {
          propertyListeners.removeElement(pcl);
        }

} // End Class
```

To make things easier for all of us, we summarize the InfoBusMember interface definition with descriptions in Table 3.1.

TABLE 3.1   InfoBusMember Interface Descriptions

Method	Type	Description
public void setInfoBus (InfoBus newInfoBus) throws PropertyVetoException	Interface	Sets the InfoBus property for the member
public InfoBus getInfoBus()	Interface	Returns the current InfoBus property
public void addInfoBusVetoableListener (VetoableChangeListener listener)	Interface	Adds a VetoableChangeListener to the members list

TABLE 3.1   *Continued*

Method	Type	Description
public void removeInfoBus VetoableListener(Vetoable ChangeListener listener)	Interface	Removes the VetoableChangeListener from the members list
public void addInfoBusPropertyListener (PropertyChangeListener listener)	Interface	Adds a PropertyChangeListener to the members list
public void removeInfoBusPropertyListener (PropertyChangeListener listener)	Interface	Removes the PropertyChangeListener from the members list

The InfoBusMemberSupport Class

Listing 3.1 showed an implementation of InfoBusMember that includes the management of the various listeners and the necessary steps for implementing setInfoBus(). As an alternative to doing this yourself, we recommend that you use the InfoBusMemberSupport class, which implements the functionality described previously for you. We do this by creating an instance of InfoBusMemberSupport in our member class and wrap the interface methods of InfoBusMember around the analogous methods contained in InfoBusMemberSupport. The InfoBusMemberSupport class then acts as a proxy to the InfoBus instance your member is a part of. Listing 3.2 shows a complete implementation of this, revising our previous IBMember class that we wrote earlier.

LISTING 3.2   **Revision of IBMember Class**

```
import javax.infobus.*;
import java.beans.*;


class IBMember_s implements InfoBusMember {

  private InfoBusMemberSupport memberSupport = null;

  public IBMember_s()
  {
```
Continues

LISTING 3.2 Revision of IBMember Class *(Continued)*

```
      memberSupport = new InfoBusMemberSupport(this);
    }


    public void setInfoBus(InfoBus newInfoBus)
    throws PropertyVetoException
    {
      memberSupport.setInfoBus(newInfoBus);
    }

    public InfoBus getInfoBus()
    {
      return memberSupport.getInfoBus();
    }

public void
    addInfoBusVetoableListener(VetoableChangeListener vcl)
      {
        memberSupport.addInfoBusVetoableListener(vcl);
      }

public void
    removeInfoBusVetoableListener(VetoableChangeListener vcl)
      {
        memberSupport.removeInfoBusVetoableListener(vcl);
      }

public void
    addInfoBusPropertyListener(PropertyChangeListener pcl)
      {
        memberSupport.addInfoBusPropertyListener(pcl);
      }

public void
    removeInfoBusPropertyListener(PropertyChangeListener pcl)
      {
        memberSupport.removeInfoBusPropertyListener(pcl);
      }


    }
```

Note that, when using this approach, we no longer have to contain or manage an InfoBus property or listeners within our InfoBusMember implementation. These tasks are delegated to the support class. You can instantiate an InfoBusMemberSupport object by providing an appropriate InfoBusMember object to the constructor. For example:

```
public InfoBusMemberSupport(InfoBusMember member)
```

When this method is invoked, the member object has its InfoBus property set to null. In addition, instances of VetoableChangeSupport and PropertyChangeSupport are created and managed within InfoBus-MemberSupport. These classes play an important role in managing the InfoBus property within the support class similar to how we handled it ourselves in Listing 3.1. You may want to alter the InfoBus property of an InfoBusMemberSupport class. That is always done through InfoBus-MemberSupport.setInfoBus(). Let's have a look:

```
public synchronized void setInfoBus(InfoBus newInfoBus)
    throws PropertyVetoException
```

When InfoBusMemberSupport.setInfoBus() is called, notification of the change is sent to the VetoableChangeSupport and Property-ChangeSupport objects. VetoableChangeSupport objects receive this notification through their fireVetoableChange() method, and Property-ChangeSupport objects receive it through firePropertyChange(). Since each ChangeSupport object manages a list of listeners, the change event is passed to every listener maintained for that member.

Finally, assuming no veto takes place, the InfoBusMemberSupport object calls InfoBus.join(support), adding itself to the active member list of the requested InfoBus. Because the support class handles and hides all the details from our InfoBusMember, the process for joining InfoBuses is accomplished through one of the following methods:

```
public synchronized void joinInfoBus(String busName)
throws StaleInfoBusException, PropertyVetoException

public synchronized void joinInfoBus(Component component)
throws StaleInfoBusException, PropertyVetoException
```

When you invoke one of these methods, the following actions take place:

1. The support class calls getInfoBus() on the member that it supports. If this method returns null, an InfoBusMembershipException is thrown; otherwise, its name is extracted.
2. It then calls InfoBus.get() and provides either the name of the InfoBus or the component depending on which flavor of joinInfoBus was called.
3. The support class calls InfoBus.join(this) on the instance it receives from Step 1. Essentially, it's the InfoBusMemberSupport class that belongs to the InfoBus and acts as liaison for our InfoBusMember.

Similarly, in order to leave an InfoBus through an InfoBusMember-Support class we use the following:

```
public synchronized void leaveInfoBus()
    throws PropertyVetoException, InfoBusMembershipException
```

This code does three primary things:

1. It calls InfoBusMember.getInfoBus(), throwing InfoBusMember-shipException if it returns null.
2. It calls getInfoBus().leave(this) to instruct the InfoBus instance to which this support class belongs and removes it from its list of active members.
3. It invokes setInfoBus(null) on the support class which, in turn, calls setInfoBus(null) on the associated InfoBusMember.

Let's take a look at Table 3.2. It shows the method mapping between InfoBusMember and InfoBusMemberSupport with additional InfoBus-MemberSupport methods not required by the InfoBusMember interface.

CONSUMERS

InfoBus consumers receive notification events about data availability and make blind requests for specific types of data. When data items become available on an InfoBus instance, notification events are sent to the list of consumers that currently belong to that InfoBus. Each consumer receives notification when data items arrive on the InfoBus and can examine the data item name to determine if it's interested in it.

TABLE 3.2   InfoBusMember-to-InfoBusMemberSupport Method Mappings

InfoBusMember	InfoBusMemberSupport
public void setInfoBus(InfoBus throws PropertyVetoException	public void setInfoBus(InfoBus newInfoBus) newInfoBus) throws PropertyVetoException
	public void setInfoBus(String busName) throws PropertyVetoException
public InfoBus getInfoBus()	public InfoBus getInfoBus()
public void addInfoBusVetoableListener (VetoableChangeListener listener)	public void addInfoBusVetoableListener (VetoableChangeListener listener)
public void removeInfoBus VetoableListener(VetoableChange Listener listener)	public void removeInfoBusVetoableListener (VetoableChangeListener listener)
public void addInfoBusPropertyListener (PropertyChangeListener listener)	public void addInfoBusPropertyListener(PropertyChange Listener listener)
public void removeInfoBusPropertyListener (PropertyChangeListener listener)	public void removeInfoBusPropertyListener(Property ChangeListener listener)
	public synchronized void leaveInfoBus() throws PropertyVetoException, InfoBusMembershipException
	public synchronized void joinInfoBus(String busName) throws StaleInfoBusException, PropertyVetoException
	public synchronized void joinInfoBus(Component component) throws StaleInfoBusException, PropertyVetoException

The InfoBusDataConsumer Interface

InfoBus consumers are created by implementing the InfoBusDataConsumer interface and are added and removed to an InfoBus instance through its InfoBus.addDataConsumer() and InfoBus.removeDataConsumer() methods, respectively. For example:

```
IBMember myMember = new IBMember();
InfoBusMemberSupport memberSupport = new
    InfoBusMemberSupport(myMember);
```

```
...
InfoBusDataConsumer consumer = new IBConsumer();

...

myMember.getInfoBus().addDataConsumer(consumer);

...
```

When a data item arrives on an InfoBus, its availability is broadcast by calling InfoBusDataConsumer.dataItemAvailable() on each consumer. Let's have a look:

```
public void
dataItemAvailable(InfoBusItemAvailableEvent event)
```

This operation is performed by the InfoBus instance on behalf of the producer that sends the data item. When a consumer receives an InfoBusItemAvailableEvent, it can inspect the data item name within it. For example:

```
public void
    dataItemAvailable(InfoBusItemAvailableEvent event)
    {
      ...
      String dataName = event.getDataItemName();

      if(dataName.equals("x-InfoBus/mydatatype")) {
        DataItem data = event.requestDataItem();
        ...
      }

    ...
    }
```

Figure 3.3 depicts the process of a consumer becoming aware of an item's availability.

As you might have guessed, data producers have the ability to revoke data items that they have previously posted to InfoBus.

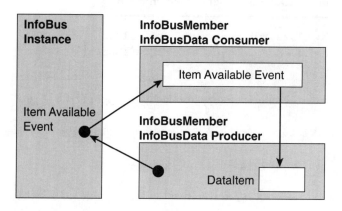

FIGURE 3.3   Consumer notification of item availability.

Consumers are made aware of item revocation through their InfoBus-DataConsumer.dataItemRevoked() method. For example:

```
public void dataItemRevoked(InfoBusItemRevokedEvent event)
```

This method is also called by the InfoBus instance on behalf of the data producer. When a consumer receives this event notification, it checks to see if it's currently using the revoked data item. We do have a suggestion for the implementation of this: Try to inspect the data item name of the revoked item and originate producer through the InfoBusItemRevokedEvent object and compare the results to data items currently held. See what happens! If it is currently held, it should take the necessary steps to ensure no further usage of that item.

When either a consumer is finished using a data item or the data item is revoked, you must release it. Releasing a data item allows the producer to properly track the resources and allocations without disrupting other users of the item. When a consumer attempts to release a data item it should inspect all subitems of that data item it may have used. When an item is released, all subitems are assumed to be released as well. Any isolated references to any subitems of a released item are no longer used. If any subitems implement the DataItem interface, it is appropriate to release them as well. A DataItem is released by invoking DataItem.release(). Take a look at Listing 3.3, which shows an example implementation of InfoBusDataConsumer.

LISTING 3.3   InfoBusDataConsumer Implementation

```
public class MyApplet extends Applet
    implements InfoBusMember, InfoBusDataConsumer
    {

      InfoBusMemberSupport memberSupport = null;

      Vector heldItems = new Vector(10,10);

      public void init()
      {
        memberSupport = new InfoBusMemberSupport(this);
      }


      public void start()
      {
        try {
            // Join the default InfoBus for this applet
            memberSupport.joinInfoBus(this);
            getInfoBus().addDataConsumer(this);
        } catch (PropertyVetoException e) {
            // Someone probably vetoed our change to our
            // infoBus property
        } catch (StaleInfoBusException f) {
            // The InfoBus instance we were attempting to join
            // is apparently stale or we're not a participating
            // member
        }


      }

      public void stop()
      {
        try {
            // release held items
            getInfoBus().removeDataConsumer(this);
            memberSupport.leaveInfoBus();
        } catch (PropertyVetoException e) {
```

LISTING 3.3 *Continued*

```
                // We were not allowed to leave this InfoBus because
                // a VetoableChangeListener vetoed our attempt to
                // change the InfoBus property.
                } catch (InfoBusMembershipException f) {
                    // The InfoBus instance we were attempting to join
                    // is apparently stale or we're not a participating
                    // member
                }
        }


        // InfoBusMember method implementations
        ////////////////////////////////////////////////////////////////

        public void setInfoBus(InfoBus newInfoBus)
        throws PropertyVetoException
        {
            memberSupport.setInfoBus(newInfoBus);
        }


        public InfoBus getInfoBus()
        {
            return memberSupport.getInfoBus();
        }

    public void
        addInfoBusVetoableListener(VetoableChangeListener vcl)
        {
            memberSupport.addInfoBusVetoableListener(vcl);
        }

    public void
        removeInfoBusVetoableListener(VetoableChangeListener vcl)
        {
            memberSupport.removeInfoBusVetoableListener(vcl);
        }

    public void
```

Continues

LISTING 3.3   InfoBusDataConsumer Implementation *(Continued)*

```
    addInfoBusPropertyListener(PropertyChangeListener pcl)
    {
        memberSupport.addInfoBusPropertyListener(pcl);
    }

public void
    removeInfoBusPropertyListener(PropertyChangeListener pcl)
    {
        memberSupport.removeInfoBusPropertyListener(pcl);
    }


    // InfoBusDataConsumer methods here
    ////////////////////////////////////////////////////////

public void
    dataItemAvailable(InfoBusItemAvailableEvent event)
    {
        String dataName = event.getDataItemName();

        if(dataName.equals("x-InfoBus/mydatatype")) {
            DataItem data = event.requestDataItem();

    // Make sure the data item we're interested
    // in has a "Name" property. Although not
    // mandatory, in our example we require it.
    // This ensures that when items are revoked,
    // we can match them quite accurately.
    if(data.getProperty("Name") != null)
                // Add this item to our list of held items
                heldItems.addElement(data);
        }
    }


public void
    dataItemRevoked(InfoBusItemRevokedEvent event)
    {
        for(int i = 0;i<heldItems.size();i++) {
```

LISTING 3.3 *Continued*

```
DataItem heldItem =
                        (DataItem)heldItems.elementAt(i);
        String itemName = event.getDataItemName();



        // This works because we've only held dataItems
        // we know have a "Name" property (or any other)
        // we would choose).
     if(heldItem.getProperty("Name").equals(itemName)) {
        if(event.getSourceAsProducer() ==
        heldItem.getSource ()) {
        heldItem.release();
        }
      }
    }
  }

} // class
```

When an applet that wishes to join an InfoBus initializes, it is common (if it is a consumer type) for it to inspect the InfoBus to see if any data is currently available for it to consume. Also, it is foreseeable that a consumer can request a certain type of information even before it has been submitted for availability. These types of requests are termed *blind* requests, because it is not known if the appropriate producer is available to satisfy the requested data item type. To invoke a blind request, a consumer calls InfoBus.findDataItem(). If no producer currently joined to the InfoBus can provide the needed data, a null value is returned. We are sure you can't get enough of this subject. So to fulfill your needs, we will cover the details in Chapter 4, "Advanced InfoBus Concepts."

SEGREGATING MEMBERSHIP

Because InfoBusMember and InfoBusDataConsumer are different interfaces, it is possible that you can separate their implementations from one another. One typical method you can use is to create an applet that would coexist on a web page with other applets, all of which would exchange information through a default InfoBus instance. In this situation, your applet would likely implement all the needed interfaces directly. That is, it would be a member and a consumer or producer, or all three. Conversely, you might have an object that implements InfoBusMember only. It would then maintain an internal list of consumers and/or producers and manage their membership to and from the InfoBus outside of its own. Situations like this may arise in Java applications where you would construct special classes using object composition whose attributes or members might be InfoBusDataConsumer or InfoBusDataProducer objects.

Consider the object UserManager that manages a list of active user objects, each of which sends and receives data items to an InfoBus. When the UserManager leaves or joins an InfoBus, all of the managed user objects move as well. Take a look at the following code segment, which will help you understand this idea in more detail:

```
public class UserManager implements InfoBusMember {

    private InfoBus infoBus = null;

// This Vector will contain the users
    // this object will maintain
    Vector users = new Vector(10,10);

    // List of VetoableChangeListeners
    Vector vetoListeners = new Vector(10,10);

    // List of PropertyChangeListeners
    Vector propertyListeners = new Vector(10,10);

    public void joinInfoBus(InfoBus infoBus)
    throws PropertyVetoException
    {
        infoBus.join(this);
    }

    public void addUser(User user)
    throws InfoBusMembershipException
    {
        users.addElement(user);
        if(user instanceof InfoBusDataConsumer)
            infoBus.addDataConsumer(user);
        if(user instanceof InfoBusDataProducer)
            infoBus.addDataProducer(user);
    }
```

```
    public InfoBus getInfoBus()
    {
        return infoBus;
    }

    public void setInfoBus(InfoBus newInfoBus)
    throws PropertyVetoException
    {
        // Notify ChangeListeners
        …

        // Remove all our current users from
        // the current InfoBus
        for(int i=0;i<users.size();i++) {
if((User)users.elementAt(i) instanceof
        InfoBusDataConsumer)
    infoBus.removeDataConsumer((User)users.elementAt(i));
if((User)users.elementAt(i) instanceof
        InfoBusDataProducer)
    infoBus.removeDataProducer((User)users.elementAt(i));
        User user = (User)users.elementAt(i);
      // Make sure we release held data
        user.releaseAll();items
    }
    infoBus.leave(this);
    infoBus=newInfoBus;     // Set new value
    infoBus.register(this);

        // Add all the users managed by
        // this object to the new infoBus.
        for(int i=0;i<users.size();i++) {
if((User)users.elementAt(i) instanceof
        InfoBusDataConsumer)
    infoBus.addDataConsumer((User)users.elementAt(i));
if((User)users.elementAt(i)
        instanceof InfoBusDataProducer)
    infoBus. addDataProducer((User)users.elementAt(i));
        }

    }

public void
    addInfoBusVetoableListener(VetoableChangeListener vcl)
```

```
        {
            vetoListeners.addElement(vcl);
        }

    public void
        removeInfoBusVetoableListener(VetoableChangeListener vcl)
        {
            vetoListeners.removeElement(vcl);
        }

    public void
        addInfoBusPropertyListener(PropertyChangeListener pcl)
        {
            propertyListeners.addElement(pcl);
        }

    public void
        removeInfoBusPropertyListener(PropertyChangeListener pcl)
        {
            propertyListeners.removeElement(pcl);
        }
}


class User implements InfoBusDataConsumer,
    InfoBusDataProducer {

    // InfoBusDataConsumer interface implementation
    ...
    // InfoBusDataProducer interface implementation
    ...

    public void releaseAll()
    {
        // Release any data items we're holding
    }
}
```

We discuss the UserManager class in a greater detail in Chapter 5, "InfoBus Design Models."

Table 3.3 shows the descriptions for the InfoBusDataConsumer interfaces.

TABLE 3.3   **InfoBusDataConsumer Interface Methods**

Method	Type	Description
public void dataItemAvailable (InfoBusItemAvailableEvent event)	Interface	Notifies the implementer of new data availability
public void dataItemRevoked (InfoBusItemRevokedEvent event)	Interface	Notifies the implementer that a specific data producer has revoked a particular data item

PRODUCERS

InfoBus producers are objects that provide specific types of data items to InfoBus instances. Producers can place data items on an InfoBus either by choice or at the request of some consumer that previously requested the data item type. Typically, an InfoBus will have a variety of producers attached to it that service certain kinds of data such as GIF images, Rowset results from a relational database, or tabular data possibly to be plotted by a separate graphing consumer Bean.

The InfoBusDataProducer Interface

As you can expect, objects that wish to become data producers implement the InfoBusDataProducer interface. Producers notify the InfoBus when data items are available and receive special events that request certain kinds of data. Producers are added and removed from the InfoBus by calling InfoBus.addDataProducer() and InfoBus.removeDataProducer(), respectively. Listing 3.4 shows an example of an InfoBusMember that contains a producer as a member object and manages its membership to InfoBus.

LISTING 3.4   An Example of an InfoBusMember Containing a Producer as a Member Object and How to Manage Its Membership to InfoBus

```
public class MyMember implements InfoBusMember {

    IBProducer ibProducer;
    InfoBusMemberSupport memberSupport;


    public MyMember(String infoBusName) {
```
Continues

LISTING 3.4 **An Example of an InfoBusMember Containing a Producer as a Member Object and How to Manage Its Membership to InfoBus** *(Continued)*

```
        memberSupport = new InfoBusMemberSupport(this);

        try {
                memberSupport.joinInfoBus(infoBusName);

                InfoBus infoBus = memberSupport.getInfoBus();

                ibProducer = new IBProducer(infoBus);
                addInfoBusPropertyListener(ibProducer);
        } catch (PropertyVetoException e) {
            // Exception handling code here
        } catch (InfoBusMembershipException f) {
            // Exception handling code here
        }
    }


    public void setInfoBus(InfoBus newInfoBus)
    throws PropertyVetoException
    {
        memberSupport.setInfoBus(newInfoBus);
    }

    public InfoBus getInfoBus()
    {
      return memberSupport.getInfoBus();
    }


public void
    addInfoBusVetoableListener(VetoableChangeListener vcl)
    {
        memberSupport.addInfoBusVetoableListener(vcl);
    }

public void
    removeInfoBusVetoableListener(VetoableChangeListener vcl)
    {
```

LISTING 3.4 *Continued*

```
            memberSupport.removeInfoBusVetoableListener(vcl);
        }

    public void
        addInfoBusPropertyListener(PropertyChangeListener pcl)
        {
            memberSupport.addInfoBusPropertyListener(pcl);
        }

    public void
        removeInfoBusPropertyListener(PropertyChangeListener pcl)
        {
            memberSupport.removeInfoBusPropertyListener(pcl);
        }

        public void propertyChange(PropertyChangeEvent event)
        {
            ibProducer.propertyChange(event);
        }
}




class IBProducer implements InfoBusDataProducer {

    public final static String DATA_TYPE  = "IBDataType";

    InfoBus infoBus;

    public IBProducer(InfoBus infoBus)
    {
        this.infoBus = infoBus;
        try {
            infoBus.addDataProducer(this);
        } catch (InfoBusMembershipException e) {
            // Apparently our infoBus instance is stale
        }
    }
```

Continues

LISTING 3.4 **An Example of an InfoBusMember Containing a Producer as a Member Object and How to Manage Its Membership to InfoBus** *(Continued)*

```
        public void propertyChange(PropertyChangeEvent event)
        {
          String name = event.getPropertyName();
          if(!name.equals("infoBus")) return;
          InfoBus newInfoBus = (InfoBus)event.getNewValue();
          if(infoBus != newInfoBus) {
                infoBus.removeDataProducer(this);
                infoBus = newInfoBus;
          }
          infoBus.addDataProducer(this);
        }


        //InfoBusDataProducer method implementations
    public void
        dataItemRequested(InfoBusItemRequestedEvent event)
        {
            String dataName = event.getDataItemName();

            if(dataName.equals(DATA_TYPE)) {
                // DataItemImpl is a hypothetical implementation
                // of DataItem.
                DataItemImpl data = new DataItemImpl();
                event.setDataItem(data);
            } else return;
        }

        public void finalize()
        {
            infoBus.removeDataProducer(this);
        }

    }
```

Producers are made aware of requests for data items when their InfoBusDataProducer.dataItemRequested() method is invoked by an InfoBus instance on behalf of a consumer. For example:

```
public void
dataItemRequested(InfoBusItemRequestedEvent event)
```

The proposed procedure for implementing this method is:

- Check the data item name obtained by calling event.getDataItem-Name() to see if it's an item this producer can provide. If not, simply return.
- Create an instance of the data item requested, or if it already exists, set it through event.setDataItem().

When an InfoBusDataProducer has information to broadcast over InfoBus, it does so by invoking InfoBus.fireItemAvailable() and likewise revokes the item by calling InfoBus.fireItemRevoked().

NOTE   A data item can be revoked only if it has already been made available.

Table 3.4 gives the description for the InfoBusDataProducer interface.

DATAITEMS

In InfoBus, DataItems are represented with objects that implement the DataItem interface. References to them are passed back and forth between DataItemProducers and DataItemConsumers. DataItems always originate at DataItemProducers and are passed over InfoBus by way of a request event.

TABLE 3.4   InfoBusDataProducer Interface Methods

Method	Type	Description
public void dataItemRequested (InfoBusItemRequestedEvent event)	Interface	Invoked by an InfoBus instance on behalf of a consumer wishing to receive a particular type of data

The DataItem Interface

The InfoBus API defines various interfaces to enable InfoBus functionality for data items. The DataItem interface itself is designed to provide details about the identity and description of a data item. For example:

```
public Object getProperty(String key)
```

The DataItem.getProperty() method is used to return property information about the data item. The only current required property data items must provide is Name. The use of other properties is optional. The following code segment shows how to retrieve an arbitrary property:

```
public void
    dataItemAvailable(InfoBusItemAvailableEvent event)
      {
          String dataName = event.getDataItemName();

          if(dataName.equals("x-InfoBus/mydatatype")) {
              DataItem data = event.requestDataItem();

String access = data.getProperty("Access");
...
// Do something useful with information contained
// in "access"
          }
          ...
      }
```

In some cases, it's necessary for the consumer of a data item to identify the source object behind that item possibly to distinguish the data item from other similarly named ones. This is done by calling DataItem.getSource().

```
public InfoBusEventListener getSource()
```

Typically, this method returns an InfoBusDataProducer, which is a subclass of InfoBusEventListener. The one exception you should keep in mind is when a consumer alters a mutable data item and gives it back to the producer. When this situation occurs, getSource() returns the consumer that provided the altered data item back to the originating producer. This allows producers to identify which consumer has made the alterations. Please note that getSource() never returns null.

In order for consumers to identify the type of data item available on the InfoBus, DataItems must maintain a list of DataFlavors that describe the data item. For instance:

```
public DataFlavors[] getDataFlavors()
```

DataFlavors are represented as mime strings that begin with x-InfoBus/. It is the owner of the data item that populates the DataFlavors array that is requested through the DataItem. We strongly advise that producers provide descriptive DataFlavors for its data items. It can, however, opt not to provide descriptive flavors by returning null. Consumers always have the ability to decide whether to inspect a data item or not, regardless of the data item descriptions.

When a producer places a data item on the InfoBus by calling InfoBus.fireItemAvailable(), it has the option of setting the DataFlavors that accurately describe the types of data contained in the data item. Because DataItems can represent collections or contain multiple member types, the producer should set all the DataFlavors that apply to the composite data item. We discuss DataFlavors in further detail in Chapter 4, "Advanced InfoBus Concepts."

```
public void release()
```

As we discussed earlier, it is mandatory for consumers to notify the producer that it has finished using a data item and any possible subitems. This is done by calling DataItem.release(). You should know that this becomes important when producers allocate and manage resources while the data item is on the InfoBus, such as maintaining a live database connection or opening file access. It's the responsibility of the producer to notice when all consumers have released a data item and free or close the appropriate resources. Likewise, in order for this to occur, consumers must utilize release() when completed.

The DataItem interface is a requirement for any top-level object that wishes to be passed in InfoBus. It is, however, optional, for any subitems in the collection hierarchy. In situations in which multiple DataItems exist as a hierarchy, calling release() on any DataItem should release that item and all subitems beneath it. It is up to your implementation to provide this capability. The producer must ensure that when release() is called on a data item from one consumer, it does not disrupt the access to that item from other consumers. As a general rule, when the producer decides to free resources associated with the DataItem it should send a DataItemRevokedEvent to change listeners on the data item and also send an InfoBusItemRevokedEvent to consumers by calling InfoBus-.fireItemRevoked(). Let's take a look at a simple DataItem object in Listing 3.5.

LISTING 3.5   An Example of a DataItem Object

```java
import javax.infobus.*;

public class Price implements DataItem
{
    private static final String NAME = "Price";

    private Double price = new Double();

    private InfoBusEventListener source = null;

    private int users = 0;

    public Price(InfoBusEventListener source)
    {
        // This will typically represent the producer that
        // instantiates this item.
        this.source = source;
    }

    public Double getPrice()
    {
        return price;
    }

    public void setPrice(Double price)
    {
        this.price = price;
    }

    public void incrementUsers()
```

LISTING 3.5 *Continued*

```
        {
            users+=1;
        }

        public Object getSource()
        {
            return source;
        }

        public void release()
        {
            users-=1;
            if(users==0) {
// Do some cleanup since there
                // are no longer any active users
            }
        }

        public void getProperty(String key)
        {
            if(key.equals("Name")) return NAME;
        }

        public DataFlavors[] getDataFlavors()
        {
            ...
        }

}
```

In Listing 3.5, the class Price contains an exposed property called *price*. In this particular example, consumers that have retrieved this price object identify its type by using instanceof, exploring the DataFlavors, or calling getProperty("Name"). Also, notice we've added a method called incrementUsers(). Whenever the producer receives a request for this item, it can tally the number of users by calling this method. Likewise, when consumers release the item, the total is decremented. This allows the producer to know when all active users have released the data item. Our example, however, is somewhat flawed. Accessing the price property requires prior knowledge of the type of object, namely Price. To illustrate this better, let's take a look at a possible consumer implementation of InfoBusDataConsumer.dataItemAvailable() in Listing 3.6.

LISTING 3.6   A Possible Consumer Implementation of infoBusDataConsumer.dataItemAvailable()

```
public void
    dataItemAvailable(InfoBusItemAvailableEvent event)
    {
      String dataName = event.getDataItemName();

      DataItem data = event.requestDataItem();

      if(dataName.equals("x-InfoBus/Price") ||
         data instanceof Price) {
          Price price = (Price)data;

          Double thePrice = price.getPrice();

          // Do something useful with 'thePrice'

          // Release the object since we're done
          data.release();
      }
    }
```

It should be obvious to you by now that a tight bond exists between the DataItem implementation, Price, and the consumer implementation of dataItemAvailable. In some cases this may be all that is necessary, but it undermines the true nature of InfoBus. Specifically, InfoBus allows consumers and producers from different origins to exchange data in an *application-independent* manner. In order to accomplish this, we need a neutral mechanism for examining or traversing data held within a DataItem. Table 3.5 summarizes all the DataItem interface methods.

TABLE 3.5 DataItem Interface Methods

Method	Type	Description
public object getProperty(String key)	Interface	Returns a property object with a specific key value. "Name" is the only mandatory property; however, other properties can be provided in the implementation of the DataItem.
public InfoBusEventListener getSource()	Interface	Returns the originator of the DataItem. In almost all cases, this is an InfoBusDataProducer.
public DataFlavors[] getDataFlavors()	Interface	Returns an array of DataFlavors that describe the DataItem.
public void release()	Interface	Informs a producer when a consumer is finished accessing a DataItem.

ACCESS INTERFACES

Access interfaces provide a standard mechanism for exploring the data within DataItems. Producers are aware of the true nature of DataItems they originate and may therefore choose to access DataItems through instance methods like setPrice. Consumers need a reliable standard for getting the information. The InfoBus API defines a variety of standard access interfaces for producers and consumers to use. In general, it is recommended that producers attempt to implement as many access interfaces as possible to ensure maximum interoperability between foreign consumers. To allow for maximum flexibility and future compatibility, the Object class is used for getting and setting DataItems. Not coincidentally, the upcoming JDK Collection classes also use Object as their primary data exchange format.

The ImmediateAccess Interface

The ImmediateAccess interface allows data values to be returned directly. The interface defines methods to return member data of the DataItem as either a string or object. For example:

```
public String getValueAsString()
```

This method returns a String representation of the data within the DataItem. The actual string returned is of an arbitrary format and need not represent Object.toString(). For the consumer, this provides an easy mechanism to get the information it needs without knowing the details of the type or organization of the data such as identifying a collection and traversing its members. This method of retrieval is not recommended for Collections, but rather as a wrapper for simple or final member types. Building upon our previous example shown in Listing 3.6, a partial implementation looks something like Listing 3.7.

LISTING 3.7   A Partial Implementation of Listing 3.6

```
public class Price implements DataItem, ImmediateAccess
{
  ...
  Double price = new Double();

  // getter/setter methods

  // DataItem interface methods
  ...

  public String getValueAsString()
  {
// Since our price currency is
    // defaulted to dollars, our
      // default representation is '$'.
    return ""+price;
  }

  public Object getValueAsObject()
  {
    return price;
  }

  // Other ImmediateAccess interface methods
  ...
}
A variation on getValueAsString() is:
public string getPresentationString(Locale locale)
    throws UnsupportedOperationException
```

This method allows data items to cater their String values according to specific locales. In the case of our Price data item, it determines the locale and adjusts the string representation accordingly. To check out the code, see Listing 3.8. When a consumer wishes to receive the data value as type Object a call to ImmediateAccess.getValueAsObject() is made. For example:

```
public Object getValueAsObject()
```

After a consumer has received an object by calling this method, it must interrogate the object type to determine its class. This can be accomplished by using instanceof or reading the Mime formatted data type and creating a properly cast version of the object. If the implementer does not wish to expose the data value in this form, a value of null can be returned. In some situations, consumers may need to change the data item's value. This is done through ImmediateAccess.setValue(). When DataItems accept changes to their data we call them *mutable*.

```
public Object setValue(Object newValue)
    throws InvalidDataException
```

It is recommended that producers recognize newValue itself as an ImmediateAccess interface to promote the standard. However, producers should allow or accept any type of object that makes sense for the application.

There are some important considerations when implementing set-Value(). Because the actual invocation of interface methods in DataItems actually occurs in the producer context by way of the InfoBus, it is up to the producer to understand the underlying implementation details around the DataItem. Specifically, implementations of setValue() should consider any change listeners on the property or value being changed and notify them accordingly before setting the value. For example, if the change request was vetoed by a VetoableChangeListener somewhere in the producer, the consumer would receive an Exception after calling set-Value(). Let's consider one possible implementation of setValue() using our Price data item in Listing 3.8.

LISTING 3.8   A Possible Implementation of setValue()

```
import javax.infobus.*;
import java.beans.*;
import java.awt.datatransfer.*;
import java.util.*;

public class Price implements DataItem, ImmediateAccess
{
  private Double price = null;

  // DataItem interface methods


  ...


  // ImmediateAccess interface methods


  public String getValueAsString()
  {
  // Since our price currency is
  // defaulted to dollars, our
  // default representation is '$'.
return "$"+price;
  }

  public Object getValueAsObject()
  {
    return price;
  }


  public synchronized void setValue(Object newValue)
  throws InvalidDataException
  {
    Double actualValue = null;
    String stringValue = "";

    if(newValue instanceof ImmediateAccess) {
ImmediateAccess priceValue =
                (ImmediateAccess)newValue;
        try {
```

LISTING 3.8 *Continued*

```
            actualValue = (Double)priceValue.getValueAsObject();
            } catch (Exception e) {
            // The value we received was not a Double, but we'll
            // acquire the string value and possibly try to
            // determine its
            // type maybe by parsing it or something.
String stringValue =
              priceValue.getValueAsString();

        // parse stringValue or attempt to
        // determine its nature
          try {
            Integer integer = new Integer(stringValue);
            } catch (Exception f) {
        // This would indicate a failure
        // to generate a legal
        // Integer object based on the string
        // representation.
          // Could try other methods here
          // or throw an exception
            throw new IllegalArgumentException();
          }
        }
      } else
      if(newValue instanceof Double) {
          actualValue = (Double)newValue;

      } else {
      // We received an unknown object
      // type or access interface
        throw new IllegalArgumentException();
      }

      price = actualValue;
    }


    public String getPresentationString(Locale locale)
      throws UnsupportedOperationException
```

Continues

LISTING 3.8 A Possible Implementation of setValue() *(Continued)*

```
        {
        if(locale == Locale.US)
            return "$"+price;
            else
        if(locale == Locale.GERMANY) {
            String representation_string = "";

            // convert to appropriate locale representation

            return representation_string;
        } else {
            // We do not support the locale requested
throw new
    UnsupportedOperationException("Locale not
                    supported.");
        }
    }

}
```

TIP InfoBus does not directly provide the facility of thread-safe access to DataItems. It is entirely up to you to protect DataItem and producer methods with proper synchronization techniques. Two possible ways of dealing with this are to use the synchronized keyword in method declarations or to use a synchronized block on the property changed. This is an issue only when data values are set, such as in DataItem.setValue() for mutable DataItems. Read access to a data item is not affected and always returns the latest obtainable value of the property either before or after a synchronized change occurs, depending when the read first initiated.

Table 3.6 summarizes all the methods for ImmediateAccess Interface.

TABLE 3.6 ImmediateAccess Interface Methods

Method	Type	Description
public String **getValueAsString**()	Interface	Returns the data item's member data as a string representation.
public String **getPresentationString** (Locale *locale*) throws *UnsupportedOperationException*	Interface	Returns a string representation that accounts for the current locale supplied by the consumer.
public object **getValueAsObject**()	Interface	Returns an object representation to the consumer.
public object **setValue** (object *newValue*) throws *InvalidDataException*	Interface	Allows the consumer to attempt a value change on the data item. newValue is typically an ImmediateAccess object as well.

The ArrayAccess Interface

Data items that represent collections are viewed as simple n-dimensional arrays. Typically, basic DataItems implementing ImmediateAccess will aggregate into collection classes that implement ArrayAccess. Combined, these two interfaces allow for an application-independent mechanism to explore data items received through InfoBus. ArrayAccess objects are bounded and therefore their size can be determined at any time. Essential to the notion of array collections is random-access capability without significant performance penalty. The first step in achieving this is determining the dimension of the array by using get-Dimensions().

```
public int[] getDimensions()
```

The number integers returned represent the number dimensions of the array data. The actual integer values contained at each index coincide with the number of elements at that array location in the ArrayAccess. For example, a return of {5,6,7} indicates a 5×6×7 three-dimensional array. To retrieve an individual data item by location in the array we call getItemByCoordinates(). For example:

```
public Object getItemByCoordinates(int[] coords)
```

For mutable type objects, the returned object type for this method should be an access interface; likewise, to set the value of an object at a particular coordinate. Have a look:

```
public Object
setItemByCoordinates(int[] coords, Object newValue)
    throws InvalidDataException
```

It is recommended that producers accept ImmediateAccess objects as a conventional standard for newValue. However, other object types that are critical to the application can be used as well. If the underlying data source is not mutable and forbids any alteration, an UnsupportedOperationException should be thrown. If newValue is of a type incompatible with the underlying data representation, a java.lang.IllegalArgumentException should be thrown. Finally, when the value given is not acceptable (e.g., out of range), an InvalidDataException is thrown.

ArrayAccess provides the capability to obtain portions of the array data it represents. This is accomplished by dividing the array into a subset of the original by supplying a coordinate range.

```
public ArrayAccess subdivide(int[] start,int[] end)
```

The subdivide method returns another ArrayAccess that represents the range beginning at start and ending at end. If end is not greater than start, or either parameter is beyond the valid range for the Array-Access, an ArrayIndexOutOfBoundsException is generated. All of the methods for ArrayAccess interface are summarized in Table 3.7.

TABLE 3.7   ArrayAccess Interface Methods

Method	Type	Description
public int[] getDimensions()	Interface	Returns the number of dimensions for the ArrayAccess.
public object getItemBy Coordinates(int[] coords)	Interface	Returns the object at the specified coordinates.
public object setItemByCoordinates (int[] coords, Object newValue) throws InvalidDataException	Interface	If the data item is mutable, this method allows the consumer to update an object at the specified location.
Public ArrayAccess subdivide (int[] start, int[] end)	Interface	Returns a subrange of the ArrayAccess beginning at start and ending at end.

As you can see, it's quite conceivable that complicated applications can have numerous, intricate relationships between data items, consumers, and producers. Often, it is necessary for consumers to monitor changes to data items. InfoBus provides various classes and interfaces that assist the developer in broadcasting and receiving event notifications about internal changes to data items.

The DataItemChangeManager Interface

A DataItem can optionally implement the DataItemChangeManager interface to track listeners on that data item interested in knowing when changes occur. To add and remove change listeners to a DataItemChangeManager, use the following methods:

```
public void
addDataItemChangeListener(DataItemChangeListener listener)

public void
removeDataItemChangeListener(DataItemChangeListener listener)
```

The DataItemChangeSupport Class

The DataItemChangeSupport class provides a convenient implementation of DataItemChangeManager and includes event firing mechanisms for notifying listeners being managed. Table 3.8 shows the descriptions for the DataItemChangeSupport Class instances.

The DataItemChangeListener Interface

After a consumer has received notification about the availability of a DataItem and has obtained a reference to that item, it can receive further event notifications when the data item changes by registering an implementation of DataItemChangeListener with the item. Registering occurs with specific DataItems on an instance-by-instance basis. This means that notification about change events emits from only the DataItem instances with which the DataItemChangeListener is registered. The DataItemChangeListener interface has a variety of specific methods used to notify the implementer of change events.

```
public void
```

```
dataItemValueChanged(DataItemValueChangedEvent event)
public void dataItemAdded(DataItemAddedEvent event)
public void dataItemDeleted(DataItemDeletedEvent event)
public void dataItemRevoked(DataItemRevokedEvent event)
public void rowsetCursorMoved(RowsetCursorMovedEvent event)
```

When this method is invoked on a DataItemChangeListener, it receives an event from which it can determine how the data was changed and what data item was changed.

Although each of these methods is more or less self-explanatory by name, we take a closer look at each event object delivered through these method calls and how to use them.

TABLE 3.8   DataItemChangeSupport Class

Method	Type	Description
public void **addDataItem ChangeListener**(DataItem ChangeListener *listener*)	Instance	Adds a DataItemChangeListener
public void **removeDataItem ChangeListener**(DataItem ChangeListener *listener*)	Instance	Removes a DataItemChangeListener
public void **removeAllListeners**()	Instance	Removes all listeners
public void **fireItemValue Changed**(object changedItem, InfoBusPropertyMap propertyMap)	Instance	Fires a DataItemValueChangedEvent to all listeners
public void **fireItemAdded** (object *changedItem*, object *changedCollection*, InfoBusProperty Map *propertyMap*)	Instance	Fires a DataItemAddedEvent to all listeners
public void **fireItemDeleted** (object *changedItem*, object *changedCollection*, InfoBus PropertyMap *propertyMap*)	Instance	Fires a DataItemDeletedEvent to all listeners
public void **fireItemRevoked** (object *changedItem*, InfoBus PropertyMap *propertyMap*)	Instance	Fires a DataItemRevokedEvent to all listeners
public void **fireRowsetCursor Moved**(object *changedItem*, InfoBusPropertyMap *propertyMap*)	Instance	Fires a RowsetCursorMovedEvent to all listeners

TIP   One typical scenario where DataItemChangeListeners are effective is on a web page with a collection of three InfoBus applets that operate independently. One applet provides various graph views of a DataModel entity on the InfoBus. Let's call it GraphApplet. Another applet stores and retrieves the DataModel from a remote database. Let's call it DBApplet. The third applet retrieves input data from the user and is called UserApplet. In this scenario, we have a combination of DataItemChangeListeners, consumers, and providers. UserApplet acts as a producer and when the user has entered in the data, it notifies InfoBus that the new DataModel is available. As a consumer of type DataModel, DBApplet retrieves the object off InfoBus and stores it in the database. GraphApplet is another consumer of DataModel, but also wants to be notified when changes to that specific DataModel occur, and therefore registers as a DataItemChangeListener. When DataModel does change as a result of user input, GraphApplet is notified of the type of change and can update its graphs accordingly.

THE DATAITEMCHANGEEVENT CLASS

DataItemChangeEvent, as shown in Figure 3.4, represents a base class under which a variety of subclasses exist to differentiate types of changes on DataItems. When a change is made on a DataItem, all registered listeners are notified that a change has occurred on that item. Depending on the nature of the change, the listeners receive a different type of event class. Typically, DataItems that arrive on an InfoBus are collections or composite objects that often contain many subitems. When a parent object or any of its children undergo a change, proper notification to registered listeners is called for. It is up to the producer to decide which levels of a data item hierarchy should allow listeners by implementing DataItemChangeManager. Let's examine how to create a base DataItemChangeEvent.

```
public
DataItemChangeEvent(Object source,Object changedItem,
  InfoBusPropertyMap propertyMap)
```

Source represents the object sending the event. The changedItem represents the object data that changed, and the propertyMap parameter represents a Map object that contains valid properties that are discovered and retrieved using getProperty() dynamically. This parameter is entirely optional, and null is an acceptable value for propertyMap. Take a look at the following:

```
public Object getProperty(String key)
```

When getProperty() is called, it in turn calls the get method of the appropriate Map supplied in the constructor and provides the object data associated with *key*. A consumer can obtain a reference to the originating listener object from the notification event by calling getSource(). For example:

```
public Object getSource()
```

In addition, to retrieve the actual object that changed, DataItem-ChangeEvent.getChangedItem() is called.

```
public Object getChangedItem()
```

In some cases such as collection size changes or simple value changes, getSource() and getChangedItem() will likely return the same object. When getChangedItem() returns a non-null value that differs from getSource(), it refers to a subitem of the value returned by getSource(). In this case, that data item that actually changed was hierarchically connected to the original DataItem, which notified the registered listeners. If the value returned from getChangedItem() is null, it means that multiple data items had changed on the collection.

DataItemValueChangedEvent

This class extends DataItemChangeEvent, but provides the same functionality and access methods as its ancestor. For each DataItem that implements ImmediateAccess and whose value has changed, the following procedure should take place:

1. A new DataItemValueChangedEvent event is created and sent to any change listeners registered for that particular DataItem.

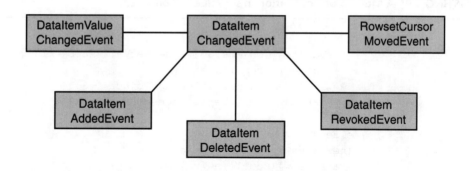

FIGURE 3.4   Class hierarchy for DataItemChangeEvents.

2. The DataItem's parent collection is notified and a similar DataItem-
    ValueChangedEvent is created and subsequently sent to any regis-
    tered listeners on the parent collection.
3. Repeat these steps until you reach the top-level DataItem that
    arrived on the InfoBus.

Listing 3.9 demonstrates one method of notification in setValue().

LISTING 3.9   A Method of Notification in setValue()

```
public class MyDataItem implements DataItem,
    DataItemChangeManager
    {
    Vector changeListeners = new Vector(10,10);

    Object data;

    // DataItem interface methods
    ...

    public synchronized Object setValue(Object newValue)
    throws InvalidDataException
    {
      Object aValue = null;

      if(newValue instanceof ImmediateAccess) {
ImmediateAccess objValue =
            (ImmediateAccess)newValue;
```
Continues

LISTING 3.9 **A Method of Notification in setValue()** *(Continued)*

```
                try {
                 aValue = (Object)objValue.getValueAsObject();
                } catch (Exception e) {
                    // Cannot get value as Object
                    throw new IllegalArgumentException();
                }
            } else
            if(newValue instanceof Object) {
                aValue = (Double)newValue;

            } else {
                // We received an unknown object type
                throw new IllegalArgumentException();
            }

            // Set the new value
            data = aValue;

             // Create the appropriate change
             // event and notify our listeners

            DataItemValueChangedEvent change = new
              DataItemValueChangedEvent(this,aValue,null);

            for(int i=0;i<changeListeners.size();i++) {
                DataItemChangeListener listener =
            (DataItemChangeListener)changeListeners.elementAt(i);
                listener.dataItemValueChanged(change);
            }
        }


    // DataItemChangeManager methods

public void
    addDataItemChangeListener(DataItemChangeListener listener)
    {
      changeListeners.addElement(listener);
    }
```

LISTING 3.9   *Continued*

```
public void
  removeDataItemChangeListener(DataItemChangeListener listener)
  {
    changeListeners.removeElement(listener);
  }

}
```

It is, as always, at your discretion to determine a convenient and practical method for notifying any interested listeners about changes to appropriate data items.

DataItemAddedEvent

This class extends DataItemChangeEvent and inherits the base class methods from it. In addition, it provides the capability to identify the actual object added to the data collection. This is done through a slightly different constructor as shown here:

```
public
DataItemAddedEvent(Object source,Object changedItem,Object
changedCollection, InfoBusPropertyMap propertyMap)
```

In this constructor, source represents the data item sending the event; changedItem represents the item added; changedCollection represents the collection to which the previous item was added.

DataItemDeletedEvent

Identical in nature to DataItemAddedEvent, this class identifies a deletion from a collection-type DataItem.

```
public
DataItemDeletedEvent(Object source,Object changedItem,
ObjectchangedCollection, InfoBusPropertyMap propertyMap)
```

Both DataItemAddedEvent and DataItemDeletedEvent contain a method for obtaining the modified collection. For example:

```
public Object getChangedCollection()
```

DataItemRevokedEvent

When a consumer receives a change event of this type, it means that the producer no longer provides that type of DataItem, possibly because the producer's source for the data item such as a database connection has gone away. When this occurs, consumers must immediately cease any access to the DataItem and release() all references to it and any subitems.

RowsetCursorMovedEvent

This event is generated when a cursor for a RowsetAccess data item has moved to a different row. This event is covered in greater detail in Chapter 4, "Advanced InfoBus Concepts."

Table 3.9 summarizes the various event classes responsible for notification of data item changes.

TABLE 3.9   DataItemChangeEvent Classes

Class	Constructor	Description
DataItemChangEvent	(Object source, object changedItem,InfoBus PropertyMap map)	This class acts a base class for specific subclasses indicating the nature of the change event.
DataItemValue ChangedEvent	Inherited	Subclass indicating a value change for a specific DataItem.
DataItemAddedEvent	(Object source, object changedItem,object collection, InfoBusPropertyMap map)	Subclass indicating the addition of an object to a collection-type DataItem.
DataItemDeleteEvent	(Object source, object changedItem,object collection, InfoBusPropertyMap map)	Subclass indicating the removal of an object from a collection-type DataItem.
DataItemRevokedEvent	Inherited	Indicates the producer of the data item can no longer provide that data item.
RowsetCursor MovedEvent	Inherited	Indicates a cursor for a RowsetAccess data item has moved to another row.

CONCLUSION

In this chapter we have explored the specifics behind the major InfoBus interfaces, including InfoBusMember, InfoBusDataConsumer, InfoBus-DataProducer, DataItem, and a host of others. Together these interfaces represent the heart of the InfoBus API, which, as we've seen, is designed in the spirit of component computing like JavaBeans. As a JavaBean developer, you will agree that InfoBus shares many of the same mechanisms used in JavaBeans to provide the maximum amount of interoperability with the Bean's computing paradigm. In addition, we've explored some example implementations of InfoBus interfaces to help understand how we can provide implementations to suit our own application needs.

CHAPTER 4

Advanced InfoBus Concepts

In the last chapter we took a look inside the major pieces of InfoBus. We will now revisit some of those components in greater detail and take a look at some new components and processes that make InfoBus a truly powerful standard for interapplet/module communication. In addition, you will learn how to link relational databases and InfoBuses together through special access interfaces. You will also learn how InfoBus policy objects and exception-handling mechanisms operate.

Having introduced the basic event objects of InfoBus in Chapter 3, "Inside the InfoBus," we now explore more thoroughly the mechanisms through which these events are generated and delivered. The process of event delivery from producer to consumer (data availability) and consumer to producer (data request) is termed *rendezvous* for the basic reason that data items and events essentially meet in one place, on the InfoBus.

RENDEZVOUS

We already know about InfoBusMembers, InfoBusDataConsumers, and InfoBusDataProducers. We've examined how they are created, how they join and leave InfoBuses, and a bit about how they make notifications about data items. In this section we explore the specific pieces that comprise an event notification. Specifically, we refer to the events themselves, how they're created, and what they provide to the recipients.

InfoBusEvent

The InfoBusEvent is simply a root class for rendezvous events and is not instantiated directly. Its primary function is to carry the common elements across all rendezvous-type events, namely the dataItemName.

```
public String getDataItemName()
```

In the spirit of good object-oriented design, the creators of the InfoBus API utilize base classes to carry common members for a variety of more specific subclasses. Table 4.1 shows the description for the InfoBusEvent method.

InfoBusItemAvailableEvent

In the previous chapter we learned event notification to consumers involved calling dataItemAvailable() on each consumer listening on an InfoBus. InfoBusItemAvailable event objects are passed to the consumer when this occurs and contain the information the consumer needs to identify the data item name extract the dataItem, or identify the source.

Consumers identify data items of interest by name and optionally by examining the DataFlavors list.

```
public DataFlavor[] getDataFlavors()
```

The flavors associated with the data item should indicate all the available named types in the data item hierarchy so the consumer can accurately determine if the content is of interest. We look more closely at how data items are described with DataFlavors in a later section of this chapter.

Often, it is necessary for consumers to acquire a reference to the source producer object that generated the event. For example, suppose a consumer applet receives a data item over a default InfoBus on a common web page that contains other applets or Beans that all belong to the same InfoBus. After the applet receives the item, it can obtain a reference to the source Bean or applet that produced the data item. This is useful if the consumer applet wishes to identify the producer of a particular data item whose name is shared by another data item possibly produced by a different producer. In this sense, it is necessary to track the producer of the item to distinguish it completely. Getting a reference to the producer of a data item is done by calling getSourceAsProducer() on the event.

```
public InfoBusProducer getSourceAsProducer()
```

TABLE 4.1 InfoBusEvent Method

Method	Type	Description
public String getDataItemName()	Instance	Returns the name associated with the data item this event is representing

The consumer can indicate the flavors that are of interest when requesting the data item through requestDataItem(). The producer may return null if it cannot provide the requested data item as one of the given flavors.

```
public Object
requestDataItem(InfoBusDataConsumer consumer,
    DataFlavor[] flavors)
```

Table 4.2 shows the method descriptions for InfoBusItemAvailableEvent.

InfoBusItemRevokedEvent

When data producers wish to revoke a data item previously made available on InfoBus, they fire an InfoBusItemRevokedEvent. As we've seen, this is done by calling InfoBus.fireItemRevoked(). InfoBus notifies consumers on behalf of the producer that fires the event. Because this type of event can originate only from an InfoBusDataProducer, it has but one method for identifying that producer, as shown here:

```
public InfoBusDataProducer getSourceAsProducer()
```

When consumers receive notification about item revocation they inspect the data item name through the InfoBusEvent base class method getDataItemName() to determine if it is currently held and releases it appropriately. Because it's possible that a variety of producers provide the indicated data type, it is useful to store the producer of a data item when it is retrieved from the InfoBus. That way, consumers can verify that a held item originated from the producer who now revokes it; otherwise, it's safe to keep the data item. Table 4.3 shows the description for the InfoBusItemRevokedEvent methods.

TABLE 4.2 **InfoBusItemAvailableEvent Methods**

Method	Type	Description
public InfoBusProducer getSourceAsProducer()	Instance	Returns the InfoBusDataProducer object that generated the event
Public object requestDataItem (InfoBusDataConsumer consumer, DataFlavor[] flavors)	Instance	Returns the data item object requested or null if the producer cannot provide the object type
Public DataFlavor[] getDataFlavors()	Instance	Returns the list of DataFlavors represented in the item hierarchy of the event

InfoBusItemRequestedEvent

This type of event is used when generating *blind* requests. As we discussed previously, blind requests are fired by consumers that wish to receive specific data item types. It is not known if a producer exists at the time the event is fired; hence the term *blind*.

> **NOTE** This contrasts with data item notification directly to consumers where the consumer can retrieve the item specifically from the producer that originates the notification. This direct process is handled by DataController objects and is discussed in the next section on DataControllers.

Similar to the way other InfoBusEvent mechanisms operate, the DataFlavors requested by the consumer can be packaged in this type of event to notify possible producers of the types of items needed.

```
public DataFlavor[] getDataFlavors()
```

In addition, the producer can retrieve the consumer object from the event by calling getSourceAsConsumer(). This bilateral mechanism for acquiring references to originators allows InfoBus components to operate more efficiently if necessary. For reasons that may be discovered, acquiring the consumer object behind the current request may prove useful.

```
public InfoBusDataConsumer getSourceAsConsumer()
```

TABLE 4.3   InfoBusItemRevokedEvent Methods

Method	Type	Description
public InfoBusDataProducer getSourceAsProducer()	Instance	Returns the InfoBusDataProducer object that originated the event

TIP Efficient Access and Notification: Suppose a consumer initializes and fires a blind request for a data item. It receives an InfoBusItemAvailable event and records the producer of the item for future use. Next time the consumer needs an item it may opt to ask for it directly from the producer that last provided it before firing another blind request. This can lead to less overhead when requesting rare item types.

When the producer receives a request for a data item and can service the request with the appropriate data item type, it either passes an existing reference of the data item or creates a new instance and places it in the event using setDataItem().

```
public void setDataItem(Object dataItem)
```

Listing 4.1 shows the setting of a non-DataItem object inside an InfoBusItemRequestedEvent. The drawback to this is that the consumer that requests the object needs to cast it specifically. That is, it needs to know before the request that it receives a chart object in order to access its data properly. This assumes the chart class itself does not implement the DataItem interface. If it did, the consumer can access properly because it casts the return to the appropriate interface, namely DataItem. An example of a consumer requesting a data item can be seen in Listing 4.2.

TIP Discerning Object Types: Note that this method receives an object-of-type Object. The conformity to DataItem interfaces is strictly used to provide reliable access mechanisms. However, depending on the nature of the application and the degree of interoperability, the developer may use discretion and provide a user-defined type in place of a DataItem object. Doing so reduces InfoBus compliance if you plan on integrating with different Beans.

LISTING 4.1 **Setting Specific Object Inside an InfoBusItemRequestedEvent**

```
    ...

public static
    final String[] supportedTypes = {"chart.101",null};

    // This DataItem would implement ArrayAccess
    ChartData chartData = null;

public void
    dataItemRequested(InfoBusItemRequestedEvent event)
    {
      String itemName = event.getDataItemName();


      for(int i=0;i<supportedTypes.length();i++)
        if(itemName.equals(supportedTypes[i])) {
          chartData = new ChartData();
          event.setDataItem(chartData);
        }


      ...
    }
    ...
```

LISTING 4.2 **Consumer Requesting a Data Item**

```
    ...
    InfoBus infoBus = null;

    // Get a reference to our InfoBus,
    // creating it if necessary
    infoBus = InfoBus.get("MyInfoBus");


    ...
    // Join our InfoBus instance
    infoBus.join(this);
    ...
```

LISTING 4.2 *Continued*

```
    // Attempt to find a chart data with the name "chart.101"
DataItem chartData =
(DataItem)infoBus.findDataItem("chart.101",null,this);

    if(chartData==null) {
    // No producers responded
    } else {
        if(chartData instanceof ArrayAccess) {
        // Cycle through our data and display an appropriate chart
        }
    }
```

When the consumer invokes a request for a data item, the InfoBus class contacts producers through their dataItemRequested() method using an InfoBusItemRequestedEvent. When the producer returns from this invocation, InfoBus passes the returned data item back to the object that issued the request. Depending on how the original request for the data item was issued, the resulting data item can be acquired in two ways:

- In the event of a blind request, the consumer receives an object-of-type Object when its call to InfoBus.findDataItem() returns.
- InfoBus retrieves the actual data item from the InfoBusItemRequestedEvent by calling the getDataItem() method after a producer has provided the item through setDataItem().

```
public Object getDataItem()
```

Table 4.4 shows the methods' descriptions for InfoBusItemRequestedEvent.

The events we just looked at represent the heart of the InfoBus event notification process. These events are generated inside an InfoBus instance and delivered to the appropriate listeners depending on the type of request. As we saw in Chapter 3, "Inside the InfoBus," the primary listeners associated with InfoBus instances are InfoBusDataProducer and InfoBusDataConsumer, both of which extend the common base class InfoBusEventListener. Similar to the way InfoBusEvent contains

TABLE 4.4   InfoBusItemRequestedEvent Methods

Method	Type	Description
public DataFlavor[] getDataFlavors()	Instance	Returns the DataFlavors requested by the consumer issuing the request for the data item
public void setDataItem (Object dataItem)	Instance	Sets the appropriate data item requested
public Object getDataItem()	Instance	Returns the data item set by the producer that responded to the event
public InfoBusData ConsumergetSource AsConsumer()	Instance	Returns the InfoBusDataConsumer requesting the data item type

general information common to all InfoBusEvent types, the InfoBus EventListener acts as a root or base interface for the various InfoBus listener interfaces that we explore now.

The InfoBusEventListener Interface

Consumers and producers represent listener objects so they can receive special notifications about data item delivery and revocation. In addition, they need to monitor changes to the *InfoBus* property associated with the member object to which the listener belongs. For this reason, they must also implement the PropertyChangeListener interface that serves as the root class of InfoBusEventListener. Because the InfoBusEventListener interface is a base interface, it is not very useful to implement directly.

In Chapter 3, "Inside the InfoBus," we briefly touched on mechanisms used to deliver events on InfoBus. InfoBus components will invoke instance methods on the InfoBus instance to which they belong, which generates the desired event notification and delivery. At this point, it is important to revisit the InfoBus class and take a closer look at the event delivery mechanisms it supports.

The InfoBus Class: Event Delivery Methods

Event delivery methods in InfoBus are designed to "fire" off specific event objects destined to notify the appropriate listeners of the type of event as well as information about any data affected by generating the event. Appropriately, you will notice that these methods begin with "fire" followed by a mnemonic representation of the type of event object that will be delivered. The following sections describe each type of event notification method.

Item Availability

When producers are ready to announce the availability of new data items, they do so by invoking InfoBus.fireItemAvailable() on the InfoBus to which they are currently joined. There are multiple flavors of this method, each with a slightly different effect.

```
public void
fireItemAvailable(String dataItemName, DataFlavor[]
flavors,InfoBusDataProducer producer)
```

This variation is called by passing the name of the data item, dataItemName, the optional flavors describing the data or null if the producer wishes not to describe it, and the producer generating the InfoBusItemAvailableEvent.

```
public void
fireItemAvailable(String dataItemName, DataFlavor[]
flavors,InfoBusDataProducer producer, InfoBusDataConsumer target)
```

Consumers can be notified directly as well. Target represents the consumer listener to which the InfoBusItemAvailableEvent is delivered via its dataItemAvailable() method. In some cases, it is necessary to broadcast an item available event to a collection of consumers, and this is indeed what DataController objects do behind the scenes of InfoBus. We get there shortly, but for now, remember that target-specific methods such as these are reserved exclusively for DataControllers.

```
public void
fireItemAvailable(String dataItemName, DataFlavor[]
flavors,InfoBusDataProducer producer, Vector targets)
```

In this case, targets represent a Vector of InfoBusDataConsumer objects to which event notification takes place. As we see later in this chapter, DataController objects utilize the last two variations of fireItemAvailable() exclusively to facilitate event notification. For most purposes, InfoBusDataProducers should be concerned only with the first variation of fireItemAvailable() that does not directly contact consumer objects.

Item Requests

It is a recommended procedure for consumers to fire a blind request for interesting data items when they initialize. Typically, this is an applet in a web page where the request is invoked in the applet's start() method to search for data items pending retrieval from a default InfoBus. Like the availability methods just described, the following blind request methods have three primary variations:

```
public Object
findDataItem(String dataItemName, DataFlavor[]
flavors,InfoBusDataConsumer consumer)
```

When this method is called, an instance of InfoBusItemRequesed-Event is sent to producers notifying them of the consumer requesting a data item with name dataItemName and an optional list of flavors describing the data types wanted. As this method is called, all producers on the InfoBus are notified in an unspecified order. The first producer capable of providing the needed data item responds with that item and the method returns. If no producer can provide the requested item, a value of null is returned.

```
public Object
findDataItem(String dataItemName, DataFlavor[] flavors,
InfoBusDataConsumer consumer, Vector targets)

public Object
findDataItem(String dataItemName, DataFlavor[] flavors,
InfoBusDataConsumer consumer, InfoBusDataProducer target)
```

These two variations behave similarly to the fireItemAvailable() methods in that the specified target or targets will receive the event notification exclusively. Because of this, these variations are designed exclusively for use by DataControllers.

When a consumer wishes to retrieve all available data items capable of being provided by all producers rather than simply the first available item, it can use InfoBus.findMultipleDataItems().

```
public Object[]
findMultipleDataItems(String dataItemName, DataFlavor[]
flavors,InfoBusDataConsumer consumer)
```

The return value of this method is an array containing all the data items provided by each producer that responded to the event. This type of request almost warrants the use of DataFlavor descriptors. It is possible that a request for a specific type of data via data name would yield many responses. In this case, the use of DataFlavors can serve as a way for producers to reduce their responses to more adequately serve the request. This really depends, again, on the application design. There are few general rules that can be applied in situations like this simply because the number of applications, conditions, and requirements are limited only by one's imagination and goals. To avoid possible problems, though, there are some basic questions you can ask before determining how to store data items for consumer retrieval.

- If the DataItem contains specific data and not default data after calling its constructor, it's usually a good idea to give it a unique name or mnemonic so chances of another producer carrying the same named object are low. This reduces the chances that consumers receive multiple ambiguous object references.
- If a producer returns a newly created instance with generic default values each time a consumer request arrives, it may prove better to avoid unique naming and simply use a class name that describes the object or some other nonunique name. That way, when requests arrive for the generic object name, it's clear that a generic nonunique object is requested.

Item Revocation

Sometimes producers may request that data items previously submitted to InfoBus be revoked. This can happen for a number of reasons. Perhaps the database connection that services a particular data item has closed and therefore the item should no longer be used by consumers. Firing an item revocation event is similar in method to the other two event notification types we just looked at. Non-DataController components should use the following method to notify consumers of item revocation:

```
public void
fireItemRevoked(String dataItemName,
          InfoBusDataProducer producer)
```

It should be relatively straightforward as to the name of the input parameters to this method. The result of this method is the creation and distribution of an InfoBusItemRevokedEvent to all consumers currently joined on the InfoBus.

Two other variations on this method exist to serve DataController objects.

```
public void
fireItemRevoked(String dataItemName,
InfoBusDataProducer producer, InfoBusDataConsumer target)

public void
fireItemRevoked(String dataItemName,
InfoBusDataProducer producer, Vector targets)
```

Note that all three types of event notification methods in the InfoBus class look relatively identical in structure with the primary invoker method and two method variations intended for DataController use as well. Get ready, DataControllers are coming up next!

Table 4.5 shows a summary of the InfoBus class methods.

TABLE 4.5   InfoBus Class and Instance Methods

Method	Type	Description
public static synchronized InfoBus **get**(Component *component*)	Class	Returns the default InfoBus.
public static synchronized InfoBus **get**(String *infoBusName*)	Class	Returns the InfoBus with the name infoBusName.
public synchronized void **join**(InfoBusMember *member*) throws *PropertyVetoException, InfoBusMembershipException*	Instance	Joins member to this InfoBus.
public String **getName**()	Instance	If the InfoBus was created by name, this method returns the name of the InfoBus. If this is the default InfoBus instance, the name returned is derived from the applet context document base, or DOCBASE.
public void **register** (InfoBusMember member)	Instance	Registers member on the list of active members for this InfoBus. It also registers this InfoBus as a PropertyChangeListener to the InfoBusMember's infoBus property.

TABLE 4.5 *Continued*

Method	Type	Description
public synchronized void leave(InfoBusMember member) throws PropertyVetoException	Instance	Causes member to be removed from the InfoBus' active member list and be removed as a PropertyChangeListener on member's infoBus property.
private synchronized void release()	Instance	This method is called internally by the InfoBus instance. When called, it determines if all event listeners and data controllers for that instance have been removed and, if so, removes the instance from the active list.
public void addDataProducer (InfoBusDataProducer producer)	Instance	Adds a data producer to this InfoBus.
public void removeDataProducer (InfoBusDataProducer producer)	Instance	Removes the specified data producer from the InfoBus.
public void addDataConsumer (InfoBusDataConsumer consumer)	Instance	Adds a data consumer to this InfoBus.
public void removeDataConsumer (InfoBusDataConsumer consumer)	Instance	Removes the specified data consumer from the InfoBus.
public void addDataController (InfoBusDataController dataController)	Instance	Adds a data controller to the InfoBus.
public void removeDataController (InfoBusDataController dataController)	Instance	Removes a data controller to the InfoBus.
public Object findDataItem (String name, DataFlavors[] flavors,InfoBusDataConsumer consumer)	Instance	A consumer requests a particular data type.
public Object findDataItem (String name, DataFlavors[] flavors,InfoBusDataConsumer consumer, InfoBusDataProducer producer)	Instance	A consumer requests a particular data type from a specific producer.

Continues

TABLE 4.5 **InfoBus Class and Instance Methods** *(Continued)*

Method	Type	Description
public Object findDataItem (String name, DataFlavors[] flavors,InfoBusDataConsumer consumer, Vector producers)	Instance	A consumer requests a particular data type from multiple producers.
public Object[] findMultiple DataItems(String name, DataFlavors[] flavors, InfoBus DataConsumer consumer)	Instance	A consumer requests a variety of data item types.
public void fireItemAvailable (String name, DataFlavors[] flavors, InfoBusDataProducer source	Instance	A producer notifies InfoBus when a particular type item is available.
public void fireItemAvailable (String name, DataFlavors[] flavors, InfoBusDataProducer source, InfoBusDataConsumer consumer)	Instance	Notifies a specific consumer when a data item is available.
public void fireItemAvailable (String name, DataFlavors[] flavors, InfoBusDataProducer source, Vector targets)	Instance	Notifies a Vector of targets that a data item is available.
public void fireItemRevoked (String name, InfoBusData Producer producer)	Instance	A producer has revoked an item it previously made available.
public void fireItemRevoked (String name, InfoBusData Producer producer, InfoBusData Consumer consumer)	Instance	Notifies a specific consumer of a data item revocation.
public void fireItemRevoked (String name, InfoBusData Producer producer, Vector targets)	Instance	Notifies a Vector of targets of a data item revocation.

DATACONTROLLERS

DataControllers are both the traffic cops and messengers of InfoBus rolled into one. Their basic responsibility is to determine who gets what kind of message. Whenever a component fires a request over an InfoBus object, the DataControllers take over inside and process the request on behalf of the sender. The notification events we've discussed are generated by the

InfoBus and delivered to the appropriate recipients through DataControllers. All of this is transparent to the originator of an event. They simply interact with their support class or InfoBus instance, and the rest is handled behind the scenes, so to speak.

DataController objects in InfoBus implement the InfoBusDataController interface. When an event notification method is fired on an InfoBus instance, it systematically polls each and every DataController currently registered. By default, each InfoBus instance has a DefaultController object that performs a simple, one-to-many transmission; that is, a source generates an event and that event reaches all possible recipients without discrimination. To draw upon what we already know, it is easy to see this working when a producer fires an event that notifies consumers of an available item. We learned in Chapter 3, "Inside the InfoBus," that each and every consumer is notified through its dataItemAvailable() method. Likewise, when a consumer places a request for an item type, all producers are polled in sequence until one can provide the item.

One of the nice features about DataControllers is that they allow us to optimize this process. In other words, we can determine which producers or which consumers receive event notifications and avoid polling or notifying every producer or consumer, respectively.

DataController Priority

InfoBus instances can have many registered controllers. Because of this, it is necessary to provide a mechanism to prioritize them. The order in which controllers are allowed to process events is important to your application and is therefore at the discretion of the developer. Because the DefaultController assumes no other controllers are present, it always has the lowest priority. There are seven defined priority settings in InfoBus for DataControllers.

InfoBus.MONITOR_PRIORITY

InfoBus.VERY_HIGH_PRIORITY

InfoBus.HIGH_PRIORITY

InfoBus.MEDIUM_PRIORITY

InfoBus.LOW_PRIORITY

InfoBus.VERY_LOW_PRIORITY

InfoBus.DEFAULT_CONTROLLER_PRIORITY

These priority levels represent integer values and determine the order in which data controllers are notified about InfoBus events first. Specifically, high-priority data controllers process incoming events before low-priority data controllers. There are two special priority levels provided. InfoBus.MONITOR_PRIORITY is designed for data controllers that act as monitors and do not specifically partake in event distribution. These monitor-type data controllers receive all incoming events but don't respond to these events, and their return values are ignored for this reason. InfoBus.DEFAULT_CONTROLLER_PRIORITY is reserved for the DefaultController we just talked about. Any attempt to set your data controller to this priority level will result in it being adjusted to InfoBus.VERY_LOW_PRIORITY. Data controllers having the same priority level will receive event notifications in an unspecified order. That is, at this time, no strict rule can define the order in which two identical priority controllers will receive events, and for this reason, no particular order shall be assumed. Bottom line here is, don't add data controllers of the same priority level and assume that they will run in the order added. They won't.

The following InfoBus methods are used to add and remove data controllers:

```
public synchronized void
addDataController(InfoBusDataController controller,
int priority) throws InfoBusMembershipException

public synchronized void
removeDataController(InfoBusDataController controller)
```

Figure 4.1 shows two DataControllers connected to an InfoBus along with three consumer objects. DataController1 maintains all three consumers and their connections indicated by the lines. This represents the default controller because it sees all consumers connected to the InfoBus. DataController2 sees only one of the consumers and restricts event notification to only that consumer. DataController2 represents a higher-priority DataController and processes events first. Depending on what DataController2 decides, it may or may not allow DataController1 to process events as well.

The InfoBusDataController Interface

We now explore the InfoBusDataController interface, which defines the methods implemented by DataControllers.

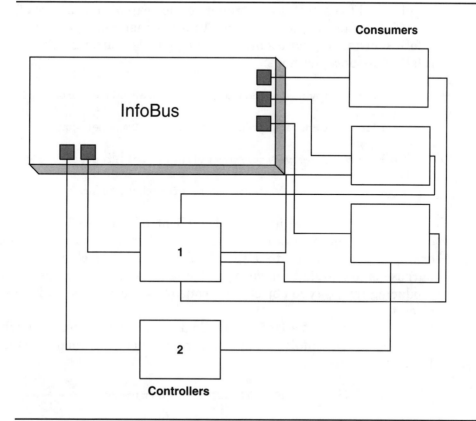

FIGURE 4.1 Two DataControllers with consumers.

If you get bored with some of the technical aspects of the API, skip along and come back and reference it at a later time. Much of the API discussions from here on out are quite syntax and technically oriented and may cause drowsiness if you don't pause periodically for breaks.

Because DataControllers can deliver events directly to consumers or producers, they must maintain their own internal list of which InfoBus-Members they notify when an event is processed. When a controller joins an InfoBus, it receives a copy of that InfoBus's master list of members. Typically, the controller is interested in only a subset of all the members on an InfoBus (unless it is the DefaultController that operates on all members). Whenever members join or leave an InfoBus, the InfoBus instance notifies the DataControllers currently joined to it that membership changes have occurred. At this time, the list of active members is published to each DataController so they can also be aware of new or retired InfoBus members. When InfoBus members join or leave an InfoBus instance, DataControllers are notified through the following InfoBus instance methods:

```
public void addDataProducer(InfoBusDataProducer producer)

public void addDataConsumer(InfoBusDataConsumer consumer)

public void removeDataProducer(InfoBusDataProducer producer)

public void removeDataProducer(InfoBusDataConsumer consumer)
```

It is the responsibility of the DataController object to decide which consumers or producers to accept to its internally managed lists. For example, you may create a specific DataController object whose only purpose is to marshal image-type objects between producers capable of producing image-type objects and consumers interested in image-type objects.

The InfoBus initializes a DataController's list of members when it initially joins the InfoBus. The following methods are used internally by InfoBus to do this.

```
public void setConsumerList(Vector consumers)

public void setProducerList(Vector producers)
```

DataControllers deliver specific events depending on which InfoBus method was fired. For example, producers that want to notify consumers of a particular item's availability would naturally call InfoBus .fireItemAvailable(). The consequence of this is the creation of an InfoBusItemAvailableEvent that's broadcast to concerned consumers as indicated by a particular DataController object. The highest-priority DataController processes the event by using its internal list of members as a basis to broadcast the associated event; in this case, it is InfoBusItemAvailableEvent. The controller calls a direct method on each member passing the newly created event. See the previous section, *The InfoBus Class: Event Delivery Methods*, for a list of DataController-to-member-specific method calls.

The activation methods for InfoBusDataControllers are almost identical to those in the InfoBus class, except invocations on data controllers occur internally through the InfoBus and are not called directly by InfoBus members.

```
public boolean findDataItem(String dataItemName, DataFlavor
flavors[], InfoBusDataConsumer consumer, Vector foundDataItem)

public boolean findMultipleDataItems(String dataItemName,
DataFlavor flavors[], InfoBusDataConsumer consumer, Vector
foundDataItems)
```

When a consumer invokes a find method on an InfoBus object, the highest-priority DataController is given control and its corresponding find method is also invoked. When this occurs, the controller polls its list of producers using target-specific methods looking for returned data items. The reference to the consumer generating the event is passed to each and every producer to provide access to the event originating from the producer. When each producer is polled directly, a non-null response indicates a found item, which should be stored in the appropriate foundDataItems vector. In the case of findMultipleDataItems(), all non-null responses are accumulated in the foundDataItems vector. When either of these methods returns a true Boolean value, this indicates to the InfoBus to *not* proceed to the next DataController with the event request. A value of false allows lower-priority DataControllers to process the incoming event as well. In the situation in which a consumer invokes findMultipleDataItems() on an InfoBus instance, nondefault DataControllers should consider simply returning false and not providing any functionality for the method. The reason for this is because the DefaultController accomplishes the basic process of collecting return values from producers already, and only in special cases should a custom controller override this functionality. If you choose to implement this feature in your controller, a few considerations are worth mentioning.

You must invoke the single-target version of findDataItem() on producers and not the flavor that contains the Vector parameter. This is because you must poll each producer separately regardless of a return value providing a Vector of targets in findDataItem() returns with the first non-null response.

Results returned by the data controllers are aggregated by the InfoBus.   The default functionality provides for elimination of duplicate object occurrences. However, because certain producers may provide multiple, different return values, you may want to allow this.

As we've seen before, producers interact with an InfoBus instance to make data items available for consumer acquisition. When a producer uses its two primary invocation methods, fireItemAvailable() and fireItemRevoked(), analogous methods in associated DataControllers are invoked.

```
public boolean
fireItemAvailable(String dataItemName, DataFlavor
flavors[],InfoBusDataProducer producer)

public boolean
fireItemRevoked(String dataItemName,
InfoBusDataProducer producer)
```

Like the other DataController interface methods, these invoke directly on consumer objects.

To help clarify how DataControllers can be useful, let's consider a hypothetical scenario that involves a department store, suppliers, and storerooms. Consider the department store as an InfoBus instance, the suppliers as producers, and the storerooms as consumers. Each department also has a corresponding DataController that maintains references to each storeroom for that department.

Storeroom 1 is registered in the men's clothing department of our department store and represents an InfoBus consumer. Storeroom 2 is registered in the sporting goods department and also represents a consumer. Supplier 1 provides a variety of goods to our department store, sometimes clothes, sometimes sporting goods, and acts as an InfoBus producer. For each department there exists a DataController that specializes in a particular type of goods and notifies only the storerooms that are interested in such goods. These controllers are called menswear and sporting goods. When each of our DataControllers initializes, it receives a list of members on the current InfoBus. In this case, it receives a list of storerooms. Because the menswear DataController is only interested in notifying the menswear storeroom, it only stores the menswear storeroom to its internal list of members. Likewise, the sporting goods Data-

Controller refuses the menswear storeroom to its internal list and keeps the sporting goods storeroom instead.

Now suppose Supplier 1 provides a variety of items, some sporting goods, some menswear. It notifies the InfoBus through fireItemAvailable() that items of interest can now be inspected. Starting with the highest-priority DataController, InfoBus invokes fireItemAvailable() on it, passing the current data item. If the highest-priority controller is our menswear DataController, it accepts the data item if it is of type menswear and notifies Storeroom 1 from its internally managed list. It then returns true indicating no other DataControllers need be notified about this item. If the item is of type sporting goods, the menswear controller will return false and InfoBus will move to the next-highest priority DataController with the current item. In our case, this is the sporting goods DataController. It recognizes the item type and notifies Storeroom 2 only.

If we were to use the DefaultController behavior in our example, both storerooms will receive notification whenever an item arrives on the InfoBus. Although they can distinguish between types that are interesting and types that are not, it is much more efficient for a DataController to notify only the interested consumers of an item. This is especially true if you are dealing with many consumers, each with specific items of interest. DataControllers can be very effective at governing the proper flow of information and reducing the amount of InfoBus traffic and consumer notification events. In our example, our DataControllers routed events from producer to consumer. DataControllers also participate in notification in the other direction; that is, from consumer to producer. When consumers issue blind requests on an InfoBus, the InfoBus polls each DataController in the same fashion we described, from highest to lowest priority. Depending on the flavor of method invoked, the DataController responds accordingly. If a consumer invokes InfoBus.findDataItem(), the InfoBus will invoke the analogous InfoBusDataController.findDataItem() method in the next-highest priority DataController. The DataController will respond to this method by polling producers directly searching for the first available result, or collecting return values from each producer it maintains and placing them in a Vector of found items.

Table 4.6 summarizes the methods descriptions for InfoBusDataController. In Chapter 5, "InfoBus Design Models," we explore various implementations of DataController objects that perform specific tasks.

TABLE 4.6 InfoBusDataController Methods

Method	Type	Description
public void setConsumerList (Vector consumers)	Interface	Sets the DataController's list of consumers
public void setProducerList (Vector producers)	Interface	Sets the DataController's list of producers
public void addDataConsumer (InfoBusDataConsumer consumer)	Interface	Adds the specified consumer to the DataController's internal list
public void addDataProducer (InfoBusDataProducer producer)	Interface	Adds the specified producer to the DataController's internal list
public void removeData Consumer(InfoBusDataConsumer consumer)	Interface	Removes the specified consumer to the DataController's internal list
public void removeDataProducer (InfoBusDataProducer producer)	Interface	Removes the specified producer to the DataController's internal list
public boolean fireItemAvailable (String dataItemName, DataFlavor flavors[], InfoBusDataProducer source)	Interface	Creates an InfoBusItemAvailableEvent and passes it to its internal list of consumers
public boolean fireItemRevoked (String dataItemName,InfoBus DataProducer source)	Interface	Creates an InfoBusItemRevokedEvent and sends to its internal list of consumers
public boolean findDataItem (String dataItemName, DataFlavor flavors[], InfoBusDataConsumer consumer, Vector foundDataItem)	Interface	Creates an InfoBusItemRequestedEvent and sends to its internal list of producers
public boolean findMultiple DataItems(String dataItemName, DataFlavor flavors[], InfoBusData Consumer consumer, Vector foundDataItem)	Interface	Creates an InfoBusItemRequestedEvent and sends to its internal list of producers

Describing DataItems

Throughout our discussions involving data items, we've indicated that they can be further described using flavors. The class involved in providing a description or flavor for an object is, naturally, DataFlavor and is provided in Java 1.1. At this point, it is important to cover DataFlavors in detail and how they play a role in describing InfoBus DataItems.

Before we get into the details about DataFlavor objects let's take a minute to discuss mime-type encoding and its application and purpose in InfoBus.

Mime Encoding Strings

Mime (Multipurpose Internet Mail Extensions) is an Internet standard that is used to describe the content and format of data. Objects formatted to the mime specification are called *mime objects*. Some typical mime objects include email packets and an HTML page. For example, an HTML page would have a mime string like text/html that indicates it's text data and, more specifically, HTML text data. In this sense, you can view the mime string as type/subtype.

The mime type of a mime object is contained in the header block that is used to properly identify the mime object to mime reader applications. Your web browser is such an application, and it understands a variety of mime objects such as pictures, HTML, and video and audio clips as well. All of this is very transparent to the user, of course, and is designed to be flexible and dynamic. This means that applications can discover at runtime the type and content of a mime object and apply the necessary reader to decipher the object's content and display it to the user. This puts the problem of reading the object into the application and allows the object itself to be exchanged between applications of a possibly different nature, but both capable of identifying and displaying similar mime objects.

If all of this sounds vaguely familiar to how InfoBus operates, it's not by accident. The marriage of InfoBus data items and descriptive naming standards like mime is a natural fit. InfoBus does not enforce the strict use of mime naming because providing DataFlavors to InfoBus objects is always optional. However, to ensure maximum flexibility and interoperability, it is probably a good idea to invest the time to incorporate proper naming conventions like mime in your object descriptions. Table 4.7 shows examples of mime types.

TABLE 4.7   Example Mime Types

Mime Type	Content Description
text/html	HTML text
Image/gif	A GIF formatted image
x-InfoBus/ArrayAccess	An InfoBus ArrayAccess object

The DataFlavor Class

You can find the DataFlavor class in java.awt.datatransfer.DataFlavor, and it is included as part of the JDK1.1 spec from Sun. It essentially provides a Java class that serves as a representation of a mime encoding string that can be associated with objects in your applet or application.

The term *DataFlavor* is pretty right on the nose. The data contained in objects within your program should be properly labeled in order for foreign entities to inspect and possibly use it in an appropriate manner. In this sense, an object hierarchy representing your data can contain various types of objects or *flavors* of data. Since the data is the heart of the matter between an interchange, flavor indicators are needed to identify the data properly.

In adherence with the InfoBus spec, object mime types should be prefaced with x-InfoBus/. In addition, it is recommended that object flavors also adopt the Access interface names we've discussed already. For example, consumers capable of using ArrayAccess objects could provide a DataFlavor such as x-InfoBus/ArrayAccess. Likewise, in order for this to work, producers would also have to announce that they provide x-InfoBus/ArrayAccess. Because the access interfaces exist to provide an agreed-upon standard for application-independent data access, it stands to follow that the standard should also be utilized when describing those data items using the mime notion and DataFlavors. Indeed, it is good practice to do so. This ensures maximum interoperability between your objects, data, and other components written for InfoBus. In addition, it may be deemed necessary by you, the developer, to provide additional mime encoded strings specific to your applet or application as well as providing the InfoBus standard naming scheme. This can be useful within a specific application where data specific to it can be properly identified and separated from other sources.

Here is a list of more InfoBus specific mime types you may want to use in your applications.

x-InfoBus/ImmediateAccess

x-InfoBus/ArrayAccess

x-InfoBus/RowsetAccess

x-InfoBus/AnyAccess

The AnyAccess descriptor can be used as an agreement that any DataFlavor is acceptable to a consumer.

We cover just the basics behind the DataFlavor API. It is beyond the scope of this book to provide an in-depth examination of that particular class, but if you'd like to know all the details you can reference the API docs that come with JDK1.1.

Creating a DataFlavor class involves providing a mime encoding string and a practical human version of the description in the constructor.

```
public
DataFlavor(String mimeString, String humanPresentableForm)
```

The resulting DataFlavor object has a variety of useful methods, some of which we'll discuss now.

Determining what type a particular DataFlavor represents involves testing for equality against specific kinds of objects. If you wish to see if a DataFlavor object is equal to x-InfoBus/ArrayAccess you can issue the method call shown in Listing 4.3.

LISTING 4.3   Identifying an Interesting DataFlavor

```
    ...

public void
   dataItemAvailable(InfoBusItemAvailableEvent event)
    {
      int i = 0;

      DataFlavor[] flavors = event.getDataFlavors();

      for(i = 0;i< flavors.length();i++) {
        if(flavors[i].equals("x-InfoBus/ImmediateAccess")){
          // We've identified an ImmediateAccess flavor!
          ImmediateAccess iaObject =
          (ImmediateAccess)event.requestDataItem(this,null);

    ...

        }
      }
    }
   }
```

In addition to this, you can compare DataFlavor objects to one another by substituting the DataFlavor object you want to compare to in place of the string we used in the previous code segment.

If you wish to use the human-represented string description for the object you can retrieve it from the DataFlavor by issuing DataFlavor.getHumanPresentableName().

> **NOTE** The scope of DataFlavors goes well beyond the surface we've brushed lightly. The java.awt.datatransfer package deals with the grander scheme of transferring mime encoded or DataFlavor objects over streams. Its applicability to InfoBus is simply to describe DataItems in a manner consistent with the state of technology on the Internet, which is driven largely by mime (in addition to lesser-known standards).

DATABASE ACCESS INTERFACES

For those of you not familiar with relational data and how an RDBMS (Relational Database Management System) stores and retrieves data, we take a minute to recap the relational data model. If you are already skilled in relational databases, you may want to skip over the next section.

Relational Data Structures

A relational database stores data in table structures. The concept of a table is derived from the two-dimensional or rectangular shape of the data and its elements. Each table has a specific number of columns and an arbitrary number of rows. Each row, in turn, contains a cell for each column in the table. Each cell holds the value for that column or field. As data is entered into a table it goes in essentially one row at a time. In other words, the tables are composed of a series of rows that can be viewed sequentially, giving the table its height. Populating and retrieving rows from a relational database typically involves constructing SQL (Structured Query Language) statements, called queries, and submitting them to the database server. When a request is made for information from the database, one of two things will occur. Either it will not return anything, meaning no information matching your query could be found, or it will return a set of rows as a table. All rows in a given table are guaranteed to conform to the topology of the table itself. Basically, this means that when you query against a specific table, any rows you receive back will have the same columns or fields as defined in the table and no more or no less. The term used to describe the set of results in the form of a table you get back from a database query is, rightfully, ResultSet.

Result sets contain row data elements. Often, with extremely large databases, the number of rows in a result set can be huge. Special objects called cursors are used to navigate a result set sequentially, one row at a time, without reissuing additional queries. Cursors have a position within a result set table. Specifically, a cursor is said to be pointing at a specific row at any given time. Through the database API in your program, you step through the rows in your result set and process them individually and sequentially. This is referred to as *scrolling*.

The InfoBus API provides a convenient, application-independent mechanism to access result sets returned from relational databases. You may be wondering at this point why a separate access interface is needed and why ArrayAccess is not sufficient to hold a simple, two-dimensional table format (if you're not wondering, skip along at your leisure). Actually, you can accomplish simple table/row access by implementing an ArrayAccess interface over your table, but for reasons we'll soon explore, you may want to avoid doing this. Luckily, the InfoBus API provides a more natural access interface that lends itself more to the structures and concepts associated with relational database models.

The family of interface specifications in InfoBus that serve relational database models is called RowsetAccess. There are a variety of interfaces designed to make database access through InfoBus more manageable than the basic access interfaces mentioned in Chapter 3, "Inside the InfoBus." We cover each type of interface in detail and hopefully make it fun and interesting along the way.

The RowsetAccess Interface

The RowsetAccess interface is implemented on objects receiving row data from a data source, typically a relational database. The interface provides convenient methods for accessing all the information you need or want to know about your result set, such as number of columns, rows, data values, and so forth. In addition, it provides the ability to insert, update, and delete rows.

Let's take a moment and discuss some high-level behavior of Rowset-Access objects. First of all, objects representing row data from a database store the corresponding result set of a query. As we mentioned earlier, the result set is a sort of mini-table representing the rows matching the query sent to the database server. Because the number of rows can potentially be enormous, all access to row data from a RowsetAccess object is done through cursors. If you skipped the section on relational data models, jump back and read about cursors!

When a RowsetAccess object returns with row data, its corresponding cursor value is set at the first row (assuming there is one). The rows representing the result of your query are not returned or stored in your RowsetAccess object, but rather scrolled through using the cursor contained within the RowsetAccess object and sequentially retrieved from your database server. As we get into the methods and details of the RowsetAccess interface, we will see how to manipulate the cursor.

Let's take a look at how this interface is defined and situations in which it is useful to employ.

RowsetAccess objects contain special methods to access the metadata (or data about data) of the result set.

```
public int getColumnCount()

public String getColumnName(int columnIndex)
    throws IndexOutOfBoundsException
```

To obtain the number of columns, consumers invoke RowsetAccess.getColumnCount(). By using an index within the range of columns on the item, a consumer can obtain the name of the column or field. In addition to this, it will be necessary at times to identify the specific type represented by a particular column in your result set.

```
public int getColumnDatatypeNumber(int columnIndex)
    throws IndexOutOfBoundsException
```

The preceding method returns an int value corresponding to standard SQL types listed in java.sql.Types. Also, to acquire the class name of the object represented by a particular column in a table you invoke the following method:

```
public String getColumnDatatypeName(int columnIndex)
    throws IndexOutOfBoundsException
```

Acquiring the name of the class used in the columns of a result set table allows the consumer to possibly load the needed class before retrieving or creating dynamic instantiations of it.

These metadata methods provide useful ways to discover, at runtime, how the result set is organized. This is important because components on an InfoBus (typically multiple applets on a single web page) are not aware of the internal states of other components. They can respond only to InfoBus events and produce or examine DataItems in an application-independent manner. This is actually a good thing. We want to be able to share information between different applets or Beans in a possibly ad hoc or dynamically constructed environment in which disparate type applications are serving and sharing data objects between them. To remain faithful to this goal, the RowsetAccess interface allows Beans or applets to discover all the necessary attributes and information about result sets when they receive them over the InfoBus.

RowsetAccess objects operate in a slightly different manner from other InfoBus type data items we've discussed. As we've already mentioned, these objects return access to a result set table. The rows representing the result of the query are not all contained within the RowsetAccess object; rather, only a single row pointed to by the current cursor is actually contained at any one time. For this reason, it is necessary to navigate through the row set using your cursor. Currently, InfoBus allows only for forward navigation of database cursors. To move your cursor to the next row in the result or row set, you simply call RowsetAccess.next().

```
public boolean next()
        throws SQLException, RowsetValidationException
```

If another row in your result set exists, this method will advance the cursor and return true, indicating as such. A return value of false indicates that no more rows exist in this object.

> **TIP Monitoring Cursor Movement:** Because RowsetAccess objects allow access only to a single row of data at a time, it is essential for interested objects to be notified whenever a new row is available by advancing the cursor on the appropriate object. This is accomplished by registering DataItemChangeListeners on the RowsetAccess object. When we do this, a notification is sent to all listeners that the cursor has moved and new data is available. This is accomplished when rowsetCursorMoved() is called on the register listeners. An appropriate DataItemChangeEvent is created and passed along as a result. (See Figure 4.2.)

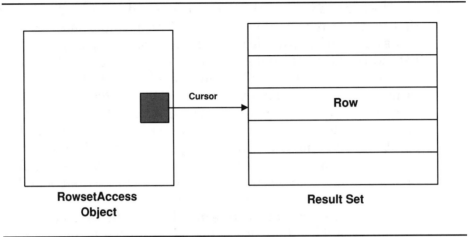

FIGURE 4.2   RowsetAccess cursor and result set.

It is also worth mentioning that, because data items that implement RowsetAccess are acquired by multiple consumers, advancing the cursor must be done with extreme caution. Whenever a cursor advances on a data item, all consumers currently holding the item will see the advancement. If two consumers advance a cursor expecting to receive the next sequenced row, they will collide and neither will be pointing to the row they think is next. To help clarify this, consider two consumers, A and B. They each receive a RowsetAccess object off of the InfoBus, call it Item C. If Item C's cursor is currently pointing to the first of 10 rows, both consumer A and B have access to row 1. If the consumers attempt to cycle through each row and process data, a collision will occur. Consumer A will receive row 1 and increment to row 2. Consumer B also receives row 1 at the same time as consumer A and increments the cursor, but because consumer A has already incremented the cursor, the cursor now points at row 3 for each consumer. Since they are expecting row 2 next, a collision occurs and problems will surely arise.

It is difficult to determine when this problem will arise if you are dealing with Beans or applets from other parties because it is not necessarily known how they will handle database items that arrive on the InfoBus. If, however, you are developing a set of Beans or applets that intend to interoperate peacefully, you may want to separate consumers that need to listen to cursor changes on a RowsetAccess object and consumers that actually manipulate the cursor. In other words, only one consumer should affect the cursor directly on any given RowsetAccess. Other consumers should be registered listeners and notified when changes occur.

When a consumer wishes to know the number of rows in a returned row set, it invokes RowsetAccess.getHighWaterMark(). If, while traversing a row set, a consumer wants to know if more rows exist, it calls RowsetAccess.hasMoreRows(), which returns true if more rows are present for retrieval.

```
public int getHighWaterMark()

public boolean hasMoreRows()
```

When you are ready to extract column data from the RowsetAccess object, you can do so in one of two possible ways. First, you can indicate the column index as an integer offset from 1.

```
public Object getColumnItem(int columnIndex)
        throws IndexOutOfBoundsException
```

Because there is only one row pointed to by the access object, you need indicate only which column in the row you wish to retrieve the value of. If all the rows were available in RowsetAccess, it is easy to see that you would need to specify both a column and a row; however, this is not currently the case.

The object value returned is typically an ImmediateAccess object, allowing the consumer a standard and expected method for examining its internal value as well. Typically, relational databases carry scalar or simple data types in their cells. For this reason, ImmediateAccess is generally used as a return value in this case. The consumer is still responsible for getting the actual data object by invoking ImmediateAccess.getValueAsObject() or ImmediateAccess.getValueAsString(). It is possible to provide objects of nonscalar type, from possibly a different kind of data source.

The second method for retrieving column values requires only the column name and provides a useful way of retrieving column values regardless of the order in which columns appear. In other words, as long as column names remain the same, it doesn't matter how your data source orders them.

```
public Object getColumnItem(String columnName)
        throws IndexOutOfBoundsException
```

> **TIP RowsetAccess Implementations:** We've talked about how RowsetAccess objects are used to access table data by querying a relational data store. However, because these interfaces are designed to provide application-independent methods to get at data stores, it is possible to provide an alternate retrieval mechanism depending on your needs. Your RowsetAccess implementation can provide custom object types from a specific data store, or it can maintain its own data storage mechanism. In the next chapter, we explore some special implementations of RowsetAccess.

In actuality, column ordering is not something that changes within a database over time, but hypothetically, your producer could be retrieving similar tables from different databases. As long as column names are identical or overlap, their values can be accessed using the second method. If the column name or index is not valid on the current object, an exception is generated and thrown.

Up until now we've talked about various methods of RowsetAccess that allow us to identify the row set configuration, size , names, and values, or generally speaking, read-type accesses. Now let's look into methods that perform write operations against your database such as insert, update, and delete, which are all basic operations supported by the relational data model and JDBC.

Once a consumer has acquired the RowsetAccess object and has accessed its underlying data, it can modify the data values and cause the current row to be updated in the database. Take a look at Listing 4.4 for a glimpse at how this might be done.

LISTING 4.4 Consumer Modifies Column Data through Access Interface

```
    ...
    DataFlavor[] flavors = new DataFlavor[1];
flavors[0] = new DataFlavor("x-InfoBus/RowsetAccess",
    "Result Set");

    RowsetAccess rowSet =
(RowsetAccess)infoBus.findDataItem(this,flavors);
```

LISTING 4.4 *Continued*

```
        if(rowSet!=null) {
          int cols = rowSet.getColumnCount();
          for(int i=1;i<=cols;i++) {
ImmediateAccess iaObj =
            (ImmediateAccess)rowSet.getColumnItem(i);
            Object value = (Object)iaObj.getValueAsObject();
            if(value!=null && value instanceof Integer)
              iaObj.setValue(new Integer(1998));
          }
          rowSet.newRow();
        }
        ...
```

Listing 4.4 shows an example of a consumer firing a blind request for a RowsetAccess item. Once it receives the item (assuming it does when the returned object is non-null), it acquires the ImmediateAccess object associated with each column. When it finds a column or cell whose type is Integer, it sets its new value to 1998.

Note that the use of access interfaces here emphasizes the need for application-independent mechanisms. It is not possible for another applet running in a web browser's VM (virtual machine) to know the specific object class of the returned data; therefore, it is unable to get at the internal data in a standard and reliable way. If all Beans or applets using RowsetAccess objects retrieve information using the standard InfoBus access interfaces for column data types, they should be able to exchange information freely without incident.

This is not to say that there will never exist a circumstance in which it is not beneficial to bypass the access interfaces in favor of common object types or base classes, but this would be specific to the system you are designing. We will explore design methodologies and decisions addressing this very issue in the next chapter on InfoBus design patterns.

Once you are satisfied with your modified data, submitting it to the backend database can be accomplished by calling RowsetAccess.newRow().

```
public void newRow()
      throws SQLException, RowsetValidationException
```

Calling this method causes a new row to be created with the current cursor set to it. Data held in the row previously pointed to by the cursor should be automatically stored in your backend database. It is really at the discretion of the developer as to how he or she implements this functionality. We are merely providing suggestions on possible implementations that remain consistent with the InfoBus spec and the recommendations of the InfoBus designers.

Listing 4.4 showed us how to modify the actual DataItem object, be it an ImmediateAccess interface or otherwise. It is also possible to modify a column value for the current row in your RowsetAccess object directly using RowsetAccess.setColumnValue(), which has two flavors. The first indexes the column by number that is always offset from 1.

```
public void setColumnValue(int columnIndex, Object object)
throws SQLException, RowsetValidationException,
IndexOutOfBoundsException

public void setColumnValue(String columnName, Object object)
throws SQLException, RowsetValidationException,
ColumnNameNotFoundException, DuplicateColumnException
```

In either case, you set the value of the column as the same type you expect to receive from getColumnItem(). Looking back at Listing 4.2, we see that our columns contain ImmediateAccess objects and not Integers that represent the type of the data value contained in the ImmediateAccess object. If we wanted to modify Listing 4.4 to use direct column access, it might look like Listing 4.5.

LISTING 4.5 Consumer Modifies Column Data Directly

```
    ...
    DataFlavor[] flavors = new DataFlavor[1];

    // This call assumes that an appropriate producer
    // can service A RowsetAccess object with the data name
    // "Result Set". In reality, this would throw a
    // ClassCastException if a producer returned a type
    // other than RowsetAccess. In our example, however,
    // we know we'll always get a RowsetAccess.
flavors[0] = new DataFlavor("x-InfoBus/RowsetAccess",
```

LISTING 4.5 *Continued*

```
    "Result Set");

    RowsetAccess rowSet =
(RowsetAccess)infoBus.findDataItem(this,flavors);


    if(rowSet!=null) {
      int cols = rowSet.getColumnCount();
      for(int i=1;i<=cols;i++) {
ImmediateAccess iaObj =
          (ImmediateAccess)rowSet.getColumnItem(i);
        Object value = (Object)iaObj.getValueAsObject();
        if(value!=null && value instanceof Integer) {
          ImmediateAccess myInt = new MyIntegerAccess(1998);
          rowSet.setColumnValue(i,myInt);
        }
      }
    }
    ...



    public class MyIntegerAccess implements ImmediateAccess {
    {
      Integer value = null;

      public MyIntegerAccess(int num)
      {
        value = new Integer(num);
      }

      public Object getValueAsObject()
      {
        return value;
      }

      public String getValueAsString()
      {
        return value+"";
      }
```

Continues

LISTING 4.5 **Consumer Modifies Column Data Directly** *(Continued)*

```
public String getPresentationString(Locale locale)
{
  return value+"";
}

public void setValue(int val)
{
  value = new Integer(val);
}
}
```

These methods can be used to perform an update on existing row data or to add value to a newly created row after calling Rowset Access.newRow(). When the call to setColumnValue() completes on a newly created row, it should ensure that the appropriate operation is called against your backend database. In concordance with the relational model, this will be either an update or insert SQL call depending on whether the row already exists in your database. A determination can be made, and the appropriate call can be issued to the database from within your RowsetAccess object.

Deleting the current row is done, predictably, by invoking Rowset Access.deleteRow().

Other database operations are supported through the following generalized method calls:

```
public void validate() throws SQLException,
RowsetValidationException

public void flush()throws SQLException,
RowsetValidationException
```

which explicitly cause any changed data to be written to the back end.

```
public void lockRow()throws SQLException,
RowsetValidationException
```

The preceding code requests that a lock be placed on the current row. This functionality should be provided in your backend database and augmented by the producer of the data item. Typically, row-level locks are implicitly held when rows are retrieved and released when the cursor advances to the next row. Your specific needs may require a slightly different implementation. In the next section, we will look at the DbAccess interface that provides a generic transaction processing model common to almost all databases. Implicit row lock can be accomplished in conjunction with the onset and subsequent finish of database transactions.

Data stores provide the ability to indicate what type of operations or combinations thereof can be done on the row data. Because of this, consumers need a way of knowing what types of actions can be done to the newly acquired DataItem. This is done through a series of Boolean methods.

```
public boolean canInsert()

public boolean canUpdate()

public boolean canDelete()
```

It should occur to you that if any of these methods returns a true value it indicates the respective operation can be issued on the Rowset Access item. Table 4.8 shows the interface methods for RowsetAccess.

TABLE 4.8   RowsetAccess Interface Methods

Method	Type	Description
public int getColumnCount()	Interface	Returns the number of columns in the current row
public String getColumnName (int columnIndex) throws IndexOutOfBoundsException	Interface	Returns the name of the column at position columnIndex, offset from 1
public int getColumn DatatypeNumber(int columnIndex) throws IndexOutOfBoundsException	Interface	Returns the data type of the column as listed in java.sql.Types
public String getColumn DatatypeName(int columnIndex) throws IndexOutOfBoundsException	Interface	Returns the string name representing the column class type

Continues

TABLE 4.8   RowsetAccess Interface Methods *(Continued)*

Method	Type	Description
public boolean next() throws SQLException, RowsetValidationException	Interface	Advances the cursor to the next row, submitting changes to the current row
public boolean hasMoreRows()	Interface	Returns true if more rows exist in your result set, false otherwise
public int getHighWaterMark()	Interface	Returns the known number of rows in the result set of your query
public Object getColumnItem (int columnIndex) throws IndexOutOfBoundsException	Interface	Returns the object associated with the column number columnIndex
public Object getColumnItem (String columnName) throws ColumnNotFoundException, DuplicateColumnException	Interface	Returns the object associated with the column whose name is columnName
public void newRow() throws SQLException, RowsetValidationException	Interface	Creates a new empty row and positions the cursor on it, submitting any previous row pointed to
public void setColumnValue (int columnIndex, Object object) throws SQLException, RowsetValidationException, IndexOutOfBoundsException	Interface	Sets the value of the specified column index to object
public void setColumnValue (String columnName, Object object) throws SQLException, RowsetValidationException, IndexOutOfBoundsException	Interface	Sets the value of the specified column name to object
public void deleteRow()	Interface	Deletes the current row
public void validate() throws SQLException, RowsetValidationException	Interface	Validates the current row by reconciling changes with values stored in the database
public void flush() throws SQLException, RowsetValidationException	Interface	Flushes any unwritten changes to the database
public void lockRow() throws SQLException, RowsetValidationException	Interface	Explicitly asks the producer for row-level lock on the current row

TABLE 4.8 *Continued*

Method	Type	Description
public boolean canInsert()	Interface	Indicates insert operations can take place on the current RowsetAccess object
public boolean canUpdate()	Interface	Indicates update operations can take place on the current RowsetAccess object
public boolean canDelete()	Interface	Indicates delete operations can take place on the current RowsetAccess object
public DBAccess getDb()	Interface	Returns the DbAccess interface object associated with this RowsetAccess

The DbAccess Interface

DbAccess objects maintain control over operations on the backend database that involve the onset and termination points of transactions on the database. In most cases, this can be provided by the producer object and therefore is relatively transparent to consumers invoking operations through RowsetAccess. However, there are situations in which only the consumer knows exactly when database operations should commence and terminate. Such situations might occur when operations against the database involve lengthy queries, unusually large result sets, or other special circumstances in which greater control is needed by a consumer to achieve the best performance.

The connect() and disconnect() methods provide a way for objects to specify exactly when connections are made to the database.

```
public void connect()
throws SQLException

public void
connect(String url, String username, String password)
throws SQLException

public void connect(String url, Properties info)
throws SQLException

public void disconnect()
throws SQLException
```

These methods mimic the analogous methods found in java.sql.DriverManager and java.sql.Driver. It was the intention of the InfoBus designers to maintain consistency between the core Java SQL classes where it made sense.

Before the disconnect() method is issued by a producer, it should fire item revocation events on all items retrieved from the data store by issuing InfoBus.fireItemRevoked() and also notifying any DataItem-ChangeListeners through their dataItemRevoked() method. This ensures that no additional database operations are performed against RowsetAccess items currently held by consumers that must immediately release() such items back to producers. Well-behaved producers resolve any allocated resources and/or connections as a result of this. If further access is made to a DbAccess object that had its disconnect() method called, unpredictable results may occur. The only reasonable action to take on a DbAccess after disconnect() is connect().

Whenever a consumer wishes to examine the properties used by the producer to establish the database connection, it can do so by invoking DbAccess.getPropertyInfo().

```
public java.sql.DriverPropertyInfo[]
getPropertyInfo(String url, Properties info)
```

This method provides the caller with DriverPropertyInfo objects as defined in the java.sql package. The returned objects represent properties required to connect to the database. It may be that no special properties are required; in which case, none are returned.

Since transferal of information into and out of a relational database requires the submission of SQL-based queries, DbAccess provides an execution method for submitting SQL-based queries and returning the results as an Object type.

```
public Object executeRetrieval(String sqlQuery,
String dataItemName, String options) throws SQLException
```

The specified sqlQuery string represents an SQL statement such as an INSERT, DELETE, or UPDATE. The result of the query is stored as an Object type and is returned from this method. Also, the producer should apply the value of dataItemName as the Name property of the resulting RowsetAccess object. The Options parameter provides a place to send special options to the data provider. The producer is not required to implement any specific options, but a few predefined standard options are provided by InfoBus. Others can be added to your specific producer. These options are summarized in Table 4.9.

```
public int executeCommand(String sqlCommand,
String dataItemName) throws SQLException
```

This method specifically submits nonretrieval-based queries such as DELETE, INSERT, UPDATE, or a stored procedure. If it succeeds, it will return the number of rows affected. If dataItemName is not null, the producer should create an ImmediateAccess object containing the number of rows affected and make it available on InfoBus. For operations such as INSERT, UPDATE, or DELETE, the returned rows affected will likely be 0. A return value of –1 indicates that returning affected rows is not applicable for the given operation. If the requested operation fails, an exception is thrown.

When change operations are submitted to a database, they are implicitly committed; that is, they take immediate effect in the database and can be seen by subsequent operations operating on the changed data. Because it is supported by a variety of databases and middle-tier applications, grouping transactions before committing them can be accomplished through the DbAccess interface as well. Essentially, grouped transactions take place as a whole; either they all succeed or none succeed. This is particularly useful in certain applications. Consider filling in an account form that gets updated in a database. If the data in the form is grouped into a transaction block, then if an error occurs with one transaction, none of the data is committed and you have to start over. This is useful because partially submitted information can create disharmony between your data tables and should explicitly be

TABLE 4.9   Default Execution Options

"ArrayAccess"	Instructs the producer to submit an object implementing the ArrayAccess interface to the InfoBus.
"Map"	Instructs the producer to submit an object implementing the Map interface to the InfoBus.
"PreFetch=n"	Requests the producer pre-fetch the specific number of rows indicated by "n." 0 means none, –1 means all.
"RowLimit=n"	Requests that the producer fetch no more than "n" rows. 0 means none, –1 means all.

avoided. This is done by setting the onset of your transaction using DbAccess.beginTransaction().

```
public void beginTransaction()
```

All operations performed after a call to DbAccess.beginTransaction() are considered inside the transaction and are explicitly committed all at once. This is accomplished, naturally, by calling commitTransaction().

```
public void commitTransaction() throws SQLException,
RowsetValidationException
```

After a call to this method is made, you are back in implicit commit mode. Any and all database operations occurring at this point can be considered committed to the database. If a transaction block that has been committed to the database is in error, most databases provide a rollback facility that will undo all previous transactions in the last committed transaction block. To issue a rollback through DbAccess, you invoke rollbackTransaction().

```
public void rollbackTransaction() throws SQLException,
RowsetValidationException
```

Similar to how commitTransaction() operates, implicit commit mode is entered once again after this method is called. Table 4.10 shows the interface methods for DbAccess.

TABLE 4.10 DbAccess Interface Methods

Method	Type	Description
public void connect() throws SQLException	Interface	Connects to the previously specified database
public void connect(String url, Properties info) throws SQLException	Interface	Attempts to connect to the database specified by url with the properties supplied by info
public void connect(String url, String username, String password) throws SQLException	Interface	Attempts to connect to the database specified by url with username and password
public void disconnect() throws SQLException	Interface	Disconnect from this database

TABLE 4.10 *Continued*

Method	Type	Description
public DriverPropertyInfo[] getPropertyInfo(String url, Properties info)	Interface	Acquire DriverPropertyInfo objects describing the connection options for the current database
public Object executeRetrieval(String retrieval, String dataItemName, String options) throws SQLException	Interface	Execute an SQL retrieval command (SELECT) and return a RowsetAccess object
public int executeCommand(String command, String dataItemName) throws SQLException	Interface	Execute a nonretrieval SQL statement such as INSERT, DELETE, or UPDATE and return the rows affected
public void beginTransaction()	Interface	Begin a transaction block entering explicit commit mode
public void commitTransaction()	Interface	Commit the current transaction block and enter implicit commit mode
public void rollbackTransaction()	Interface	Undo or rollback the previously commited transaction block
public void validate()	Interface	Without commiting items, perform an explicit validationof changes
public void flush()	Interface	Flush all changes to the database

CONCLUSION

In this chapter we looked deeper into InfoBus at more advanced topics such as DataControllers, DataFlavors, and database Access interfaces. We've seen how the internal hierarchy of interface definitions is laid out and how the event mechanisms known as *rendezvous* operate between InfoBus components. You should have a deeper understanding of the usefulness of InfoBus standards and interfaces and how they facilitate interoperability and allow for seamless transparent access of nonuniform data types across applications. In addition, we've explored to some detail how to access databases from our InfoBus applications through the use of specialized interfaces for controlling retrieval and transactions under the relational database model. In Chapter 6, "Creating a Data Controller," we will see how to create a full–blown data controller application built upon the backgrounds discussed here.

CHAPTER 5

InfoBus Design Models

So far we've covered in great detail all of the major components and operations provided by InfoBus. In this chapter, we introduce some interesting and, hopefully, useful design ideas that can be adapted to solve a variety of application needs. Because it's the intent of these ideas to be reusable in a number of different applications or circumstances, we refer to them as *design models*. We define a design model here as a template that describes a set of objects and functionality that is sufficiently generic for domain-specific parameters to be inserted into the model without altering its definition or functionality. If that seems a bit long-winded, it should become clearer as we delve into our examples.

We approach this chapter similarly to the previous ones in that the sections represent a breakdown of the InfoBus components we wish to discuss; namely, members, consumers, producers, DataItems, and Data-Controllers. In each section we address useful design models that you can adapt to your applications based on that specific component. In some cases the boundaries overlap, but you'll figure that out as you go.

MEMBERS

We're already familiar with InfoBus members and how they join and leave InfoBus. Depending on the kind of applet or application you design, certain models for managing InfoBus memberships may prove useful. In Chapter 3, "Inside the InfoBus," we introduced the notion of a UserManager object that hosts a common InfoBus membership among all of its constituents. We now take a closer look at this particular model and pose a few scenarios in which it may prove useful.

UserManager

Our UserManager object is designed to service InfoBus membership to all of its participating user objects. We distinguish between members and Users for the sake of separating our own class and object names versus InfoBus names. In doing this, we hope to reduce any confusion about what is native InfoBus and what is not. Let's continue to look at this class.

Each UserManager object belongs to a variety of InfoBuses, or you can restrict it to only one InfoBus per object instantiation. We look at both implementations and discuss the benefits of each. First, we finish talking about how the class operates. A UserManager object also allows user objects to join and leave it; therefore, it must maintain an internal list of active participants at all times. User objects themselves don't directly interact with InfoBus instances. This is similar to how InfoBusMember-Support objects work. If you remember back in Chapter 3, "Inside the InfoBus," InfoBusMemberSupport objects are delegated the responsibility of routing membership events from the InfoBus instance to the member. Keep in mind that when using a delegate object like InfoBusMemberSupport, or in some cases (as we'll soon see) our UserManager object, your member may not actually be joined to an InfoBus instance.

One useful idea behind this concept is that objects joined to a User-Manager object do not need to be InfoBusMembers. You're probably wondering why. The reason for this is that the UserManager object itself is the member of a given InfoBus instance. The UserManager class receives events from any InfoBus it may currently be joined to and processes data items from those InfoBuses. It's therefore up to the UserManager to decide what to do with certain data items it receives, possibly repackaging and delivering them to its own member objects using a nonstandard application-specific manner. InfoBus is useful for notifying members about data availability; however, not all parts of an application may require the use of an InfoBus to receive and transmit information. User-Manager, therefore, acts as an envoy on behalf of other non-InfoBus objects that may need InfoBus data but don't necessarily know how to talk InfoBus. In this sense, UserManager may be a bit inadequate as a name, but you can certainly call your version anything you like.

Another important concept we mentioned earlier about this class is the management of membership. Users joining a UserManager may or may not specify a specific InfoBus they wish to talk to. This specification would be by name or would fall back to the default InfoBus, if one is provided. The UserManager has the ability to shift its membership to various InfoBuses on the fly. By doing this, it essentially changes the perceived membership among all its members. In the case in which your UserManager is managing real InfoBusMember objects, it can either act as a delegate member to a specific InfoBus or simply assign its own membership InfoBus to all the User members directly. In the second situation, user objects would, in fact, implement InfoBusMember except they would not be responsible for joining InfoBuses directly. In both situations, the UserManager controls the membership to and from InfoBuses on behalf of its Users.

This capability nicely provides for a way to corral InfoBus members whether they directly implement InfoBus interfaces or not. The logic contained within UserManager centrally manages which members belong to which InfoBus and which members (or groups of members) receive data from which InfoBus. This allows user objects to be essentially unaware of the rules governing each InfoBus they listen to and whether they are allowed access to certain InfoBuses. We will revisit this later in the chapter when we discuss security mechanisms that can be employed in your applets or applications. The following sections recap the UserManager class and some of its different incarnations.

First Variation

The UserManager object accepts user objects that implement InfoBus-Member and directly joins those user objects to a predetermined InfoBus known only to the UserManager. As the UserManager changes or is requested to change its InfoBus, all user objects leave the old InfoBus and subsequently are joined to the new one. Event notification in this model occurs directly to the user member objects and therefore the UserManager need not act as a consumer and process incoming event notifications or data items.

Second Variation

This version of UserManager accepts independent object types *not* implementing InfoBusMember. The user objects of this variation are guaranteed to not be InfoBusMembers and are therefore not directly joined to InfoBuses. Rather, this UserManager also implements InfoBusDataConsumer and InfoBusDataProducer and marshals data between its user objects and its corresponding InfoBus. Here, the UserManager has the added responsibility of packaging other objects into data items and announcing their availability. In addition, it receives event notifications and must determine what is of interest to its user objects. This may be only known to the UserManager where it is centrally managed. User objects of this type of UserManager may operate using their normal object data classes rather than expecting InfoBus-type data items. The UserManager is responsible for translating incoming data items to their native class equivalents and sending them directly to user objects without the need for event notification. In addition, this variation may receive a single data item type and duplicate that item and send it to all of its members as specific object type rather than DataItem. This could reduce the overhead involved in the consumer notification-item request process we examined in Chapter 3, "Inside the InfoBus." Items can be directly delivered with only one request from the producer that occurs through the UserManager class.

Third Variation

This variation can operate like either of the other two variations with the added capability to allow members to request a channel or InfoBus to which they prefer to be joined. In the previous two variations, the UserManager dictated which InfoBus its members are joined to and control of that membership was done through it. In this variation, a user object can request that it listen to a specific InfoBus much like a channel. This name is a simple String type. The UserManager must further maintain a list of InfoBus instances that have been requested in addition to a list of members listening to that InfoBus. This implementation diminishes that ability to shift members on the fly. Also, other components would have to be aware of what InfoBus channels are available if you wish for these components to exchange data with your UserManager and its respective user objects. In this sense, it might better be referred to as a ChannelManager. You can choose names you feel are appropriate.

In Listings 5.1 through 5.3, notice example implementations for the three variations described. In some cases, method implementation has been deferred where it does not directly illustrate the example. Also, you'll find that some method implementations rely heavily on the type of application you are writing. Use these classes as guidelines or templates to create your own more specialized versions.

LISTING 5.1   UserManager Variation 1

```
import javax.infobus.*;
import java.util.*;
import java.beans.*;

public class UserManager
```

LISTING 5.1 *Continued*

```
    {
        InfoBus infoBus = null;
        Vector members = new Vector(10);

        public UserManager(String infoBusName)
        {
            infoBus = InfoBus.open(infoBusName);
        }

        public void addMember(InfoBusMember member)
throws InfoBusMembershipException,
        PropertyVetoException
        {
            infoBus.join(member);
            members.addElement(member);
        }

        public void removeMember(InfoBusMember member)
        {
            members.removeElement(member);
        }

        public void setInfoBus(InfoBus infoBusL)
        {
            for(int i=0;i<members.size();i++) {
InfoBusMember member =
        (InfoBusMember)members.elementAt(i);
                try {
                infoBus.leave(member);
                infoBusL.join(member);
                } catch (Exception e) {
                    members.removeElement(member);
                }
            }

        }

    }
```

LISTING 5.2   UserManager Variation 2

```
import javax.infobus.*;
import java.util.*;
import java.beans.*;

public class UserManager2 implements InfoBusMember,
        InfoBusDataConsumer, InfoBusDataProducer
{
    InfoBus infoBus = null;
    Vector members = new Vector(10);
    InfoBusMemberSupport support = null;
    Vector listeners = new Vector();

    public UserManager2(String infoBusName)
    {
        support = new InfoBusMemberSupport(this);
        infoBus = InfoBus.open(infoBusName);
    }

    public void addMember(Object member)
    {
        members.addElement(member);
    }

    public void removeMember(Object member)
    {
        members.removeElement(member);
    }

    public InfoBus getInfoBus()

    {
     return support.getInfoBus();
    }

public void
    addInfoBusVetoableListener(VetoableChangeListener
     listener)
      {
       listeners.addElement(listener);
      }
```

LISTING 5.2 *Continued*

```
public void
    removeInfoBusVetoableListener(VetoableChangeListener
      listener)
      {
        listeners.removeElement(listener);
      }

public void
    addInfoBusPropertyListener(PropertyChangeListener
      listener)
      {
        listeners.addElement(listener);
      }

public void
    removeInfoBusPropertyListener(PropertyChangeListener
      listener)
      {
        listeners.removeElement(listener);
      }

    public void setInfoBus(InfoBus infoBusL)
    throws PropertyVetoException
    {
        try {
          try {
              for(int i=0;i<listeners.size();i++) {
PropertyChangeEvent event = new

PropertyChangeEvent(this,"infoBus",infoBus,infoBusL);
EventListener listener =
(EventListener)listeners.elementAt(i);
if(listener instanceof
                  VetoableChangeListener)
((VetoableChangeListener)
        listeners.elementAt(i)).vetoableChange(event);
if(listener instanceof
                  PropertyChangeListener)
((PropertyChangeListener)
        listeners.elementAt(i)).propertyChange(event);
```
Continues

LISTING 5.2 UserManager Variation 2 *(Continued)*

```
                    }
                } catch (PropertyVetoException f) {
                    throw f;
                }
            support.leaveInfoBus();
            support.joinInfoBus(infoBusL.getName());

            } catch (InfoBusMembershipException e) {

            }
        }

        public void sendObject(Object object)
        {
            // Create data item and fire event over infoBus
        }

    public void
        dataItemAvailable(InfoBusItemAvailableEvent event)
        {
            // Get the data and send it to my members.
            // Here, I will act directly on my members
            // depending on what type of object they are.
            // This user manager class will translate infobus
            // DataItem data to objects usable by my members.

        }

    public void
        dataItemRevoked(InfoBusItemRevokedEvent event)
        {
            // your implementation would go here
        }

        public void propertyChange(PropertyChangeEvent event)
        {
            // your implementation would go here.
        }
```

LISTING 5.2   *Continued*

```
public void
    dataItemRequested(InfoBusItemRequestedEvent event)
        {
        // Package the object as a data item and send it out.
        }


    }
```

LISTING 5.3   **UserManager Variation 3**

```
        import javax.infobus.*;
        import java.util.*;
        import java.beans.*;

        public class UserManager3
        {
            Hashtable channels = new Hashtable();
            Hashtable channelMembers = new Hashtable();

            public UserManager3()
            {
            }

            public void createChannel(String channelName)

            {
                InfoBus infoBus = InfoBus.open(channelName);
                channels.put(channelName,infoBus);
                Vector members = new Vector(10);
                channelMembers.put(infoBus,members);
            }

    public void
        addMember(InfoBusMember member, String channel)
    throws InfoBusMembershipException,
            PropertyVetoException
            {
```

Continues

LISTING 5.3 **UserManager Variation 3** *(Continued)*

```
            InfoBus infoBus = (InfoBus)channels.get(channel);
            infoBus.join(member);
Vector members =
        (Vector)channelMembers.get(infoBus);
            members.addElement(member);
        }


public void
    removeMember(InfoBusMember member, String channel)
        {
            InfoBus infoBus = (InfoBus)channels.get(channel);
Vector members =
        (Vector)channelMembers.get(infoBus);
            members.removeElement(member);
        }



    }
```

Security Object

Since your InfoBus members can have their InfoBus properties changed, the InfoBusMember interface also supports the addition and removal of JavaBeans PropertyChangeListeners. One such listener may be a special kind of listener called a VetoableChangeListener, also part of the JavaBeans spec. A VetoableChangeListener can prevent or *veto* changes that occur to an InfoBusMember to which it is currently listening. It can do this because when the infoBus property of a member is attempting to change, notification messages are sent to all property listeners including VetoableChangeListeners. When a VetoableChangeListener rejects the change by examining the current and requested change value, the current value remains unchanged. You can ensure that certain members cannot have their InfoBus property changed to an unsecure channel or InfoBus by adding a security listener to it to veto any unauthorized changes. In a system in which security is important, there may be multiple InfoBuses used as channels of information flowing from producers to consumers securely. That is, the system may guarantee that consumers of a certain security level can listen only on InfoBuses serving that security level and nothing else. The security object examines current and requested InfoBus values on change attempts in a member and determines whether the change is authorized or not. The conditions for authorization are entirely up to the developer and are likely specific to the particular application.

PRODUCERS

As mentioned, producer objects provide specific types of InfoBus DataItems. They are able to place objects on the InfoBus and inform consumers currently joined to the InfoBus of the newly available data, or they can provide objects at the specific request of a consumer looking for that kind of data.

Inspection Producers

Let's now take a look at some useful ideas that represent special kinds of producers. Our first idea concerns a producer that is aware of some kind of backend database, probably a relational database. This particular producer is concerned with a subset of the data served by the back end. It provides a specific kind of object data over the InfoBus. Let's call this data item AssetItem. For the sake of consistency, let's also call our producer AssetProducer since it produces only AssetItems and nothing else. Now, as we know in InfoBus, there may be a variety of consumers that need AssetItems and, of course, the exact number of consumers is not known by our producer. This is something a DataController more likely knows. Given that our consumers want to be informed whenever the asset data in the data store changes, our producer has to accommodate them in this manner. First, it sets a timed interval at which it checks a date stamp marking when the asset data last changed. To do this, it actually makes a call to the backend database and gets a single value back representing the timestamp of the asset data. It must keep this value handy to compare against subsequent calls to the database. As it inspects the timestamp in the database at the end of each interval, it determines if it has changed. If it has, it knows to retrieve the latest asset information and create an AssetItem object to hold it. AssetItem can either implement the necessary access interfaces, such as ArrayAccess or ImmediateAccess, or represent a collection object containing many access interface objects. Once it has created the data item to hold the data, it can then call InfoBus.fire-ItemAvailable(), notifying all interested consumers that new data is available. The outcome of this procedure is that whenever data changes in the database, it is sure to be propagated to all interested consumers by any InfoBuses that contain our AssetProducer. The data in the data store can be changed by any other type of application and does not have to have an InfoBus application.

Consider another example in which you have a live feed of information coming into your network. Maybe it's up-to-the-minute stock quote information, or maybe it's a Reuters news feed providing constant news information. Specialized producers can monitor changes in repositories for these dynamic information wires and extract the information and provide it in an application-independent manner to any interested consumers. In this sense, it is possible to create a generic information provider that is capable of keeping consumers up to date on changes to that information regardless of where it happens to come from.

These producers are not perfect and do have some weaknesses that are worth mentioning. Depending on how you set your interval for checking changes to the data, you might actually miss changes. In other words, if your inspection interval is set to every 10 seconds, and the data has changed three times in 10 seconds, your consumers will not receive notification about two of the three changes (specifically, the first two). This may or may not be important to your application. Much of this depends on how the data is stored. One way of avoiding this problem is to ensure that the data store does not overwrite previously stored data when updating. This leaves a history trail of all incoming changes that can easily be followed by your producer regardless of interval. Also, this ensures that consumers are provided with all subsequent changes to the data. Because you may not have control over how the data is stored, use caution before deciding to use an interval inspection producer (see Listing 5.4).

LISTING 5.4 AssetProducer

```
import javax.infobus.*;
import java.util.*;
import java.beans.*;

public class AssetProducer implements
```

LISTING 5.4 *Continued*

```
InfoBusDataProducer, Runnable
{

  public final static String DATA_TYPE  = "IBDataType";

  InfoBus infoBus;

  // This serves for illustration
  // purposes only. In reality,
  // you will provide your own algorithm
  // for determining when
  // new data is available.
  boolean newdata = true;

  // Also for illustration purposes.
  // You will create a DataItem
  // implementation that suits your application.
  DataItem dataItem = null;

  public AssetProducer(InfoBus infoBus)
  {
    this.infoBus = infoBus;
    try {
        infoBus.addDataProducer(this);
    } catch (InfoBusMembershipException e) {
      // Apparently our infoBus instance is stale
    }
    Thread thread = new Thread(this);
    thread.start();

  }


  public void run()
  {
     while(true) {

         // This conditional is intentionally simplistic
         // and serves only to show where you would
         // place your own algorithm, possibly connecting
```

Continues

LISTING 5.4 **AssetProducer** *(Continued)*

```
              // to a database and examining timestamps.
               if(newdata) {
                   dataItem = new MyDataItem();
         InfoBus.fireItemAvailable("dataItemName",null,this);
                   newdata=false;
               }
               try {
                 Thread.sleep(1500);
               } catch (InterrupedException e) {

               }
         }
      }


      public void propertyChange(PropertyChangeEvent event)
      {
        String name = event.getPropertyName();
        if(!name.equals("infoBus")) return;
        InfoBus newInfoBus = (InfoBus)event.getNewValue();
        if(infoBus != newInfoBus) {
            infoBus.removeDataProducer(this);
            infoBus = newInfoBus;
        }
         try {
        infoBus.addDataProducer(this);
        } catch (InfoBusMembershipException e) {

        }
      }


      //InfoBusDataProducer method implementations
  public synchronized void
   dataItemRequested(InfoBusItemRequestedEvent event)
      {
          event.setDataItem(dataItem);
      }

      public void finalize()
```

LISTING 5.4 *Continued*

```
        {
            infoBus.removeDataProducer(this);
        }

    }
```

CONSUMERS

Consumers receive data item objects over the InfoBus to which they are joined. Consumers typically will request specific kinds of DataItems that will be provided by the appropriate producer capable of providing it.

ConsumerManager

Consumer objects can be managed in much the same way as we managed our members in our UserManager class described earlier. Applying the same functionality to consumers allows us to manipulate a variety of different consumers as a group based on some centralized logic or condition. The ConsumerManager can have intelligence about what to do when an InfoBus instance becomes invalid, possibly switching to another InfoBus and providing necessary security information that may not be known by the consumers because they may be Beans from another vendor (see Listing 5.5).

LISTING 5.5 **ConsumerManager Example**

```
import javax.infobus.*;
import java.util.*;
import java.beans.*;

public class ConsumerManager {

    private Hashtable members = new Hashtable();
    private InfoBus infoBus = null;
```
Continues

LISTING 5.5   ConsumerManager Example *(Continued)*

```
public ConsumerManager(InfoBus infoBus)
{
    this.infoBus = infoBus;
}

public void addMember(InfoBusMember member, String name)
throws InfoBusMembershipException, PropertyVetoException
{
    members.put(name,member);
    infoBus.join(member);
}

public void setInfoBus(InfoBus infoBus)
throws InfoBusMembershipException
{
    Enumeration m = members.elements();
    InfoBusMember member = null;

    while(m.hasMoreElements()) {
        member = (InfoBusMember)m.nextElement();
        try {
            this.infoBus.leave(member);
            infoBus.join(member);
        } catch (PropertyVetoException e) {
            members.remove(member);
        }

    }
}

}
```

Translators

Following the idea that InfoBus consumer Beans may be shielded from specific information about the InfoBus application or applet environment, it is conceivable that certain kinds of data items provided may be incompatible with some consumers. In this case, consider a special version of the ConsumerManager that supplies its constituents with data items that are known to be acceptable. In this case, the ConsumerManager manages an array of consumers that require data items to be of a specific type. This type may not currently be provided by producers on the InfoBus, but the ConsumerManager may contain specific knowledge about related types and make necessary translations of the data and either resubmit it over the InfoBus (as a producer) or supply it directly to its consumer members. One example of this might be a Consumer-Manager that contains a variety of consumers that can read GIF-type images. Each consumer can process only GIF format images; however, producers on the current InfoBus are providing image data in JPEG format. A special ConsumerManager for GIF consumers can recognize a variety of image-type data and convert it to a useable format for its consumers. This normalization process further allows producers and consumers to share similarly typed data regardless of the specific format. ConsumerManager objects can specialize in a broad spectrum of normalization types, thereby improving interoperability between data producers and consumers from possibly different vendors, environments, or applets. When a ConsumerManager resubmits the newly translated data item back on the InfoBus, it must also implement the InfoBusDataProducer interface. In addition, depending on whether InfoBus membership is hosted by the constituents or delegated to the ConsumerManager, it may not be necessary to act as a producer and resubmit data items.

It may be noticeable from our discussion on translators that they can just as easily function as independent consumer/producer objects as well. In this sense, there may not be a ConsumerManager, but an unknown (or unmanaged) number of consumers joined to the current InfoBus. The translator consumer object represents another consumer on the InfoBus and may not necessarily know about other consumers. Rather, it simply takes items off the InfoBus, translates them appropriately, and puts new data items back on the InfoBus where other consumers can identify and retrieve them.

InfoBusGateway

The InfoBusGateway is probably one of the most interesting and useful models we present. It receives events off an InfoBus and beams them to another InfoBusGateway object connected to a remote InfoBus. In essence, this provides a simple mechanism for distributing InfoBus events across multiple applications over a network. In actuality, each gateway object is both a consumer and a producer. InfoBusGateways employ the buddy system. By this we mean that each gateway object has a buddy somewhere else on a network to which it is connected. For each gateway, there is exactly one other gateway or buddy to which it will send and receive events. To further clarify this, let's walk through an example of how they operate together.

Suppose you have two applications running on a network, each with its own InfoBus. When each application initializes, it creates an InfoBus instance and joins it. It also creates an instance of an InfoBusGateway object and assigns it to the InfoBus as well. When the InfoBusGateway object is created, a port value is supplied so the gateway knows where to listen for incoming events from its buddy. In order for two gateways to communicate, they must be aware of the other's port. Typically, an instantiation of a given gateway class provides a default port value so every instantiation of that gateway will know to what port its potential buddy will be listening. Keep in mind, only one gateway can occupy a port on the same machine at any given time. Multiple gateways on the same machine must use different port values. Now, back to our applications. Suppose Application A instantiates the class InfoBusGateway that defaults to port 2001. Application B also instantiates class InfoBusGateway on port 2001, but Application B is running on another machine, so this is okay. The gateway object in Application A is joined to the InfoBus as a consumer and a producer and will receive events as such. Whenever Gateway A receives a notification, it retrieves the data item from the corresponding producer local to Application A and sends it to its buddy Gateway B. Gateway B receives the incoming data item and posts it as a producer to the InfoBus it is joined to in Application B. Consumers in Application B are notified about the newly available data item and request it from Gateway B, which is now the local producer of the data item. Likewise, when Gateway B receives a data item off its InfoBus in Application B, it retrieves it as a consumer and beams it to its buddy gateway in Application A, which posts it as a producer to its local InfoBus (see Listing 5.6).

LISTING 5.6   InfoBusGateway Example

```
import javax.infobus.*;
import java.beans.*;
import java.net.*;
import java.io.*;
```

LISTING 5.6   *Continued*

```java
import java.util.*;
import java.awt.datatransfer.*;

public abstract class InfoBusGateway implements
InfoBusMember, InfoBusDataProducer,
InfoBusDataConsumer, Runnable
{
    private InfoBusMemberSupport support;
    protected String peer;
    protected int eventPort = 4880;
    protected int peerPort  = 4880;
    protected Hashtable dataItems = new Hashtable();

    public InfoBusGateway( InfoBus infoBusName)
    {
        init(infoBusName);
    }

    private void init(InfoBus infoBus)
    {
        try {
          support = new InfoBusMemberSupport(this);
          support.setInfoBus(infoBus);
          support.getInfoBus().addDataConsumer(this);
          support.getInfoBus().addDataProducer(this);
          Thread thread = new Thread(this);
          thread.start();
          } catch (Exception e) { e.printStackTrace();}
    }

    public InfoBusGateway( InfoBus infoBus,int port)
    {
        this.eventPort = port;
        init(infoBus);

    }

    public void setInfoBus(InfoBus newInfoBus)
    {
```

Continues

LISTING 5.6 **InfoBusGateway Example** *(Continued)*

```
        try {
          support.setInfoBus(newInfoBus);
        } catch (Exception e) {}
    }


    public InfoBus getInfoBus()
    {
        return support.getInfoBus();
    }

public void
    addInfoBusVetoableListener(VetoableChangeListener
        listener)
    {
        support.addInfoBusVetoableListener(listener);
    }

public void
    removeInfoBusVetoableListener(VetoableChangeListener
        listener)
    {
        support.removeInfoBusVetoableListener(listener);
    }

public void
    addInfoBusPropertyListener(PropertyChangeListener
        listener)
    {
        support.addInfoBusPropertyListener(listener);
    }

public void
    removeInfoBusPropertyListener(PropertyChangeListener
        listener)
    {
        support.removeInfoBusPropertyListener(listener);
    }

    public void run()
```

LISTING 5.6 *Continued*

```
        {
            ServerSocket servsock = null;

            try {
                servsock = new ServerSocket(eventPort);
            } catch (Exception e) {
                    e.printStackTrace();
                    return;
            }
            Socket sock = null;
        while(true) {

                try {
            System.out.println("Waiting for connection...");
                    sock = servsock.accept();
                    System.out.println("Got connection...");
InputStream iostream =
                sock.getInputStream();
ObjectInputStream oistream = new
                    ObjectInputStream(iostream);

IBDataItem data =
                    (IBDataItem)oistream.readObject();
                System.out.println("Data is: "+data);
            System.out.println("Received: "+data.getName());

                    // Set the data item we're servicing
                dataItems.put(data.getProperty("Name"),data);
support.getInfoBus().
fireItemAvailable((String)data.getProperty("Name"),null,this);

                sock.close();
            } catch (Exception f) {
                f.printStackTrace();
            }

            }
        }

        public void setPeer(String peer)
```

Continues

LISTING 5.6   InfoBusGateway Example *(Continued)*

```
    {
        this.peer=peer;
    }

    public String getPeer()
    {
        return peer;
    }

     public void setEventPort(int port)
     {
         this.eventPort=port;
     }

     public int getEventPort()
     {
         return eventPort;
     }

    public void setPeerPort(int port)
    {
       peerPort = port;
    }

    public void propertyChange(PropertyChangeEvent event)
    {
       // Has our infoBus property been changed?
    }

public void
    dataItemRevoked(InfoBusItemRevokedEvent event)
    {
       DataItem data =
       (DataItem)dataItems.get(event.getDataItemName());
       data.release();
    }

public void
    dataItemAvailable(InfoBusItemAvailableEvent event)
    {
```

LISTING 5.6   *Continued*

```
              Socket socket = null;
              System.out.println("Item is available!");
              String  infobusURL = event.getDataItemName();

              // Need a way to identify which items are outbound
              // while preserving the items true name
              if(!infobusURL.equals("remote")) return;


          try {
              socket = new Socket(peer,peerPort);
              OutputStream ostream = socket.getOutputStream();
ObjectOutputStream oostream = new
              ObjectOutputStream(ostream);

        // Gets the data item from the
        // producer that fired the available event.
IBDataItem data =
              (IBDataItem)event.requestDataItem(this,null);
            oostream.writeObject(data);
          } catch (Exception e) {
              e.printStackTrace();
          }


    }

public void
    dataItemRequested(InfoBusItemRequestedEvent event)
    {

        // This assumes handling one data item at a time.
        // Realistically, we'd have to fetch the proper
        // data item from a collection based on its name
        // or other criteria since we're managing the
        // flow of many data items onto an infobud.

        // Consumers who don't request them right away
        // eventually, will want them.
DataItem data =
        (DataItem)dataItems.get(event.getDataItemName());    Continues
```

LISTING 5.6 InfoBusGateway Example *(Continued)*

```
            event.setDataItem(data);
        }


    }



class IBDataItem implements DataItem
{
    private InfoBusEventListener source = null;
    private String name = "";
     private int users = 0;

public
    IBDataItem(InfoBusEventListener source, String name)
        {
            // This will typically represent the producer that
            // instantiates this item.
            this.source = source;
            this.name = name;
        }

    public String getName()
    {
       return name;
    }

    public InfoBusEventListener getSource()
    {
            return source;
    }

    public void release()
    {
      // This item has been released from the consumer
    }

    public Object getProperty(String key)
    {
            if(key.equals("Name")) return name;
```

LISTING 5.6   *Continued*

```
            else return null;
    }

    public DataFlavor[] getDataFlavors()
    {
        //
        return null;
    }

}
```

DATACONTROLLERS

We've already discussed a bit about DataControllers. To recap, Data-Controllers handle the notification and event delivery across InfoBus between the various InfoBus constituents. Custom DataControllers can be provided to alter the order in which event notification takes place or to mask delivery to certain objects.

Priority Router

The priority router DataController is capable of segregating its constituents and assigning an order of precedence based on some identification criteria. The order of precedence is arbitrary from the standpoint that the developer is responsible for implementing exactly what the precedence is for that particular controller. The basic idea is that when listeners are added to the priority controller they are grouped based on some characteristic. It might be that all listeners of the same type or that implement some other interface are grouped collectively and assigned a priority. Based on the internal grouping and priorities, the DataController routes certain events to corresponding groups first. Again, the algorithm behind this type of controller will vary depending on application and developer. Let's consider a simple scenario to help clarify how a priority router might work.

Suppose there are two classes of consumers and two classes of producers. Let's call them consumers A and B and producers A and B.

Although consumers A and B can accept data items produced by both producers, each prefers data from its corresponding counterpart. That is, consumer A prefers to receive data from producer A and likewise for consumer B and producer B. However, if the situation arises in which a particular producer cannot provide the needed data, it is acceptable to receive it from the other. Because of the conditional logic in this scenario, a DataController must direct events according to the priority of the given situation. In other words, it must prevent supplying consumer A with events from producer B except in certain circumstances.

Our DataController inspects incoming members to determine their class type. For consumer A, it tests against instanceof ConsumerA and similarly for the other classes. Internally, our DataController has a Vector containing each class of InfoBusMember. Whenever a fireItem-Available() method is invoked telling our controller to notify consumers, a check is made against the producer originating the event. If it turns out it is a ProducerA, then only consumers in our ConsumerA list are notified of the event. Likewise, when a findDataItem() method is invoked on our controller through the InfoBus, it is determined the class type of the consumer issuing the find. The controller will then first check the producer list corresponding to the consumer class type. If no data items are returned, the controller may proceed to the other producer list to obtain a data item (see Listing 5.7).

The are other possible scenarios that could evolve using member grouping and priorities. We hope this stimulates more ideas for you as you explore various ways to implement controllers in your applications.

LISTING 5.7   Priority Router

```java
import javax.infobus.*;
import java.beans.*;
import java.util.*;
import java.awt.datatransfer.*;

public class ABPriorityRouter implements
InfoBusDataController {

    Vector consumerPriorityA = new Vector(10);
    Vector consumerPriorityB = new Vector(10);
    Vector producerPriorityA = new Vector(10);
    Vector producerPriorityB = new Vector(10);
```

LISTING 5.7 *Continued*

```
    public void addDataConsumer(InfoBusDataConsumer consumer)
    {
        if(consumer instanceof PriorityA) {
            consumerPriorityA.addElement(consumer);
        }
        if(consumer instanceof PriorityB) {
            consumerPriorityB.addElement(consumer);
        }
    }

    public void addDataProducer(InfoBusDataProducer producer)
    {
        if(producer instanceof PriorityA) {
            producerPriorityA.addElement(producer);
        }
        if(producer instanceof PriorityB) {
            producerPriorityB.addElement(producer);
        }
    }

public boolean findDataItem(String name,
DataFlavor flavors[], InfoBusDataConsumer consumer,
Vector targets)
    {
        if(consumer instanceof PriorityA) {
if(searchPriorityList(consumer,producerPriorityA))
        return true;
if(searchPriorityList(consumer,producerPriorityB))
        return true;
        }
        if(consumer instanceof PriorityB) {
if(searchPriorityList(consumer,producerPriorityB))
        return true;
if(searchPriorityList(consumer,producerPriorityA))

        return true;
        }
        return false;
    }
```

Continues

LISTING 5.7   Priority Router *(Continued)*

```
public boolean
searchPriorityList(InfoBusDataConsumer consumer,
Vector list)
    {
        for(int i=0;i<list.size();i++) {
InfoBusDataProducer producer =
          (InfoBusDataProducer)list.elementAt(i);
        // Create InfoBusItemRequested event and send to
        // producer.
        }
        return true;
    }

public boolean
findMultipleDataItems(String name, DataFlavor flavors[],
 InfoBusDataConsumer consumer, Vector foundItems)
    {
        // implementation here
        // All non-null response from producers
        // should be stored in foundItems
        return true;
    }

public boolean
fireItemAvailable(String name,DataFlavor
flavors[],InfoBusDataProducer producer)
    {
        // implementation here
        return true;
    }

public boolean
fireItemRevoked(String name, InfoBusDataProducer producer)
    {
        // implementation here
        return true;
    }

public void
removeDataConsumer(InfoBusDataConsumer consumer)
    {
```

LISTING 5.7   *Continued*

```
                    if(consumer instanceof PriorityB)
                        consumerPriorityB.removeElement(consumer);
                    if(consumer instanceof PriorityA)
                        consumerPriorityA.removeElement(consumer);
            }

        public void
        removeDataProducer(InfoBusDataProducer producer)
            {
                    if(producer instanceof PriorityB)
                        producerPriorityB.removeElement(producer);
                    if(producer instanceof PriorityA)
                        producerPriorityA.removeElement(producer);
            }

        public void setConsumerList(Vector list)
            {
                for(int i=0;i<list.size();i++) {
                    if(list.elementAt(i) instanceof PriorityA)
                    consumerPriorityA.addElement(list.elementAt(i));
                    if(list.elementAt(i) instanceof PriorityA)
                    consumerPriorityB.addElement(list.elementAt(i));
                }
            }

        public void setProducerList(Vector list)
            {
                for(int i=0;i<list.size();i++) {
                    if(list.elementAt(i) instanceof PriorityA)
                    producerPriorityA.addElement(list.elementAt(i));
                    if(list.elementAt(i) instanceof PriorityA)
                    producerPriorityB.addElement(list.elementAt(i));
                }
            }

        }

    }

    interface PriorityA {}
    interface PriorityB {}
```

Best-Guess Controller

Another interesting DataController design is the best-guess controller that acts as a primitive fuzzy logic device. This type of controller hosts a set of special producer Beans capable of supplying data items with additional information used by the controller to determine certainty. The controller queries all producers in its internal list regardless of return value. It examines all return values from each producer and examines a special field associated with the return value that indicates a degree of certainty from the producer Beans. It then chooses the data item response with the highest degree of certainty and returns it to the requesting consumer. Let's take a closer look at how this might be useful.

Suppose there are various special producer Beans connected to our controller. Each Bean searches a separate database for information based on an incoming query or possibly a data item type or flavor. As each search Bean returns a data item representing records or pages of data matching or closely matching the requested data, it also supplies an indicator value (possibly based on 0–100 percent) specifying the degree of match or certainty of the return data. The DataController can feasibly collect results from all search Beans, but the request may indicate an interest in only the closest match and not all returned data. The DataController simply chooses the highest degree of certainty associated with a particular data item and returns that item. It can also be specified by the consumer as the threshold for certainty with which the controller uses to qualify or disqualify return results. The benefits of this algorithm are obvious. In many cases where we're searching for something, we'd much rather see the most closely related item(s) and not the entire phone book!

Blackboard Construct

Another useful design for InfoBus is acting as a Blackboard for experts in an expert system. The term *Blackboard* is used when describing structures in expert systems where problems and solutions can be posted much like a blackboard in elementary school. The basic idea is quite simple. Suppose you have an expert system composed of a variety of experts. Each expert is good at solving a particular class of problem. When attempting to break down and solve large, complex problems, expert systems will post subproblems to a blackboard where the expert best able to produce the result can see it, remove it, and post the solution in its place. It should be quite obvious how this model resembles the basic nature of InfoBus. Even the best-guess controller can be used to mitigate solutions to the same problem provided by multiple experts. The combination of these two notions can prove to be quite useful in expert system design. If your system is distributed, you may need the InfoBusGateway or something similar to notify experts located around a network.

CONCLUSION

In this chapter we looked at some interesting design models and ideas that can be used over and over again to address a variety of application needs. We looked at other ways we can manage member objects collectively in our UserManagers, we also explored how to marshal InfoBus events across a network using an InfoBusGateway, and we talked briefly about how InfoBus can contribute to expert system design by providing a nice implementation of a Blackboard mechanism. Surely, there are many more ideas and models awaiting discovery. InfoBus is an exciting new technology that will bring data exchange and interoperability between applets and applications to new levels. As more and more developers adopt InfoBus into their own projects, we will see newer and better ways to do things.

CHAPTER 6

Creating a Data Controller

So far we have learned how the InfoBus technology works. We learned its core, but we really didn't see how to create an application using the InfoBus. In this chapter we talk again about the data controller. As we mentioned previously, a data controller is a component that regulates or redirects the flow of events between data producers and consumers. A data controller is a module that is added to an InfoBus in order to optimize some aspect of the communication on the InfoBus. To elaborate the details of the data controller object further, we create an application that depicts the use of the data controller at the end of this chapter.

WHAT IS A DATA CONTROLLER?

A data controller is an object that implements the InfoBusDataController interface. The object helps in the distribution of the InfoBusEvents to consumers and producers on an InfoBus. The InfoBus supports multiple Data Controllers on one bus. The InfoBus passes the requests generated by the producers, and the consumers are passed to the registered Data Controllers by polling each in turn. The Data Controller that is able to process the request informs the InfoBus about its ability for the request generated by returning true from the method used to pass in the request. This also indicates that the other controllers in the bus should not process the request further. The InfoBus then does not poll the remaining controllers and returns the result, if any, to the requester of this action. The polling order in which the controllers receive requests is determined by the controller priority that is specified when the controllers are added to the bus.

As mentioned previously, the data controller implements the InfoBusDataController interface. For an object to be called a Data Controller, it must implement the InfoBusDataController interface to register with an InfoBus. A Data Controller can implementz any other interface in addition to the InfoBusDataController interface, which includes InfoBusMember, InfoBusDataConsumer, and InfoBusDataProducer, but is eligible to become a Data Controller only if it implements the InfoBusDataController interface.

Data Controller Priority Levels

The priority defines the order in which the controller receives requests. Internally, it determines the insertion order in the linked list of established controllers in the InfoBus. The order in which the controller is inserted also determines the order in which the controller is given a chance to handle events. Once the event gets handled it is removed from the list of events to be handled. A lower-priority event may not get a chance to see all the events that a higher-priority controller handles.

There are seven levels of priorities defined by the InfoBus class, where the higher value indicates the higher priority. If the priority level is the same for two controllers then the order of delivery is unspecified. The following are the constants defined by the InfoBus for the priority values:

InfoBus.DEFAULT_CONTROLLER_PRIORITY

InfoBus.VERY_LOW_PRIORITY

InfoBus.LOW_PRIORITY

InfoBus.MEDIUM_PRIORITY

InfoBus.HIGH_PRIORITY

InfoBus.VERY_HIGH_PRIORITY

InfoBus.MONITOR_PRIORITY

The DEFAULT_CONTROLLER_PRIORITY is the lowest possible priority, but it is reserved for the javax.infobus.DefaultController that is always present in an InfoBus. The DefaultController is, as the name suggests, a default controller that is always present in each InfoBus instance. The DefaultController is discussed later in this chapter. The DefaultController always handles requests that have not been processed by any controller. VERY_LOW_PRIORITY is the lowest available priority level. If a controller is added with a priority lower than VERY_LOW_PRIORITY, the value is adjusted to the value of VERY_LOW_PRIORITY.

The MONITOR_PRIORITY is reserved for controller objects that need to be aware of all requests that arrive at the InfoBus, and is therefore the highest available priority for the controllers. Data controllers that have MONITOR_PRIORITY assigned are usually used for monitoring processes, and do not participate actively in event distribution. The values returned by the data controllers having MONITOR_PRIORITY are ignored, and the requests are usually passed to the data controllers with nonmonitor status. If no such controllers exist, then the request is passed down to the DefaultController. If a controller has a priority level assigned higher than VERY_HIGH_PRIORITY and lower than MONITOR_PRORITY, the object is treated as VERY_HIGH_PRIORITY because of the special restriction on MONITOR level controllers.

DefaultController

DefaultController is a data controller that is present in every instance of InfoBus and is responsible for ensuring the distribution of all requests that are not handled by any other data controller. The DefaultController insures a basic, unoptimized level of operation, where a consumer's request is sent to all producers and a producer's announcements are sent to all consumers. If no other data controller ahead of the Default-Controller in priority handles the request, the DefaultController gets the request and processes it.

InfoBus Methods for Data Controller

Now let's talk about a few important functions for the data controller. The methods describe the ways of managing a data controller, which include adding and removing data controllers, maintaining a list of consumers and producers, and event handling. An overview of these functions will help you to better understand the application presented later in this chapter.

Method for Adding Data Controllers

```
public synchronized void addDataController(
                InfoBusDataController controller,
                int priority)throws InfoBusMembershipException
```

The previous method adds the *controller* to the list of registered data controllers by the indicated *priority*. As mentioned earlier, the *priority* parameter determines the position of the data controller in the list of registered controllers. Once added to the list, the priority for the data controller cannot be changed. For changing the priority, the controller has to be removed from the list and added again. A controller cannot be added to the same list twice; on doing so, the bus will cause an InfoBus-MembershipException to be thrown.

Method for Removing Data Controller

```
public synchronized void removeDataController(
                InfoBusDataController controller )
```

The removeDataController method removes the controller passed as the parameter from the list of registered controllers. A controller does not automatically remove itself from the list of registered controllers. Henceforth, a registered data controller has to be removed from the list from their InfoBus as they exit.

Methods for Maintaining the Producer and Consumer List in Data Controller

Every data controller maintains a list of the producers and consumers that it wishes to serve. When the data controller joins the InfoBus, it is provided a copy of its master list of producers and consumers. The data controller internally maintains the subset of the list for the producers and consumers that are of interest to it. Therefore, all changes happening to the list maintained by the InfoBus may not be visible to the list maintained by the individual data controllers. However, when an InfoBus producer or consumer indicates that it is leaving the bus, all data controllers that have that producer/consumer in their list have to remove it from their distribution lists. If a data controller does not include a producer or a consumer to its list at the time it is added, there is no mechanism for a data controller to re-request the master list from the InfoBus. If the controller is not interested in adding the new member right now but might be interested in the future, then it is the responsibility of the data controller to remember that member for later usage.

When a request is generated in the InfoBus, it passes the request to the data controllers. The data controller decides whether the request applies to the members of the list it maintains. If so, it invokes the target-specific event-firing methods on the InfoBus to initiate delivery of the appropriate event to the member to which the event concerns. If the request does not apply to the members handled by this data controller, the controller simply returns.

Maintaining Producer and Consumer List

```
public void setConsumerList(Vector consumers)
public void setProducerList(Vector producers)
```

The previous two functions are called by the InfoBus for the data controller joining the bus to provide the data controller with the list of available producers and consumers at that time. As mentioned earlier, the list is provided only at the time of joining and the controller cannot request the list again from the InfoBus.

Maintaining New Additions to the InfoBus

```
public void addDataConsumer(InfoBusDataConsumer consumer)
public void addDataProducer(InfoBusDataProducer producer)
public void removeDataConsumer(InfoBusDataConsumer consumer)
public void removeDataProducer(InfoBusDataProducer producer)
```

These four methods are called by the InfoBus for the data controller whenever a producer or consumer joins and leaves the bus. This allows the controllers to make appropriate modifications to their lists.

Methods for Data Controller Event Distribution

```
public boolean fireItemAvailable(String dataItemName,
DataFlavor[] flavors,
InfoBusDataProducer producer)
```

This method is called by an InfoBus to pass a producer's request for an ItemAvailable broadcast. A data controller can distribute an InfoBusItemAvailableEvent to any of its consumers by calling the target-specific versions of fireItemAvailable () on the InfoBus. The value of the source parameter from the calling of the data controller's method should be copied to all target-specific calls to preserve the identity of the original requester. The return value indicates whether processing is complete; if true, no other data controllers are called regarding this request.

```
public boolean fireItemRevoked(String dataItemName,
InfoBusDataProducer producer)
```

This method is called by an InfoBus to pass a producer's request for an ItemRevoked broadcast. A data controller can distribute an InfoBusItemRevokedEvent to any of its consumers by calling the target-specific versions of fireItemRevoked () on the InfoBus. The value of the source parameter from the calling of the data controller's method should be copied to all target-specific calls to preserve the identity of the original requester.

```
public boolean findDataItem(String dataItemName,
DataFlavor[] flavors,
InfoBusDataConsumer consumer,
Vector foundItem)
```

This method is called by an InfoBus to pass a consumer's request for the named data item. A data controller uses the InfoBus' target-specific versions of findDataItem () to query any of its producers. The value of the consumer parameter from the calling of the data controller's method should be copied to all target-specific calls to preserve the identity of the original requester.

The foundItem Vector is passed by the InfoBus as a location for storing a response if one is found. If foundItem is not empty when the call completes, the element at 0 in the Vector is taken as the result and passed by the InfoBus back to the consumer. In this case, the Boolean return value is ignored and no other controllers receive the request. If the foundItem Vector is empty after the method completes, the return value indicates whether processing is complete; if true, no other data controllers are called regarding this request and null is passed to the requesting consumer.

```
public boolean findMultipleDataItems(String dataItemName,
DataFlavor[] flavors,
InfoBusDataConsumer consumer,
Vector foundItems)
```

This method is called by an InfoBus to pass a consumer's request for the named data item. A data controller uses the InfoBus' target-specific versions of findDataItem() to query any or all producers it is managing. The value of the consumer parameter from the calling of the data controller's method should be copied to all target-specific calls to preserve the identity of the original requester.

The foundItem Vector is passed by the InfoBus as a location for storing responses if found. If foundItem is not empty when the call completes, the elements in the Vector are concatenated by the InfoBus with results from other controllers polled (with elimination of duplicate occurrences of an object). The return value indicates whether processing is complete; if true, no other data controllers are called regarding this request. Although a consumer's findMultipleDataItems() request is sent to data controllers, it should only be handled in special cases. The desired behavior of a findMultipleDataItems() is that each producer on the bus be queried exactly once for the named data, and the collection of all responses is returned in foundItem. This behavior is exactly that performed by the DefaultController. Therefore, custom data controllers should usually simply defer to the DefaultController for handling the find-multiple case by returning false and leaving foundItems empty. In situations in which a custom controller decides to handle findMultipleDataItems(), there are some special considerations.

- The single-target version of findDataItem() should be used to query each producer being managed in turn. The Vector version will stop on the first response and is therefore unsuitable for gathering multiple response data.
- Results returned by the data controllers are concatenated by the InfoBus. The InfoBus will remove redundant responses by eliminating duplicate objects from the concatenated array; however, producers that are queried more than once may return different response objects (based, for example, on the security clearances on inquiring classes, which will include the controllers themselves).

In short, the two safest ways to handle a findMultipleDataItems() within a data controller are to either do nothing (rely on the Default-Controller) or, conversely, to query all producers on the bus and then return true to stop further processing. Firing an event to a component and then returning false to allow handling by other controllers will always result in an event being fired more than once to the same component, and should be avoided.

FILE LOCKING APPLICATION

Now let's put our discussed theory into practice. The application simulates a file locking application. This application does not have a user interface; instead we implement com.comware.InfoBusBook.TestInfoBus to test the application using the command line mode. The producer, consumer, and controller connect to our example Bus InfoBusBook. We discuss the application using parts of codes from different classes. The complete code is available with the CD provided with this book. Other classes implemented are:

FileLockController.   This class defines a controller and a producer. The controller maintains a cache of locked/in-use components. It also implements the lockable interface that serves as an identifier to the controller. The producer and the controller as mentioned earlier connect to the InfoBusBook at the time of creation.

EditorBean.   This class defines the data consumer that subscribes to the InfoBusBook. It denotes the file being edited. The class implements Lockable, which is simply a placeholder for identifying the class category. It is used by the data consumer to denote a category of producers and/or consumers. It uses the dataItemName in the findItem requests to identify a file to open.

FileInfo.   This is the data item that is passed between the producer and consumer to identify a particular file. It is currently a wrapper object.

TestInfoBusClass

First we start by implementing the TestInfoBusClass class. The main for this class first opens two files and then tries to open a file that is already in use. Finally it closes one of these files and reopens it. The class does not require any command line parameters. The code for class TestInfoBusClass is shown in Listing 6.1.

LISTING 6.1   TestInfoBus.java

```java
package com.comware.InfoBusBook;

import java.lang.String;
import java.lang.System;
import javax.infobus.InfoBus;
import com.comware.Logger.Logger;

public class TestInfoBus
{
//The main line attempts to opens 2 files, it then attempts
//to open a file that it already in use. Finally it closes
//one file and reopens it. No command line arguments
//are required


    public static void main(String[] args)
    {
        FileLockController controller = new
FileLockController();
        EditorBean editor1 = new EditorBean();
        EditorBean editor2 = new EditorBean();
        EditorBean editor3 = new EditorBean();

        if (System.getProperty("InfoBusDebug") != null)
        {
            InfoBus.setDebugOutput(true);
        }


        logger__.logTraceMessage("=====> OPENING FILE
TestModeFile1");
        editor1.open("TestModeFile1");

        logger__.logTraceMessage("=====> OPENING FILE
TestModeFile2");
        editor2.open("TestModeFile2");
```

Continues

LISTING 6.1 TestInfoBus.java *(Continued)*

```
        logger__.logTraceMessage("=====> OPENING FILE
TestModeFile1");
        editor3.open("TestModeFile1");
        logger__.logTraceMessage("=====> CLOSING FILE
TestModeFile1");
        editor1.close();
        logger__.logTraceMessage("=====> OPENING FILE
TestModeFile1");
        editor3.open("TestModeFile1");
        logger__.logTraceMessage("=====> END OF TEST");
    }

    private transient static Logger logger__ = new
Logger("com.comware.InfoBusBook.TestInfoBus");
}
```

FileLockController

The FileLockController class as mentioned before defines the producer and controller. At the time of initialization, it joins our test InfoBus InfoBusBook. If it succeeds in joining the InfoBus, it adds a Property-ChangeListener that will be alerted whenever the InfoBusMember's setInfoBus method is called and not vetoed. If it fails to join the InfoBus, it logs a fatal error message and exits from the program. It then registers this Bean as a data consumer. For it to operate as a data controller it has to implement InfoBusDataController methods in the FileLock-Controller class. The different methods used for maintaining the data controller are explained in this class. The code for this class is shown in the Listing 6.2.

LISTING 6.2 FileLockController.java

```
public class FileLockController
    implements        InfoBusMember,
                      InfoBusDataController,
```

LISTING 6.2 *Continued*

```
                    InfoBusDataProducer,
                    Lockable
{

    // Default constructor
    public FileLockController()
    {
     logger__.logTraceMessage("FileLockController()");
       init();
    }

    // Joins the InfoBus and Initializes the controller
    protected synchronized void init()
    {
        logger__.logTraceMessage("init");
        infoBusHolder_ = new InfoBusMemberSupport(this);

        try
        {
            infoBusHolder_.joinInfoBus(InfoBusName);
        }
        catch (InfoBusMembershipException exception)
        {
            logger__.logWarningMessage("init failed join : " +
                                exception.toString());
        }
        catch (PropertyVetoException exception)
        {
            logger__.logWarningMessage(
                "init failed join since voter vetoed
                setInfoBus: " + exception.toString());
        }

        infoBusHolder_.addInfoBusPropertyListener(this);
        addDataController();
        registerProducer();
    }
```

The function registerProducer attempts to register itself with the InfoBus. It assumes that the InfoBusHolder instance attribute has already been initialized. If the member is stale, then the program tries again to rejoin the Bus. If the join fails again because of any reason, then we log a fatal message and exit from the application.

```
private synchronized void registerProducer()
{
    logger__.logTraceMessage("registerProducer");
    InfoBus bus = infoBusHolder_.getInfoBus();
    if (bus != null)
    {
        try
        {
            logger__.logTraceMessage(
            "Registering itself with infobus " +
            bus.getName());
            bus.addDataProducer(this);
        }
        catch (InfoBusMembershipException exception)
        {
            logger__.logWarningMessage(
            "registerProducer : stale handle");
            try
            {
                logger__.logTraceMessage(
                "Registering itself with infobus " +
                bus.getName());
                infoBusHolder_.joinInfoBus(
                            bus.getName());
                infoBusHolder_.getInfoBus(). \
                addDataProducer(this);
            }
            catch (Exception busException)
            {
                logger__.logFatalMessage(
                "registerProducer: Failed to join bus"
                 + busException.toString());
            }
        }
    }
}
```

The function addDataController adds the data controller to the InfoBus. Similar to the registerProducer function, it also assumes that the InfoBusHolder instance attribute has already been initialized. If it is not able to join the InfoBus, then it logs a fatal message and exits from the application. To add the data controller to the InfoBus the class uses the addDataController function discussed earlier. We use HIGH_PRIORITY as priority for this controller.

```
private synchronized void addDataController()
{
    logger__.logTraceMessage("addController");
    InfoBus bus = infoBusHolder_.getInfoBus();
    if (bus != null)
    {
        try
        {
            bus.addDataController(this,
                        InfoBus.HIGH_PRIORITY);
        }
        catch (InfoBusMembershipException exception)
        {
            logger__.logWarningMessage(
            "addController : stale handle");
            try
            {
                infoBusHolder_.joinInfoBus(
                        bus.getName());
                infoBusHolder_.getInfoBus().
                addDataController(this,
                        InfoBus.HIGH_PRIORITY);
            }
            catch (Exception busException)
            {
                logger__.logFatalMessage(
                "addController : Failed to join bus "
                + busException.toString());
            }
        }
    }
}
```

For locking the file the class uses three functions: Lock, unlock, and isLocked. As the name suggests, the functions lock/unlock the filename passed by putting or removing the file from the lock table. The isLocked function returns the status of the file in Boolean terms indicating if the file is locked or not.

```
// Adds the following entry to the lock table
// @param         String              item to lock

private synchronized void lock(String name,
            InfoBusDataConsumer consumer)
{
    logger__.logTraceMessage("locking " + name);
    locks_.put(name, consumer);
}




// Remove the specified entry from the lock table
// @param         String         item to unlock

private synchronized void unlock(String name)
{
    logger__.logTraceMessage("unlocking " + name);
    locks_.remove(name);
}




// Removes all the entries held by the specified
// consumer from the lock cache
// @param  InfoBusDataConsumer   release all locks
//                                owned by this consumer

private synchronized void unlock(InfoBusDataConsumer
                        consumer)
{
    logger__.logTraceMessage("unlock by consumer");
    Enumeration iterator = locks_.keys();

    while (iterator.hasMoreElements())
    {
        String key = (String)iterator.nextElement();
```

```
        logger__.logTraceMessage("Checking if it has a
        lock on " + key);

        InfoBusDataConsumer element =
                (InfoBusDataConsumer)locks_.get(key);

        if (element == consumer)
        {
            logger__.logTraceMessage("unlocking " +
                                            key);
            locks_.remove(key);
        }
    }
}


// checks if the file is locked.
private boolean isLocked(String name)
{
    boolean status = false;

    if (locks_.containsKey(name))
    {
        logger__.logTraceMessage(name + " is locked");
        status = true;
    }
    else
    {
        logger__.logTraceMessage(name + " is
                                NOT locked");
    }

    return status;
}
```

The class also implements methods for InfoBusDataController, InfoBusMember, InfoBusDataProducer, and PropertyChangeListener classes. These methods are common for the EditorBean class as well. The EditorBean class will be explained later in the chapter. The methods for InfoBusDataController help in maintaining the list of the producers and consumers maintained by the data controller. As mentioned earlier, for a class to be called a data controller it has to implement these

functions for InfoBusDataController object. We give the part of the code
for the producer. The code for the consumer is available on the CD.

InfoBusDataController Method Implementations
This method is called on by the InfoBus to which the controller is added
at the time the controller is joining the bus. This is done so the data controller can discover what producers were on the bus already when it
joined. This implementation does nothing since it is only concerned with
producers that come on after it has joined.

```
public synchronized void setProducerList(

                                    Vector producers)
{
    logger__.logTraceMessage("setProducerList");
    Enumeration iterator = producers.elements();

    while (iterator.hasMoreElements())
    {
        consumers_.addElement(iterator.nextElement());
    }
}


// Registers a Data Producer with this data
// controller only if the producer implements the
// interface Lockable
// @param   InfoBusDataProducer   producer to add

public synchronized void addDataProducer(
                InfoBusDataProducer producer)
{
    logger__.logTraceMessage("addDataProducer");

    if (producer instanceof Lockable)
    {
        producers_.addElement(producer);
    }
}


// Removes the specified producer from the list,
```

```
// if it exists
// @param  InfoBusDataProducer  producer to remove

public synchronized void removeDataProducer(
                    InfoBusDataProducer producer)
{
    logger__.logTraceMessage("removeDataConsumer");
    producers_.removeElement(producer);
}
```

InfoBusMember Method Implementations

The methods implemented for InfoBusMember include setting the InfoBus property and methods for handling the exceptions. The setInfoBus method attempts to set the InfoBus property and ID. If any listener vetoes this request, the PropertyVetoException exception is raised. It provides methods to handle the exception and add the listener for these events.

```
// Return a reference to the InfoBus.
// @return  InfoBus       reference to the subscribed
// infobus

public InfoBus getInfoBus()
{
    logger__.logTraceMessage("getInfoBus");
    return infoBusHolder_.getInfoBus();
}




// @param  InfoBus  reference to the subscribed infobus
// @exception    PropertyVetoException

public synchronized void setInfoBus(InfoBus bus)
throws PropertyVetoException
{
    logger__.logTraceMessage("setInfoBus");
    infoBusHolder_.setInfoBus(bus);
}
```

```java
// Adds a VetoableChangeListener to the list
// of listeners that will be alerted whenever the
// InfoBusMember's setInfoBus method is called
// @param  VetoableChangeListener  listener to add

public synchronized void addInfoBusVetoableListener(
        VetoableChangeListener listener)
{
    logger__.logTraceMessage(
        "addInfoBusVetoableListener");
    infoBusHolder_.addInfoBusVetoableListener(
        listener);
}




// Removes a VetoableChangeListener from the list of
// listeners that will be alerted whenever the
// InfoBusMember's setInfoBus method is called
// @param  VetoableChangeListener  listener to remove

public synchronized void
                removeInfoBusVetoableListener(
                VetoableChangeListener listener)
{
    logger__.logTraceMessage(
            "VetoableChangeListener");
    infoBusHolder_.removeInfoBusVetoableListener(
            listener);
}




// Adds a PropertyChangeListener that will be alerted
// whenever the InfoBusMember's setInfoBus method is
// called and not vetoed
// @param  PropertyChangeListener  PCL to add

public synchronized void
                addInfoBusPropertyListener(
                PropertyChangeListener listener)
{
    logger__.logTraceMessage("
```

```
                        addInfoBusPropertyListener");
        infoBusHolder_.addInfoBusPropertyListener(
                        listener);
    }



    // Removes a PropertyChangeListener from the list of
    // listeners requesting notification of an
    // InfoBus change
    // @param   PropertyChangeListener   PCL to remove

    public synchronized void
                    removeInfoBusPropertyListener(
                    PropertyChangeListener listener)
    {
        logger__.logTraceMessage(
                "removeInfoBusPropertyListener");
        infoBusHolder_.removeInfoBusPropertyListener(
                    listener);
    }
```

Finally, we discuss the destroy function. This function is called when we want the class to unregister itself, as a consumer, from the Bus and then leave the InfoBus. The finalizer should be the only one to call this function.

```
    private synchronized void destroy()
    {
        logger__.logTraceMessage("destroy");
        try
        {
            if (getInfoBus() != null)
            {
                getInfoBus().removeDataProducer(this);
            }
            infoBusHolder_.leaveInfoBus();
        }
        catch (Exception exception)
        {
            // we ignore the exception..and simply continue
        }
    }
```

EditorBean

This class manages the file being edited, and defines the data consumer that subscribes to the InfoBusBook. It is used by the data consumer to denote a category of producers and/or consumers. It maintains in itself an indicator if a file has been opened already. If some other EditorBean object tries to access a file that is already open it notifies the user by writing an error in the log. The code for the class is explained in the code Listing 6.3.

LISTING 6.3   EditorBean.java

```java
public class EditorBean
                implements InfoBusMember,
                InfoBusDataConsumer,
                Lockable

    {
        // Default constructor calls the generic
        // initialisation routine

        public EditorBean()
        {
            logger__.logTraceMessage("EditorBean()");
            init();
        }


        // Construct a instance of this bean using the
        // specified file name
        // @param  String  name of file to edit

        public EditorBean(String name)
        {
            :
            init();
            :
        }
```

The init function is used to do the initialization. It creates an instance of an InfoBus to join the Bus and adds a PropertyChange-

Listener that will be alerted whenever the InfoBusMember's setInfoBus method is called and not vetoed. It also registers this Bean as a data consumer. If the instance fails to join the InfoBus, it logs a fatal error message and exits the application.

```
protected synchronized void init()
{
    logger__.logTraceMessage("init");

    infoBusHolder_ = new InfoBusMemberSupport(this);

    try
    {
        infoBusHolder_.joinInfoBus(InfoBusName);
    }
    catch (InfoBusMembershipException exception)
    {
        logger__.logWarningMessage(
                "init failed join : " +
                exception.toString());
    }
    catch (PropertyVetoException exception)
    {
        logger__.logWarningMessage(
        "init failed join since voter vetoed
        setInfoBus: " +
        exception.toString());
    }

    infoBusHolder_.addInfoBusPropertyListener(this);
    register();
}
```

In our test class com.comware.InfoBusBook.TestInfoBus we use the open function to open the files. This function makes a call to the InfoBus and requests a file with the specified name to be opened. If the InfoBus grants permission, then we display the opened file; otherwise, we display a message informing the client that another consumer has locked the file.

```
public void open(String name)
{
```

```
FileInfo file =
            (FileInfo)getInfoBus().findDataItem(
                                name,
                                null, this);


if (file != null)
{
    logger__.logTraceMessage("Access granted for
    file " + name);
}
else
{
    logger__.logTraceMessage(name +
    " is currently in use.");
}
}
```

The function shown next is used to register the component with the InfoBus. It assumes that the infoBusHolder instance attribute has already been initialized. If the member is stale, then it tries to rejoin the Bus one more time. If the join fails, then the function logs a fatal message after which it subsequently exits the application.

```
private synchronized void register()
{
    logger__.logTraceMessage("register");
    InfoBus bus = infoBusHolder_.getInfoBus();
    if (bus != null)
    {
        try
        {
            bus.addDataConsumer(this);
        }
        catch (InfoBusMembershipException exception)
        {
            logger__.logWarningMessage("register :
                    stale handle");

            try
            {
```

```
            infoBusHolder_.joinInfoBus(
                            bus.getName());

            infoBusHolder_.getInfoBus().
            addDataConsumer(this);
        }
        catch (Exception busException)
        {
            logger__.logFatalMessage("register :
            Failed to join bus " +
            busException.toString());
        }
    }
  }
}
```

The destroy function is called at the time of exit. The function's job is to unregister the consumer from the bus and then leave the InfoBus. This function should ideally be called by the finalizer.

```
private synchronized void destroy()
{
    logger__.logTraceMessage("destroy");
    try
    {
        if (getInfoBus() != null)
        {
            getInfoBus().removeDataConsumer(this);
        }
        infoBusHolder_.leaveInfoBus();
    }
    catch (Exception exception)
    {
        // ignore the exception...simply continue
    }
}
```

These two classes, FileLockController, and EditorBean, take care of all the elementary methods needed for explaining the InfoBus. The File-Info object is used to open the files and is passed between the producer and consumer to identify a particular file. The code for the file can be obtained from the CD included with this book.

CONCLUSION

In this chapter we talked about the data controller. The data controller acts as an event handler for events generated on the Bus. It processes the data that is of importance to it or allows it to be passed to the next controller down in the hierarchy of data controllers on the InfoBus. In the end we used a simple example to elaborate the functions used by the data controller to manage and redirect events generated. The role of the default controller and priorities of the data controller were also discussed. Now let's move to creating more complex applications using CORBA, RMI, and JDBC.

CHAPTER 7

InfoBus and JDBC

In the last chapter, we saw how to create a data controller using the InfoBus technology alone. The next few chapters show how to use InfoBus with other technologies such as JDBC, CORBA, and RMI. As you may already know, JDBC is a Java API for executing SQL queries. In this chapter we explain the need and the working of JDBC. We also talk about the connection between JDBC and ODBC. We also build an InfoBus application using JDBC, as well as discuss consumers and the producer package as it relates to JDBC. Finally, we explain the advantages JDBC offers with respect to various system models and platforms.

WHAT IS JDBC?

JDBC is a complete definition of how to implement database connectivity using Java as the programming language. Commonly mistaken as an acronym for "Java Database Connectivity," JDBC is actually a trade-marked name. It is based on the X/Open SQL Call Level Interface (CLI) specification that defines how client/server interactions are implemented in the case of database systems. As a point of interest, ODBC is also based on the same specifications.

JDBC consists of a set of classes and interfaces written in Java. The focus of the classes and the interfaces is on executing raw SQL statements and retrieving the results. Its definition ranges from the low-level API required for the JDBC driver that actually connects to and communicates with the database to the high-level API used to retrieve data from an application or applet. The implementation of the API has been included in JDK 1.1 in the java.sql package. These interfaces are database independent and can be used for any relational database. Therefore, a program written with JDBC can be used for any underlying database, keeping in mind that the SQL statements used in the program are database independent. With Java as the programming language, the program becomes database as well as platform independent.

JDBC provides a number of advantages for the developers and the end user. Based on Java as the programming language, it gets a strong, secure, and easy-to-use platform. It is truly cross platform at both the source and the binary level; thus, switching the backend database among competing products should not have any impact on the application code. It can run as an applet or a program that runs over the Internet or an intranet. It does not require a client computer to have any database software installed in order to access the database. The end user can keep his or her existing databases and use JDBC for connecting to the database. Being platform independent, it can be used across the enterprise and on different platforms. It is now widely accepted by all major database vendors. Further, the JDBC-ODBC bridge product developed jointly by Intersolv and JavaSoft enables JDBC to run on any database that supports ODBC.

WAYS TO ACCESS A DATABASE WITH JDBC

The Java Development Kit provides three components that are part of JDBC:

JDBC driver manager.   This is the primary component and forms the backbone of JDBC architecture. It helps the application to connect to the correct JDBC driver. This is the only responsibility of the manager. Once it has helped the application connect to the correct JDBC driver, it gets out of the way.

JDBC driver test suite.   Only the drivers that pass the test suite can be designated JDBC compliant. The JDBC compliant designation indicates that the vendor's JDBC has passed the conformance test provided by JavaSoft. This provides reliability to the drivers provided by the database vendors.

JDBC-ODBC bridge.   This component allows the ODBC drivers to be used as JDBC drivers.

To access the database using the JDBC, a JDBC driver or a JDBC-ODBC bridge product is required. JavaSoft has provided specification for four different types of JDBC drivers:

Native-protocol pure Java driver. As the name suggests, this is a pure Java database driver. It converts the JDBC calls into the network protocol used by the DBMSs directly. The driver uses TCP/IP sockets to talk directly to the database engine. This allows direct call from the client machine to the database server on the network. The database vendor must generally provide this type of driver. Currently, drivers for Sybase, Oracle, MS SQL Server, and Interbase are available. Several more vendors are working on providing proprietary drivers for their databases.

JDBC-Net pure Java driver. This type of driver communicates from a client to a server using generic networking APIs through TCP/IP sockets. The driver translates JDBC calls into a DBMS-independent net protocol by a server. At the server side, a middleware application translates the generic APIs to the database-specific calls required. This type of driver does not require that any special code be installed on the client, thus providing the maximum flexibility for the clients. Also, the same middleware application may be used to access different types of databases. Several vendors are adding JDBC drivers to their existing database middleware products.

Native-API partly Java driver. This kind of driver generates native API calls for the underlying database. In particular, the driver invokes the C/C++ methods provided by the database vendor for the given DBMS. This approach requires that some binary code be loaded on each client machine.

JDBC-ODBC bridge plus ODBC driver. The drivers of this kind use an existing technology like ODBC to make database calls. Its bridge provides JDBC access via ODBC drivers. Similar to the Native-API driver, this driver requires ODBC binary code as well as in many cases the database client code. The function of the JDBC driver is to translate the Java methods to the appropriate native calls required by the access technology. This kind of driver is not suitable for Internet applications, but would work in a corporate scenario.

JDBC AS AN API

JDBC is a low-level interface that is used to call the SQL statements directly. It is easier to use than other database connectivity APIs and provides an interface that is similar to several higher-level, user-friendly interfaces. ODBC right now has a wider base and provides more support for a larger number of databases than JDBC. JDBC takes advantage of this drawback with the help of a JDBC-ODBC bridge and provides access to the databases using the JDBC driver, but it is a much simpler programming interface than ODBC.

Higher-Level APIs Using JDBC

With JDBC as a low-level underlying API there are several vendors that are building high-level APIs on top of the string foundation of JDBC. At the time of this writing there are currently two higher-level APIs that are under development and will come out very soon:

Embedded SQL for Java, or SQLJ.   As a standard JDBC procedure, it requires that the SQL commands be passed as strings to the Java methods. An embedded SQL preprocessor allows a programmer to mix SQL statements directly with Java; for example, a Java variable can be used in a SQL statement to receive or provide SQL values. The preprocessor then translates this Java/SQL mix into Java with JDBC calls.

Direct mapping of relational database to Java classes.   In this mapping, each row in a table becomes an instance of that class, and each column corresponds to an attribute of that instance. This allows programmers to directly work with those objects, and all the underlying SQL happens automatically beneath the higher-level APIs.

Support for Two-Tier and Three-Tier Models

The JDBC API supports both the two-tier and the three-tier models for database access. From a layman's point of view, a two-tier architecture is made of two components: the user interface and the business logic. The two components comprise the first tier and the database server makes up the remaining part—the second tier—of a two-tier model. In contrast, the three-tier model separates the user interface and the business logic into two different tiers and makes the database the third tier. In either approach, all three of the tiers can run on the same computer.

Following this logic, every system that uses JDBC is at least a two-tier system. For a two-tier system, the client side contains the JDBC API calls that are invoked by the GUI, which has the visual controls associated with the underlying database structure. Various data access builder tools usually provide this approach.

In the three-tier model, the business logic layer usually takes care of the entire database interaction. It is responsible for invoking database queries using JDBC and returns the results to the visual component, the user interface layer. The UI part generally has no idea of how the data is stored in the database and how it is gathered to satisfy a particular request. With the JDBC taking care of the middle tier, the end user gets the advantage of Java's robustness, multithreading, and security features.

Structured Query Language (SQL) and JDBC

SQL is a standard language for accessing relational databases. Though all the databases use a standard form of SQL for standard functionality, depending on the requirements and additional features given by the database, they have their own few commands to enhance their product. The JDBC only supports the standard API as it is. We can use database-specific queries as well, but then there is no guarantee that the application using those commands will be able to access any other database without affecting the program in any way.

A way to avoid problems like these is to have ODBC-like *escape clauses*. An escape clause provides a standard JDBC syntax for several of the common areas in which the SQL statements are not common; for example, there are escapes for date literals and for stored procedure calls.

For complex applications in which it is difficult to avoid some of the database-dependent features, JDBC provides descriptive information about the DBMS by means of the DatabaseMetaData interface so that the applications can adapt to the requirements and capabilities of each DBMS.

An important indication of a driver being truly multiplatform with respect to the databases is the designation of being JDBC compliant. As mentioned earlier, having this designation indicates that the implementation has passed the conformance tests provided by JavaSoft. The drivers that are JDBC compliant support at least ANSI SQL-2 Entry Level. ANSI SQL-2 refers to the standards adopted by the American National Standards Institute in 1992. Entry Level refers to a specific list of SQL capabilities. For testing the drivers for JDBC compliance, the JDBC driver test suite is used, which comes as a standard component as part of the Java Development Kit. The conformance tests check for all the classes and the methods defined in the JDBC API and check as much as possible if the SQL Entry Level functionality is available. The tests are not exhaustive and do not cover all the areas possible, but the designation offers some level of confidence to the end user in the JDBC implementation.

JDBC is an API that comes as a standard package with JDK 1.1. JDBC allows any application or an applet written in Java, using JDBC to do database operations on a relational database. The JDBC can be used to access any database that provides a JDBC driver or, through the use of the JDBC-ODBC bridge, any database that provides an ODBC driver. No extra database software is required on the client side to access a database through a browser running an applet using JDBC. JDBC gets many performance and platform benefits because of the base being Java. More and more users are using JDBC as an alternative language for programming the middle tier for three-tier applications.

AN INFOBUS APPLICATION USING JDBC

Virtually all the business applications we write involve some sort of data repository. Of course, the most common storage medium for information is the reliable, if somewhat dated, relational database engine. As we discussed earlier in the chapter, the Java API provides a basic access mechanism to these databases through JDBC. We now combine some of the JDBC access techniques described earlier with some sophisticated InfoBus interfaces to expose this structured data on the InfoBus. In this section, we first build a producer that exposes a collection of data items that are gathered from an access database. Then we write two consumer components that use and modify this data in varying ways. But first, let's examine the needs of our user, Dr. SpamLove.

Every month, one of Dr. SpamLove's backend systems provides a list of potential customers for each of his marketers, which is loaded into an access database. Each marketer may then access this information to make phone calls, send personalized letters, or spam the individual with a customized email message. During the course of their activities, the marketers may make corrections to this information, which will be replicated to the backend systems. All these marketers use browser-based terminals and a variety of InfoBus-enabled applications. The goal of these activities, of course, is the sale of Dr. SpamLove's unique, get-rich-quick scheme to the unsuspecting public.

Dr. SpamLove has approached us to develop an extensible set of components that allow his staff to efficiently run their direct marketing business. Because so many of his applications are already InfoBus enabled, our developed components should just plug in to this environment. The three components he has requested are a contact information producer, a contact information maintenance consumer, and the Spaminator. In our application, the producer will be responsible for managing the data items and providing some status information. The contact information maintenance will permit the user to update the current contact's information and scroll through the result set. The Spaminator, which also happens to be Dr. SpamLove's personal favorite, automatically generates an email message for the current contact, permits the user to modify it, and sends it off to an email program.

Application Overview

In Figure 7.1, we see the application's basic architecture as it interacts with the InfoBus. Our producer will be responsible for managing the contact data item that is responsible for its collection of data items. The contact data item will also perform all the interactions with the database, the results of which are propagated down to each of its sub-data items. The sub-data items are simple data items that hold either an integer or string. The contact maintenance consumer interacts with the sub-data items to store changes made by the user while interacting with the contact data item to request both permanent storage of these changes and scroll through the result set. Our Spaminator performs only light interaction with our data items, since it is only concerned with read-only operations on a few data items.

In this application we use the InfoBus' change management features to propagate changes throughout between our sub-data items and their interested consumers. This structure is shown in Figure 7.2. When our producer instantiates a contact data item, a record is read from the DB, and sub-data items are instantiated to hold the information. When each sub-data item is instantiated and the producer fires an ItemAvailable event, the consumers that are interested in that data item not only grab a reference, but also register their interest in any changes to the data item. Once registered, the consumers may be assured of receiving immediate notification of changes when they occur. For example, if the user changes an email address on the current record through the Maintenance object, the Spaminator instantly knows the change has occurred and redraws the screen accordingly.

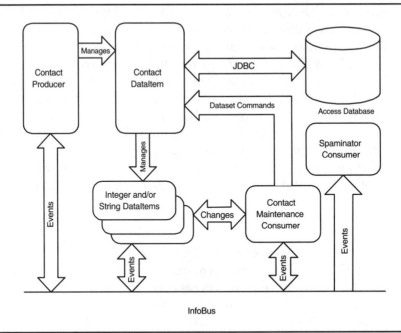

FIGURE 7.1 The application architecture.

The application is divided into three components that we develop in the following sections. Each component will be a fully viable, independent InfoBus member, whose interactions with one another will be compliant with the InfoBus' specification. Because of the volume of code required to produce this application, we will selectively explore in detail the sections which hold special interest to us, while discussing the high level functionality of areas containing the more generic housekeeping code. Although we will not examine the option, each of these components could easily be modified to include a whole suite of configurable features that are accessible through a JavaBeans property sheet.

THE PRODUCER PACKAGE

The first place to start is with our producer package. This package is composed of the ContactProducer, ContactDataItem, StringDataItem, and IntegerDataItem classes, which we will cover in this order. We examine in detail the inner workings of the ContactProducer and Contact DataItem. In the remaining data items, which we will call sub-data items, we examine only a few code snippets that are of interest.

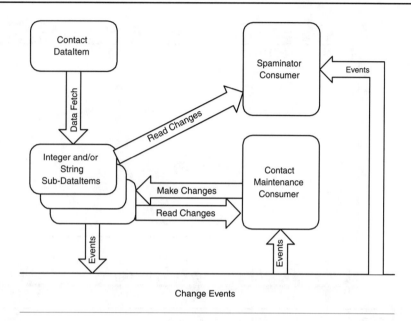

FIGURE 7.2   Change events.

ContactProducer

The ContactProducer is responsible for managing our data items interface with the InfoBus, which displays a simple monitor GUI (see Figure 7.3), and permits the user to reexecute queries against the database. During startup, this producer adds references to all of the data items under its supervision to an internal list. During shutdown, this producer uses its internal list of data item references to inform the InfoBus members that these same items are no longer available.

In Listing 7.1, we see the first section of the ContactProducer class. After declaring this is a member of our producer class and performing our required imports, we enter our class definition. The class definition is pretty typical of our previous applications, except for extending Panel class. Because our ContactProducer displays some GUI, we use a panel to contain it. The first variable definition of interest is the Contact-DataItem; that is, the data item responsible for executing database requests and maintaining our collection of data items representing the results of these requests. The next variable defines a hashtable object that we use to store references to each collection member, with the key

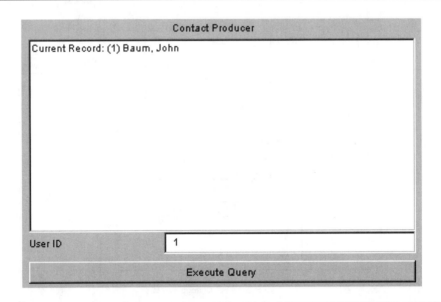

FIGURE 7.3 The ContactProducer component.

being the data item's name and the value the data item's object reference. It is interesting to note that although the ContactDataItem is
responsible for creating and maintaining the collection of members' content, the producer in our design is ultimately responsible for registering
and unregistering their availability on the InfoBus. Wait a minute,
where are the definitions for all the GUI components? Well, to keep our
discussion focused, we placed most of the code relating to the GUI at the
bottom of the file. Have no fear, we explore that in more detail later on.

Moving to the constructor, we see a few interesting things happening. First, we make a call to the drawComponent method that tosses
some GUI onto this panel. Next we assign a name to a button press
event and register an inner class that will be handling the event (don't
worry, more on this later). Next we do our normal InfoBus startup stuff.
The new area of interest here is the instantiation of the Contact-
DataItem class. Immediately after instantiating the object, we call its
method responsible for creating a query to the database for the passed
user ID. Using this information, the object builds and executes the
query, creates and populates its sub-data items, and calls a method
located in the ContactProducer called subItemAvailable to notify the

world when each of these data items are available. When it returns, we call our displayRow method to show some information about the results of our query.

LISTING 7.1   Partial Listing for ContactProducer.java

```java
package producer;

import javax.infobus.*;
import java.beans.*;
import java.util.*;
import java.awt.*;
import java.awt.event.*;
import utilities.Util;

public class ContactProducer extends Panel
    implements InfoBusMember, InfoBusDataProducer
{

    private InfoBusMemberSupport ibHandle;
    private String ibName          = "myBus";
    private ContactDataItem contactDataItem;
    private String contactDataName = "Contact Data";
    private Hashtable subDataItems = new Hashtable();
    private Object syncAvailRevokeEvent = new Object();

    public ContactProducer()
    {

        drawComponent();

        //Register our button listeners
        reQueryBtn.setActionCommand("reQueryBtn");
        reQueryBtn.addActionListener(
            new Panel_actionAdapter());

        ibHandle = new InfoBusMemberSupport(this);
        try
        {
            ibHandle.joinInfoBus(ibName);
            InfoBus ib = ibHandle.getInfoBus();
            ib.addDataProducer(this);
```
Continues

LISTING 7.1 **Partial Listing for ContactProducer.java** *(Continued)*

```
            // Load up our Data
            contactDataItem = new ContactDataItem(this);
            contactDataItem.runQuery(userIDTxt.getText());
            displayRow();
        }
        catch (Exception e)
        {
            // Well, something went wrong...
            System.out.println(
                "ERROR - Failed to initialize InfoBus \n"

                + e);
            e.printStackTrace();
        }


        // Open for business
        synchronized (syncAvailRevokeEvent)
        {
            // Inform the bus that data is available.
            InfoBus ib = ibHandle.getInfoBus();
            ib.fireItemAvailable(
                contactDataName, null, this );


        }

    } // ContactProducer
```

In Listing 7.2, we have the code required to gracefully remove our producer from the InfoBus. Within our synchronize block, our first task is to revoke the sub-data items first, then revoke our Collection object. To revoke our sub-data items, we first ask our hashtable to provide an Enumeration object containing the keys (data item names). Next we iterate through these items, firing ItemRevoked events for each one. Then we revoke the contactDataItem and remove ourselves from the Bus, and then ask the contactDataItem to close its database connection. Although the garbage collector will take care of the clean-up activities when the contact producer object is dereferenced, it is usually a good idea to close any database connection explicitly.

LISTING 7.2   Continuing with ContactProducer.java

```
public void stop()
{
    try
    {
        synchronized (syncAvailRevokeEvent)
        {
            InfoBus ib = ibHandle.getInfoBus();
            for (Enumeration en = subDataItems.keys();
                en.hasMoreElements();)
            ib.fireItemRevoked(
                (String)en.nextElement(), this);

            ib.fireItemRevoked(contactDataName, this );
            ib.removeDataProducer ( this );
        }

        ibHandle.leaveInfoBus();
        contactDataItem.stop();
    }
    catch (Exception ex)
    {
        System.out.println("ERROR - " + ex.getMessage());
        ex.printStackTrace();
    }

} //stop
```

In Listing 7.3, we now see a number of new method definitions. The first two methods are described as *protected* because they are called by the ContactDataItem class. The displayRow method is called by ContactDataItem when the data item has moved on to another row in the data set. As noted in our architectural diagram earlier, the contact maintenance consumer may request that the ContactDataItem object move to its next row. Since our producer is not responsible for receiving this request, it relies on the ContactDataItem object to call this method to update the row status information on the screen. Entering our code, this method makes calls to the ContactDataItem's RowsetAccess methods to obtain references to the sub-data items that contain the fields in which we are interested. Next, we place a nicely formatted string on the screen by calling one of the ImmediateAccess methods.

Our next method is an implementation of the subItemAvailable method. This method receives calls from ContactDataItem when new sub-data items are created. The method first places the data item's name and object reference in the hashtable, then notifies the InfoBus that a data item is born. Our final method in the listing is the strangely named reQueryBtn_actionPerformed. The method structure is designed to convey two pieces of information, <component>_<event>. Using this structure for event handler naming helps to keep us organized when designing a complex GUI composed of a large number of components. When the user presses this button, it first places a notification string on the GUI indicating that a new query has been performed. It then calls our ContactDataItem's query execution method, passing it the most recent user ID entry.

LISTING 7.3   Continuing with ContactProducer.java

```java
    protected void displayRow()
    {
        try
        {

            IntegerDataItem contactID =(IntegerDataItem)
                contactDataItem.getColumnItem("CONTACT_ID");
            StringDataItem lastName =(StringDataItem)
                contactDataItem.getColumnItem("LAST_NAME");
            StringDataItem firstName =(StringDataItem)
                contactDataItem.getColumnItem("FIRST_NAME");
            producerStatusList.addItem("Current Record: " +
                "(" + contactID.getPresentationString(null)
                + ") " +

                lastName.getPresentationString(null) + ", " +
                firstName.getPresentationString(null));
        }
        e.printStackTrace();
            {
        catch (Exception e)
        }
```

LISTING 7.3 *Continued*

```
        } //displayRow

        protected void subItemAvailable(String s, Object o)
        {
            subDataItems.put(s, o);
            InfoBus ib = ibHandle.getInfoBus();
            synchronized (syncAvailRevokeEvent)
            {
                ib.fireItemAvailable(s, null, this );
            }
        } //subItemAvailable

        private void reQueryBtn_actionPerformed()
        {
            producerStatusList.addItem(
                "—— New Query ——");

            contactDataItem.runQuery(userIDTxt.getText());
            displayRow();
        } //reQuery
```

In Listing 7.4, we implement our InfoBus interfaces. The first, dataItemRequested, checks to see if we have a ContactDataItem event available, then finds the requested data item name and places a reference to the object in a temporary variable, o. Next, after determining we actually found something, we place the object reference on the Bus. The next group of methods are the required InfoBus member methods. We follow the same design pattern as the previous applications. They are included for completeness.

LISTING 7.4 Continuing with ContactProducer.java

```
        public void dataItemRequested(
            InfoBusItemRequestedEvent ibItemRequested)
        {
            if ( contactDataItem == null ) return;

            String s = ibItemRequested.getDataItemName();    Continues
```

LISTING 7.4   Continuing with ContactProducer.java *(Continued)*

```
        Object o;

      if (s.equals(contactDataName))
          o = contactDataItem;
      else
          o = subDataItems.get(s);

      if (o != null)
          synchronized (o)
              ibItemRequested.setDataItem(o);

  } //dataItemRequested

  public InfoBus getInfoBus()
  { return ibHandle.getInfoBus(); }

  public void setInfoBus(InfoBus ib)
      throws   PropertyVetoException

  { ibHandle.setInfoBus(ib); }

  public void addInfoBusVetoableListener(
      VetoableChangeListener vcListener)
  { ibHandle.addInfoBusVetoableListener(vcListener); }

  public void removeInfoBusVetoableListener(
      VetoableChangeListener vcListener)
  { ibHandle.removeInfoBusVetoableListener(vcListener); }

  public void addInfoBusPropertyListener(
      PropertyChangeListener pcListener)
  { ibHandle.addInfoBusPropertyListener(pcListener); }

  public void removeInfoBusPropertyListener(
      PropertyChangeListener pcListener)
  { ibHandle.removeInfoBusPropertyListener(pcListener); }

  public void propertyChange ( PropertyChangeEvent pce ) {}
```

In Listing 7.5, we have a section of code containing an inner class that we use to respond to button presses. An inner class permits us to define classes that are only within the scope of the parent class (in this case, ContactProducer). Inner classes are defined and act identical to externally defined classes except that they also have access to private variables and methods within the parent. During compile time, these classes actually get written as separate files in the format <Parent Class>$<Inner Class>. The first line contains the class definition that implements the ActionListener interface. Next we enter the class's only method, actionPerformed. Earlier in the discussion, in the class constructor, we instantiated class and added the instance to reQueryBtn's addActionListener method. This method then issues calls to the actionPerformed method each time a button is pressed. This method simply forwards the request to the reQueryBtn_actionPerformed method we discussed earlier.

Why use an inner class? In order to capture the event, we have to implement the ActionListener interface somewhere. As is often the case, we have a number of choices. One option is to take the traditional approach and create a separate Java class file, which ContactProducer then passes its "this" reference to so the separate class can issue callbacks to the reQueryBtn_actionPerformed method. The second option is to implement ActionListener in the ContactProducer class. Since this option requires the implementation of only one method, actionPerformed, this is an easy, viable method (in fact, we used it in our previous applications!). We are electing to use inner classes for two reasons. First, in more complex screen designs an adapter class is required in order to implement each of a myriad of event handling calls (and who wants to write a separate class for two lines of code). Second, the code becomes not only more segmented but also much easier to read.

LISTING 7.5   Continuing with ContactProducer.java

```
class Panel_actionAdapter implements ActionListener
{
    public void actionPerformed(ActionEvent e)
    {
        reQueryBtn_actionPerformed();
    }
} //Panel_actionAdapter
```

We now enter the magic kingdom of the GUI development. Since the other components follow a similar design pattern, we will discuss the generation of the UI for this component only. For the interested (and brave!) reader, the complete GUI code for other components is available on the CD. Now let's put on our armor, grab a sword, and slay some AWT.

Our next task is to draw the screen. Throughout this application we use the GridBagLayout manager for component placement. Grid-BagLayout! The thought of late nights tweaking position, size, and weight values tends to inspire a sense of dread. In complex GUI development, GridBagLayout can easily cause a number of gray hairs (we have a few here as well!), but this screen design is pretty straightforward. Although the screen painters in some of the newer development tools make this task easier, we will approach the layout design from a more traditional approach. Our first task is to lay out the screen on a piece of graph paper to determine how many equally sized grid boxes we will need to display the screen in our desired format. In Figure 7.4, we see our screen layout overlaying a 2×4 grid.

Setting GridBagConstraints usually involves setting value, then variable, value, variable, and so on, and adding the component to the screen using these layout settings. Then, it is back to setting variable/value pairing for the next component. To make things a bit easier, we have defined a set of utilities, contained in the utilities package, that allow us to pass a GridBagConstraints object and a list of values to assign it. The full signature for this method call is shown next, and the class defines various polymorphic calls to the same method signature to reduce the parameter count on simple operations.

```
public static void setGBC(
    GridBagConstraints gbc, int x, int y,
        int w, int h, double wx, double wy, int anchor)
```

In Listing 7.6, we have the code required to build our screen. Our variable definitions are placed at the bottom of the listing. First, we reduce our font size a bit and color our panel's background to distinguish it from the applet's default white background. Next we inform our parent Panel class that we will be using the GridBagLayout manager and we instantiate a new constraints object that we will use to set our components' display attributes. Next we indicate that our first component, the component label, will be placed starting at cell 0,0 and extending to

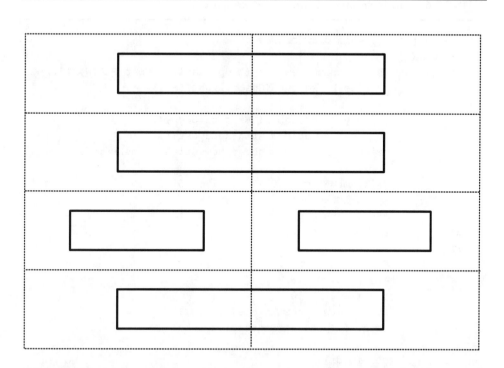

FIGURE 7.4 Screen layout.

cell 1,0 (a length of 2 and a height of 1), have a basic weighting, and be centered within the two cells.

Our next component, the list box containing the status information, is added to row 1. We specify that the component's default size should be changed, and that its location in the panel should be indented by 10 pixels on both the left and right sides. Our next row contains two components: the label stating User ID and a text component to receive this input. We add this label in the first grid column (notice the length is 1) and ensure the label will sit on the left (west) margin . The text component's size is increased to 130 pixels in width, and should always extend itself horizontally to occupy its entire display area. We increase the text field's default size simply to increase the proportional area it occupies, which in effect moves it closer to the label. Finally, we add a button that triggers our query.

LISTING 7.6   Continuing with ContactProducer.java

```java
        private void drawComponent()
        {
            this.setFont(new Font("AppDefault", Font.PLAIN, 10));
            this.setBackground(Color.lightGray);

            reQueryBtn.setLabel("Execute Query");
            this.setLayout(new GridBagLayout());
            GridBagConstraints gbc = new GridBagConstraints();

            Util.setGBC(gbc, 0, 0, 2, 1, 1.0, 1.0,
                GridBagConstraints.CENTER);
            gbc.insets = new Insets(0,0,0,0);
            this.add(label0, gbc);

            Util.setGBC(gbc, 0, 1, 2, 1);
            gbc.ipadx = 216;
            gbc.ipady = 130;
            gbc.insets = new Insets(0,10,0,10);
            this.add(producerStatusList, gbc);

            gbc.ipadx = 0;
            gbc.ipady = 0;
            gbc.fill = GridBagConstraints.NONE;
            Util.setGBC(gbc, 0, 2, 1, 1);
            gbc.anchor = GridBagConstraints.WEST;
            gbc.insets = new Insets(0, 10, 0, 0);
            this.add(label1, gbc);

            gbc.ipadx = 130;
            gbc.fill = GridBagConstraints.HORIZONTAL;
            gbc.insets = new Insets(0, 0, 0, 10);
            Util.setGBC(gbc, 1, 2, 1, 1);
            this.add(userIDTxt, gbc);

            gbc.ipadx = 0;
            gbc.ipady = 0;
            gbc.insets = new Insets(7,10,7,10);
            gbc.fill = GridBagConstraints.HORIZONTAL;
            Util.setGBC(gbc, 0, 3, 2, 1);
            this.add(reQueryBtn, gbc);
```

LISTING 7.6 *Continued*

```
      } //drawComponent

      // GUI
      Label label0 = new Label("Contact Producer");
      List producerStatusList = new List();
      Button reQueryBtn = new Button();
      Label label1 = new Label("User ID");
      TextField userIDTxt = new TextField("1");

} // Class ContactProducer
```

ContactDataItem

The ContactDataItem forms the core of our application's interaction with the database. It is responsible for establishing a connection to the database, retrieving records for the passed user ID, managing its collection of data items, and supporting its consumer's data update requests. In Listing 7.7, we start to have our first section of code for the class. After our requisite package and import statements, we have our class definition. Here we indicate we will be implementing the Rowset-Access interface for our consumers.

Our first set of class variables will be used for our data access code for our JDBC connection. The first variable, the database's URL, contains the string the JDBC connection manager will interpret to find our access database. The string indicates we will be using JDBC, communicating through the ODBC driver, and should connect to the Contacts data source. Next we have the query string we will run against the database. This simple select statement will join the CONTACTS and PROFESSION tables, and filter by the user ID that we append to the string before passing to the database for execution. The next four variables provide the handles to the resources we use to manage our interaction with the database.

Our next chunk of variables provides some housekeeping functions. The first is a count of the columns the database has returned to us. The next, moreRows, indicates whether there is another record in the database—well, sort of. Unfortunately, this variable actually is stating, "as far as we know, there are more records," since the only way we will really find we have run out is if our next fetch is unsuccessful. The array curRowDataItems stores references to the sub-data items in our collection. Each of these data items contains the value for one of the fields in our currently retrieved row. Finally, the firstQuery variable is tested by our application to determine if we should instantiate sub-data items for the first execution of a query. Finally, we have a reference back to our producer for callbacks to indicate our status.

LISTING 7.7 Partial Listing for ContactDataItem.java

```java
 package producer;

import java.sql.*;
import javax.infobus.*;
import java.util.*;

public class ContactDataItem implements
    DataItem, RowsetAccess
{

    private String url   = "jdbc:odbc:Contacts";
     private String query =
        "select * from CONTACTS, PROFESSION where " +

        "CONTACTS.PROFESSION_ID = PROFESSION.PROFESSION_ID "+
        "AND CONTACTS.ASSIGNED_USER_ID = ";
    private Connection con;
    private Statement stmt;
    private ResultSet rs;
    private ResultSetMetaData rsmd;
    private int colCnt;
    private boolean moreRows;
    private Object curRowDataItems[];
    private boolean firstQuery = true;

    private ContactProducer cp;
```

In Listing 7.8, we see our class constructor and stop method. The constructor takes the passed ContactProducer and assigns it to our internal variable. Our next task is to request that our JVM load the class file responsible for instantiating the management resources required for our ODBC connection. Next, using the DriverManager, we request a connection to our access database. From this connection, we request a statement object that we use to pass SQL requests to the database and to request result set objects that will store the information returned by the queries.

LISTING 7.8   Continuing with ContactDataItem.java

```
public ContactDataItem(ContactProducer cp)
  {
      this.cp = cp;

      try
      {
          Class.forName ("sun.jdbc.odbc.JdbcOdbcDriver");
          con  = DriverManager.getConnection(url, "", "");
          stmt = con.createStatement();
      }
      catch (Exception ex)
      {
          ex.printStackTrace();
      }
  } //ContactDataItem
```

After establishing our connection to the database and returning control to our ContactProducer, we can expect to receive a call to populate our collection query. In Listing 7.9, we have a protected method that ContactProducer calls to execute our query. Our first step asks our statement object to run our query string, appended with the user ID, and return a ResultSet object. Each field of the record is segmented and stored in the ResultSet object. From this object, we may call one of the many accessor methods to retrieve the field's value, mapped to a Java data type, or to move our record pointer to the next row of information. Our next statement requests the metadata information about our ResultSet. The layman's definition of metadata is "data about data." Essentially, we use the metadata's information to determine the data types of each field, their display information (if available), the row's table name, and so forth. We use one of ResultSetMetaData's methods in the next line of code to determine the number of columns (fields) returned from our query.

When we receive our ResultSet object back from our executed statement, the record pointer is placed before the first row. Executing the next() method moves us to the first row. Since our runQuery method may be executed more than once, we first test if this was the initial call. If so, we create our sub-data items. Next we call a method that populates these items our ResultSet's information.

LISTING 7.9   Continuing with ContactDataItem.java

```
    protected void runQuery(String UserID)
    {
        try
        {
            rs   = stmt.executeQuery (query + UserID);
            rsmd = rs.getMetaData();
            colCnt = rsmd.getColumnCount();

            moreRows = rs.next();

            if (firstQuery) CreateDataItems();
            firstQuery = false;

            loadRow();
        }
        catch (SQLException e)
        {
            e.printStackTrace();
        }

    } //runQuery
```

The next two methods in Listing 7.10 are responsible for creating sub-data items and loading their values with the results of our query. The CreateDataItems first allocates array space to store our data item object references. Notice we are initializing the array 1 element larger than we need. Why? The JDBC implementation, in its infinite wisdom, uses the number 1 to reference the first element, rather than the 0-

based reference standard used in most other APIs. To keep things simple, we just leave the curRowDataItems' first element empty. Our next task is to loop through each element in the ResultSet and create the proper data item dictated by its data type. We perform the test by using the ever-handy ResultSetMetaData object. After instantiating the data item, we ask our ContactProducer to fire a DataItemAvailable event to the rest of the InfoBus.

Our next method takes our sub-data items and loads them with the values of our ResultSet. Our first task is to define an ImmediateAccess handle and begin looping through the ResultSet. For each data item in our internal list, we cast it to an ImmediateAccess type. Next, using our metadata information, we call the accessor method for the data item designed to store the specified data type.

LISTING 7.10   Continuing with ContactDataItem.java

```
private void CreateDataItems() throws SQLException
    {
        curRowDataItems =
            new Object[rsmd.getColumnCount() + 1];

      for (int i = 1; i <= colCnt; i++)
      {
          if (rsmd.getColumnType(i) == Types.INTEGER)
              curRowDataItems[i] =
                  new IntegerDataItem(cp);
          else
              curRowDataItems[i] =
                  new StringDataItem(cp);
            cp.subItemAvailable(getColumnName(i),
                curRowDataItems[i]);

      }
    } //CreateDataItems

    private void loadRow()  throws SQLException
    {
        ImmediateAccess ia;
        for (int i = 1; i <= colCnt; i++)
        {
            try
```

Continues

LISTING 7.10 Continuing with ContactDataItem.java *(Continued)*

```
        {
            ia = (ImmediateAccess)curRowDataItems[i];
            if (rsmd.getColumnType(i) == Types.INTEGER)
                ia.setValue(new Integer(rs.getInt(i)));
            else
                ia.setValue(rs.getString(i));
        }
        catch(InvalidDataException e)
        {
            System.out.println(
                "ERROR - Invalid Data at " + i);

        }
    }
} //loadRow
```

The ContactMaint object, which we describe later, allows the user to move through the ResultSet. Additionally, it also captures updates to the data items and permits the user to request these changes be saved, or *flushed*, to the database. ContactDataItem receives a flush request through its RowsetAccess interface, and we call the updateRow method to perform the operation. A condensed version of the code, and a little utility method, is shown in Listing 7.11.

The first task is the creation of a SQL update string that properly pairs the database fields with our internal sub-data items. In each block, we call our public getColumnItem requesting the data item reference representing the database field we intend to store. Using the data item's immediate access method, we retrieve its value and append it to our string. We continue this process for each field, finally adding our where clause to insure our update occurs against the current record only. Our next step is to request a new statement object from the connection, then request the execution of a SQL update statement. Since our SQL statement does not produce a results set, we call executeUpdate rather than the executeQuery.

Our remaining method is a handy little utility that we use to test to see if a passed array index reference is within the boundaries defined by our column count. Since so many of the RowsetAccess methods accept an index parameter, this little guy saves us from replicating the same test everywhere. If the passed index exceed the boundaries, the method throws an exception that bubbles up to the calling method.

LISTING 7.11   Continuing with ContactDataItem.java

```
private void updateRow()  throws SQLException
    {
        try
        {
            String sql = "Update CONTACTS set " +
                " LAST_NAME = " + "`" +
                ((ImmediateAccess)getColumnItem(

                    "LAST_NAME")).getPresentationString(null)
                    + "`," +

                " FIRST_NAME = " + "`" +
                    ((ImmediateAccess)getColumnItem(

                    "FIRST_NAME")).getPresentationString(null)
                    + "`," +


                        .
                        .
                        .

                " where CONTACT_ID = " +
                    ((ImmediateAccess)getColumnItem(

                    "CONTACT_ID")).getPresentationString(null);


            Statement updateStmt = con.createStatement();
            updateStmt.executeUpdate(sql);

        }
        catch(DuplicateColumnException e)
            .
            .
            .
    } //updateRow
    private void testBounds(int columnIndex) throws
```

Continues

LISTING 7.11 **Continuing with ContactDataItem.java** *(Continued)*

```
        IndexOutOfBoundsException
    {
        if (columnIndex > colCnt  || columnIndex < 0)
            throw new IndexOutOfBoundsException(
                "ERROR - Passed " + columnIndex +
                " Column count " + colCnt);
    } //testBounds
```

In Listing 7.12, we have the first chunk of code for implementing the RowsetAccess interfaces. RowsetAccess defines a large number of methods, most of which we implement here, with varying degrees of completeness. The ever complicated getColumnCount() does the obvious. Next is a method for retrieving a column's name that simply queries the metadata and returns the string that describes the field's name in the database. Following this method, we have the implementation code for two methods that return the data type information about a column. The first returns an int which is a number corresponding to one of the descriptor types found in the java.sql.Types class. The second method, simply returns the same data type in a string format.

Following the UpdateRow method is the next() method. This method is called by the consumer when it wishes to move to the next row in the results set. Since most of the functionality was defined earlier in our code, this method simply calls to move our results set to the next row, requests that our sub-data items be refreshed with the new data, and asks ContactProducer to refresh its status display. Of course, there is a bit of a bump in the road. When the rs.next() method is called and there are no more rows available, the ODBC driver for Access throws an exception rather than simply returning a failure code. Rather than having printStackTrace barfing all over our Java console, we trap that particular exception. The two methods following next() return obvious little bits of data.

LISTING 7.12 **Continuing with ContactDataItem.java**

```
    public int getColumnCount()
        {
        return colCnt;
```

LISTING 7.12   *Continued*

```
        }

        public String getColumnName(int columnIndex) throws
            IndexOutOfBoundsException
        {
            testBounds(columnIndex);
            String s = "";
            try
            { s = rsmd.getColumnName(columnIndex); }
            catch (SQLException e)
            {    e.printStackTrace(); }

            return s;
        }

        public int getColumnDatatypeNumber(int columnIndex)
            throws IndexOutOfBoundsException
        {
            testBounds(columnIndex);
            int i = -1;
            try
            { i = rsmd.getColumnType(columnIndex); }
            catch (SQLException e)
            {    e.printStackTrace(); }

            return i;
        public String getColumnDatatypeName(int columnIndex)
            throws IndexOutOfBoundsException

        {
            testBounds(columnIndex);
            String s = "";
            try
            { s = rsmd.getColumnTypeName(columnIndex); }
            catch (SQLException e)
            {    e.printStackTrace(); }

            return s;
        }
```

Continues

LISTING 7.12 Continuing with ContactDataItem.java *(Continued)*

```
public boolean next() throws
    SQLException, RowsetValidationException

{
    try
    {
        if (moreRows)
        {
            moreRows = rs.next();
            loadRow();
            if (cp != null) cp.displayRow();
        }
    }
    catch (SQLException e)
    {
        System.out.println("STATE: " + e.getSQLState());
        if (!e.getSQLState().equals("24000")) throw e;
        else moreRows = false;
    }
    return moreRows;
}
public int getHighWaterMark() { return 0; }
public boolean hasMoreRows()  { return moreRows; }
```

Stay with us! The remaining code for implementing RowsetAccess is shown in Listing 7.13. The first two methods provide accessors to our member sub-data items, with the first accepting an int value and the second a string. Both return references to the data item located at the index position requested. Following the data item accessors, we have the data item setters. The first sets the data item located at a specified index point to the value contained in the passed object. The second method accepts a string reference, looks up the index, and asks its sister method to do its stuff.

In our next block of methods, we leave a number without implementation code. The first, deleteRow, permits a consumer to request the removal of the current results set's row from the database. This obviously becomes more complicated if the row represents information gathered from a number of tables. The next method, validate, might be called by a consumer to test if the latest updates could be written to the database. The flush method was already discussed earlier. It simply indicates the current changes should be moved from memory into an area of permanent storage. The final method in this block is lockRow. Consumers might call this method to ensure they have exclusive access to the data when operating in a multiuser environment.

The next three methods from the RowsetAccess interface answer certain questions that a generic consumer might ask, such as "Can I insert?" or "Can I update?" The final method is getDb(), which returns an object implementing the DbAccess interface. DbAccess permits the consumer to exercise even greater control over the database, such as establishing connections to multiple databases, executing queries, and controlling transaction logic.

LISTING 7.13   Continuing with ContactDataItem.java

```java
public Object getColumnItem(int columnIndex) throws
    IndexOutOfBoundsException
{
    testBounds(columnIndex);
    return curRowDataItems[columnIndex];
}
public Object getColumnItem(String columnName) throws
    ColumnNotFoundException, DuplicateColumnException
{
    int i = 0;
    try
    {
        i = rs.findColumn(columnName);
    }
    catch (SQLException e)
    {   e.printStackTrace(); }

    if (i == 0) throw new ColumnNotFoundException(
        "ERROR - Column " + columnName + " Not Found");

    return curRowDataItems[i];
}
    public void newRow() throws SQLException,
    RowsetValidationException
{
```

Continues

LISTING 7.13 Continuing with ContactDataItem.java *(Continued)*

```java
            throw new UnsupportedOperationException(
                "ERROR - Gotta Code this one");
    }

    public void setColumnValue(
        int columnIndex, Object object)
        throws IndexOutOfBoundsException, SQLException,
        RowsetValidationException
    {
        testBounds(columnIndex);

        try
        {

            ImmediateAccess ia =

                (ImmediateAccess) curRowDataItems[columnIndex];

            ia.setValue(object);
        }
        catch (InvalidDataException e)
        {
            throw new

                RowsetValidationException(
                    e.getMessage(), this, null);
        }

    } //setColumnValue
    public void setColumnValue(
        String columnName, Object object) throws
        ColumnNotFoundException, DuplicateColumnException,

        SQLException, RowsetValidationException
    {
        int i = rs.findColumn(columnName);
        if (i == 0) throw new ColumnNotFoundException(
            "ERROR - Column " + columnName + " Not Found");
        setColumnValue(i, object);
    }
```

LISTING 7.13   *Continued*

```
    public void deleteRow() throws SQLException,
        RowsetValidationException
    {

        throw new UnsupportedOperationException(
            "ERROR - Code me");
    }

    public void validate() throws
        SQLException,RowsetValidationException

{}
    public void flush() throws
        SQLException, RowsetValidationException

    {
        updateRow();
    }
    public void lockRow() throws
        SQLException, RowsetValidationException

    {}
    public boolean canInsert() { return false; }
    public boolean canUpdate() { return true; }
    public boolean canDelete() { return false; }
    public DbAccess getDb()     { return null; }
```

In Listing 7.14, we have our typical data item methods, with which we are already familiar. The only point of interest here is the release method. We have provided a release method to this class to explicitly release any database resources before we close our connection. Although the JVM's garbage collector eventually cleans up these unreferenced objects, the amount of resources these connections consume is quite substantial. Further, if we begin to manage a large number of connections in a high transaction volume, we want to make sure a connection awaiting garbage collection is not still accessing, or worse, locking a row in the database. Within this method we close our resources in the reverse order in which they were created.

LISTING 7.14 Finishing up with ContactDataItem.java

```
public java.awt.datatransfer.Transferable
    getTransferable ()

{ return null; }

public InfoBusEventListener getSource()
{ return (InfoBusEventListener) cp; }

public Object getProperty( String propertyName )
{ return null; }

public java.awt.datatransfer.DataFlavor[]
    getDataFlavors()

{ return null; }

public void release()
{
    try
    {
        rs.close();
        stmt.close();
        con.close();
    }
    catch (SQLException e)
    {
        e.printStackTrace();
    }
} //release

} //ContactDataItem
```

Integer and String Data Items

Both the integer and string sub-data items follow the design pattern similar to that followed by our previous applications. Both store a simple object type of either the integer or string variety. Both also provide an ImmediateAccess interface. So what's new? Well, we have added change management support to both. In this short section, we will examine the section of code responsible for providing the change management functionality. Since the implementation philosophy is identical between the two data items, we will use the integer data item for our sample code.

Our IntegerDataItem implements the DataItemChangeManager interface. In doing so, we are telling the InfoBus consumer community that we will register its interest in data item changes and publish events to these consumers when the changes occur. Fortunately, the InfoBus package provides a ready-made change manager class called DataItemChangeSupport. The code snippet in Listing 7.15 shows the constructor DataItemChangeManager implementation. First we instantiate the dataItemChangeSupport, then simply pass on listener requests as we receive them.

LISTING 7.15   IntegerDataItem.java (Code Snippet)

```
public IntegerDataItem(InfoBusEventListener source)
{
    this.source = source;
    dataItemChangeSupport =
        new DataItemChangeSupport(source);

}


public void addDataItemChangeListener(
    DataItemChangeListener l)
{ dataItemChangeSupport.addDataItemChangeListener(l); }


public void removeDataItemChangeListener(
    DataItemChangeListener l)

{dataItemChangeSupport.removeDataItemChangeListener(l);}
```

After registering our consumers we are required to notify them when the data we are representing changes. To accomplish this, we ask dataItemChangeSupport to fire these change events for us. Our IntegerDataItem has only one accessor method by which an external object may change its value, the setValue method. When this method is called, we simply check if it is a new value and fire the change event. The code for this functionality is in Listing 7.16.

LISTING 7.16   IntegerDataItem.java (Code Snippet)

```
    public void setValue(Object obj)
    {
        Integer newItem = (Integer)obj;
        if (newItem.intValue() != item.intValue())
        {
            item = newItem;
            dataItemChangeSupport.fireItemValueChanged(
                this, null);


        }
    } //setValue
```

THE CONSUMERS

We have built two consumers for this application, the Spaminator and the ContactMaint classes. These classes are stored in the spamconsumer and mainconsumer classes, respectively. Because each of these classes contains a great deal of code that we have already examined, we are focusing on only a couple of key areas during this discussion.

Spaminator

The Spaminator, the crown jewel of Dr. SpamLove's nefarious empire, is responsible for taking the current record from our ContactDataItem, creating a personalized email message using the ContactDataItem's sub-data items, and calling his spam mailer. The GUI portion of the screen is shown in Figure 7.5. The Spaminator handles the job of staying current with its data items through the use of the change management process. In this section, we focus on the change management implementation only.

In Listing 7.17, we have the code for the Spaminator's dataItemAvailable method. When this method is called by the InfoBus, we first get the data item name that just became available. Next, we check

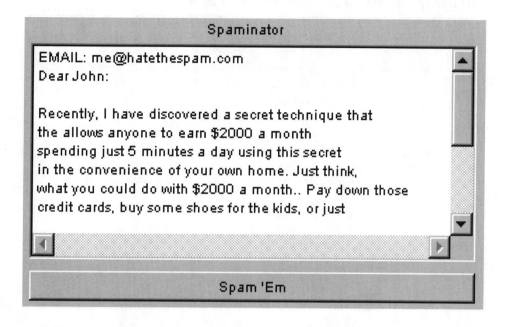

FIGURE 7.5 The Spaminator component.

this name against the constants containing data item names in which we are interested. If we have a match, our first action is to gain a reference to the DataItemChangeManager interface. With this reference, we add ourselves as a change listener. Finally, we gain a reference to the ImmediateAccess interface of the data item and call the internal method createMessage, which refreshes our display to reflect the newly personalized message from the good Doctor.

LISTING 7.17   Spaminator.java (Code Snippet)

```
public void dataItemAvailable(
    InfoBusItemAvailableEvent event)

{
    String dataName = event.getDataItemName();

    if (dataName.equals(emailAddressDataName))
    {
```
Continues

LISTING 7.17 Spaminator.java (Code Snippet) *(Continued)*

```
            DataItemChangeManager cm =

(DataItemChangeManager)event.requestDataItem(this,null);
            cm.addDataItemChangeListener(this);
            emailAddressDataItem =
                (ImmediateAccess) event.requestDataItem(
                    this, null);

            createMessage();
        } else if (dataName.equals(firstNameDataName))
        {
            DataItemChangeManager cm =
            (DataItemChangeManager)event.requestDataItem(
                this,null);
                        .

                        .

                        .
```

The next area of the code in which we are interested is the DataItem-ChangeListener implementation. In order for the data item to be able to call us back with changes, we have to implement this interface. In Listing 7.18, we have the required implementation code (or nonimplementation code, depending on your viewpoint!). Because we are not supporting row adds and deletes in this application, the only method requiring any work is the dataItemValueChanged method. Simply ask the createMessage method to update itself with the new information.

LISTING 7.18 Spaminator.java (Code Snippet)

```
public void dataItemAdded(DataItemAddedEvent event) {}
public void dataItemDeleted(
    DataItemDeletedEvent event) {}

public void dataItemRevoked(
    DataItemRevokedEvent event) {}

public void dataItemValueChanged(
    DataItemValueChangedEvent event)
```

LISTING 7.18   *Continued*

```
{ createMessage(); }

public void rowsetCursorMoved(
    RowsetCursorMovedEvent event) {}
```

ContactMaint

The ContactMaint class, shown in Figure 7.6, is responsible for displaying the user-modifiable information contained in the results set we received from the database. Like the Spaminator, it updates itself through the use of change listeners. Besides the obvious GUI differences, this class interacts with the InfoBus using a technique identical to the Spaminator. The only two differences are a call to the proper

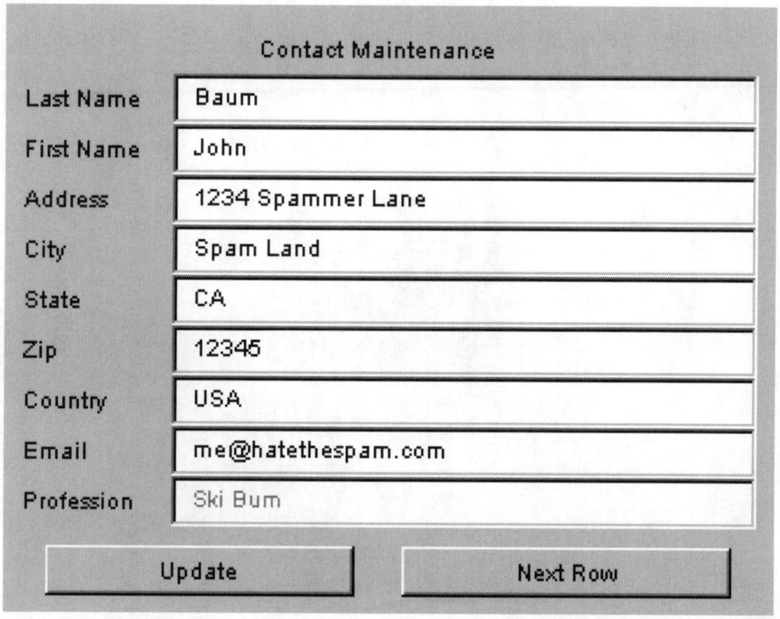

FIGURE 7.6 The ContactMaint component.

ContactDataItem method for the button clicks and a call to the sub-data item's setValue() method after a user enters a change to a field's value.

CONCLUSION

The only activity remaining to us is the creation of an applet that displays the three components together. The code for this effort is very straightforward and may be viewed on the included CD under the Directory applet. In a nutshell, the init section of the code simply establishes a layout manager, instantiates each of our classes (ContactProducer first!), and displays them on the screen.

During the development of this application, we explored a lot of structure provided by the InfoBus to move data freely between components. In the interest of keeping this chapter under 200 pages, we tended to focus on executing reading results sets and executing updates against current data. It would definitely be a very worthwhile exercise for the reader to enhance the base application, adding implementation code for the add and delete activities. Further, exploration into the change DbAccess interface will be a very productive endeavor.

CHAPTER 8

InfoBus and RMI

The current InfoBus specification includes robust functionality for encapsulating data bits and sharing them among many Beans within both applets and applications that are running on the same JVM instance. While running a single instance of a web page or a Java application, you can have data flying about between a dozen different Beans, all connected to a shared InfoBus(s). In the previous chapters, we focused our discovery on the InfoBus that runs locally to one JVM. In this chapter, we explore some of the techniques used to "network enable" the InfoBus using Java's own Remote Method Invocation (RMI). The applications we write in this chapter allow us to pass InfoBus information between JVMs located in the same room or on the other side of the world.

We first explore the basic capabilities of RMI and then build a simple RMI-enabled remote applet and host application to get our feet wet. Next, we use this new knowledge to develop our first sample, the Info-Bridge. Finally, we'll summarize our efforts.

A BIT OF RMI HISTORY

There has been a lot of talk recently about terms such as *remote objects*, *distributed objects*, and *distributed component architectures*. Besides adding to our already lengthy list of buzzwords, what do these terms really mean to the developer who wants to build a system? These terms describe a very powerful concept that we can leverage when building robust, scalable solutions for our users. As is often the case, it's best to examine our industry's history in order to understand the present and the future. So, let's pull the lever of our time machine and venture back to the "bad ol' days" of centralized computing.

> **NOTE** Before we get started, let's first establish a few guidelines to some of the terms we use frequently in our discussions. The first term is *remote application* or *remote applet*. A remote application/applet can be a wholly dependent "client" in the client/server model or simply another server that wants to access an RMI service. Another term we use frequently is *host application*. This is the "server" in a client/server model or a "distributed-object service" in distributed-object speak. The host application is responsible for exposing one or more RMI-enabled objects for use by the remote application as well as implementing the host code required to provide the remote object's host-side functionality. The host application must be a Java application. If this sounds a little confusing, don't worry! Just remember, a remote application is the "client" and a host application is the "server."

Until the early 1980s, most corporate software was developed internally by the company's IT staff. If the software was purchased, it probably came from one of a handful of independent software developers. Because software development was not as prolific as it is today, the pace of innovation was slower. With fewer competitors in the market, the software that was developed was quite expensive. Add to this mix the cost of the hardware to run the stuff (we didn't always have a supercomputer on our desktop) and you have some big bucks spent for a single implementation project. This leads us to the equation: Big $$ = fewer projects. During this era, a few critical systems were implemented on a common, centralized hardware platform. Application integration was (relatively) easy and scalability involved slapping more hardware into the data center.

As we know, things changed when computing power became smaller, cheaper, and more widely understood by the masses. All of the sudden, a division manager could build/buy a system that used a department's slush funds. As the years passed, the demand for specialized systems continued to blossom. When client/server came along, the users' workstations were leveraged to add their computing power to the already powerful servers that resided throughout the enterprise; hence the rise of *distributed computing*. As more servers appeared in the enterprise, these servers could also share data between themselves. In the theoretical world, each client and server performs the tasks that it is best at and collaborate with remote computing resources in the areas for which *they* are best suited. In the early days of client/server, programmers had to "roll their own" communication libraries to transport information between these computers. Today, a few, competing, standards have evolved from which we can choose as our transport medium. Some of the most popular standards include CORBA, DCOM, and RMI.

In release 1.02 of the JDK, the basic APIs included a robust set of both input/output classes and networking classes that the developer could use for passing raw data streams. In response to developer requests for a more robust, standardized approach for a distributed object architecture, JavaSoft released the 1.1 JDK with the RMI API. Because it's easy to use, and entirely Java based, RMI is one of the most popular choices for transmitting information between multiple JVMs running on the same, or multiple, hosts.

A CRASH COURSE IN RMI

The objective of RMI is to allow us to expose certain key objects of our application to other hosts and applications running in their own, separate address space. In order for the remote application to understand the structure of your host class, you first define an interface file that contains the methods we expose. To "RMI enable" this interface file you must extend java.rmi.Remote and each of your methods must throw java.rmi.RemoteException. That's it, well, almost. The other caveat is that any object passed to or from the method must implement the java.io.Serializable interface or be a Java primitive such as byte, char, int, and so forth. As we saw earlier in our discussion of JavaBeans, a Bean saves its customization information by storing a copy of its instance variables to an output stream. This same technique is used to pass a copy of an object between two JVMs.

> **NOTE** Remember that objects and primitives are passed by copy between two JVMs during a remote method call. The only object(s) accessed directly by reference are objects whose structure is defined by a remote interface.

After defining the interface, or signature, of the object we provide on the host, we next need to define what it does for the remote application. The implementation code for the interface is usually written in a file named <interface name>Impl.java, although this is not a requirement.

This class must inherit or extend the java.rmi.server.UnicastRemote-Object and implement the one (or more) interfaces we defined earlier. Within this class, we write the code that is executed when the remote application calls our method. Listing 8.1 shows a sample interface.

LISTING 8.1   ServerStatus.java

```
import java.rmi.*;

public interface ServerStatus extends Remote
{
    public String howYaDoing() throws RemoteException;


} // ServerStatus
```

What if an exception occurs on our host object? We need to trap the exception and package it as a java.rmi.RemoteException for transmission back to the client. The easiest way to do this is to throw a new RemoteException that calls the default constructor. Since we are writing a generic service that can be used by a large number of suitors, it's better to send back a descriptive message that calls the RemoteException(String s, Throwable ex) constructor. If the remote application is run directly by a user, the string may be displayed to a popup dialog on his or her screen. If the application is another server, this message is probably logged in some exception file with the stack trace. Listing 8.2 demonstrates a simple host implementation.

LISTING 8.2   ServerStatusImpl.java

```
import java.rmi.*;
import java.rmi.server.UnicastRemoteObject;

public class ServerStatusImpl extends UnicastRemoteObject
    implements ServerStatus
{
    public String howYaDoing() throws RemoteException
    {
        String s;
        try
        {
```

LISTING 8.2 *Continued*

```
        // Check on our day....
        s = "Doing Great, I love this RMI stuff!";
    }
    catch (Exception e)  // Must be a bad day after all !
    {
        throw new RemoteException("SERVER ERROR", e);
    }
    return s;

    } //howYaDoing

}//ServerStatusImpl
```

After we define the host object's interface and implementation, we then have to apply a little bit of magic to enable RMI to remotely execute it. This magic comes in the form of the rmic command. This command is included with the JDK 1.1 distribution and is stored in the ./bin directory. To run rmic against the host implementation of remote object's interface creates a *skeleton* and a *stub* class that RMI uses to move the requests between the remote application and the host. The stub code is used by the remote application to proxy its requests through RMI. The stub and remote interface file must be placed on the client's JVM. The skeleton file remains on the host side and is used to invoke the host's implementation of the interface. For the example shown in Listing 8.2, you would run rmic ServerStatusImpl.

> **TIP** In most systems development, it makes sense to keep all the code and rmic-generated class files associated with a distributed object in one location on the server. Often, it's wise to bundle the code logically within a *package*. When the project is built, it can copy into a separate directory the class files that are exposed to the client.

Before you start a host object, it's necessary to also start an RMI registry instance on the server. The registry is a separate process that's responsible for the collection of the name(s) of "bootstrap" objects. During the initial contact between the remote application and our host services, the remote application needs to have a place to go to retrieve its first object reference. Any additional remote objects created by the server don't need to be registered; instead, their object reference can be returned to the client through a method call. The remaining coding task on the host side to expose our ServerStatus object is the creation of code necessary to start the application and register our object with an RMI repository. The first step is to override the JVM's default security manager to allow a remote application to access our distributed object. Next, we instantiate a host object. Finally, we indicate to the RMI registry that our object is open for business. The code required to start a host object is shown in Listing 8.3.

LISTING 8.3   StartHost.java

```java
import java.rmi.*;

public class StartHost
{

    public static void main(String args[])
    {
        System.setSecurityManager(new RMISecurityManager());
        ServerStatus ss = new ServerStatus();
        Naming.bind("ServerStatus", ss);

    } //main

} //StartHost
```

The Remote Applet

Next, we move on to the remote (or client) side of things. Stay with us; the code that's required for a remote applet to access a host's remote object is surprisingly simple. First the applet builds a string that contains the object's name. The format of this string is a familiar one: a URL. The URL string is usually in the form //myhost/RemoteObject. It has the following characteristics:

- The myhost is the server name from which we access the remote object. If this name is omitted, the name defaults to the local machine.

RMI calls and the RMI registry both default to port 1099 for the transmission pathway. If you wish to override this port to, say, 5000, then you specify the following URL: //myhost:5000/RemoteObject.

■ RemoteObject is the object name registered in the RMI registry.

Next, the applet calls the java.rmi.Naming object's static lookup-(String s) method, passing it the URL. The Naming object returns a remote object reference to which the applet refers when running lookup. Finally, the applet calls any of the methods on the remote reference. RMI handles all the packaging of method calls and returned values through its stub and skeleton structure. Sound simple? Well, it is! In Listing 8.4, we show the code required to access our sample distribute object.

LISTING 8.4   CheckOnServer.java

```java
import java.awt.*;
import java.rmi.*;

public class CheckOnServer extends java.applet.Applet
{
    String s = "";

    public void init()
    {
        try
        {
            String url = "//" + getCodeBase().getHost() +
                "ServerStatus";


            ServerStatus ss =
                (ServerStatus)Naming.lookup(url);

            s = ss.howYaDoing();
        }
        catch(Exception e)
        {

    } //init
```

Continues

LISTING 8.4 **CheckOnServer.java** *(Continued)*

```java
    public void paint(Graphics g)
    {
        g.drawString(s, 25, 75);
    }

} // CheckOnServer
```

Finally, we need an HTML wrapper to run our applet code. This code is described in Listing 8.5.

LISTING 8.5 **index.html**

```html
<HTML>
<BODY>

<CENTER><H1>Server Status</H1></CENTER>
<P><APPLET codebase=""
        code="CheckOnServer"
        width=500 height=120></APPLET>
</BODY>
</HTML>
```

> **TIP** Systems that use a distributed object model have a lot of moving parts. Among them are basic network connections, routers, domain name servers, RMI server registries, corporate firewalls, and browser security restrictions. It's very important to get a basic application up very early on in the design stage of your project. Next, evolve the prototype to include a basic framework of your distributed objects. Ideally, this includes all of your RMI interface files, but little or no implementation code. Having developed a basic framework and a simple "end-to-end" test case, set it up and run it in a production environment. Use the test application to determine where your roll-out issues are and make sure your corporate infrastructure supports your design. It's surprising how many projects omit this initial test, only to discover a large reengineering effort is required during pilot testing.

Putting It Together

The code described in the previous listings are located on the accompanying CD-ROM under the directory Chapter8/SimpleRMI. After either typing the code or copying it to your hard disk, it is time to give it a go. Please refer to Figure 8.1 to see a logical view of our application's execution.

First, compile the code using javac *.java. Then create your stubs and skeletons by running the command rmic ServerStatusImpl. Next, start the RMI registry bootstrap with start /min rmiregistry and fire up the server with Java StartHost. We now have an RMI-enabled object instantiated and registered as "open for business."

Next, in a separate window, start our remote applet with appletviewer index.html. The applet locates the registry at the URL specified in the code and asks for an object reference to the host object that implements ServerStatus. With this reference, the applet invokes the howYaDoing() method. The host object does some processing (real or imagined) and returns a string object that is copied to the applet for display to the user.

AN RMI-ENABLED INFOBUS APPLICATION

Now that we have a general understanding of RMI, let's explore how the InfoBus can use this technology to pass its information to a remote JVM. To explore how these techniques apply to the real world, we build an application to satisfy the needs of Mr. Big—the loud, impatient, cigar-chomping executive who runs the ACME Scissors factory. In this section, we build two InfoBus components: a producer and a consumer. They interact normally with one another if they are run on the same JVM. Next, we build an InfoBridge to allow any number of producers to send their data to a centrally located consumer. But first, let's see what Mr. Big wants.

Mr. Big has a large number of automated machines distributed throughout his scissors factory. At the start of each day, trucks dump raw materials into a hopper at one end of his factory and at the end of the day, his factory produces a pile of scissors at the other end of the factory. In their production duties, each of the automated machines produces a wealth of data. The painting machine knows how much paint it has used, how many widgets it has painted, and when its next scheduled maintenance should occur. The spot welding machine knows how many welds it has completed, and the stamping press knows the number of widgets it has created. Unfortunately, Mr. Big purchased all of this modern equipment

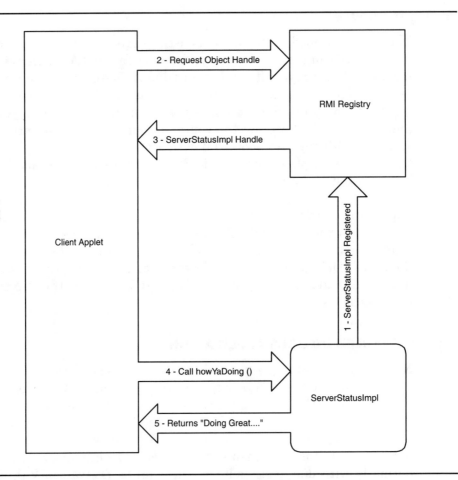

FIGURE 8.1 Execution diagram of a simple RMI application.

for his factory, but no comprehensive factory management software. He has turned to you, his best developer, to engineer an application that permits open data sharing between the factory management systems and the automated machines.

The data produced by our production machines can be useful to a wide audience of consumers. The production operations department may need to know how many widget operations each machine has produced. The production staffing may use production data to determine labor requirements for the next shift. The maintenance staff may want to know which machines have reached their next maintenance interval.

This data is produced dynamically, as the machines perform their tasks in the production cycle. A great deal of this data may be generically represented, filling one guideline for using the InfoBus. A number of consumer applications may exist that would be interested in this data, filling a second guideline.

In our application, we assume that each of these machines is an InfoBus-enabled data producer. To keep things simple, we assume each machine produces two pieces of data: the machine's name and a machine fault alert. The recipient of this information is our factory floor fault monitor application. This application immediately displays any errors encountered by our factory equipment. We also assume that each data producer and consumer runs on a separate JVM, thereby requiring the use of a distributed object transport protocol for bridging the JVMs. To keep things focused on the InfoBridge, we won't spend too much time discussing the basic producer and consumer components. These are based on simple InfoBus components you have already built earlier in the book.

The Producer and Consumer Components

In our application, our producer resides in the machines package. Within this package are three files that make up the functionality of the machine. As we mentioned earlier, each machine has the ability to transmit its name and a text string describing the production problem (machine fault) it encountered. To simulate this activity, the component throws up a simple GUI that allows you to dynamically enter a fault and send it to the fault monitor. The data item managed by this component is accessible through the ImmediateAccess InfoBus interface. As with all well-behaved InfoBus components, this component is used on any InfoBus instance to exchange data. Here is a brief description of the three files:

MachineFaultDataItem.java. Implements our DataItem and ImmediateAccess interfaces for the InfoBus. The data item's contents are the machine's name and a description of the most recent fault. This information is stored in a string format.

MachineStatus.java. Our basic producer component. The component displays a simple GUI for the user to enter machine fault data and to create fireItemAvailable and fireItemRevoked events. For simplicity, the producer does not concern itself with change management and instead always revokes the first data item before sending a data item available event. It implements the InfoBus-Member, InfoBusDataProducer, and ActionListener interfaces.

StartMachine.java.   Displays a basic frame, instantiates and displays a MachineStatus component, and establishes the connection to the InfoBridge. We explore this connection in more detail when we build our bridge. For this application we start the machine as an application rather than an applet. Changing the start code into an applet is merely a matter of extending the applet and changing the main method to an applet init method.

Our target consumer for this data is the fault monitor located in the package monitor. This package contains only two Java files. The fault monitor's job is to listen to its InfoBus connection and display the presentation string of any machine faults it discovers. Like the MachineStatus component described previously, the fault monitor is a component with a simple GUI presentation. As a simple InfoBus component, it stands alone. The two files in the monitor package are the following:

FaultMonitor.java.   Draws a simple TextArea to which it appends machine fault information as it receives it from the InfoBus. The implementation code for this object is rather unexceptional. It implements the InfoBusMember and InfoBus-Consumer interfaces.

StartMonitor.java.   Like StartMachine, it displays a basic frame, instantiates and displays a FaultMonitor component, and calls the InfoBridge to create and export the RMI objects. Where the program differs is that it must be run as an application.

The Distributed InfoBus

As of this writing, the InfoBus specification did not include a recommended implementation for distributing InfoBus structured information to and from remote consumers and producers. The specification did allude to the possibility of using a data controller. As we have already seen, a data controller is responsible for the distribution of events among the InfoBus participants. A data controller is often introduced to optimize (in some way) the flow of information to and from the various components on the InfoBus. Can a data controller be used to somehow propagate the events as they occur on the machines? Because the flow of data in our scenario is unidirectional and to only one host, we really do not need a smart distribution monitor. Separate from the data controller issue is still the not-so-small matter of moving and representing data items on two or more remote InfoBuses.

When we think about the InfoBus, we have a picture of producers and consumers all hooked up asynchronously to a common event distribution model. Within our model, our InfoBus data items all implement, to varying degrees, a common set of interfaces that define access to the data. Our challenge, therefore, is twofold. First, the host InfoBus wants to know that a remote InfoBus has a data item available. Second, the host needs a copy of the data item from the remote instance. Remember, values are passed by copy through RMI. Let's see, both the remote data producer and its data item are representatives on the host side while the host needs a representative on the remote side. In Hollywood, we would call for a stunt double. In the computer world, we call for a proxy!

Figure 8.2 shows the logical architecture of our InfoBridge when one machine connects to one fault monitor. The consumer proxy first establishes a connection with its sister producer proxy over on the host. The consumer then registers itself to the machine's InfoBus and snoops for machine faults. When a fault occurs, it queries the data item and forwards the information to the producer proxy. The producer proxy creates a data item local to the host machine and fires its Item available/revoked events as normal.

Note that the architecture described in the diagram allows only a single machine to connect to a single fault monitor. Why can't multiple machines connect to the producer proxy? When connecting to a remote object, the object's instance is on the host. When a second machine is instantiated, a unique consumer proxy is created. This consumer needs to speak to a producer proxy, so it can connect to the host and start to share the same producer reference that the first machine uses. Mr. Big may get a little disappointed if the latest machine's fault message stepped on current data from another machine—data integrity issues usually upset the Mr. Bigs of the world.

The method used to solve this issue is the creation of a remote object factory or *factory object*, as it's often called. A factory is responsible for receiving a new object request, creating a new instance of an object(s), and handing back a reference to the requester. At that point, the requester speaks directly to the new object and the factory moves on to create objects for the next requesters. The factory is also responsible for the disposal of objects when they are no longer needed. Ideally, the requester makes a call to the factory and says, "I'm finished." The factory

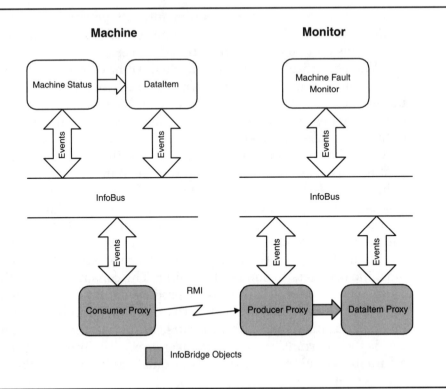

FIGURE 8.2 **The InfoBridge architecture.**

determines which objects the requester used, tells the object to dispose of itself, and removes the last reference to the object from its internal list so the object can be garbage collected. As we know, the ideal doesn't always happen. Any number of things can occur: The requesting application may have crashed, had a power cut-off, lost its network connection, or perhaps the user just left for vacation with his PC logged in. Obviously, our host object doesn't know it's no longer needed, so most designers also put a life expectancy on the objects created by the factory. There are a number of strategies for implementing this procedure, but the basic result is the factory automatically disposes of objects that the designer has determined are probably just clutter.

In Figure 8.3, we removed the InfoBus and drilled into the functionality of our factory object. In this diagram, the consumer proxy first connects to the InfoBridge factory and requests a producer proxy. The InfoBridge instantiates the producer proxy and then sends back the unique reference to the consumer proxy. The consumer proxy is now free to interact with its unique instance of the producer. Later, when all the work is completed, the consumer proxy notifies the InfoBridge factory that its producer proxy is no longer needed. The InfoBridge tells its producer proxy to clean up its activities, then the last object reference to the producer is removed and the Java garbage collector comes along and deletes the object. We have not only satisfied Mr. Big, but we developers can also sleep better at night.

The Producer Proxy

Okay, enough of the design stuff, let's cut some code! Our producer proxy is a good place to start in our development process, since its only dependency is the data item proxy. Because the producer proxy is exposed directly through RMI, we first need to define its interface. Please refer to Listing 8.6. The first line in that listing is a package statement. This indicates that this file is part of the infobridge bundle. We bundle our code in

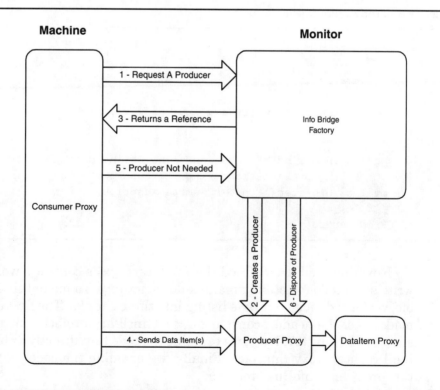

FIGURE 8.3   The InfoBridge factory object.

order to define clear groups of functionality and to allow the sharing of protected methods and variables. When code outside of this package refers to one of its classes it must either import the package such as import infobridge.* or use a fully qualified name such as infobridge.fooClass.

Next, we import our java.rmi package and define an interface called ProducerProxy that extends java.rmi.Remote—a requirement for an RMI-based interface. Next, we define the method(s), which we expose to our consumer proxies. The only one we need for our application is the sendPresentationString method, which is invoked by the consumer proxy to pass a data element to our proxy. The ProducerProxy's implementation code then creates a data item, if needed, and indicates to the InfoBus that data is available. We define a second method that the InfoBridgeImpl object calls to perform some house-cleaning. Obviously, we are not limited to just two methods. To expose more flexibility and functionality to our host consumer(s), the ProducerProxy can have additional method calls for passing parameters, raw objects, and so forth.

LISTING 8.6   ProducerProxy.java

```
package infobridge;

import java.rmi.*;

public interface ProducerProxy extends java.rmi.Remote
{

    public void sendPresentationString(String dataName,
        String presentationString) throws RemoteException;
    public void stop() throws RemoteException;

}// ProducerProxy
```

Now that we have defined the ProducerProxy's contract, we need to write some code to actually make it do something. To make things sensible, we have divided our code listing into three chunks. The first chunk is made up of the header, constructor, and ancillary protected methods as shown in Listing 8.7. Next, we examine the code that directly implements the ProducerProxy interface. Finally, we examine the code that makes this proxy and InfoBus producer.

Our first code chunk defines the package and import statements, then moves on to indicate the class that inherits from UnicastRemote-Object, a requirement for RMI. Our class header also implements the InfoBusMember and InfoBusDataProducer to be a valid producer, while implementing our ProducerProxy interface to become an RMI class. Next, we define a few global class variables such as the InfoBus name with which we are associated and the dataName for storing the name of the data the data item is currently publishing. The next two lines are handles to the InfoBus services and our data item that stores the data from the remote consumer. Next, we get our interesting little sync object, which we use to ensure that we exclusively have access to the JVM when firing the item available and revoke events.

The next section of code is our constructor. It throws a RemoteException if we have problems with RMI. First, the super() method executes the code in the UnicastRemoteObject class to create and export the proxy as a remote object. Next, the code is a straightforward join to the InfoBus. Notice that our exception handling status messages always begin with ERROR, WARNING, or MESSAGE. This should help you pinpoint problem areas quickly, while ignoring "noise" from messages that indicate things are going fine.

Our final method is the stop() method. The stop() method's job is to clean up ProducerProxyImpl's membership to the InfoBus and allow it to terminate gracefully. Because the ProducerProxyImpl's instance is created by the InfoBridge's factory object and is responsible for managing this instance, this method should be called from the factory. The next section of code synchronizes our revoke event, ensuring that we have exclusive access to our event mechanism.

LISTING 8.7   ProducerProxyImpl.java

```
package infobridge;

import java.beans.*;
import java.awt.*;
import java.awt.event.*;
import javax.infobus.*;
import java.rmi.*;
import java.rmi.server.UnicastRemoteObject;

public class ProducerProxyImpl extends UnicastRemoteObject
    implements                                          Continues
```

LISTING 8.7   ProducerProxyImpl.java *(Continued)*

```java
            InfoBusMember, InfoBusDataProducer, ProducerProxy

{

    // Beanbox configurable items
    private String ibName   = "myBus";
    private String dataName = null;

    // InfoBus related var's
    private InfoBusMemberSupport ibHandle;
    private DataItemProxy dataItemProxy = null;

    //Synchronize Avail & Revoke events
    private Object syncAvilRevokeEvent = new Object();

    public ProducerProxyImpl() throws RemoteException
    {

        super();

        // Establish the connection to the InfoBus
        ibHandle = new InfoBusMemberSupport(this);

        // Hop on the 'Bus
        try
        {
            ibHandle.joinInfoBus(ibName);

            InfoBus ib = ibHandle.getInfoBus();
            ib.addDataProducer(this);
        }

        catch (Exception e)
        {
            // Well, something went wrong...
            System.out.println(
              "ERROR - Failed to initialize InfoBus \n" + e);

        }

    }//ProducerProxyImpl()
```

LISTING 8.7   *Continued*

```
protected void stop () throws RemoteException
{
    try
    {
        synchronized (syncAvilRevokeEvent)
        {
            // Let the world know our data
            //is gonna disappear
            InfoBus ib = ibHandle.getInfoBus();
            ib.fireItemRevoked(dataName, this);
            ib.removeDataProducer(this);
        }

        // Get off the bus.
        ibHandle.leaveInfoBus();
    }
    catch ( Exception e )
    {
        System.out.println("
            ERROR - Could not exit gracefully " + e);
        e.printStackTrace();
    }
} // stop()
```

Well, so far so good! Now we get to the implementation code for the ProducerProxy interface. In Listing 8.8, we include the code for the sendPresentationString. First we present the method signature where the consumer proxy will pass the data item's name and nicely formatted value. Notice that the method throws a RemoteException if anything goes wrong. A RemoteException is a nice feature of RMI that passes back to the remote object both the stack trace of the error as well as any string you wish to define. The next statement, this.dataName = dataName, assigns the passed string dataName to the class global variable dataName. This statement could have just as easily been dataName = s where s was the passed dataName. Next, if the DataItemProxy does not already exist, we instantiate it; otherwise, we revoke the previous published availability of the DataItemProxy. Finally, we tell the InfoBus there is data available. Notice the exception handler blindly traps all exceptions but ensures that a RemoteException is sent back to the remote object if there is an error.

LISTING 8.8   Continuing with ProducerProxyImpl.java

```
public void sendPresentationString(String dataName,
       String presentationString) throws RemoteException
   {
       this.dataName = dataName;
       try
       {
           InfoBus ib = ibHandle.getInfoBus();
           if ( dataItemProxy == null )
           {
               //DataItem from our remote consumer
               dataItemProxy =
                   new DataItemProxy(
                       presentationString, this);

           }
           else
           {
               // DataItem has changed
               synchronized (syncAvilRevokeEvent)
               {
                   //Not doing a DataItemChangeManager,
                   // so remove this item from the bus
                   // and then re-add.

                   ib.fireItemRevoked(dataName, this);
               }
               dataItemProxy.setValue(presentationString);
           }
           synchronized (syncAvilRevokeEvent)
           {
               // Inform the bus that data is available.
               ib.fireItemAvailable(dataName, null, this );
           }
       }
       catch (Exception e)
       {
```

LISTING 8.8   *Continued*

```
                    System.out.println(
                        "ERROR - sendPresentationString " + e);
                    throw new RemoteException(e.toString(), e);
                }
        } //sendPresentationString
```

> **TIP** The Java exception handling model is one of the most innovative developments in the language. The model allows you to concentrate on writing the functional code, without cluttering it up by checking the return values of every method call you make. As a rule, production code should determine which exceptions may occur and handle each one in a separate catch statement. To keep the discussion focused, we violate this rule and generically handle most exceptions with the catch (Exception e). At a minimum, we recommend running the printStackTrace() method when an exception occurs. The stack trace that's dumped to the console can provide invaluable information on where in the code your error occurred, and the call history leading up to it.

Now we round out our code with the additional methods required to be a data producer, shown in Listing 8.9. The only code of significance we have added is for the dataItemRequested method. If we receive a request from the InfoBus for a data item, we first check if we even have an Item. If we do, we next check if the name requested by the InfoBus is the same as the data item we have available. Assuming it is, we set the event's data item reference and within a synchronized block and return. The remaining method calls and performs the minimal functionality required by the InfoBus.

LISTING 8.9   Continuing with ProducerProxyImpl.java

```
public void dataItemRequested(
    InfoBusItemRequestedEvent ibItemRequested)
{
```
Continues

LISTING 8.9 Continuing with ProducerProxyImpl.java *(Continued)*

```java
        if ( dataItemProxy == null )
            // Nothing to send.
            return;

        String s = ibItemRequested.getDataItemName();
        if (s != null && s.equals( dataName ))
        {
            synchronized (dataItemProxy)
            {
                // Place our DataItem object reference on the bus
                ibItemRequested.setDataItem(dataItemProxy);
            }
        }
    }

}

public InfoBus getInfoBus()
    {return ibHandle.getInfoBus();}


public void setInfoBus(InfoBus ib)
    throws PropertyVetoException
    {ibHandle.setInfoBus(ib);}

public void addInfoBusVetoableListener(
    VetoableChangeListener vcListener)
    {ibHandle.addInfoBusVetoableListener(vcListener);}

public void removeInfoBusVetoableListener(
    VetoableChangeListener vcListener)
    {ibHandle.removeInfoBusVetoableListener(vcListener);}

public void addInfoBusPropertyListener(
    PropertyChangeListener pcListener)
    {ibHandle.addInfoBusPropertyListener(pcListener);}

public void removeInfoBusPropertyListener(
    PropertyChangeListener pcListener)
    {ibHandle.removeInfoBusPropertyListener(pcListener);}
```

LISTING 8.9   *Continued*

```
public void propertyChange ( PropertyChangeEvent pce )
    {}
}
}//ProducerProxyImpl
```

The DataItem Proxy

Now that we have reviewed the functionality of the ProducerProxy implementation, let us quickly look at the data item it manages. As we mentioned earlier, our data item is responsible for providing the local representation of data contained in a remote object. In our application, the DataItemProxy is interested only in the formatted-string value passed to the ProducerProxy through an RMI call. This allows us to keep its implementation simple and focused. Please refer to Listing 8.10 for the complete code listing of the DataItemProxy.

This is a rather run-of-the-mill data item, so we focus on just a few points of interest. After the class header information, notice that our data item inherits the ImmediateAccess interface as well as implementing the required data item interface. In the constructor, our data item is instantiated with the presentation string of the machine fault that occurred. After the DataItemProxy is instantiated, the Producer-ProxyImpl instance sets the next value by making direct calls to the class's setValue(Object) method. The only other methods of interest are the getValueAsString() and getPresentationString(Locale). Both of these methods return our machine fault description.

LISTING 8.10   **DataItemProxy.java**

```
package infobridge;

import javax.infobus.*;

public class DataItemProxy
    implements ImmediateAccess, DataItem

{
```
                                                                    Continues

LISTING 8.10   DataItemProxy.java *(Continued)*

```
        // These are the data elements of the proxy's data
        private String         presentationString;

        // Vars for managing the object's
        // involvement w/ the InfoBus

        private InfoBusEventListener  source;

        public DataItemProxy(String presentationString,
            InfoBusEventListener source)
        {
            this.presentationString = presentationString;
            this.source = source;
        }

        /////////////////////////////////////
        // ImmediateAccess methods          //
        /////////////////////////////////////
        public void setValue(Object o)
        {this.presentationString = (String)o;}

        public Object getValueAsObject()
        {return presentationString;}

        public String getValueAsString()
        {return presentationString;}

        public String getPresentationString(
            java.util.Locale locale)

        {return presentationString;}

        /////////////////////////////////////
        // DataItem methods                 //
        /////////////////////////////////////

        public java.awt.datatransfer.Transferable
            getTransferable ()

        {return null;}
```

LISTING 8.10   *Continued*

```
      public InfoBusEventListener getSource()
      {return source;}

      public Object getProperty( String propertyName )
      {return null;}

      public java.awt.datatransfer.DataFlavor[]
         getDataFlavors()

      {return null;}

      public void release()
      { }
} //DataItemProxy
```

So those are our ProducerProxy interface and ProducerProxyImpl and DataItemProxy classes. One thing to note is how little of the code actually deals with RMI. The data item has no ties whatsoever with RMI and can be used generically within any InfoBus type application. The only effect RMI has on our ProducerProxyImpl involves extending the UnicastRemoteObject class, performing a couple of things in the constructor, and implementing the exposed method sendPresentationString dictated by the ProducerProxy interface. While our goal in this application is to simply send a presentation string to the host InfoBus, these three files can easily be enhanced to fully implement any one of a number of InfoBus interfaces.

The InfoBridge Factory

Up to now, we have built objects that perform our proxy services on the host. In order to finish the work on our host, we now need to build our factory object. As with all RMI objects, first we need to define the interface that will be exposed to the world. In Listing 8.11 we have the code to define our interface. If you refer back to Figure 8.3, notice that some similarities exist between the methods defined by our interface and the services we noted in the diagram.

As with our ServerStatus application earlier in the chapter, the InfoBridge implementation registers itself with the RMI registry and waits for requests. There is only one instance of the InfoBridge implementation on the host. The first method exposes the retrieveProducerProxy(), which returns an instance of the ProducerProxy we built earlier. The other item to note is that this method must be synchronized in the implementation code. Because there is only one instance of our factory object, we can have multiple, concurrent requests for a ProducerProxy. As we see in the implementation, we must ensure that each request is completely fulfilled before the next is serviced. By synchronizing this method, the other requests queue up and are serviced sequentially until they are all completed.

The other method in our interface is removeProducerProxy(Producer-Proxy). As the name suggests, this tells our factory object to remove a previously instantiated ProducerProxy. The remote application should call this method when it wishes to disconnect itself from the InfoBridge. You may ask, "Should this method be synchronized as well?" Although we can have concurrent requests, the code is thread safe. When the remote application calls the method, it's passed a unique reference to an object that it uniquely owns. We can safely remove that object with a 100-percent assurance that no other remote application is interested in its instance.

LISTING 8.11   InfoBridge.java

```
package infobridge;

import java.rmi.*;

public interface InfoBridge extends Remote
{

    public ProducerProxy retrieveProducerProxy()
        throws RemoteException;
    public void removeProducerProxy(ProducerProxy pp)
        throws RemoteException;

}// InfoBridge
```

Now it's time to dig into the implementation of the InfoBridge interface. We have a great deal to discuss here, so we take a walk through the code in chunks. First, we look at the class, class variables, and constructor definition. Next, we examine the retrieveProducerProxy method, then removeProducerProxy, and finally a funny static method call startInfo-Bridge. Let's start with Listing 8.12.

Things look pretty normal until we hit the proxyServerName. What do all those keywords mean in front of the variable name? Well, this is Java's long-winded way of defining a protected constant. The *static* keyword means the class does not need to be instantiated in order to access the variable or method. The *final* keyword indicates its value may not be changed. Now, on to the contents of the two strings. The proxy-ServerName is used to uniquely identify our ProducerProxy in our list of active proxies. This string can actually say anything, but we have chosen to stick with the traditional URL-based naming scheme. The second string, infoBridgeServerName, contains the URL used by the remote consumer to connect to this object instance. The format of this URL is very important. For this example, we have left the Machine Name empty, which causes the remote object to default to the name of the computer on which it is running. This is fine for testing, but when we run multiple consumers on different computers, we must define the Machine Name to be the host computer on which the InfoBridgeImpl instance runs.

Next, notice that we define a class global hashtable object called producerProxies. A Java hashtable is a convenient way to store key/value pairs that are represented as objects. The hashtable indexes these entries and makes quick retrieval easy. The other global class variable is proxyNumber. This variable is incremented each time we add a new proxy to the hashtable. Moving on, we see our constructor explicitly call the constructor in the UnicastRemoteObject. Because the constructor has no other code, we can leave it out altogether.

LISTING 8.12   InfoBridgeImpl.java

```
package infobridge;

import java.util.*;
import java.rmi.*;
import java.rmi.server.UnicastRemoteObject;

public class InfoBridgeImpl extends UnicastRemoteObject
    implements InfoBridge
{
// The format is "//<Machine Name>/<RMI object name>"    Continues
```

LISTING 8.12   InfoBridgeImpl.java *(Continued)*

```
protected static final String
    proxyServerName = "///ProducerProxy";
protected static final String
    infoBridgeServerName = "///infoBridge";

private Hashtable producerProxies = new Hashtable();
private int proxyNumber = 0;

public InfoBridgeImpl() throws RemoteException
{
    super();
}
```

In Listing 8.13, we get down to the business of implementing the InfoBridge interface. In our synchronized retrieveProducerProxy method, we first define a ProducerProxyImpl object reference called ppi. We then enter our try block where we create a string with a unique name of ProducerProxyImpl, which we instantiate for ppi. After calling ProducerProxyImpl's constructor, we place a reference to the object in the hashtable. Note that we are specifically casting the stored reference to a ProducerProxy type object. We are allowed to do this because the ProducerProxyImpl specifically implements the ProducerProxy interface. But why not just store the ProducerProxyImpl reference? Recall that when our remote consumer is ready to leave the InfoBridge, it calls the removeProducerProxy method passing the ProducerProxy. Because our remote object can directly access only objects defined by an interface, it's never as a direct handle to the entire ProducerProxyImpl instance.

After adding our ProducerProxyImpl reference to the hashtable, we increment our proxyNumber unique and print a message to the console that a new ProducerProxy has been created. Next, we have code that deals with exception handling, both generating a descriptive message for our host instance as well as formulating a RemoteException to pass back to our consumer. Finally, we return our new ProducerProxyImpl cast as a ProducerProxy.

TIP Virtually all larger projects have a constant(s) file for storing paramaters, messages, labels, development time configuration information, and so forth. All constants should be stored with the keywords *static final* to ensure that no ill-behaved class file can change the constant's value.

Java handles static final variables a bit differently internally than you might expect. Each class file that references a static final variable actually compiles the constant's *value* into its code, rather than dynamically accessing the value during runtime. Unfortunately, most of us discover this little fact after questioning why an obvious piece of logic in a class file that refers to a recently changed constant does not work properly. Consider the following example:

```
public class Constants
{
    // Pun intended!
    public static final boolean iAmNotAFoo = true;


}



public class FooTest
{
    <Some code>
    if (Constants.iAmNotAFoo == true)
        System.out.println("I read the Developer Tips!");

}
```

In this code sample, if you compile both Constants.java and FooTest.java, you get the message "I read the Developer Tips!". However, if you now make iAmNotAFoo = false and compile only Constants.java, you still get the message "I read the Developer Tip!". This is because the JVM does not compare (Constants.iAmNotAFoo == true) but rather (true == true), based on FooTest's most recent compile.

In the code snippet, the effect is pretty obvious. But in systems composed of hundreds of class files, it may take a little longer to figure out.

LISTING 8.13   Continuing with InfoBridgeImpl.java

```
public synchronized ProducerProxy retrieveProducerProxy()
    throws RemoteException
{

    ProducerProxyImpl ppi;
    try
    {
        String currentProxy =
            proxyServerName+proxyNumber;

        ppi = new ProducerProxyImpl();
        producerProxies.put(
            (ProducerProxy)ppi, currentProxy);

        proxyNumber++;
        System.out.println("MESSAGE - Created " +
            currentProxy);
    }
    catch (Exception e)
    {
        System.out.println(
            "ERROR - retrieveProducerProxy " + e);
        e.printStackTrace();
        throw new RemoteException(
            "ERROR - Could not create a Producer Proxy",
            e);

    }
    return (ProducerProxy)ppi;

} //retrieveProducerProxy
```

In Listing 8.14, we explore the functionality of the removeProducer-Proxy method. When our remote consumer decides it's no longer interested in the ProducerProxy it used, it calls this method passing its ProducerProxy reference. The method first stores the instance name of the ProducerProxy we assigned previously in retrieveProducerProxy. Next, we remove its entry from the hashtable, then call the producer's stop() method to allow it to clean itself up. Finally, we display a message to the console that a ProducerProxyImpl has been removed from our list of externally referenced objects. Sometime later, the Java garbage man will make his rounds and discover that no other object on the host JVM has a reference open to this ProducerProxyImpl instance. The object is deallocated from the heap and the memory marked as available for the next object.

LISTING 8.14   Continuing with InfoBridgeImpl.java

```
public void removeProducerProxy(ProducerProxy pp)
    throws RemoteException
{

    String producerProxyName =
        (String)producerProxies.get(pp);
    producerProxies.remove(pp);
    pp.stop();
    System.out.println(
        "MESSAGE - Removed " + producerProxyName);

} //removeProducerProxie
```

The final method in our InfoBridgeImpl class is the startInfoBridge shown in Listing 8.15. Notice the method's signature once again contains that funny static reference. Just like the protected constants we defined earlier in the class, a static method may be accessed without first instantiating an object. Here we use this static method to instantiate the InfoBridgeImpl object. Why did we place this static method in this class, rather than in another, separate file? Actually, it does not have to be in this class or even in the infobridge package. We decided to place it here so the main statement in the monitor package has to refer to only one class. It helps to keep things tidy.

When the method is called, we assume that the host RMI registry has already been started on the computer as a separate process. The InfoBridgeImpl object's reference is first identified, then a security manager friendly to our RMI cause replaces the default security manager for this JVM. Next, we enter our try block, where we self-instantiate the InfoBridgeImpl (seems odd, huh?). Next, we register ourselves with the RMI bootstrap registry with the name defined by our infoBridgeServerName constant. Finally, we print a message to the console indicating we were successful. The remainder of the code includes our basic error handling logic.

LISTING 8.15   Continuing with InfoBridgeImpl.java

```java
    public static InfoBridgeImpl startInfoBridge()
    {
        InfoBridgeImpl infoBridgeImpl = null;
        // Create and install the security manager
        System.setSecurityManager(new RMISecurityManager());

        try
        {
            infoBridgeImpl = new InfoBridgeImpl();
            Naming.bind(infoBridgeServerName,
                infoBridgeImpl);


            System.out.println(
                "InfoBridgeImpl created and bound to " +
                infoBridgeImpl);

        } catch (Exception e) {
            System.out.println("ERROR - During Bind");
            e.printStackTrace();
        }

        return infoBridgeImpl;
    } //startInfoBridge

}// InfoBridgeImpl
```

This completes our discussion of the InfoBridgeImpl factory object class. There are some obvious improvements that we could still make to our factory as our system became more complex. The first item that comes to mind is to include a time-out function. Earlier in our discussion, we noted that a remote object that has obtained a ProducerProxyImpl object reference may never call the removeProducerProxy method. If this happens frequently, we would begin to see more and more unused ProducerProxyImpls clogging up the works of our otherwise smoothly running host. A technique that we could use is to store the date/time-stamp for the object reference in a separate hashtable. Periodically, a monitor thread might start up and scan the table looking for old, dusty

object references. It could gain a reference to the ProducerProxy in producerProxies and call removeProducerProxy itself. Obviously, if our
remote application suddenly woke up and wanted its ProducerProxy to
do something, it would be disappointed to find a RemoteException being
thrown instead.

Another idea might be to have the same monitor start up and display
a list of currently active ProducerProxyImpls in the hashtable list. We
could even require the remote consumers to provide retrieveProducer-
Proxy with even more information such as machine name and location.
Further, we might have the ProducerProxyImpl update some statistics
on the factory object such as date/time last contacted and last data item
reference updated. This information could also be dumped when the
monitor checks its active list.

The Consumer Proxy

Our host InfoBus needs a consumer out on the remote machine to relay
a copy of the data item(s) as they appear on the remote InfoBus. Our
ConsumerProxy class is responsible for both connecting itself to the
remote InfoBus as well as establishing a direct connection to its ProducerProxy located on the host machine. We will break this file listing
into three parts. The first will be the class header, instance variables,
constructor, and stop method. Next we will examine the code that actually sends the data item's information over to the host object. Finally, we
will show simple implementations of the remaining code required to
implement the InfoBusMember interface.

In Listing 8.16, the class ConsumerProxy first implements the interfaces required to make it an InfoBus member. Next, we see some of the
variables typical of a simple consumer such as which InfoBus name we
will be joining and a handle to the InfoBusMemberSupport. Now we get
to some RMI-based object references. First is the InfoBridge factory reference that we call to retrieve and remove our host ProducerProxy.
Finally, there is a reference to that ProducerProxy that we will use
throughout the life of this object.

Moving on to the constructor. We first retrieve the infoBridgeServer-
Name constant from InfoBridgeImpl and use it to retrieve an object reference from the specified URL. Because we know this reference will be
to an InfoBridge, we cast it as such and store it in infoBridge. Next, we
use our infoBridge reference to call the factory, requesting the creation

of a ProducerProxy for our exclusive use. This reference is stored in our local producerProxy object reference. Next, we get to the task of joining the InfoBus and adding ourselves as an InfoBusDataConsumer. After the constructor, we have our stop method. This method is called by our owner when it wants us to terminate our activities. This method first removes the consumer from the InfoBus, then notifies the factory object that the services of our ProducerProxy are no longer required.

> **NOTE** Once again in our code, we are generically trapping all exceptions. It is interesting, however, to note some of the RMI-related exceptions that may be thrown. The first, Malformed-URLException, may be thrown if our reference string to the InfoBridge is not in a URL format. Next, NotBoundException will occur if our previously received InfoBridge reference has gone stale or never existed. Finally, our remote catchall RemoteException will be triggered if our host encounters some sort of problem executing its own code.

LISTING 8.16   ConsumerProxy.java

```
package infobridge;

import javax.infobus.*;
import java.util.*;
import java.awt.datatransfer.*;
import java.beans.*;
import java.rmi.*;
import java.net.*;

public class ConsumerProxy
    implements InfoBusMember, InfoBusDataConsumer
{

    // Beanbox configurable items
    private String ibName          = "myBus";

    // InfoBus related var's
    private InfoBusMemberSupport ibHandle;
```

LISTING 8.16   *Continued*

```
        // RMI related var's
        private InfoBridge infoBridge;
        private ProducerProxy producerProxy;

        public ConsumerProxy()
        {
            try
            {
                String theBridge =
                    infobridge.InfoBridgeImpl.infoBridgeServerName;

                infoBridge =
                    (InfoBridge)Naming.lookup(theBridge);

                producerProxy =
                    infoBridge.retrieveProducerProxy();
                // Retrieve our Infobus reference support object
                ibHandle = new InfoBusMemberSupport(this);

                // Join our specified bus
                ibHandle.joinInfoBus(ibName);

                // Register ourselves as a DataConsumer
                InfoBus ib = ibHandle.getInfoBus();
                ib.addDataConsumer(this);
            }
            catch(Exception e)
            {
                // Guess we are unwanted.
                System.out.println(
                    "ERROR - Could not create ConsumerProxy " + e);

                e.printStackTrace();
            }

        } // ConsumerProxy

        public void stop()
        {
            try
```

Continues

LISTING 8.16   ConsumerProxy.java *(Continued)*

```
        {
            InfoBus ib = ibHandle.getInfoBus();
            ib.removeDataConsumer(this);
            infoBridge.removeProducerProxy(producerProxy);
        }
        catch (Exception e)
        {
            System.out.println(
                "ERROR - Could not exit gracefully " + e);
            e.printStackTrace();
        }
    } //stop
```

In Listing 8.17, we continue the ongoing saga of our ConsumerProxy. The dataItemAvailable method is required by the InfoBus when a new data item is placed on the Bus. Our first step is to get the name of the data and the actual object reference to the data item. At this point, we could simple check if this data name is a MachineFault type, call an ImmediateAccess method, and be done with it. Instead, we take a more generic approach. The goal here is to forward all data items appearing on our specified InfoBus that implement the ImmediateAccess interface.

NOTE The technique of generically sending data items is useful, but it needs to be used with care. In our current architecture, one ConsumerProxy talks to one ProducerProxy. Therefore, each time the ConsumerProxy sends a piece of data, the ProducerProxy revokes the previous data item and creates a new one. Obviously, if our remote InfoBus has a lot of traffic from a large number of local producers, the ProducerProxy will be creating and removing data items so fast that consumers local to the host will not have time to examine them. Solutions for this dilemma abound. Your producer might cache the data items for timed release, or it might create multiple data items. Another idea could be to design the consumer to create ProducerProxies for each local producer.

The ProducerProxy on the host will place a DataItemProxy on its InfoBus, and the host's consumers may decide if they are interested in the specified data name. First we use the Java operator instanceof to determine if the data item implements the ImmediateAccess interface. If so, we call the object's getPresentationString and send it to our ProducerProxy. For debugging purposes, we display a message to the console on the remote application indicating the data item has been sent. It always helps to have this little bit of information when your RMI requests appear to be disappearing into a vacuum!

LISTING 8.17   Continuing with ConsumerProxy.java

```
public void dataItemAvailable(
    InfoBusItemAvailableEvent event)
{
    String dataName = event.getDataItemName();
    try
    {
        Object aDataItem =
            event.requestDataItem(this, null);

        if (aDataItem instanceof ImmediateAccess )
        {
            // We can access the data
            String presentationString =
                ((ImmediateAccess)
                 aDataItem).getPresentationString(null);

            // Off it goes
            producerProxy.sendPresentationString(
                dataName,presentationString);
            System.out.println(
                "Sent: " + presentationString + '\n');
        }
    }
    catch(Exception e)
    {
        System.out.println(
            "ERROR - Transmitting DataItem");

        e.printStackTrace();                        Continues
```

LISTING 8.17   Continuing with ConsumerProxy.java *(Continued)*

```
        }
    } //dataItemAvailable
    public void dataItemRevoked(
        InfoBusItemRevokedEvent event)

    {
        System.out.println("MESSAGE - DataItemRevoked");
    }
```

Finally, we have the implementation of the required InfoBusMember methods. The methods shown next contain the minimum amount of code necessary to allow our ConsumerProxy to perform its function. Please refer to Listing 8.18.

LISTING 8.18   Continuing with ConsumerProxy.java

```
    public InfoBus getInfoBus()
    {return ibHandle.getInfoBus();}

    public void setInfoBus(InfoBus ib)
        throws PropertyVetoException

    {ibHandle.setInfoBus(ib);}

    public void addInfoBusVetoableListener(
        VetoableChangeListener vcListener)
    {ibHandle.addInfoBusVetoableListener(vcListener);}

    public void removeInfoBusVetoableListener(
        VetoableChangeListener vcListener)
    {ibHandle.removeInfoBusVetoableListener(vcListener);}

    public void addInfoBusPropertyListener(
        PropertyChangeListener pcListener)
    {ibHandle.addInfoBusPropertyListener(pcListener);}

    public void removeInfoBusPropertyListener(
        PropertyChangeListener pcListener)
    {ibHandle.removeInfoBusPropertyListener(pcListener);}
```

LISTING 8.18   *Continued*

```
        public void propertyChange ( PropertyChangeEvent pce )
        {}
}// ConsumerProxy
```

Putting It All Together

Now that we have defined and built our InfoBridge, the only remaining matter is write the code required to start the host and remote applications. In our monitor package is a Java file called StartMonitor.java. This file contains the code to draw a basic frame, instantiate our Fault-Monitor, and start the host-side InfoBridge. The line to instantiate the InfoBridge is shown here:

```
infoBridgeImpl = InfoBridgeImpl.startInfoBridge();
```

After our host application is up and the InfoBridge is bound to the RMI registry, we can start any number of machines. The code for starting a machine is contained in the machine's package within a file called StartMachine.java. The file performs a set of operations similar to Start-Monitor. First, we draw a basic frame, instantiate and draw a MachineStatus object, and finally instantiate a ConsumerProxy to carry our local InfoBus data to the host application. The code to start the Con-sumerProxy is:

```
cp = new ConsumerProxy();
```

Now all we have to do is transmit our machine faults. Mr. Big will be pleased, indeed.

CONCLUSION

We have covered a lot of ground in this chapter. After reading this chapter, you should have a firm foundation in RMI development to start creating your own distributed objects. The InfoBridge application we built earlier will provide you with an invaluable starting structure from which you can develop some very comprehensive distributed InfoBus applications. If you need to explore RMI's secrets more deeply, we suggest you purchase one of the more comprehensive texts available that describe the Zen of distributed objects in more detail. Now let's move on to CORBA and InfoBus.

CHAPTER 9

InfoBus and CORBA

In Chapter 8, "InfoBus and RMI," we looked into RMI and InfoBus and built an application using RMI. Now we focus on how to build the same application using CORBA. The reason we rebuild the same application is to keep things simple. As you know, when you work in a distributed environment, things can get a little complicated. Therefore, instead of confusing you with a whole new application, we would like to revisit the application introduced in the previous chapter. As before, we start with a little background of the technology. After that, we concentrate on the application itself.

A PRIMER ON CORBA

CORBA, or Common Object Request Broker Architecture, is the set of specifications that define the ways in which software objects should work together in a distributed environment. An independent body called OMG (Object Management Group) manages these specifications. OMG is a coalition of around 750 member companies from different parts of the software industry that includes vendors, developers, and end users. These companies work together to make specifications that allow software objects to be developed independently and yet work together in a harmonic fashion.

The architecture of CORBA is based on the Object Management Architecture (OMA) as defined by OMG and shown in Figure 9.1. The OMA is a high-level design of a distributed system as formulated by the members of OMG. The main components, which define the OMA, are Object Request Broker (ORB), object services, common facilities, domain interfaces, and application objects. These components help in

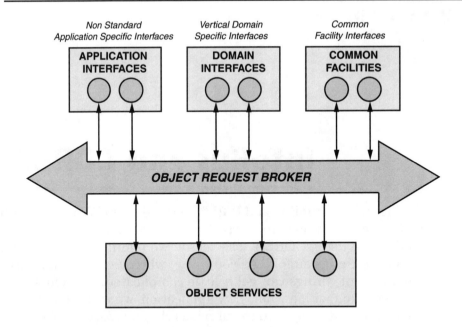

FIGURE 9.1   Object Management Architecture.

handling different segments of the software industry, mainly *application-oriented*, *system-oriented,* and *vertical market-oriented* systems. For the application-oriented systems, the OMA characterizes interfaces and common facilities as solution-specific components that rest closest to the user. The ORBs and object services help in defining the system and infrastructure aspects of distributed object computing and management. The vertical market segment is handled by domain interfaces, which are vertical applications, or domain-specific interfaces.

OMA Components

The heart or the main component of the OMA is the *ORB*, commercially also known as CORBA. The ORB provides the foundation and underlying operation for the distributed objects and their management. It provides an infrastructure that allows objects to talk to one another, independent of the specific platforms and techniques used to implement the objects. Compliance with the ORB standard guarantees portability and interoperability for objects over a network of heterogeneous systems.

Object services are a collection of services that support basic functions for using and implementing objects. They help in standardizing the life cycle management of objects. Interfaces are provided to create objects, to control access to objects, to keep track of relocated objects, and to control the relationship among styles of objects (class management). Also provided are the generic environments in which single objects can perform their tasks. Object services provide for application consistency and help to increase programmer productivity. Object services are independent of application domains; they do not tell how objects are implemented in the application.

The collection of services that many applications can share but are not as fundamental as object services is called *common facilities*. Commercially known as CORBA facilities, common facilities provide a set of generic application functions that can be configured to the specific requirements of a particular configuration. These are facilities, such as printing, document management, database, and electronic mail facilities, that sit closer to the user. Standardization leads to uniformity in generic operations and to better options for end users for configuring their working environments. CORBA facilities also include facilities for use over the Internet.

Application objects constitute the uppermost layer of the reference model. They are built by independent vendors who control the interfaces of the objects. The *application interfaces* represent component-based applications that perform specialized tasks for the user. As these are essentially applications developed by private vendors, they are not standardized by OMG.

Domain interfaces represent vertical areas that provide functionality of direct interest to end users, particularly application domains. Domain interfaces may combine some common facilities and object services, but they are designed to perform particular tasks for users within a certain vertical market or industry.

Of all these components, the ORB is the one that constitutes the foundation of OMA and manages all communication among components. It is responsible for allowing different objects that are lying across the network and unaware of one another's implementation methods to interact in a heterogeneous, distributed environment. In performing its task it relies on object services that are responsible for general object management such as creating objects, access control, and keeping track of relocated objects. Common facilities and application objects are the components closest to the end user, and in their functions they invoke services of the system components.

These components that make up OMA are standard components of OMA and are available to the developer at the time of development. The developer does not have to develop them for making the applications that are CORBA compliant.

OMG's Object Model

The OMG's object model underlies the CORBA architecture and acts as a basis for developing objects in a distributed environment. The object model helps in defining concepts so that an object system can define services for the client in an implementation-independent manner. The implementation-independent principle is important because it allows different object technologies to grow and define the solution in their own manner. It provides an organized presentation of object concepts and terminology. The object model first describes concepts that are meaningful to clients, including such concepts as object creation and identity, requests and operations, and types and signatures. It then describes concepts related to object implementations, including such concepts as methods, execution engines, and activation.

The OMG object model defines a core set of requirements defined on the basis of basic concepts of objects, methods, attributes, types, requests, creation and destruction of objects, which must be supported in any system that complies with the object model standard. While the core object model serves as a common ground for the OMG object model, extension to the core model is allowed to enable even greater commonality amongst different technology domains.

Object Request Broker (ORB)

The heart of CORBA is the ORB. ORB provides the foundation and the underlying operation for the distributed objects and their management. It provides an infrastructure that allows objects to talk to each other, independent of the specific platforms and techniques used to implement objects. The ORB acts like an object Bus that lets the objects interoperate across address spaces, networks, operating systems, and languages; in other words, across the distributed environment where the objects could be on the same machine or on a completely different machine. This Bus allows the objects to discover each other. The ORB helps the client to connect to the object from which it requires the services or that it wishes to use. The client application need not know whether the object resides on the same computer or on a computer across the network. For the client, the only information that is required is the name of the object and how to use its interfaces. The ORB takes care of locating the object, routing the request, and returning the result back to the client.

Figure 9.2 shows the structure of the ORB. To make a request, the client can use an OMG IDL stub, or it may dynamically connect to the remote object using an interface known as *dynamic invocation interface*, whereby the client can dynamically discover the interfaces supplied by the remote object. The client can also interact directly with the ORB by calling some of its functions.

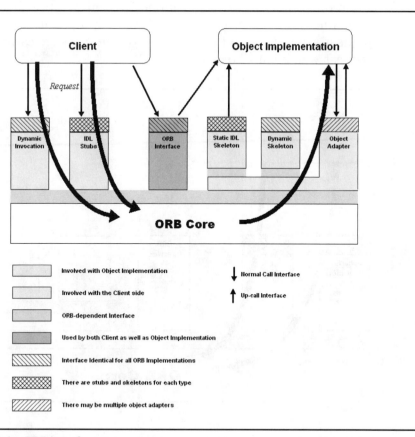

FIGURE 9.2   ORB interfaces.

Interfaces to objects can be defined in two ways. They can be defined statically using IDL. This language defines the types of objects according to the operations that may be performed on them and the parameters to those operations. Alternatively, or in addition, interfaces can be added to an interface repository service; this service represents the components of an interface as objects, permitting runtime access to these components. In any ORB implementation, the Interface Definition Language (IDL) and the interface repository have equivalent expressive power.

The client performs a request by having access to an object reference for an object and knowing the type of the object and the desired operation to be performed. The client initiates the request by calling stub routines (OMG IDL stubs) that are specific to the object or by constructing the request dynamically (Dynamic Invocation Interface, or DII). The dynamic and stub interfaces for invoking a request satisfy the same request semantics, and the receiver of the message cannot tell how the request was invoked (see Figure 9.3).

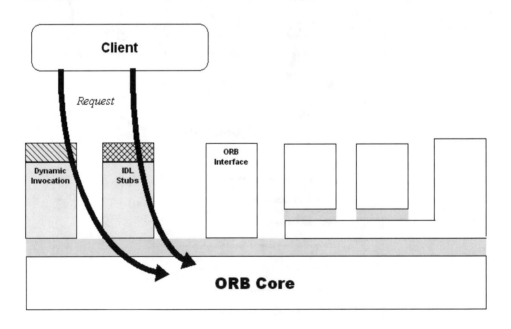

FIGURE 9.3   Client that uses stubs or dynamic invocation interface.

The ORB locates the appropriate implementation code, transmits parameters, and transfers control to the object implementation through an IDL skeleton or a dynamic skeleton. Skeletons are specific to the interface and the object adapter. In performing the request, the object implementation may obtain some services from the ORB through the object adapter. When the request is complete, control and output values are returned to the client. The object implementation may choose which object adapter to use. This decision is based on what kind of services the object implementation requires (see Figure 9.4).

Client Stubs

CORBA can be used in both object-oriented languages such as C++ and Java and procedural languages such as C. Object-oriented languages provide methods and interfaces that let the user define and access properties of the object. This is lacking in nonobject-oriented languages, which require a programming interface to the stubs for each interface type. Usually, the stubs will present access to the OMG IDL-defined

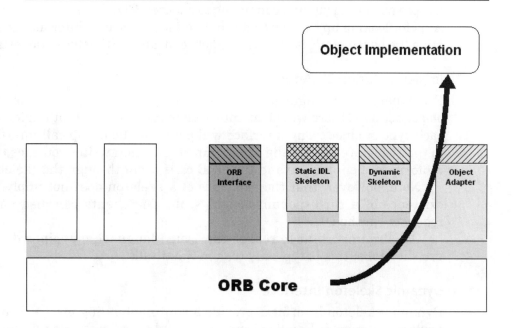

FIGURE 9.4   **An object implementation that receives a request.**

operations on an object in a way that is easy for programmers to predict once they are familiar with the OMG IDL and the language mapping for the particular programming language. The stubs make calls on the rest of the ORB using interfaces that are private to and presumably optimized for the ORB core. If there are more ORBs available, then there may be different stubs corresponding to the different ORBs. In this case, it is necessary for the ORB and language mapping to cooperate to associate the correct stubs with the particular object reference.

Dynamic Invocation Interface (DII)

For situations in which the client would like to specify the object to be invoked and the operations to be performed, instead of specifying a particular operation for a particular object, an interface that allows the dynamic construction of object invocations is available. In such cases, the client code must supply the information about the operation to be performed and the types of parameters being passed. This information is usually obtained from a runtime source such as an interface repository. The nature of the dynamic programming interface may vary substantially from one programming language mapping to another. CORBA defines standard APIs for looking up the metadata that defines the server interface, generating the parameters, issuing the remote call, and getting back the results.

Implementation Skeleton

For a particular language mapping, and possibly depending on the object adapter, there will be an interface to the methods that implement each type of object. The interface will generally be an up-call interface in that the developer of the object implementation writes routines that conform to the interface and the ORB calls them through the skeleton.

Note, however, that the existence of a skeleton does not imply the existence of a corresponding client stub. The clients can also make requests via the DII.

It's also important to realize that some language mappings do not use skeletons; this is typically true in Smalltalk.

Dynamic Skeleton Interface

Dynamic skeleton interfaces provide a runtime binding mechanism for servers that need to handle incoming method calls for objects that do not have IDL-based compiled skeletons or stubs. The dynamic skeleton looks at the parameter values in an incoming message to figure out which object is being called and what method is being invoked. This is in contrast to using normal compiled skeletons, which are defined for a particular object and expect a method implementation for each IDL-defined method.

The implementation code must provide descriptions of all the operation parameters to the ORB, and the ORB provides the values of any input parameters for use in performing the operation. The implementation code provides the values of any output parameters, or an exception, to the ORB after performing the operation. The nature of the dynamic skeleton interface may vary substantially from one programming language mapping or object adapter to another, but it will typically be an up-call interface. Dynamic skeletons may be invoked both through client stubs and through the dynamic invocation interface; either style of client request construction interface provides identical results.

The ORB Interface

The ORB interface is made up of few APIs to local services that are of interest to an application. It is an interface that directly goes to the ORB and is the same for all ORBs. It does not depend on the object adapter or the object's interfaces. As most of the functionality of the ORB is provided through the object adapter, stubs, skeletons, or dynamic invocations, there are only a few operations that are common across all objects. These operations are useful to both the client and implementation of objects. The common operations include functions like get_interface and get_implementation, which work on any object reference and are used to obtain an interface repository object or an implementation repository object, respectively.

Interface Repository

The interface repository is a service that provides IDL information in a format available at runtime. The ORB, in order to perform requests from clients, may use the interface repository information. Client programs may also use this information. Using the information available in the interface repository, it is possible for a such a program to encounter an object whose interface was not known when the client program was compiled, yet be able to determine what operations are valid on it and make an invocation on it. The interface repository is also a common database that stores additional information associated with interfaces to ORB objects, such as object definitions, debugging information, and libraries of stubs or skeletons.

Implementation Repository

The implementation repository contains information that allows the ORB to locate and activate implementations of objects. It provides a runtime repository of information about the classes the server supports, the objects that are instantiated, and their IDs. Although most of the information in the implementation repository is specific to an ORB or operating environment, the implementation repository is the conventional place for recording such information. Ordinarily, installation of implementations and control of policies related to the activation and execution of object implementations are done through operations on the implementation repository.

In addition to its role in the functioning of the ORB, the implementation repository is a common place for the ORB to store additional information associated with the implementations of ORB objects, such as debugging information, administrative control, resource allocation, and security.

Object Adapters

If you look at Figure 9.2, the primary way that an object implementation accesses services provided by the ORB is through an object adapter. The object adapter, which is part of a CORBA library, sits on top of the ORB's core communication services and accepts requests on behalf of the server's objects. It provides the runtime environment for instantiating server objects, passing requests to them and assigning them object IDs. The object adapter also registers the classes it supports and their runtime instances with the *implementation repository*. CORBA specifies that each ORB must support a standard adapter called the *Basic Object Adapter* (BOA). A server may support more than one object adapter.

Services provided by the ORB through an object adapter often include generation and interpretation of object references, method invocation, security and interactions, object and implementation activation and deactivation, mapping object references to implementations, and registration of implementations. Through object adapters, it is possible for the ORB to target particular groups of object implementations that have similar requirements with interfaces tailored to them.

Structure of an Object Adapter

An object adapter is the primary means for an object implementation to access ORB services such as object reference generation. An object adapter exports a public interface to the object implementation and a private interface to the skeleton. It is built on a private ORB interface. An object adapter is responsible for various functions, including:

- Generation and interpretation of the object reference
- Method invocation
- Security and interactions
- Object and implementation activation and deactivation
- Mapping object references to the corresponding object implementations
- Registration of implementations

All these functions are performed with the help of ORB core and additional components if required.

As shown in Figure 9.5, the object adapter is implicitly involved in the invocation of methods. The object adapter defines most of the services from the ORB that the object implementation can depend on. With the object adapters, it is possible for an object implementation to have access to a service whether or not it is implemented in the ORB core. If the ORB core provides the service, then the adapter simply provides an interface to it; if not, then the adapter must implement it on top of the ORB core. Every instance of the adapter provides the same interface and service for all the ORBs it is implemented on. It is also important for the object adapters to provide the same interface. Depending on the requirement, the object adapter should be tuned for special kinds of object implementations so that it can take advantage of particular ORB core details to provide the most effective access to the ORB.

Implementations of CORBA

There are many implementations of CORBA currently available; they vary in the degree of CORBA compliance, quality of support, portability, and availability of additional features.

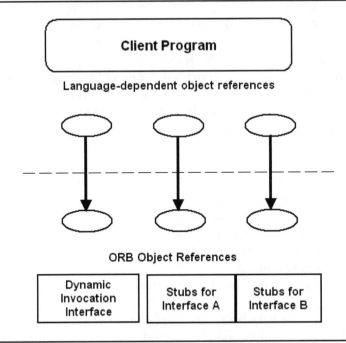

FIGURE 9.5 **Structure of an object adapter.**

Orbix from Iona is a very solid, fully compliant, commercial implementation with excellent support. VisiBroker from Visigenic, which is now a part of Inprise, is also 2.0 compliant and offers interoperability with Java. ObjectBroker from BEA Systems is 1.2 compliant. Other implementations include Expersoft's XShell, a Distributed Object Oriented Management (DOME) system, which also is CORBA compliant, and Hewlett-Packard's DistributedSmalltalk product, which also implements OMG CORBA 1.1 Object Request Broker.

APPLICATION EXAMPLE

In Chapter 8, "InfoBus and RMI," we completed an InfoBus example that allowed our remote data producers to send fault information to a central fault monitor using RMI. As we discussed in Chapter 8, RMI is just one method in which a distributed object may be exposed. In the following application example, we port the code we developed previously over to a CORBA-based architecture. For our example, we use the Visigenic ORB version 3.1 to build the application. A fully functional trial version of the ORB may be downloaded from Visigenic's Web site at www.visigenic.com.

> **N**OTE At the time of this writing, Borland International had just completed the purchase of Visigenic. According to Borland, Visigenic will continue to offer a separate product line of CORBA products. The merged company is also releasing a suite of products in the near future that integrate the CORBA distributed object structure into Inprise's existing development tools.

After we deployed our application at the ACME Scissors factory, word got out that Mr. Big had a very talented development team in his IT organization. As the word spread, a number of other ACME factories became interested in the distributed InfoBus technology for managing their factory floor. We were contacted by Ms. Bigger, the president and CEO of ACME Holdings, to deploy the fault monitoring technology throughout the enterprise. In exploring the deployment options, we find that all the ACME factories do not use a homogeneous technology for controlling their machines. The control logic on the machines is written in a variety of languages such as C++, Java, BASIC, PL/1, and so on. Fortunately, the talent exists in other areas of IT to write code for these machines; we just need to define how their logic is encapsulated for distributed access.

As we saw earlier, CORBA is a technology that allows virtually any language to be used in implementing a distributed object. The key is to find an ORB vendor who supports the platform and language one is using. From our more Java-centric perspective, we will assume that Ms. Bigger has a group of concurrent project teams running to create CORBA-compliant interfaces to the non-Java controlled machines. Further, we will assume that Ms. Bigger has decided that the entire enterprise will standardize on CORBA, not RMI, so we will port both the remote and host sides of the InfoBridge over to a CORBA standard.

Of course, Ms. Bigger is not just interested in a straight port of the application (she wouldn't be "Bigger" if she just took Mr. Big's application!). Ms. Bigger wants each of the machines to store its fault history in an InfoBus-compatible data item and the fault monitor to be enhanced to allow the user to "drill into" the fault history of any machines that have recently produced faults. We assume that the reader has already experimented with the application developed in Chapter 8. Rather than reexamining the previous application's functionality, we will focus mainly on the areas that have changed. We also assume that the Visigenic ORB has been installed and tested.

The Producer and Consumer Components

As with our previous RMI-based application, the data producer component is located in the machine package. Because of our additional requirements to include the machine's history, the MachineStatus class is modified to now manage two data items. The first data item is the MachineFaultDataItem, which serves the same purpose as it did previously: It contains the data related to a current machine's fault. It has received a minor modification to include a date/timestamp when the fault is registered. The second data item, called MachineFaultHistoryDataItem, is contained in a class that implements the ArrayAccess interface. A duplicate MachineFaultDataItem is passed to MachineFaultHistoryDataItem by the producer when a fault occurs.

Figure 9.6 is a screenshot of the remote application's user interface. The functional components of the machine's package are listed here:

MachineFaultDataItem.java.   Implements our DataItem and ImmediateAccess interfaces for the InfoBus. The data item's contents are the machine's name, date/time of the fault's occurrence,

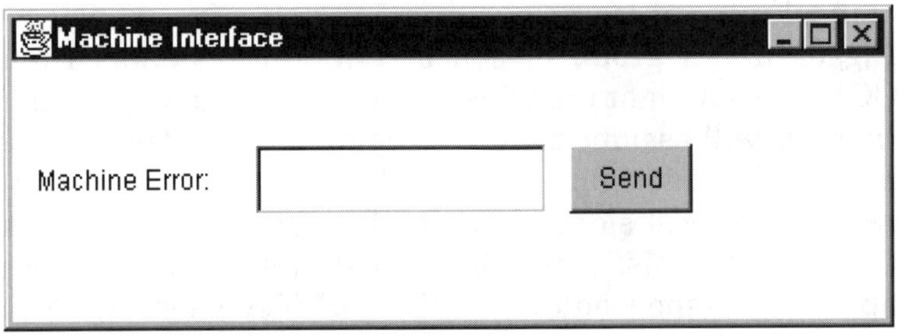

FIGURE 9.6   The machine component.

and a description of the most recent fault. This information is stored in a string format.

MachineFaultHistoryDataItem.java.   Implements the DataItem and ArrayAccess interfaces. The object stores a collection of Machine-FaultDataItems in a Vector and supports the standard ArrayAccess methods for reading the information.

MachineStatus.java.   This is our basic producer component. The component displays a simple GUI for the user to enter machine fault data and to create fireItemAvailable and fireItemRevoked events. For simplicity, the producer does not concern itself with change management and instead always revokes the first data item before sending a data item available event. After creating a current machine fault, it also adds a machine fault to the history. It implements the InfoBusMember, InfoBusDataProducer, and ActionListener interfaces.

StartMachine.java.   Displays a basic frame, instantiates and displays a MachineStatus component, and establishes the connection to the InfoBridge.

FaultMonitor, our data consumer for our fault information, has to be modified substantially over its predecessor. The component displays an enhanced GUI that contains two list boxes and a button. The first list box contains any current machine faults as they have occurred in real time. At any time, the user may highlight one of the real-time machine faults and click the Show History button to drill into the machine's fault and discover any additional fault history. When a drill down occurs, the component determines who the previous data producer was and issues a findDataItem request to get the history data item. The fault monitor then iterates through the list of items contained in the array access object, populating the Machine History list box.

A sample screenshot of the fault monitor in action is shown in Figure 9.7. The files composing the monitor package are shown in the following list:

FaultMonitor.java.   Draws the monitor GUI, attaches itself to the InfoBus, and responds dynamically to both user and InfoBus events. It implements the InfoBusMember and InfoBusConsumer interfaces.

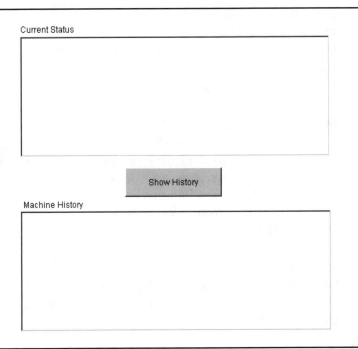

FIGURE 9.7 **The fault monitor component.**

StartMonitor.java. Like StartMachine, it displays a basic frame, instantiates and displays a FaultMonitor component, and calls the InfoBridge to create and export the CORBA objects.

The CORBA-Enabled InfoBus

At a basic level, both RMI and CORBA share a large number of similarities. Both use a similar stub and skeleton technique for marshaling calls between the remote and host applications. Both the remote and host objects are required to inherit from a common hierarchy. When the remote application wishes to gain access to the host, it follows a similar binding procedure to gain access. Invocation of host methods is performed in a similar manner, and both implementations share the same requirements that any object passed to or from the method must implement the java.io.Serializable interface or be a Java primitive.

Figure 9.8 shows the logical architecture of our enhanced application. In CORBA-enabling, or shall we say "CORBA-tizing," we will use most of the basic services of CORBA. The basic application architecture will not change much during this effort. For the interested reader, we have included on the CD a straight port of the application from RMI to CORBA. It is located in the directory chapter09\RMI_Port and contains modifications to the IDL, InfoBridgeImpl, ProducerProxyImpl, and Consumer-Proxy. The source code for this project, which is essentially the port plus new enhancements, is contained on the CD under the directory chapter09\CORBA_App. For our discussion, we cover the following areas:

- Defining interfaces for our objects using the Interface Definition Language (IDL)

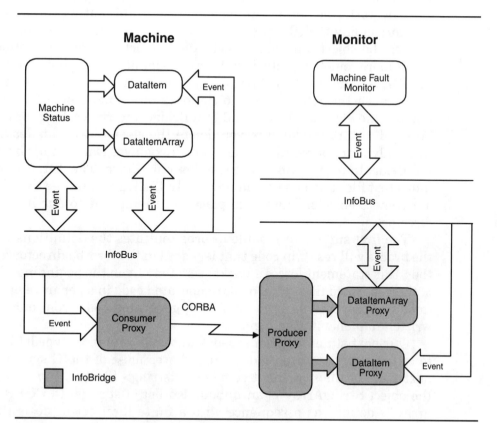

FIGURE 9.8   The InfoBridge architecture.

- Performing a little heart surgery on the InfoBridgeImpl to CORBA-enable it
- Modifying to both CORBA-enable and functionally enhance Producer-ProxyImpl and ConsumerProxy
- Creating a new proxy data item called DataItemArrayProxy

The IDL

In the previous chapter, we created interfaces to define the remote object we intended to expose through RMI. In these interfaces we described our remote object names and method signatures. From these interfaces, we ran the rmic executable to create stubs and skeletons that RMI used to proxy the connection between the client and server. In the CORBA world, we define our remote objects differently using the IDL. The core of any CORBA-based remote object resides in the IDL, which defines the object names, methods, data structures, and exceptions of one or more remote objects. For those of us familiar with SQL databases, the IDL is to distributed objects what the schema is to a database.

Because the IDL is used in defining our remote objects, we can remove the ProducerProxy and InfoBridge interfaces from our info-bridge directory (make sure you delete the class files). This leaves us with only four source files: ConsumerProxy.java, DataItemProxy.java, InfoBridgeImpl.java, and ProducerProxyImpl.java. The IDL is entered into a text file called <some name>.idl. In Listing 9.1, we see the IDL for our remote objects. The file is placed in the parent to our infobridge directory.

The first statement module ibcorba indicates the definitions within the braces will result in code that is placed in the ibcorba directory. Further, this statement forces a package statement on the beginning of each of the generated files. Placing our generated code in a separate package (module) prevents us from confusing generated code from our hand-written implementation logic.

Our next statement is a typedef statement. As in C, typedef is used to create new data type names and shares most of the C syntax. The next piece of the statement sequence, <string> StringArray, indicates the object StringArray is an unbounded list of strings. In CORBA, an array is defined as a sequence with a finite limit set at design time, while a sequence is unbounded. Both arrays and sequences are translated to Java as array data types in our method signatures. The biggest difference in bounding an array is simply a performance boost, since memory is preallocated. Following the typedef, we see a RemoteException defined. CORBA actually provides very robust exception trapping logic for such things as network faults, security violations, object mismatches, and others. We are defining a RemoteException to pass back non-CORBA-related runtime errors on the host.

TIP Exceptions in CORBA: Although CORBA does not require the developer to define an exception for transmission back to the remote application, it does not relieve us of the responsibility of good error handling. Some good steps to follow are:

- Early in the design phase of the project, a common set of exception objects should be discussed and defined (remember that not just Java applications might be using your CORBA service).
- Each of the IDL defined methods should be examined to determine if the remote application will be interested in the success of the functional logic on the host.
- If the remote application is interested in the execution of the host's logic, then one or more of our previously defined exceptions should be thrown.

Next, we get to our first remote object definition, the ProducerProxy. This first method in the interface is our sendPresentationString. Things look pretty normal until we get to that in string dataName thing. In CORBA, parameters must be defined as in, out, or inout. In Java method calls, parameters are passed by value if it is one of the Java primitive types or by reference if it is an object. In the CORBA world, we actually define what will happen to the parameter in the implementation code. If the parameter is an in, then it is essentially passed by value. The method will not change the value of the parameter when invoked. Defining an out type indicates the remote caller will be passing in a reference that it expects to be populated by this method after invocation. Finally, an inout is a parameter more closely akin to the pass by reference method. The remote application has assigned a value to the parameter, but its value might be changed by the method. All of our parameters in this application are of the in flavor. Finally, in our method signature we have the raises statement. This is similar to the throws statement in Java.

The second interface definition sendArrayOfPresentationStrings is used by the consumer proxy to transmit the machine's fault history to the host. This method signature is similar to the previous send method, except it will be receiving an array of strings. Finally, we see our stop method that is called by the InfoBridgeImpl to remove the producer proxy when the consumer proxy's connection is terminated.

Finally, we arrive at our InfoBridge interface. Just as in our RMI application, this interface defines the method call signatures to our factory object. The only item to note here is that retrieveProducerProxy returns a ProducerProxy object, which must be defined previously. The IDL compiler requires that objects be defined before they are used. If we reversed the order of the interfaces, then a forward definition would be required to prevent a compile error.

LISTING 9.1   ibcorba.idl

```
module ibcorba
{
    typedef sequence<string> StringArray;

    exception RemoteException
    {
        string reason;
    };

    interface ProducerProxy
    {
        void sendPresentationString(in string dataName,
            in string presentationString)
                raises (RemoteException);

        void sendArrayOfPresentationStrings(
            in string dataName,

            in StringArray presentationStringArray)

   raises (RemoteException);
        void stop() raises (RemoteException);
```

LISTING 9.1 *Continued*

```
    };

    interface InfoBridge
    {
        ProducerProxy retrieveProducerProxy()
            raises (RemoteException);

        void removeProducerProxy(in ProducerProxy pp)
            raises (RemoteException);

    };
}; // Module ibcorba
```

After completing our IDL definition and saving it as ibcorba.idl in the parent to our infobridge directory, we next need to generate the Java code. From the DOS prompt, run the Visigenic executable idl2java. This program will create a subdirectory called ibcorba and populate it with a whole bunch of files. For our purposes, these files should just be treated as a black box through which our CORBA requests flow. These files should never be manually modified, since regenerating the code from the IDL would overwrite our modifications.

The InfoBridge Factory

The InfoBridge factory contains the majority of the changes we need to make in our conversion effort. To put the changes in context, we have included the entire code listing for the InfoBridgeImpl.java file. The areas of the code that have changed from the RMI implementation are noted in bold and are discussed in detail. Please refer to Listing 9.2.

The first change we encounter is in our import statements. We are now importing our previously generated code in the ibcorba directory rather than the RMI package. Next, notice that we extend a funny thing called _InfoBridgeImplBase rather than UnicastRemoteObject. The _InfoBridgeImplBase Java file is automatically generated by the idl2java executable and contains some of the interface-specific logic for invoking our exposed methods. Next, notice we are still implementing the InfoBridge interface. The difference now is that the interface file was automatically generated by idl2java. Following the class definition, we now see the format for our constants have changed and a new host-Name constant has been added. In Visigenic's implementation, the host name is separated from the object name.

Moving on, we get to the orb and boa reference declaration. Both references provide our basic access to the services provided by the ORB for common tasks such as registering and unregistering objects. Next we enter the constructor. Here we first call _InfoBridgeImplBase's constructor, then get a handle to the previously initialized ORB. Finally, we see that retrieveProducerProxy and removeProducerProxy are completely unchanged.

LISTING 9.2   InfoBridgeImpl.java

```
package infobridge;

import java.util.*;
import infobridge.ibcorba.*;

public class InfoBridgeImpl extends _InfoBridgeImplBase
    implements InfoBridge
{
    protected static final String
        proxyServerName = "ProducerProxy";

    protected static final String
        infoBridgeServerName = "infoBridge";

    protected static final String
        hostName = "yourComputerName";


    private Hashtable producerProxies = new Hashtable();
    private int proxyNumber = 0;

    private org.omg.CORBA.ORB orb;
    private org.omg.CORBA.BOA boa;

    public InfoBridgeImpl() throws RemoteException
    {
        super(infoBridgeServerName);
        orb = org.omg.CORBA.ORB.init();
```

LISTING 9.2 *Continued*

```
        boa = orb.BOA_init();
    }
public synchronized ProducerProxy retrieveProducerProxy()
    throws RemoteException
{
    ProducerProxyImpl ppi;
    try
    {

        String currentProxy =
            proxyServerName+proxyNumber;
        ppi = new ProducerProxyImpl();
        producerProxies.put(
            (ProducerProxy)ppi, currentProxy);

        proxyNumber++;
        System.out.println(
            "MESSAGE - Created " + currentProxy);

    }
    catch (Exception e)
    {
        System.out.println(
            "ERROR - retrieveProducerProxy " + e);

        e.printStackTrace();
        throw new RemoteException(
            "ERROR - Could not create a Producer Proxy");
    }
    return (ProducerProxy)ppi;
} //retrieveProducerProxy

public void removeProducerProxy(ProducerProxy pp)
    throws RemoteException
{
    try
    {
        String producerProxyName =
            (String)producerProxies.get(pp);
        producerProxies.remove(pp);
```

Continues

LISTING 9.2   InfoBridgeImpl.java *(Continued)*

```
            pp.stop();
            System.out.println("MESSAGE - Removed " +
                producerProxyName);
        }
        catch (Exception ex)
        {
            throw new RemoteException(
                "WARNING - Exception occurred " +
                + " on removeProducerProxy " +

                ex.getMessage());
        }

    } //removeProducerProxy
```

In Listing 9.3, we have the InfoBridge startup routine. First, notice we have the orb and boa references defined again. Why? Because this is a static method, it is not permitted to instance variables with an instantiated object. We need this reference to initialize the ORB. Because there can be only one ORB instance per running JVM, repeated calls to orb.init() always return the same reference. After initialization, we notice a call to boa.obj_is_ready. This call is similar to the Naming.bind call we made in RMI. This call indicates to the CORBA object locator service that this object is available under the name specified when it was constructed with the super(infoBridgeServerName) statement. Our final call is to boa.impl_is_ready(). This call is actually just precautionary. The statement ensures that a thread remains alive after the execution of the startInfoBridge method. This is not necessary in this application because our GUI will keep the server running. If, however, we attempted to start the application without the GUI screen, it would create an InfoBridge object, initialize the ORB, register the object, and quit back to the command prompt—a rather anticlimactic event.

LISTING 9.3   Continuing with InfoBridgeImpl.java

```
    public static InfoBridgeImpl startInfoBridge()
    {
        InfoBridgeImpl infoBridgeImpl = null;
```

LISTING 9.3   *Continued*

```
        try
        {
            infoBridgeImpl = new InfoBridgeImpl();

            org.omg.CORBA.ORB orb;
            org.omg.CORBA.BOA boa;

            orb = org.omg.CORBA.ORB.init();
            boa = orb.BOA_init();
            boa.obj_is_ready(infoBridgeImpl);
            boa.impl_is_ready();

            System.out.println(
                "InfoBridgeImpl created and bound to " +

                infoBridgeImpl);

        } catch (Exception e) {
            System.out.println("ERROR - During Bind");
            e.printStackTrace();
        }

        return infoBridgeImpl;

    } //startInfoBridge

}// InfoBridgeImpl
```

The Producer Proxy

The producer proxy requires only some minor CORBA modifications, one new method, and some changes to the dataItemRequested method. For this discussion, we examine only a partial code listing of class signatures and methods that have actually changed in this enhanced application.

In Listing 9.4, we see our class header for ProducerProxyImpl. First, we replaced the rmi imports with import ibcorba.*. Next, we modified the class definition so it inherits from the framework generated by our ProducerProxy IDL definition. Then we define a string to hold the name of our ArrayAccess data item. Next, we declare our handle to the Array-Access proxy.

LISTING 9.4   ProducerProxyImpl.java (Class Header)

```
package infobridge;

import java.beans.*;
import java.awt.*;
import java.awt.event.*;
import javax.infobus.*;
import ibcorba.*;

public class ProducerProxyImpl
    extends _ProducerProxyImplBase

    implements InfoBusMember, InfoBusDataProducer, ProducerProxy


    private String ibName   = "myBus";
    private String dataName = null;
    private String arrayDataName = null;

    private InfoBusMemberSupport ibHandle;
    private DataItemProxy dataItemProxy          = null;
    private DataItemArrayProxy dataItemArrayProxy = null;

    private Object syncAvilRevokeEvent = new Object();
```

Let's skip the constructor, stop, and sendPresentationString methods, which have not changed. Our next method to tackle is the sendArrayOf-PresentationStrings, which is shown in Listing 9.5. Like sendPresenta-tionString, this method is called by the consumer proxy on the remote application in order to pass remote data item strings to the host. The first thing to note is the method signature. In our IDL, we typedef'd a sequence called presentationStrings, which is represented in the Java world as an array. Next, we store a global reference to the data's name, get our InfoBus reference, and instantiate an array proxy if required. If we already had an array proxy, we inform our InfoBus member(s) the item will be invalid for a short period of time while we populate it.

Now that we are assured of an array proxy reference that is also not currently being accessed, we pass our string array to the object. Next, we let the world (well, the InfoBus world) know our array proxy is stable and ready for consumption. Finally, we get to our exception trapping logic that dumps the exception information to the host's console and creates and sends back to the remote application a RemoteException.

LISTING 9.5   ProducerProxyImpl.java (sendArrayOfPresentationStrings Method)

```java
public void sendArrayOfPresentationStrings(
    String arrayDataName,
    String[] presentationStrings) throws RemoteException
{
    this.arrayDataName = arrayDataName;
    try
    {
        InfoBus ib = ibHandle.getInfoBus();
        if ( dataItemArrayProxy == null )
        {
            dataItemArrayProxy =
                new DataItemArrayProxy(this);

        }
        else
        {
            synchronized (syncAvilRevokeEvent)
            {
                ib.fireItemRevoked(arrayDataName, this);
            }
        }
        synchronized (syncAvilRevokeEvent)
        {
            dataItemArrayProxy.setArray(
                presentationStrings);
                arrayDataName, null, this );

        }
    }
    catch (Exception e)
    {
        System.out.println(
            "ERROR - sendArrayOfPresentationStrings "    Continues
```

LISTING 9.5   ProducerProxyImpl.java (sendArrayOfPresentationStrings Method) *(Continued)*

```
                        + e);
                e.printStackTrace();
                throw new RemoteException(e.getMessage());
        }
} //sendArrayOfPresentationStrings
```

The dataItemRequested method is called by the InfoBus when a consumer fires a findDataItem event. In our RMI application, we wrote some code to handle the call (required to implement an InfoBusData-Producer), but never exercised it with a findDataItem event from our consumer. With our fault history requirement, we now have a reason to fire the event. When our fault monitor receives a fault data item, it now internally stores the DataItem's producer reference. When the user clicks to drill into the machine's fault history, our consumer fires a findDataItem event with a producer reference. The InfoBus then fires InfoBusItemRequestedEvent to the instance specified by the consumer. In our code shown in Listing 9.6, we simply check the data name the consumer is requesting and pass the event's setDataItem method the reference to our array. The InfoBus will then return the reference to the consumer, which will then display the array's contents using the standard ArrayAccess methods.

LISTING 9.6   ProducerProxyImpl.java (dataItemRequested Method)

```
public void dataItemRequested(InfoBusItemRequestedEvent ibItemRequested)
    {

        if ( dataItemProxy == null )
            // Nothing to send.
            return;

        String s = ibItemRequested.getDataItemName();
        if (s != null && s.equals( dataName ))
        {
            synchronized (dataItemProxy)
            {
                ibItemRequested.setDataItem(dataItemProxy);
            }
```

LISTING 9.6

```
        } else if (s != null && s.equals(arrayDataName))
        {
            synchronized (dataItemArrayProxy)
            {
                ibItemRequested.setDataItem(dataItemArrayProxy);

            }
        }
    }
```

The Consumer Proxy

In the consumer proxy object we also have only a few minor tweaks to make to CORBA-tize code and then one new and one modified method to examine. As before, we note the changes to the previous RMI application in bold. The CORBA changes are noted in Listing 9.7. First, we removed the rmi and net packages from our import statement. For a change, we won't import ibcorba directly, but instead use a full object reference in our code. Our next change is to the object references for the interfaces. Rather than referring to the interface we created manually in the RMI application, we instead refer to the interface generated by the IDL compiler (idl2java).

In the constructor, we encounter our final group of changes. The first is to get our host name constant from InfoBridgeImpl. Next, we start up the ORB on the remote side and obtain a reference to the object. The ORB instance will continue to run for the life of the JVM or until it is explicitly stopped by a call to shutdown(). Finally, we issue a bind operation to attach ourselves to the instance of the InfoBridge running on the host. Once bound to InfoBridge, our object can make calls to its services in a manner identical to RMI.

LISTING 9.7 ConsumerProxy.java (Class Header and Constructor)

```
package infobridge;

import javax.infobus.*;
import java.util.*;
```
Continues

LISTING 9.7 ConsumerProxy.java (Class Header and Constructor) *(Continued)*

```java
import java.awt.datatransfer.*;
import java.beans.*;

public class ConsumerProxy
    implements InfoBusMember, InfoBusDataConsumer
{

    // Beanbox configurable items
    private String ibName          = "myBus";

    // InfoBus related var's
    private InfoBusMemberSupport ibHandle;

    // CORBA related var's
    private ibcorba.InfoBridge infoBridge;
    private ibcorba.ProducerProxy producerProxy;

    /**
     * Construct a new Consumer Proxy
     */
    public ConsumerProxy()
    {
        try
        {
            String theBridge =
                infobridge.InfoBridgeImpl.infoBridgeServerName;

            String hostName  =
                infobridge.InfoBridgeImpl.hostName;

            org.omg.CORBA.ORB orb =
                org.omg.CORBA.ORB.init();

            infoBridge = ibcorba.InfoBridgeHelper.bind(
                orb, theBridge, hostName, null);

            producerProxy =
                infoBridge.retrieveProducerProxy();

                            .
                            .
                            .
```

Skipping around a bit, let's examine the dataItemAvailable method shown in Listing 9.8. This method is called by the InfoBus when a new item appears with which we have registered an interest. Our job is to take the passed event, pull it apart, and determine both if the data item is interesting and if we can access it. Since our new mission is now to also transmit a list of previous machine faults encapsulated in a data item implementing the ArrayAccess interface, we have written a separate handler for ArrayAccess interfaces. If we have an ArrayAccess type data item, we make a call to our private getArrayAccessPresentation-Strings method that returns a string array. The array is then sent to the host through a call to the producer proxy. Finally, we drop a message to the console of our transmission, as a sanity check for debugging.

LISTING 9.8 ConsumerProxy.java (dataItemAvailable)

```
public void dataItemAvailable(
    InfoBusItemAvailableEvent event)

{
    String dataName = event.getDataItemName();
    Object aDataItem = event.requestDataItem(this, null);

    try
    {
        if (aDataItem instanceof ImmediateAccess )
        {
            String presentationString =
                ((ImmediateAccess)
                aDataItem).getPresentationString(null);


                presentationString);
            producerProxy.sendPresentationString(dataName,
            System.out.println( "Sent: " + presentationString);

        }
        if (aDataItem instanceof ArrayAccess)
        {
            String[] tmpStrings =
            getArrayAccessPresentationStrings(
```

Continues

LISTING 9.8 ConsumerProxy.java (dataItemAvailable) *(Continued)*

```
                    (ArrayAccess)aDataItem);
                producerProxy.sendArrayOfPresentationStrings(
                    dataName, tmpStrings);
                System.out.println(
                    "Sent: Array of Presentation Strings");
            }
        }
        catch(Exception e)
        {
            System.out.println("ERROR - Transmitting DataItem");

            e.printStackTrace();
        }
    } //dataItemAvailable
```

> **TIP** **Sending nulls through Visigenic's ORB:** It is important
> to note that you may never make a CORBA call that passes or
> sends a Java null object. This includes sending an array that has one
> or more null elements. There are a number of methods for avoiding
> this problem if sending a null is necessary. One of the most common
> is to define a constant to which a variable is set if it should be treated
> as a null. For example, a string might be null if it contains a single
> space, or an integer is null if its value is −12345.

In Listing 9.9, we have added to our consumer proxy another private
method that returns an array of strings ready to be passed back to the
host. This method takes as a parameter a data item that supports the
ArrayAccess method. Entering the method, we call the getDimensions
method that returns both the dimensions as well as the size of each of the
dimensions. For a three-dimension array, for example, we might get a
return value of {3,5,2}. In our example, we will assume only a single dimension. Next, we create a Vector to gather the elements from the ArrayAccess object, create an ImmediateAccess handle, and a string array handle
to store our return values. Rounding off our variable initialization, we create an array of integers that we pass to the ArrayAccess object to specify
the item number with which we are interested.

Dropping into our loop, we increment our integer array through all the elements contained in the ArrayAccess object. Notice that we are using the variable arraySize[0] to define our upper boundary rather than making a call to aa.getDimensions. The reason? After each loop, we don't want the for statement to make another call to aa.getDimensions, since it would slow its execution. Next, we retrieve our data item at the coordinates specified by our array and check to see if it supports an access interface we can use. If the data item supports ImmediateAccess, we place the reference in our tmpIA handle and extract a string value from it. Finally, we print a sanity check to the console and add the element to our Vector.

When we exit our loop, we initialize the return array to the size of the Vector. Finally, we place all the Vector's elements into our array and return it to the calling function. Why use a dynamic storage method like a Vector when we know the array's size from our call to getDimensions? Because each of the ArrayAccess elements may not be a homogeneous collection of the same data item type. We first check if each element implements the ImmediateAccess interface before accessing the value using the getPresentationString method.

LISTING 9.9 ConsumerProxy.java (getArrayAccessPresentationStrings)

```
private String[]
    getArrayAccessPresentationStrings(ArrayAccess aa)


{
    // Setup Tmp Vars for reading all the data items
    int arraySize[] = aa.getDimensions();
    Vector presentationElements = new Vector();
    ImmediateAccess tmpIA;
    String[] tmpStrings;
    int[] i = new int[1];
    for ( i[0] = 0;i[0] < arraySize[0];i[0]++)
    {
        if ((Object)aa.getItemByCoordinates(i)
            instanceof ImmediateAccess)
        {
            // OK! Element is of an ImmediateAccess type.

            // Add to our vector.                    Continues
```

LISTING 9.9   ConsumerProxy.java (getArrayAccessPresentationStrings) *(Continued)*

```
                    tmpIA =
                    (ImmediateAccess)aa.getItemByCoordinates(i);

                    String s =
                        tmpIA.getPresentationString(null);

                    System.out.println("Added : " + s);
                    presentationElements.addElement(s);
            }
        }
        String[] strings =
            new String[presentationElements.size()];

        presentationElements.copyInto(strings);

        return strings;
    } //getArrayAccessPresentationStrings
```

Array Access Proxy

Our final class file we need for our InfoBridge is a proxy that implements the ArrayAccess interface. Just like our DataItemProxy class file we created before, this data item will sit on the host side and respond to standard InfoBus requests to access our array of machine faults. In version 1.2 of the JVM, JavaSoft will be implementing standard interfaces for "collections" of items such as a table, set, or list of objects. The InfoBus will support this implementation, but for this proxy we will stick to the standard methods supported in ArrayAccess.

Let's look at some code! In Listing 9.10, we have the first section of the DataItemArrayProxy class. After declaring we are part of the infobridge package and declaring our import statements, we see our class declaration that implements the ArrayAccess and DataItem interfaces. Unlike our DataItemProxy, this class does not directly implement an easy ImmediateAccess method since it would not provide any benefit to the consumer. Rather, we will allow our consumer to access individual data items from our collection and access their ImmediateAccess methods. Next we define a Vector for dynamically storing our collection of

TIP Balancing the "coolness factor": After coding a few complex Java projects, it is easy for a developer to start writing one-liners that perform a large number of functions. Although complex one-liners are fun to create, might save a few keystrokes, and even receive complements such as "Cool!" or "Wow!" from fellow developers, they often make the code hard to read. For example, the code listed previously for adding elements to our vector could have been written:

```
presentationElements.addElement(
    ((ImmediateAccess)aa.getItemByCoordinates(i)
    ).getPresentationString(null));
```

On a scale of 1 to 10, this might get us a "Coolness" rating of 6, but a readability factor of 1. Writing unreadable code will just make the next developer's job much more difficult when he needs to debug or enhance the code.

data items and our standard InfoBusEventListener so the InfoBus can determine who the producer is who is controlling this data item. This InfoBusEventListener is set by our constructor method in the following two lines.

The final method in this code listing is a method our producer will use for setting the values of this data item. As noted earlier in our consumer proxy, our strategy calls for sending a complete collection of ImmediateAccess objects to the host (which are represented by strings). The array of strings is passed into the setArray method. Within this method, we first clear our Vector of any previous elements. Next, we tell our Vector how many elements we plan to insert. This optional statement permits the Vector object to preallocate its internal storage size. Finally, we iterate through the passed array of strings creating DataItemProxy's and adding them to our Vector.

LISTING 9.10 Partial Listing for DataItemArrayProxy.java

```
package infobridge;

import javax.infobus.*;                              Continues
```

LISTING 9.10   Partial Listing for DataItemArrayProxy.java *(Continued)*

```java
import java.util.*;
public class DataItemArrayProxy
    implements ArrayAccess, DataItem

{

    private Vector DataItems = new Vector();
    private InfoBusEventListener  source;

    public DataItemArrayProxy(InfoBusEventListener source)
    { this.source = source; }

    public void setArray(String[] presentationStrings)
    {
        DataItems.removeAllElements();
        DataItems.setSize(presentationStrings.length);
        for (int i = 0; i < presentationStrings.length;i++)
        {
            DataItems.addElement(
                new DataItemProxy(presentationStrings[i], source));

        }
    } //setArray
```

After the DataItemArrayProxy is instantiated and populated with values, we now must provide methods for a consumer to access the elements. In Listing 9.11, we have the implementation code for the Array-Access interface. Our first responsibility is to provide our consumer with our array dimensions and sizes of each of these dimensions. For our application, we always assume a single dimension array. We first initialize our integer array to carry a single element. Then we set this array's first dimension to the size of our Vector and return it to the caller.

Our next task is to return an object at the coordinates specified by the caller in the passed integer array. We first make a check to ensure the consumer is not requesting an element outside of our Vector's boundaries. Since our Java uses zero-based references for array and Vector elements, we subtract 1 from the Vector's returned size to perform the comparison. If we exceed the boundaries, we throw an ArrayIndexOutOfBoundsException. Hmm . . . but why didn't we declare this exception in the throws clause? We could (and in many instances should), but it is not required. Exceptions declared to inherit from RuntimeException are trapped by the JVM and displayed to the console, if not previously trapped by our code. Finally, we return the data item requested wrapped as an object.

Our next two methods are unsupported in this proxy. The first, setItemByCoordinates, would allow a consumer to change the values of the array's elements at the specified coordinate. Of course, we could have written implementation code for this method, rather than creating the setArray method described earlier, to permit the producer to add items to the array. However, doing so would also allow any consumer to also change the values that should not be permitted since our proxy's implementation is a one-way recipient of information from our machines. The final unsupported method would permit the consumer to receive a subsection of the array at the passed coordinates. Both methods throw a subclass of the RuntimeException called UnsupportedOperationException.

LISTING 9.11   DataItemArrayProxy.java (ArrayAccess Implementation)

```
public int[] getDimensions()
    {
        int[] i = new int[1];
        i[0] = DataItems.size();
        return i;
    } //getDimensions


public Object getItemByCoordinates(int[] coordinate)
    {
        if (coordinate[0] > DataItems.size()-1)
            throw new ArrayIndexOutOfBoundsException(
                "ERROR - Total elements of " + DataItems.size() +

                " exceeded by " + coordinate[0]);
        else
            return DataItems.elementAt(coordinate[0]);
    } //getItemByCoordinates


public void setItemByCoordinates(
```
Continues

LISTING 9.11   DataItemArrayProxy.java (ArrayAccess Implementation) *(Continued)*

```
        int[] coordinate, Object newValue)

    throws InvalidDataException
{
    throw new UnsupportedOperationException(
        "ERROR - Consumer may not update the array");
} // setItemByCoordinates

public ArrayAccess subdivide(
    int[] startCoordinates, int[] endCoordinates)

{
    throw new UnsupportedOperationException(
        "ERROR - subdivides are not supported");
} // subdivide
```

The final chunk of code for our proxy is shown in Listing 9.12. This code fills the requirement for implementing a data item. The only method requiring any implementation is the InfoBusEventListener method that is used by the InfoBus to determine the data item's producer reference.

LISTING 9.12   DataItemArrayProxy.java (DataItem Implementation)

```
public java.awt.datatransfer.Transferable getTransferable ()

{return null;}
public InfoBusEventListener getSource()
{return source;}

public Object getProperty( String propertyName )
{return null;}

public java.awt.datatransfer.DataFlavor[] getDataFlavors()

    {return null;}

public void release()
{ }
```

CONCLUSION

Well, it has been quite a journey! We have completed all the modifications necessary to CORBA-tize our application and add the new functionality requested by Ms. Bigger. Because our application now conforms to the CORBA standard, virtually any compliant ORB adhering to the Object Management Group's 2.0 specification can speak to our host application. It is also interesting to note that our machine and monitor applications continue to remain blissfully unaware of the network-enabling logic contained in our InfoBridge.

To run our newly minted applications, first we start Visigenic's osagent process. The osagent serves a purpose similar to rmiregistry and becomes a place where distributed objects references are placed for lookup by remote applications. Next, we start our monitor application that creates an InfoBridge instance and register it with osagent. Finally, we start one or more machines. When each machine starts, the consumer proxy first connects to the osagent to find the InfoBridge factory, binds to the instance, and requests a producer proxy. The producer proxy then begins to service requests for our host-based InfoBus consumer.

In building this application, we have touched on a large number of concepts for bridging the InfoBus across multiple instances of the JVM. Using this foundation, you can take these concepts and expand on them in a number of ways. Some possibilities include modifying the consumer, producer, and data item array proxies to handle arrays of an unspecified number of dimensions. Another enhancement might include providing a bidirectional means of passing InfoBus data items between both the host and remote instances. Still another might include using CORBA's event handling logic to actually wrap native InfoBus events and pass them to listeners located throughout the enterprise. Hmm . . . perhaps these enhancements will be requested by Mr. Biggest.

JavaBeans Classes and Interfaces

The API for JavaBeans consists of the java.beans package. At this point, the package consists of 6 interfaces, 15 classes, and 2 exception handling classes. Following is a list, with accompanying descriptions, of all of the interfaces in the package.

INTERFACE JAVA.BEANS.BEANINFO

```
public interface BeanInfo
```

The interface, if implemented, provides information about the methods, properties, events, and so on, of the Beans. It allows you to choose the information that you want to provide through this interface.

Member Variables

- `public final static int ICON_COLOR 16x16`
  Constant that indicates a 16×16-color icon
- `public final static int ICON_COLOR 32x32`
  Constant that indicates a 32×32-color icon
- `public final static int ICON_MONO 16x16`
  Constant that indicates a 16×16 monochrome icon
- `public final static int ICON_MONO 32x32`
  Constant that indicates a 32×32 monochrome icon

Methods

- `public abstract BeanInfo[] getAdditionalBeanInfo()`
  Returns an arbitrary collection of other BeanInfo objects that provide additional information on the current Bean. If there are conflicts or overlaps between the information provided by different BeanInfo objects, then the current BeanInfo takes precedence over the getAdditionalBeanInfo objects, and later elements in the array take precedence over the earlier ones.

- `public abstract BeanDescriptor getBeanDescriptor()`
  Returns a BeanDescriptor object that provides overall information about the Bean. Returns null if the information should be obtained by automatic analysis.

- `public abstract int getDefaultEventIndex()`
  Returns the default event that was set in the EventSetDescriptor array. If no such event was set, then returns –1.

- `public abstract int getDefaultPropertyIndex()`
  Returns index of the default property in the PropertyDescriptor array. If no default property was set, then returns –1.

- `public abstract EventSetDescriptor[] getEventDescriptors()`
  Returns an array of EventSetDescriptors describing the kinds of events fired by this Bean. May return null if the information is supposed to be obtained by automatic analysis.

- `public abstract Image getIcon(int iconKind)`
  Returns the image that is used to represent the current Bean. Icons are usually GIF right now, but in future may include other formats. Icons are not necessary for Beans and in cases where the Bean does not have an icon, this function returns null. Icons are preferred in a transparent background so that they blend with the existing background.

- `public abstract MethodDescriptor[] getMethodDescriptors()`
  Returns an array of MethodDescriptors describing externally visible methods supported by this Bean. Returns null if the information has to be obtained by automatic analysis.

- `public abstract PropertyDescriptor[] getPropertyDescriptors()`
  Returns an array of PropertyDescriptors describing the editable properties supported by this Bean. May return null if the information should be obtained by automatic analysis.

INTERFACE JAVA.BEANS.CUSTOMIZER

```
public interface Customizer
```

The class provides a complete GUI for customizing a target Java-Bean. It is important that the customizer should inherit from the java.awt.Component class so that it can be instantiated inside an AWT dialog or panel. Every customizer should have a null pointer.

Methods

- `public abstract void addPropertyChangeListener(`
  `PropertyChangeListener listener)`
  The method registers a listener for PropertyChange event. The customizer should fire the PropertyChange event when the Bean has changed so the displayed properties will be refreshed.
- `public abstract void removePropertyChangeListener(`
  `PropertyChangeListener listener)`
  Removes the listener passed as the parameter for the property change event.
- `public abstract void setObject(Object bean)`
  This method sets the object to be customized and is supposed to be called only once before the customizer object has been added to a parent AWT container.

INTERFACE JAVA.BEANS.PROPERTYCHANGELISTENER

```
public interface PropertyChangeListener extends EventListener
```

PropertyChangeListener object handles the PropertyChange event whenever a bound property changes. The object is registered with a source Bean so as to be notified of any bound updates.

Methods

- `public abstract void propertyChange(`
  `PropertyChangeEvent event)`

This method is called whenever a bound property is changed. The parameter received describes the event source and the property that is changed.

INTERFACE JAVA.BEANS.PROPERTYEDITOR

```
public interface PropertyEditor
```

The interface PropertyEditor provides different ways of displaying properties and updating property values. Most PropertyEditors support only a subset of APIs that are available from this object. It is required that every PropertyEditor support at least one of the three simple display styles. The styles are:

- Support isPaintable
- Return a non-null String[] from getTags() and return a non-null value from getAsText()
- Return a non-null String from getAsText ()

It is also important that the PropertyEditor must support a call on setValue when the argument object is of the type for which this is the corresponding PropertyEditor. The PropertyEditor must also support either a custom editor or setAsText ().
Each PropertyEditor should have a null constructor.

Methods

- `public abstract void addPropertyChangeListener(`
  `                    PropertyChangeListener listener)`
  This method registers a listener for the PropertyChange event. When a PropertyEditor changes its value, then it should fire a PropertyChange event for all registered PropertyChangeListeners, specifying a null value for the property name and itself as the property source.
- `public abstract String getAsText()`
  This method returns a property value as string, which can be edited. If the value to be returned cannot be edited, then it returns null.

- `public abstract Component getCustomEditor()`

  A PropertyEditor can choose to make available a full custom Component that edits its property values. It is the property of the PropertyEditor to hook itself up to its editor and Component itself and to report property value changes by firing a PropertyChange event.

- `public abstract String getJavaInitializationString()`

  This method is used for generating Java code to set the value of the property. The function returns the subset of code, which can be used for initializing a variable with the current property value.

- `public abstract String[] getTags()`

  This returns the tag values for this property. If the property value must be one of the set of known tagged values, then this method should return an array of the tags. If this property cannot be represented as a tag value, then it returns a null. If the PropertyEditor supports tags, then it should support the use of setAsText and getAsText methods for setting and getting the tag values, respectively.

- `public abstract Object getValue()`

  This returns the value for the property. Built in types such as int will be wrapped as the corresponding object type such as java.lang.integer.

- `public abstract boolean isPaintable()`

  Returns true if the calls will support the paintValue method; false otherwise.

- `public abstract void paintValue(Graphics gfx,`
                       `Rectangle box)`

  This paints the graphics object specified in the rectangular box. The PropertyEditor is responsible for doing its own clipping so that it fits into the rectangle. If the PropertyEditor does not support paint, it requests that nothing happens when using this function.

- `public abstract void removePropertyChangeListener(`
                    `PropertyChangeListener listener)`

  Removes the listener specified for the PropertyChange event.

- `public abstract void setAsText( String text)`
                    `throws IllegalArgumentException`

  This sets the property value by parsing the string passed. If the property type is not supported, or the string is badly formatted, or the value and the property type do not match, then raises java.lang.IllegalArgumentException.

- `public abstract void setValue( Object value)`
  This method sets or changes the object that is to be edited. Built-in types such as int must be wrapped as the corresponding object type, such as java.lang.Integer.
- `public abstract boolean supportsCustomEditor()`
  Returns true if the PropertyEditor can provide a custom editor.

INTERFACE JAVA.BEANS.VETOABLECHANGELISTENER

```
public interface VetoableChangeListener extends EventListener
```

VetoableChangeListener object handles the VetoableChange event whenever a constrained property for a Bean changes. The object VetoableChangeListener is registered with a source Bean so as to be notified of any constrained property updates.

Methods

- `public abstract void vetoableChange(`
  `                    PropertyChangeEvent event)`
  This method is called whenever a constrained property is changed. The parameter received describes the event source and the property that is changed. The recipient may throw a PropertyVetoException if it wishes the property change to be rolled back.

INTERFACE JAVA.BEANS.VISIBILITY

```
public interface Visibility
```

This interface inquires the Bean about its requirements for a GUI. In cases where GUI is not available on servers, the interface also advises the Bean about the unavailability of a GUI.

Methods

- `public abstract boolean avoidingGui`
  Returns true if the Bean is avoiding the use of GUI because of call on dontUseGui().
- `public abstract void dontUseGui()`
  Instructs the Bean not to use the GUI.
- `public abstract boolean needsGUI()`
  Returns true if the Bean absolutely needs the GUI in order to work.
- `public abstract void okToUseGui()`
  This method instructs the Bean that it is okay to use the GUI. The package also contains 15 classes. The description and the methods supported by these objects are described next.

CLASS JAVA.BEANS.BEANDESCRIPTOR

```
public class BeanDescriptor extends FeatureDescriptor
```

The object provides global information about the Bean, including its Java class, its display name, and so forth. This descriptor is one of the descriptors returned by a BeanInfo object. The object also returns descriptors for properties, methods, and events.

Constructor

- `public BeanDescriptor(Class beanClass)`
  This creates a BeanDescriptor for a Bean that doesn't have a customizer. The parameter passed is the object that implements the Bean.
- `public BeanDescriptor(Class beanClass,`
  `            Class customizerClass)`
  This constructor creates a BeanDescriptor that has a customizer.

Methods

- `public Class getBeanClass()`
  Returns the class object for the Bean.
- `public Class getCustomizerClass()`
  This returns the object for the Bean's customizer. If the Bean does not have a customizer, then this value is null.

CLASS JAVA.BEANS.BEANS

```
public class Beans extends Object
```

Provides methods for controlling Beans.

Constructor

- `public Beans()`
  Creates a Beans object.

Methods

- `public static Object getInstanceOf(Object bean,`
            `Class targetType)`
  This returns a view of the object passed as the parameter, of the type specified by targetType. The result may be the same object or a different object depending on if the requested type is available when the given Bean is returned.
- `public static Object instantiate(ClassLoader cls,`
            `String beanName)`
            `throws IOException, ClassNotFoundException`
  This function instantiates a Bean. The Bean is created based on the name relative to the class loader specified as the parameter. The name specified must be separated by dots, like x.y.z. The beanName passed can either be a serialized object or a class.
  If the beanName is a serialized object, then we convert the bean-Name to a resource pathname and then add a trailing .ser suffix.

We then try to load that serialized object from the resource. The function first tries loading the serialized object and if that fails, then loads the class as specified by the beanName and then creates an instance of the class.

- `public static boolean isDesignTime()`

  This tests if we are in design mode. Returns true if we are running the application in a construction environment.

- `public static boolean isGuiAvailable()`

  This returns true if the Bean can assume that the running environment supports interactive GUI. Usually returns true in case of windowing environment and false if the Bean is running in either a server environment or as a part of a batch job.

- `public static boolean isInstanceOf(Object bean,`

  `                Class targetType)`

  This checks if the Bean can be viewed as the given target type. Returns true if the getInstanceOf method can be used on the given Bean to obtain an object that represents the specified target type view.

- `public static void setDesignTime(boolean isDesignTime)`

  `                throws SecurityException`

  This function is used to indicate if we are running in an application builder environment. The method is security checked and is not available to untrusted object/applets.

- `public static void setGuiAvailable(`

  `                boolean isGuiAvailable)`

  `                throws SecurityException`

  This function is used to indicate if we are running in an environment where GUI interaction is available. This method is security checked and is not available to untrusted objects/applets.

CLASS JAVA.BEANS.EVENTSETDESCRIPTOR

```
public class EventSetDescriptor extends FeatureDescriptor
```

EventSetDescriptor object describes the group of events that a given JavaBean fires. The given group of events are all delivered as method calls on a single event listener interface, and an event interface object can be registered via a call on a registration method supplied by the event source.

Constructor

- ```
  public EventSetDescriptor(
                  Class sourceClass,
                  String eventSetName,
                  Class listenerType,
                  String listenerMethodName)
                  throws IntrospectionException
  ```
  This creates an EventSetDescriptor object based on the information provided as constructor arguments. The sourceClass denotes the class that is firing the event. The listenerType object receives the event eventSetName and handles the event using the method listenerMethodName.

- ```
  public EventSetDescriptor(
                  Class sourceClass,
                  String eventSetName,
                  Class listenerType,
                  String listenerMethodNames[],
                  String addListenerMethodName,
                  String removeListenerMethodName)
                  throws IntrospectionException
  ```
  This creates an EventSetDescriptor object. The listenerMethod-Names provides an array of names of methods that will get called when the event gets delivered to its target listener object, unlike the previous constructor, which only provides only one method name for handling the specified event. The addListenerMethod-Name and removeListenerMethodName denote names of methods on the event source that can be used to register and unregister an event listener object, respectively.

- ```
  public EventSetDescriptor (
                  String eventSetName,
                  Class listenerType,
                  Method listenerMethods[],
                  Method addListenerMethod,
                  Method removeListenerMethod )
                  throws IntrospectionException
  ```
  ```

This creates an EventSetDescriptor object. The parameters passed are similar to the ones described earlier. This constructor does not have the source of the event passed at the time of creating the object.

- `public EventSetDescriptor (`
  `        String eventSetName,`
  `        Class listenerType,`
  `        MethodDescriptor listenerMethodDescriptors[],`
  `        Method addListenerMethod,`
  `        Method removeListenerMethod)`
  `        throws IntrospectionException`

This creates an EventSetDescriptor object. The listenerMethodDescriptor is an array of MethodDescriptor objects describing each of the event handling methods in the target listener.

Methods

- `public Method getAddListenerMethod()`
  This is the method used to register a listener at the event source.
- `public MethodDescriptor[] getListenerMethodDescriptors()`
  This returns an array of MethodDescriptor objects for the target methods within the target listener interface that will get called when events are fired.
- `public getListenerMethods()`
  This method returns an array of method objects for the target methods within the target listener interface that will get called when events are fired.
- `public Method getRemoveListenerMethod()`
  This function returns the method used to register a listener at the event source.
- `public void setInDefaultEventSet(boolean inDefaultEventSet)`
  This method is used to mark an event set as being in the default set, true indicating that the event is part of the default set. It is by default to true.
- `public boolean isUniCast()`
  Events by default are multicast by nature; however, some exceptions are unicast. The method helps in finding if the current event is set as unicast.

- `public boolean isInDefaultEventSet()`
  Returns TRUE if the event is part of the default set.
- `public void setUnicast(boolean unicast)`
  Marks an event as being in unicast mode if the value passed is true.

CLASS JAVA.BEANS.FEATUREDESCRIPTOR

`public class FeatureDescriptor extends Object`

FeatureDescriptor class is the common base class for PropertyDescriptor, EventSetDescriptor, MethodDescriptor, and so forth. It provides an extension mechanism so that arbitrary attribute/value pairs can be associated with a design feature. The object supports some common information that can be set and retrieved for any of the introspection descriptors.

Constructor

- `public FeatureDescriptor()`
  Creates an object of type FeatureDescriptor.

Methods

- `public Enumeration attributeNames()`
  Returns an enumeration of locale-independent names of any attributes that have been registered by setValue method.
- `public String getDisplayName()`
  This function returns the localized display name for the property or method or the event. This name is the same as its programmatic name retrieved from getName.
- `public String getName()`
  Returns the programmatic name for the property/method/event.
- `public String getShortDescription()`
  This function retrieves the localized short description associated with this property/method/event. This by default is the display name of the object.

- public Object getValue(String attibuteName)

  This function returns a value of the attribute requested. The attributeName is the locale-independent name of the attribute. If the attribute is unknown to the object, then returns null.

- public boolean isExpert()

  The Expert flag is used to differentiate between those features that are for expert users and those that are for normal users. The return value of true indicates the feature as that for use by experts only.

- public boolean isHidden()

  The Hidden flag indicates that the feature is intended to be hidden from the end users and to be used for tool use only.

- public void setDisplayName(String displayName)

  Sets the localized display name for the property/method/event.

- public void setExpert(boolean expert)

  This is used for setting the Expert flag. The flag indicates if the feature is meant to be used by experts only.

- public void setHidden(boolean hidden)

  This sets the Hidden flag. If set as true indicates that the feature is to be hidden from the human users.

- public void setName(String name)

  Sets the programmatic name of the property/method/event.

- public void setShortDescription(String text)

  This is used for associating a short descriptive string about this feature. The descriptive strings should not be more than 40 characters.

- public void setvalue(String attributeName, Object value)

  Associates a value for the given attribute names.

CLASS JAVA.BEANS.INDEXEDPROPERTYDESCRIPTOR

```
public class IndexedPropertyDescriptor
                    extends PropertyDescriptor
```

An IndexedPropertyDescriptor describes a property that acts like an array and has indexed read and/or write methods to access specific elements of the array. The indexed properties also provide nonindexed read and write methods. If they are present, then they read and write arrays of the type returned by the indexed read method.

Constructor

- ```
  public IndexedPropertyDescriptor(
              String propertyName,
              Class beanClass)
              throws Introspectionexception
  ```
  This creates an object of type IndexedPropertyDescriptor for a property that provides general Get and Set accessor methods for both indexed access and array access. The parameter passed indicates the programmatic property name and the class name for the target Bean.

- ```
  public IndexedPropertyDescriptor(
              String propertyName,
              Class beanName,
              String getterName,
              String setterName,
              String indexedGetterName,
              String indexedSettername)
              throws Introspectionexception
  ```
  This creates an object of type IndexedPropertyDescriptor. At the time of construction it also takes the name of the methods for reading and writing the property for both indexed and nonindexed cases.

- ```
  public IndexedPropertyDescriptor(
              String propertyName,
              Method getter,
              Method setter,
              Method indexedGetter,
              Method indexedSetter)
              throws IntrospectionException
  ```
  This creates an object of type IndexedPropertyDescriptor for a given property and takes the method objects for reading and writing the property at the time of construction.

Methods

- ```
  public Class getIndexedPropertyType()
  ```
  This returns the Java class for the indexed property types. This type is also returned by the indexedReadMethod.

- `public Method getIndexedReadMethod()`

  This function returns the method for indexed reading. The returned value is null if the property is not indexed or is write only.

- `public Method getIndexedWriteMethod()`

  This returns the method that is to be used for writing an indexed property value. Returns null if the property isn't indexed or is read only.

CLASS JAVA.BEANS.INTROSPECTOR

```
public class Introspector extends Object
```

The introspector object provides methods for tools to learn about the properties, events, and methods supported by the target JavaBean.

Methods

- `public static String decapitalize(String name)`

  This method provides a way for converting the strings to normal Java variable name capitalization. This usually involves converting the first character from uppercase to lowercase, but in cases where the first two characters are in uppercase, then we leave it alone.

- `public static BeanInfo getBeanInfo(Class beanClass)`
  `throws IntrospectionException`

  This method returns a BeanInfo object describing the target Bean for the class passed as the parameter to be analyzed.

- `public static BeanInfo getBeanInfo(`
  `Class beanClass,`
  `Class stopClass)`
  `throws IntrospectionException`

  This gets the BeanInfo for the beanClass passed as the parameter. The stopClass is the base class at which we should stop the analysis. Any methods/properties/events in the stopClass or in its base classes will be ignored in the analysis.

- `public static String[] getBeanInfoSearchPath()`
  This returns an array of package names that will be searched in order to find BeanInfo classes. This value is initially set to sun.beans.info.
- `public static void setBeanInfoSearchPath(`
            `String path[])`
  Changes the list of package names that will be used for finding BeanInfo classes as specified by the array of package names passed as the parameter.

CLASS JAVA.BEANS.METHODDESCRIPTOR

    `public class MethodDescriptor extends FeatureDesrciptor`

A MethodDescriptor describes a particular method that a JavaBean supports for external access from other components.

Constructor

- `public MethodDescriptor(Method method)`
  Creates an object of type MethodDescriptor, for the low-level method information passed as the parameter.
- `public MethodDescriptor(`
        `MethodDescriptor method,`
        `ParameterDescriptor parameterDescriptors[])`
  Creates an object of type MethodDescriptor for the low-level method and descriptive information about the method's parameters.

Methods

- `public Method getMethod()`
  Returns the low-level description of the method.
- `public ParameterDescriptor[] getParameterDescriptors()`
  Returns locale-independent names of the parameters. If the parameter names are not known, then the method may return null array.

CLASS JAVA.BEANS.PARAMETERDESCRIPTOR

```
public class ParameterDescriptor extends FeatureDesrciptor
```

An object of type ParameterDescriptor allows Bean implementers to provide additional information on each of their parameters, beyond the low-level type information as provided by the java.lang.reflect.Method class.

Constructor

- `public ParameterDescriptor()`
  Creates an object of type ParameterDescriptor.

CLASS JAVA.BEANS.PROPERTYCHANGEEVENT

```
public class PropertyChangeEvent extends EventObject
```

This class handles the PropertyChange event, which is delivered whenever a Bean changes a bound or constrained property. A PropertyChangeEvent object is sent as an argument to the PropertyChangeListener and VetoableChangeListener methods.

The name and the old and new values of the changed property accompany a PropertyChangeEvent object. The property is wrapped as the corresponding java.lang.* object type if the new value of the property is a built-in type. If the true values of the new and old values are not known, then null values may be provided. An event source may also send a null object as the name to indicate that an arbitrary set of its properties has changed. Usually in this case the old and the new values are also null.

Constructor

- `public PropertyChangeEvent(`
            `Object source,`
            `String propertyName,`
            `Object oldValue,`
            `Object newValue)`

This creates an object of type PropertyChangeEvent. The constructor tells what Bean fired the event, the name of the property that changed, and the new and old values of the property.

Methods

- `public Object getNewValue()`
  This returns the new value of the property. If multiple properties have changed, then it may be null.
- `public Object getOldValue()`
  This returns the old value for the property. It may be null if multiple properties have changed.
- `public Object getPropagationId()`
  The field propagationId is reserved for future use. In Beans 1.0, the sole requirement is that if a listener catches a PropertyChangeEvent, then it should make sure that it propagates the propagationId field from its incoming event to its outgoing event that it fires as the response to the event received.
- `public String getProperyName()`
  This returns the programmatic name of the property that was changed and may be null if multiple properties have changed.
- `public void setPropagationId(Object propagationId)`
  Sets the propagationId object for the event.

CLASS JAVA.BEANS.PROPERTYCHANGESUPPORT

```
public class PropertyChangeSupport extends Object
              implements Serializable
```

This class is a utility class that is used by Beans that support bound properties. The Bean can either inherit from this class or can be used as a member field of the Bean and delegate various work to it.

Constructor

- `public PropertyChangeSupport()`
  Creates an object of type PropertyChangeSupport.

Methods

- `public synchronized void addPropertyChangeListener(`
            `PropertyChangeListener listener)`
  This method adds the PropertyChangeListener passed as the parameter to the listener list.
- `public synchronized void removePropertyChangeListener(`
            `PropertyChangeListener listener)`
  Removes a PropertyChangeListener from the listener list.
- `public void firePropertyChange(`
            `String propertyName,`
            `Object oldValue,`
            `Object newValue)`
  This method reports the registered listeners for any updates to a bound property. If the newValue and the oldValue are equal and non-null, then no event is fired.

CLASS JAVA.BEANS.PROPERTYDESCRIPTOR

`public class PropertyDescriptor extends FeatureDescriptor`

A PropertyDescriptor describes one property that a JavaBean exports via a pair of assessor methods.

Constructor

- `public PropertyDescriptor(`
            `String propertyName,`
            `Class beanClass)`
            `throws IntrospectionException`
  This constructs a PropertyDescriptor object for the property passed for the given target Bean. It is important that the property follows the standard Java convention by having Get and Set methods for the given property.

- `public PropertyDescriptor(`
    `String propertyName,`
    `Class beanClass,`
    `String getterName,`
    `String setterName)`

    This constructor creates an object of type PropertyDescriptor and takes the name of the property, the target Bean object, and the method names for reading and writing the property.
- `public PropertyDescriptor(`
    `String propertyName,`
    `Method getter,`
    `Method settor)`
    `throws IntrospectionException`

    This constructor takes the name of the property and the method names for reading and writing the property.

Methods

- `public Class getPropertyEditorClass()`

    This returns the class that has been registered as a property editor for this property. If the value returned is null, which indicates that no property editor has been assigned to the property, the PropertyEditorManager should be used to find out the appropriate property editor.
- `public Class getProperytType()`

    This method returns the Java type information for the property. The result returned may be null if the property in question is an indexed property and does not support nonindexed access.
- `public Method getReadMethod()`

    This returns the method used for reading the property. If the property cannot be read, then the return value is null.
- `public Method getWriteMethod()`

    This function returns the method, which is used for writing the property value. If the property cannot be written, then returns null.
- `public boolean isBound()`

    This method is used to find out if the property is a bound property. Any updates to the bound property cause a PropertyChange event to be fired.

- `public boolean isConstrained()`

  This method is used to find out if the property is a constrained property. Any updates to such property will cause a VetoableChange event to be fired when the property is changed.

- `public void setBound(boolean bound)`

  This method is used for setting the property characteristic as being bound.

- `public void setConstrained(boolean constrained)`

  This method is used for setting the property characteristic as being constrained.

- `public void setPropertyEditorClass(`
  `        Class propertyEditorClass)`

  Associates a propertyEditorClass with this property.

CLASS JAVA.BEANS.PROPERTYEDITORMANAGER

```
public class PropertyEditorManager extends Object
```

PropertyEditorManager is used to locate a property editor for any given type name. This property editor must support the java.beans .PropertyEditor interface for editing a given object.

The PropertyEditorManager provides three methods for locating an editor for a given type name. It provides a registerEditor method to allow an editor to be assigned for a given type. For built-in types like int, default property editors are provided. The PropertyEditorManager tries to locate a suitable class by adding Editor to the full qualified class name of the given type. It then takes this combined name and looks in the search path of packages for a matching class.

Constructor

- `public PropertyEditorManager()`

  Constructs a PropertyEditorManager object.

Methods

- `public static PropertyEditor findEditor(Class targetType)`
  This method is used for finding a value editor for a given target type.
- `public static String[] getEditorSearchPath()`
  This method returns the array of package names that will be searched in order to find property editors.
- `public static void registerEditor(`
  `        Class targetType,`
  `        Class editorClass)`
  This function registers an editor class for editing values of a given target type.
- `public static void setEditorSearchPath(String path[])`
  Changes the list of package names that will be used for finding property editors.

CLASS JAVA.BEANS.PROPERTYEDITORSUPPORT

```
public class PropertyEditorSupport extends Object
            implements PropertyEditor
```

This is a utility class that can be used by Beans that support PropertyEditor object. You can either inherit from this class, or you can use an instance of this class as a member field of your work and delegate work to it.

Constructor

- `protected PropertyEditorSupport()`
  Constructs a PropertyEditorSupport object for use by derived PropertyEditor class.
- `protected PropertyEditorSupport(Object source)`
  This constructor is used when a PropertyEditor is delegating to us. The source is the source to use for any events that we fire.

Methods

- `public synchronized void addPropertyChangeListener(`
  `PropertyChangeListener listener)`

  This method registers a listener for the property change event. The class fires a PropertyChange value whenever the value is updated.

- `public void firePropertyChange()`

  Notifies the interested listeners of the property about the change in value.

- `public String getAsText()`

  This returns the property value in an editable fashion. If the value cannot be expressed as a string, then it returns a null. If a non-null value is returned, then the PropertyEditor should be prepared to parse that string back as setAsText().

- `public Component getCustomEditor()`

  A PropertyEditor is allowed to choose a custom component that edits its property value. It is the responsibility of the property editor to attach itself to its editor component and report all the value changes by firing a property change event. The method returns a java.awt.Component that will allow a user to directly edit a property value.

- `public String getJavaInitializationString()`

  This method returns a fragment of Java code representing the initializer for the current value. The value returned is in the form of a string and can have values like new color(255, 255, 255).

- `public String[] getTags()`

  This returns the tag values for this property. If a property editor supports tags, then it should support the use of setAsText with a tag value as a way of setting the value. If this property cannot be represented as a tagged value, then returns null.

- `public Object getValue()`

  Returns the value of the property.

- `public boolean isPaintable()`

  Returns true if the class will support the paintValue method.

- `public void paintValue( Graphics gfx, Rectangle box)`

  This paints a representation of the graphics value into the given rectangular area. The propertyEditor is responsible for doing its own clipping so that the graphics object fits in the given area.

- ```
  public synchronized void removePropertyChangeListener(
                   PropertyChangeListener listener)
  ```
  Removes the given listener from the list of listeners for the PropertyChange event.
- ```
  Public void setAsText(String text) throws
                   IllegalArgumentException
  ```
  This sets the property value by parsing a given string. If the string is badly formatted or has invalid value for the property, then it raises an exception.
- ```
  public void setValue(Object value)
  ```
  Sets or changes the object that is to be edited.
- ```
  public boolean supportsCustomEditor()
  ```
  Returns true if the propertyEditor can provide a custom editor.

CLASS JAVA.BEANS.SIMPLEBEANINFO

```
public class SimpleBeanInfo extends Object
                implements BeanInfo
```

This class is a support class and is used to provide BeanInfo classes in an easier fashion. The class defaults to providing noop information and can be selectively overridden to provide more explicit information on chosen topics. The Introspector applies low-level introspection and design patterns to automatically analyze the target Bean whenever it sees the noop values.

Constructor

- ```
  public SimpleBeanInfo()
  ```
  Constructs a SimpleBeanInfo object.

Methods

- ```
  public BeanInfo[] getAdditionalBeanInfo()
  ```
  This method claims that there are no relevant BeanInfo objects. The method is overridden in cases like this where we want to return a BeanInfo for base class.

- `public BeanDescriptor getBeanDescriptor()`

    This method is overridden to provide any explicit information about the Bean. It denies any knowledge about the class and customizer of the Bean.

- `public int getDefaultEventIndex()`

    This method denies knowledge of a default event. The user can override this function to define a default event for this Bean.

- `public int getPropertyIndex()`

    This method denies knowledge of a default property. The method can be overridden if the user wishes to define a default property for the Bean.

- `public EventSetDescriptor[] getEventSetDescriptors()`

    This method denies knowledge of event sets. The method can be overridden if the user wishes to provide event set information.

- `public Image getIcon(int iconKind)`

    This method can be overridden if the user wishes to provide icons for the Bean.

- `public MethodDescriptor[] getMethodDescriptor()`

    This method can be used to provide explicit method information if required. The user then has to override this method to do so.

- `public PropertyDescriptor[] getPropertyDescriptors()`

    This method can be overridden to provide explicit property information if required. The method denies knowledge of property by default.

- `public Image loadImage(String resourceName)`

    This method is used for loading icon images. It takes the name of the resource file associated with the current object's class file and loads an image object from that file. Usually the images are in GIF format.

CLASS JAVA.BEANS.VETOABLECHANGESUPPORT

```
public class VetoableChangeSupport extends Object
            implements Serializable
```

This class is a utility class that can be used by Beans that support constrained property. The user is allowed to either inherit from this class or use an object of this class as a member field of the Bean and then delegate the work to this object.

Constructor

- ```
  public VetoableChangeSupport()
  ```
  Constructs a VetoableChangeSupport object.

Methods

- ```
  public synchronized void addVetoableChangeListener(
          VetoableChangeListener listener)
  ```
  This method adds a VetoableChangeListener to the listener list.
- ```
  public void fireVetoableChange(
          String propertyName,
          Object oldValue,
          Object newValue)
          throws PropertyVetoException
  ```
  This method reports any vetoable property to any registered listeners. If anyone vetoes the change, then it fires a new event reverting everyone back to the old value and then rethrows the PropertyVetoException. If the new and the old values are equal and non-null, then no event is fired.
- ```
  public synchronized void removeVetoableChangeListener(
          VetoableChangeListener listener)
  ```
  Removes a VetoableChangeListener from the listener list.

  The package also consists of two exceptions. Following is the list of all available exceptions and their respective descriptions.

CLASS JAVA.BEANS.INTROSPECTIONEXCEPTION

```
public class IntrospectionException extends Exception
```

This exception is thrown when an exception happens during Introspection. The general causes for this exception being raised are not being able to map a string class name to a class object, not being able to resolve a string method name, or specifying a method name that has the wrong type signature for its intended use.

Constructor

- `public IntrospectionException( String errormessage)`
  Constructs an IntrospectionException with the errormessage as the descriptive message for the exception raised.

CLASS JAVA.BEANS.PROPERTYVETOEXCEPTION

`public class PropertyVetoException extends Exception`

A PropertyVetoException is thrown when a proposed change to a property represents an unacceptable value.

Constructor

- `public PropertyVetoException(`
      `String message,`
      `PropertyChangeEvent evt)`
  This constructs a PropertyVetoException object. The Property-ChangeVeto object describes the vetoed change, with the message describing the descriptive message.

Methods

- `public PropertyChangeEvent getPropertyChangeEvent()`

InfoBus Classes and Interfaces

The API for InfoBus consists of the javax.infobus package. The package currently consists of 17 interfaces, 14 classes, and 7 exception handling classes. Following is the list and the accompanying descriptions for all interfaces in the package.

INTERFACE JAVAX.INFOBUS.ARRAYACCESS

```
public interface ArrayAccess
```

The interface provides methods for data items that are part of a collection of data items organized in an n-dimensional array. The methods provided are to determine the dimensions, obtain individual items depending on the index provided for the array, to iterate over all elements in the data set, and subdivide the ArrayAccess object into another ArrayAccess object.

Methods

- `public abstract int[] getDimensions()`

  Provides the dimension of the ArrayAccess object as an integer array, where the array has the same number of elements as that of the ArrayAccess object. Each integer value in this returned array represents the number of elements in the respective array dimension.

- `public abstract Object getItemByCoordinates(`
    `int coordinates[])`

    Returns the data item corresponding to the passed coordinate. Valid values for coordinates of an ArrayAccess with dimension n are 0 to (getDimension ()[n] − 1).

- `public abstract void setItemByCoordinates(`
    `int coordinates[],`
    `Object newValue)`
    `throws InvalidDataException`

    This method is used for setting a new value for an item at the indicated coordinates in an ArrayAccess object. The method throws an exception when newValue is not a legal value for the object, or if the object does not support changes.

- `public abstract ArrayAccess subDivide(`
    `int startCoordinates[],`
    `int endCoordinates[])`

    Returns the subset ArrayAccess object for this ArrayAccess. For each dimension n, the endCoordinates[n] must be greater than the startCoordinates[n]. The returned ArrayAccess has its index readjusted to be zero based.

INTERFACE JAVAX.INFOBUS.DATAITEM

```
public interface DataItem
```

This interface helps in providing descriptive information about a data item and methods for identifying the data item. The data described in the DataItem interface is accessed through one of the InfoBus access interfaces, which are ImmediateAccess, ArrayAccess, RowsetAccess, ScrollableRowsetAccess, and DbAccess.

Methods

- `public abstract Object getProperty(String propertyName)`

    Returns the property or the metadata information about the item. The propertyName supplies the name of the property requested and must not contain a * character.

- `public abstract InfoBusEventListener getSource()`

  Returns the source of the data item. It is very important that the source returned by this method be the same as that of the one that calls the InfoBus.fireItemAvailable for this data item, so that the consumers can associate the data item with the InfoBusEvent that announced it.

- `public abstract void release()`

  This method allows a producer to know when a consumer has finished using a data item. Consumers must call this method when they are about to release the last reference to the data item, either directly or indirectly. The reference includes the subitems and the transfer data.

INTERFACE JAVAX.INFOBUS.DATAITEMCHANGELISTENER

```
public interface DataItemChangeListener
```

This interface is implemented by the recipients of data items so that they can register with a data item's optional DataItemChangeManager. DataItemChangeManager helps in sending the change notifications to the DataItemChangeEvents as its data changes. Listeners register via the DataitemChangeManager's addDataItemChangeListener method.

Methods

- `public abstract void dataItemAdded(`
  `        DataItemAddedEvent event)`

  Indicates using the event, the reference of the data item that was added, and the one that gained the data item. The item is added to an aggregate data item like ArrayAccess, JDK collection, and so forth.

- `public abstract void dataItemDeleted(`
  `        DataItemDeletedEvent event)`

  Indicates that an item was deleted from an aggregate data item. Like the dataItemAdded function, the event gives the reference to the items that lost the item and the one that was deleted.

- ```
  public abstract void dataItemRevoked(
              DataItemRevokedEvent event)
  ```
  Indicates if an item has been revoked or is temporarily unavailable.
- ```
  public abstract void dataItemValueChanged(
              DataItemValueChangedEvent event)
  ```
  Indicates a changed value in the data item.
- ```
  public abstract void rowsetCursorMoved(
              RowsetCursorMovedEvent event)
  ```
  Indicates that the cursor for a RowsetAccess item has changed. The event provides the reference to the Rowset data item.

INTERFACE JAVAX.INFOBUS.DATAITEMCHANGEMANAGER

```
public interface DataItemChangeManager
```

This interface manages the DataItemChangeListeners registered by the consumers and provides notifications to the consumer when the data item is changed. Data items that implement this interface must support the registration and unregistration of event listeners.

Methods

- ```
  public abstract void addDataItemChangeListener(
              DataItemChangeListener listener)
  ```
  Adds a listener to the list of objects, which request notifications of modifications to the DataItem's data.
- ```
  public abstract void removeDataItemChangeListener(
              DataItemChangeListener listener)
  ```
  Removes the listener object from the list of objects that request notifications of modifications to the DataItem's data.

INTERFACE JAVAX.INFOBUS.DATAITEMVIEW

```
public interface DataItemView
```

This interface can be used to optimize the management of view of the contents of a particular subset of records. The view is a two-dimensional
```

ArrayAccess data item, which represents the window of data that is currently visible to the consumers. The ViewStart property is used to index the views and access records at any given record position. There is no relationship with the current row of the Rowset and the ViewStart. It is possible to scroll the view without affecting or changing the current row.

Methods

- ```
  public abstract void setViewStart(int absoluteRow)
  ```
  Sets the ViewStart to absoluteRow.
- ```
  public abstract int getViewStart()
  ```
  Returns the current value of the ViewStart property.
- ```
  public abstract ArrayAccess getView(int viewSize)
  ```
  Returns an object that implements a two-dimensional ArrayAccess to represent the row and column view with viewSize rows. The array is only a two-dimensional array that is read only and throws an exception if any attempt is made to set a new value.
- ```
  public abstract void scrollView(int relativeAmount)
  ```
  Changes ViewStart by relativeAmount relative to its current position.

INTERFACE JAVAX.INFOBUS.DBACCESS

```
public interface DbAccess
```

Data items that implement the DbAccess interface represent a database. The methods of this interface include functions to connect to the database, to disconnect from the database, to execute queries, to control transactions, and to validate changes made to the database.

Methods

- ```
  public abstract void connect() throws SQLException
  ```
- ```
  public abstract void connect(
              String url,
              String username,
  ```

```
                        String password)
                        throws SQLException
```
■ `public abstract void connect(`
```
                        String url,
                        Properties info)
                        throws SQLException
```
Connect to the data source using the current connection settings.

■ `public abstract void disconnect() throws SQLException`
Disconnect from the database.

■ `public abstract DriverPropertyInfo[] getPropertyInfo(`
```
                        String url, Properties info)
```
Discovers what connection arguments are required.

■ `public abstract Object excuteRetrieval(`
```
                        String retrieval,
                        String dataItemName,
                        String options)
                        throws SQLException
```
Executes the specified retrieval query and returns the result as a DataItem.

■ `public abstract int executeCommand(`
```
                        String command,
                        String dataItemName)
                        throws SQException
```
Executes the specified nonretrieval query and returns the count of rows affected, or −1 if this is not applicable.

■ `public abstract void beginTransaction()`
Begins an explicit transaction. All transactions are committed only after the call to commitTransaction.

■ `public abstract void commitTransaction()`
```
                        throws SQLException, RowsetValidationEception
```
Commits all changes that were made since the last begin transaction. There may be no such transaction.

■ `public abstract void rollbackTransaction()`
```
                        throws SQLException, RowsetValidationException
```
Undo all changes made since the last beginTransaction.

■ `public abstract void validate()`
```
                        throws SQLException, RoqsetValidationException
```
Validates all the changes made to the database without committing them. This may be done by the data producer without interacting with the database.

- `public abstract void flush()`
         `throws SQLException, RowsetValidationException`
    Explicitly propagate all changes to the database without committing them.

INTERFACE JAVAX.INFOBUS.IMMEDIATEACCESS

`public interface ImmediateAccess`

This interface provides access to those data items that are not collections of other data items and offer methods to extract the contained data as either a string or an object.

Methods

- `public abstract void getPresentationString(Locale locale)`
    Extracts the contained data in the string presentation that includes appropriate formatting of characters like $ for a specified locale. Localization of the symbols and the format are the responsibility of the DataItem and its source.
- `public abstract Object getValueAsObject()`
    Extracts the contained data as an object.
- `public abstract String getValueAsString()`
    Extracts the value contained in a string format. The embedded data is returned as a single string representation.
- `public abstract void setValue(Object newValue)`
         `throws InvalidDataException`
    The method sets a new value for the data in the Immediate Access. The data item whose setValue has been called must do a deep copy of newValue rather than adopt a reference to it.

INTERFACE JAVAX.INFOBUS.INFOBUSDATACONSUMER

`public interface InfoBusDataConsumer`
         `extends InfoBusEventListener`

InfoBus users that wish to seek data from the InfoBusDataProducer do so by implementing the InfoBusDataConsumer interface. An InfoBus-

DataConsumer must track the InfoBus property of the InfoBusMember that obtained the Bus for them, so that if the setInfoBus method is called with a new InfoBus, then the producer will know to register with new Bus and unregister with the old InfoBus.

Methods

- `public abstract void dataItemAvailable(`
        `InfoBusItemAvailable event)`
  The InfoBus class on behalf of a data producer that is announcing the availability of a new data item calls this method. The consumer that obtains a data item from the producer should be prepared to release it when the producer announces the item is being revoked using InfoBusDataConsumer.dataItemRevoked ().

- `public abstract void dataItemRevoked(`
        `InfoBusItemRevokedEvent event)`
  The InfoBus class on behalf of a data producer that is revoking the availability of a previously announced data item calls this method. The consumer that is using this data item should release it upon receiving this notification.

INTERFACE JAVAX.INFOBUS.INFOBUSDATACONTROLLER

        `public interface InfoBusDataController`

This interface allows the user to add custom implementations to optimize the distribution of InfoBusEvents to InfoBusDataProducers and InfoBusDataConsumers. The InfoBus maintains a list of these InfoBusDataControllers and passes every incoming request to this list until one of the data controllers handles the request. DefaultController is always present in a list of data controllers, which is the last controller in the priority to get any request.

Methods

- `public abstract void AddDataConsumer(InfoBusDataConsumer)`

This is called by the InfoBus every time a new InfoBusDataConsumer joins the Bus, so that the Bus can inform the list of controllers of the addition of this consumer.

- `public abstract void AddDataProducer(InfoBusDataProducer)`

  Same as the preceding function except that this time InfoBus informs the controllers about the new producer.

- `public abstract boolean FindDataItem(`
  ```
            String dataItemName,
            DataFlavor flavors[],
            InfoBusDataConsumer consumer,
            Vector founditems)
  ```
  Called by the InfoBus when a consumer wishes to find a data item as specified by the parameter.

- `public abstract boolean findMultpleDataItems(`
  ```
            String dataItemName,
            DataFlavor flavors[],
            InfoBusDataConsumer consumer,
            Vector founditems)
  ```
  Called by the InfoBus when the consumer wishes to find all data items matching the given data item name.

- `public abstract boolean fireItemAvailable(`
  ```
            String dataItemName,
            Dataflavor flavors[],
            InfoBusDataProducer source)
  ```
  Called by the InfoBus when the source producer requests the distribution of an InfoBusItemAvailable event to the consumers on the InfoBus.

- `public abstract boolean fireItemRevoked(`
  ```
            String dataItemName,
            InfoBusDataProducer producer)
  ```
  Called by the InfoBus when a producer requests the distribution of an InfoBusItemRevoked event to the consumers on the InfoBus.

- `public abstract void removeDataConsumer(`
  ```
            InfoBusDataConsumer consumer)
  ```
  Called by the InfoBus each time when the InfoBusDataConsumer leaves the InfoBus so as to inform all the data controllers of the change.

- `public abstract void removeDataProducer(`
  ```
            InfoBusDataProducer producer)
  ```
  Same as the preceding function except for InfoBusDataProducer.

- `public abstract void setConsumerList(Vector consumers)`
  Called once by the InfoBus when the data controller adds itself.
- `public abstract void setProducerList(Vector producers)`
  Called once by the InfoBus when the data controller adds it.

INTERFACE JAVAX.INFOBUS.INFOBUSDATAPRODUCER

```
public interface InfoBusDataProducer
```

Objects that implement this interface act as data providers on an InfoBus. InfoBusDataProducers can announce and revoke the availability of data. They also register with their InfoBus in order to hear requests for data from consumers on the InfoBus.

Methods

- `public abstract void dataItemRequested(`
  `        InfoBusItemRequested event)`
  InfoBus invokes this method on behalf of the data consumer that is requesting data by name. The method on its turn checks if it can supply the data item. If not, it just returns and lets some other data producer handle the event. If the producer is able to cater the request, then it creates an instance of the data item, or gets a reference if the data item already exists.

INTERFACE JAVAX.INFOBUS.INFOBUSEVENTLISTENER

```
public interface InfoBusEventListener
        extends EventListener, PropertyChangeListener
```

This is a base interface for InfoBusDataProducers and InfoBusData-Consumers. As both the data producers and consumers need to track the InfoBus property of the InfoBusMember that obtained the Bus on which they reside, InfoBusEventListener extends PropertyChangeListener.

INTERFACE JAVAX.INFOBUS.INFOBUSMEMBER

```
public interface InfoBusMember
```

The implementation of this interface is provided in the InfoBus-MemberSupport class. All InfoBusMembers are required to implement a constrained property called InfoBus. The InfoBus attempts to set it when a connection is requested by the Member, and the attempt may be vetoed if the property has already been set by a builder tool.

Methods

- ```
  public abstract void setInfoBus( InfoBus newInfoBus)
          throws PropertyVetoException
  ```
  Sets the InfoBus object for this InfoBusMember, if not vetoed. When an InfoBusMember joins an InfoBus, the responding InfoBus uses this method to set the member's InfoBus property to itself.
- ```
  public abstract InfoBus getInfoBus()
  ```
  Method used to get the InfoBus that is currently assigned to the InfoBusMember's InfoBus property.
- ```
  public abstract void addInfoBusVetoableListener(
          VetoableChangeListener vcl)
  ```
  Adds a VetoableChangeListener to the list of listeners that will be alerted whenever the InfoBusMember's setInfoBus method is called.
- ```
  public abstract void removeInfoBusVetoableListener(
          VetoableChangeListener vcl)
  ```
  Removes a VetoableChangeListener from the listeners that will be alerted whenever a listener is removed from the list of available listener from the InfoBus.
- ```
  public abstract void addInfoBusPropertyListener(
          PropertyChangeListener pcl)
  ```
  Adds a PropertyChangeListener that will be alerted whenever the InfoBusMember's setInfoBus method is called and not vetoed.
- ```
  public abstract void removeInfoBusPropertyListener(
          PropertyChangeListener pcl)
  ```

Removes a PropertyChangeListener from the list of listeners requesting notification of InfoBus change.

INTERFACE JAVAX.INFOBUS.INFOBUSPOLICYHELPER

```
public interface InfoBusPolicyHelper
```

Several security decisions and default InfoBus name generation are encapsulated in this interface.

Methods

- `public abstract void canAddDataConsumer(`
        `InfoBus infobus,`
        `InfoBusDataConsumer consumer)`
  Helps in finding out if the specified InfoBus' canAddDataConsumer method can be executed and throws a runtime exception if not.
- `public abstract void canAddDataController(`
        `InfoBus infobus,`
        `InfoBusDataController controller,`
        `int priority)`
  Finds out if specified InfoBus' canAddDataController method can be executed and throws a runtime exception if not.
- `public abstract void canAddDataProducer(`
        `InfoBus infobus,`
        `InfoBusDataProducer producer)`
  Finds out of the specified InfoBus' canAddDataProducer method can be executed and throws a runtime exception if not.
- `public abstract void canFireItemAvailable(`
        `InfoBus infobus,`
        `String dataItemName,`
        `InfoBusDataProducer)`
  Determines if the canFireItemAvailable method of the InfoBus can be executed and raises an exception if not.
- `public abstract void canFireItemRevoked(`
        `InfoBus infobus,`
        `String dataItemName,`
        `InfoBusDataProducer producer)`

Determines if the canFireItemRevoked method of the InfoBus can be executed and raises an exception if not.

- `public abstract void canGet(String busname)`

  Determines if the static InfoBus open method can be executed and throws a runtime exception if not.

- `public abstract void canJoin(`

      `InfoBus infobus,`

      `InfoBusMember member)`

  Determines that for the given InfoBus, the specified InfoBus' join method can be executed.

- `public abstract void canRegister(`

      `InfoBus infobus,`

      `InfoBusMember member)`

  Determines if the specified InfoBus' register method can be executed and throws an exception if not.

- `public abstract void canPropertyChange(`

      `InfoBus infobus,`

      `PropertyChangeEvent event)`

  Determines if the specified InfoBus's propertyChange method can be executed and throws an exception if not.

- `public abstract void canRequestItem(`

      `InfoBus infobus,`

      `String dataItemName,`

      `InfoBusDataConsumer consumer)`

  Determines if the specified InfoBus's canRequestItem method can be executed and throws an exception if not.

- `public abstract String generateDefaultName(Object object)`

  Generates a default InfoBus name from the given object.

INTERFACE JAVAX.INFOBUS.INFOBUSPROPERTYMAP

```
public interface InfoBusPropertyMap
```

This interface is a temporary interface that is designed to provide a mechanism for use with InfoBus 1.1 components that wish to supply properties on DataItemChangeEvents. To use it, the producer implements this interface and provides a reference to the implementation class in the change event constructor.

Methods

- `public abstract Object get(Object key)`
  Returns the object to which the specified key is mapped. Returns null if the map contains no mapping or this key maps to null. Key has to be in a string format; invalid formats will raise ClassCastException exception.

INTERFACE JAVAX.INFOBUS.ROWSETACCESS

`public interface RowsetAccess`

RowsetAccess interface represents a set of rows resulting from a query against the data items. Data items implement this interface to get the query results. The interface contains methods to get the metadata, to read rows, to extract column values, to update rows, to validate changes and send changes to the database, and to obtain a DbAccess object for the associated database.

Methods

- `public abstract boolean canDelete()`
  Determines if deleting rows is allowed.
- `public abstract boolean canInsert()`
  Determines if inserting rows is allowed.
- `public abstract boolean canUpdate()`
  Returns true if modifying the items in all columns in the existing rows is allowed; false otherwise.
- `public abstract boolean canUpdate(String columnName)`
  `            throws ColumnNotFoundException,`
  `            DuplicateColumnException`
- `public abstract boolean canUpdate(int columnNumber)`
  `            throws IndexOutOfBoundsException`
  Returns true if modifying the items in the specified column is allowed; false otherwise.
- `public abstract void deleteRow()`
  `            throws SQLException, RowsetValidationException`
  Deletes the current row.

- `public abstract void flush()`
      `throws SQLException, RowsetValidationException`
  Flush all changes to the underlying database.
- `public abstract int getColumnCount()`
  Returns the number of columns in the Rowset.
- `public abstract String getColumnDatatypeName(`
      `int columnIndex)`
      `throws IndexOutOfBoundsException`
  Given the one-based column index, returns the column's data source specific type name.
- `public abstract int getColumnDatatypeNumber(`
      `int columnIndex)`
      `throws IndexOutOfBoundsException`
  Given the one-based columnIndex, returns the data type for the column using the encoding specified by java.sql.Types.
- `public abstract Object getColumnItem(`
      `int columnIndex)`
      `throws IndexOutOfBoundsException, SQLException`
  Given the one-based column index, returns an object, which can be used to obtain the current value of the specified column.
- `public abstract Object getColumnItem(`
      `String columnName)`
      `throws ColumnNotFoundException,`
      `DuplicateColumnException, SQLException`
  Given the name of the column, returns an object, which can be used to obtain the current value of the column.
- `public abstract String getColumnName(`
      `int columnIndex)`
      `throws IndexOutOfBoundsException`
  Returns the name of the column indicated by columnIndex if a name is available.
- `public abstract DbAccess getDb()`
  Gets the RowsetAccess item's database.
- `public abstract int getHighWaterMark()`
  Returns the total number of rows known to the producer so far.
- `public abstract boolean hasMoreRows()`
  Returns true if there may be more rows to fetch.
- `public abstract void lockRow()`
      `throws SQLException, RowsetValidationException`
  Locks the current row.

- ```
  public abstract void newRow()
                  throws SQLException, RowsetValidationException
  ```
  Creates a new, empty row and set the row cursor to this row.
- ```
  public abstract boolean next()
                  throws SQLException, RowsetValidationException
  ```
  Advances the row cursor to the next row.
- ```
  public abstract void setColumnValue(
              int columnIndex, Object object)
              throws IndexOutOfBoundsException,
              SQLException,
              RowsetValidationException
  ```
  Given the one-based index of a column, sets the value of the column in the current row.
- ```
  public abstract void setColumnValue(
              String columnName,
              Object object)
              throws ColumnNotFoundException,
              DuplicateColumnException,
              SQLException,
              RowsetValidationException
  ```
  Given the name of a column, sets the value of the column in the current row.

INTERFACE JAVAX.INFOBUS.ROWSETVALIDATE

```
public interface RowsetValidate
```

RowsetValidate interface is implemented by data producers that wish to validate the contents of a Rowset data item. This interface is an optional interface, and the consumer can opt not use it.

Methods

- ```
  public abstract void validateCurrentRow()
                  throws RowsetValidationException
  ```
  Explicitly validates data in the current row only.
- ```
  public abstract void validateRowset()
                  throws RowsetValidationException
  ```

The method validates data in the current row that was taken as a result of a set of rows.

INTERFACE JAVAX.INFOBUS.SCROLLABLEROWSETACCESS

```
public interface ScrollableRowsetAccess extends RowsetAccess
```

This interface gives the user the ability to navigate across the Rowset. The interface represents a set of rows that can be navigated backwards and forwards.

Methods

- `public abstract boolean absolute(int rowIndex)`
  `throws SQLException, RowsetValidationException`
  Sets the row cursor to the specified row. If any changes are pending to the currently selected row, then the producer may validate the changes and/or send them to the database before changing the cursor.
- `public abstract boolean first()`
  `throws SQLException, RowsetValidationException`
  Moves the row cursor to the first row. Producer validates and updates the current row if required.
- `public abstract int getBufferSize()`
  Gets the current buffer size. If no buffer size is set, then returns 1.
- `public abstract int getRow()`
  Gets the row number of the current row.
- `public abstract int getRowCount()`
  Gets the total number of rows in the Rowset.
- `public abstract boolean last()`
  `throws SQLException, RowsetValidationException`
  Moves the row cursor to the last row. The producers validate and update the current row if required.
- `public abstract ScrollableRowSetAccess newCursor()`
  Gets a new independent cursor for the Rowset.
- `public abstract boolean previous()`
  `throws SQLException, RowsetValidationException`
  Moves the row cursor to the previous row.

- ■ `public abstract boolean relative( int numRows)`
  `throws SQLException, RowsetValidationException`

  Moves the row cursor forwards or backwards by the specified number of rows.

- ■ `public abstract void setBufferSize(int size)`

  Asks the data provider to keep a specified number of rows immediately available.

The package also consists of 14 classes. Following is the list and the accompanied descriptions of all classes in the package.

CLASS JAVAX.INFOBUS.DATAITEMADDEDEVENT

```
public final class DataItemAddedEvent
            extends DataItemChangeEvent
```

The class describes a change to a data item that is a collection or is being added to a collection. The constructor and the methods are described below.

Constructor

- ■ `public DataItemAddedEvent(`
  `Object source,`
  `Object changedItem,`
  `Object changedCollection,`
  `InfoBusPropertyMap propertyMap)`

  Shows that a new item was added to an aggregate data item (for example, an ArrayAccess or JDK Collection).

Methods

- ■ `public Object getChangedCollection()`

  Returns a reference to the collection data item that lost or gained subitems.

CLASS JAVAX.INFOBUS.DATAITEMCHANGEEVENT

```
public class DataItemChangeEvent extends EventObject
```

This event is propagated by the DataItemChangeManager to all the DataItemChangeListeners that have registered on its addDataItemChangeListener method whenever the data item's data has been modified. The event includes two fields:

source.   The data item change manager that fixed the event.

changedItem.   The data item that has changed.

If the source and the changedItem fields are not equal then the event conveys information about a change in a data item that is in a collection of data items or is itself a collection.

Methods

- `public Object getChangedItem()`
  Returns the DataItem that changed.
- `public Object getProperty(String propertyName)`
  Returns the property or metadata information about the change event. When this method is called, the DataItemChangeEvent in turn calls the get method for either the Map or InfoBusMap provided by the event constructor.
- `public Object getSource()`
  Returns the DataItem that sent the DataItemChangeEvent.

CLASS JAVAX.INFOBUS.DATAITEMCHANGESUPPORT

```
public class DataItemChangeEvent extends Object
```

The class provides support for managing events with DataItemChangeManager by providing methods that manage the event listeners. The class provides specialized methods for firing each type of change notification. A class that implements DataItemChangeManager can delegate the work for its methods to the methods defined here, and various methods in access interface that allow changes to data can fire events using methods defined here.

Member Variables

- protected Vector m_chanageListeners
  A Vector containing all registered DataItemChangeListeners.
- protected Object m_source
  The object that implements DataItemChangeManager, representing the source of the event.

Constructor

- public DataItemChangeSupport(Object source)
  Initializes an event indicating a change to the data item passed as the parameter.

Methods

- public synchronized void addDataItemChangeListener(
              DataItemChangeListener listener)
  Change listener passed as the parameter is added as requested by a consumer or other InfoBus component.
- protected synchronized Enumeration enumerateListeners()
  Returns an enumeration of a clone of the listener list. The clone returned is unaffected by additions or removals to the master list. This method is used by all fire methods.
- public void fireItemAdded(
              Object changedItem,
              Object changedCollection,
              InfoBusPropertyMap propertyMap)
  This method is invoked when one or more new items are being added to a collection. The changedItem indicates the item being added, and the changedCollection indicates the collection that received the new item.
- public void fireItemRevoked(
              Object changedItem,
              InfoBusPropertyMap propertyMap)

This method is invoked when an item or a collection is no longer available. This event is sent to the data item passed during the rendezvous and to all subitems in a collection hierarchy.

■ `public void fireRowsetCursorMoved(`
          `Object changedItem,`
          `InfoBusPropertyMap propertyMap)`

This method is called when a Rowset's cursor has moved to a different row.

■ `public void fireItemValueChanged(`
          `Object changedItem,`
          `InfoBusPropertyMap propertyMap)`

This method is invoked when an item changes value; usually this item is ImmediateAccess.

■ `public synchronized void removeAllListeners()`

This method allows the owner of the data item using the DataItemChangeSupport to force the removal of all registered listeners. It should be called only after those listeners were delivered a DataItemRevoked event by calling DataItemChangeSupport .fireRevokedEvent and an InfoBusItemRevokedEvent was sent on the InfoBus.

■ `public synchronized void removeDataItemChangeListener(`
          `DataItemChangeListener listener)`

Removes the change listener as requested by a consumer or other InfoBus component.

CLASS JAVAX.INFOBUS.DATAITEMDELETEDEVENT

```
public class DataItemDeletedEvent
          extends DataItemChangeEvent
```

Describes a change to a data item that is a collection or is being deleted from a collection.

Constructor

■ `public DataItemDeletedEvent(`
          `Object source,`

```
Object changedItem,
Object changedCollection,
InfoBusPropertyMap propertyMap)
```

Methods

- ```
  public Object getChangedCollection()
  ```
  Returns a reference to the collection data item that lost subitems.

CLASS JAVAX.INFOBUS.DATAITEMREVOKEDEVENT

```
public class DataItemRevokedEvent
            extends DataItemChangeEvent
```

Producer revokes the changedItem. The event should be sent for all listeners for the rendezvous item and for listeners of subitems in the hierarchy. The consumers must cease making calls to this item and release any reference to it. This item differs from DataItemDeleted Event in that the item may be available in the future.

Constructor

- ```
  public DataItemRevokedEvent(
            Object source,
            Object changedItem,
            InfoBusPropertyMap propertyMap)
  ```
  Shows that an item (as well as any sub-items) has been revoked and is temporarily unavailable.

CLASS JAVAX.INFOBUS.DATAITEMVALUECHANGEDEVENT

```
public final class DataItemValueChangedEvent
            extends DataItemChangeEvent
```

Class describes the change in a data item's value. If the data item is a collection, a value change is noted when one of the members of the collection changes value. Additions and removals from the list are not noted as value changes.

Constructor

- public DataItemValueChangedEvent(
                Object source,
                Object changedItem,
                InfoBusPropertyMap propertyMap)

Indicates that a data item value has been changed.

CLASS JAVAX.INFOBUS.DEFAULTPOLICY

```
public class DefaultPolicy extends Object
            implements InfoBusPolicyHelper
```

The DefaultPolicy class generates the default InfoBus name based on DOCBASE from an AppletContext. This class implements the InfoBusPolicyHelper interface and is a policy helper that is used if the javax-.infobus.InfoBusPolicy system property is nonexistent or unreadable.

Constructor

- public DefaultPolicy()

Methods

- public void canAddDataConsumer(
                InfoBus infobus,
                InfoBusDataConsumer consumer)
- public void canAddDataController(
                InfoBus infobus,
                InfoBusDataController controller)
- public void canAddDataProducer(
                InfoBus infobus,
                InfoBusDataProducer producer)

- ▪ `public void canFireItemAvailable(`
                `InfoBus infobus,`
                `String dataItemName,`
                `InfoBusDataProducer producer)`
- ▪ `public void canFireItemRevoked(`
                `InfoBus infobus,`
                `String dataItemName,`
                `InfoBusDataProducer producer)`
- ▪ `public void canGet(String busName)`
- ▪ `public void canJoin(InfoBus infobus, InfoBusMember member)`
- ▪ `public void canPropertyChange(`
                `InfoBus infobus,`
                `PropertyChangeEvent event)`
- ▪ `public void canRegister(`
                `InfoBus infobus,`
                `InfoBusMember member)`
- ▪ `public void canRequestItem(`
                `InfoBus infobus,`
                `String dataItemName,`
                `InfoBusDataConsumer consumer)`
- ▪ `public String generateDefaultName(Object object)`

CLASS JAVAX.INFOBUS.INFOBUS

```
public final class InfoBus extends Object
            implements PropertyChangeListener
```

An InfoBus object maintains a list of InfoBusMembers that have attached to it and enables communication among those members. The members use methods provided by the InfoBus to create InfoBusEvents, which are distributed to other members to request, announce, and revoke the data items.

InfoBus members should know of an InfoBus, but can call on InfoBus .get to find the InfoBus they need.

InfoBus provides a security module called InfoBusPolicyHelper that determines which methods called on the InfoBus perform the permission checking. If the policy helper in use determines that a caller does not have the proper security clearance to perform the requested action, then it will throw a RuntimeException. The policy helper can inspect all methods on the InfoBus.

Member Variables

- `public static final int HIGH_PRIORITY`
- `public static final int LOW_PRIORITY`
- `public static final int MEDIUM_PRIORITY`
- `public static final int MONITOR_PRIORITY`
- `public static final int VERY_HIGH_PRIORITY`
- `public static final int VERY_LOW_PRIORITY`

  A priority for a data controller.

Methods

- `public synchronized void addDataConsumer(`

  `InfoBusDataConsumer consumer)`

  Registers an InfoBusDataConsumer with the InfoBus, so that the consumers can receive announcements of data availability.

- `public synchronized void addDataController(`

  `InfoBusDataController controller,`

  `int priority)`

  `throws InfoBusMembershipException`

  Adds and registers the Data Controller to the InfoBus, adding to the list of controllers sorted by priority.

- `public synchronized void addDataProducer(`

  `InfoBusDataProducer producer)`

  Adds and registers an InfoBusDataProducer on the InfoBus, so that the producer can receive request notifications from the consumers in the form of InfoBusItemRequestedEvents.

- `public Object findDataItem(`

  `String dataItemName,`

  `FataFlavor flavors[],`

  `InfoBusDataConsumer consumer)`

- `public Object findDataItem(`

  `String dataItemName,`

  `DataFlavor flavors[],`

  `InfoBusDataConsumer consumer,`

  `InfoBusDataProducer target)`

- `public Object findDataItem(`

  `String dataItemName,`

  `DataFlavor flavors[],`

```
        InfoBusDataConsumer consumer,

        Vector targets)
```

Finds a data item for the given parameter by creating an InfoBusItemRequestedEvent and distributing it to producers on the Bus. InfoBusDataConsumer calls this function.

- `public Object[] findMultipleDataItems(`

```
        String dataItemName,

        FataFlavor flavors[],

        InfoBusDataConsumer consumer)
```

Finds all available data items for the given data item name. The function polls all producers and returns an array of data items containing all responses.

- `public void fireItemAvailable(`

```
        String dataItemName,

        DataFlavor flavors[],

        InfoBusDataProducer producer)
```

- `public void fireItemAvailable(`

```
        String dataItemName,

        DataFlavor flavors[],

        InfoBusDataProducer producer,

        InfoBusDataConsumer target)
```

- `public void fireItemAvailable(`

```
        String dataItemName,

        DataFlavor flavors[],

        InfoBusDataProducer source,

        Vector targets)
```

Announces the availability of a data item by creating an InfoBusItemAvailableEvent and sending it to all registered InfoBusDataConsumers. If the target consumer is specified, then sends the message to the target consumer.

- `public void fireItemRevoked(`

```
        String dataItemName,

        InfoBusDataProducer source)
```

- `public void fireItemRevoked(`

```
        String dataItemName,

        InfoBusDataProducer source,

        InfoBusDataConsumer target)
```

- `public void fireItemRevoked(`

```
        String dataItemName,
```

```
               InfoBusDataProducer source,
               Vector targets)
```
The function notifies that a data item will no longer be available from a given source. The InfoBus creates an InfoBusRevoked-Event and distributes it to the registered InfoBusConsumers. If the target is specified, then the InfoBus distributes the event to the concerned consumers.

- `public static synchronized InfoBus get(Component component)`

  Returns the default InfoBus for a component. The function determines the default Bus name from the given component and then searches for an existing InfoBus with that Bus name on it. If no match is found for that name, then creates a new InfoBus by that name and returns it.

- `public static synchronized InfoBus get(String busname)`

  Returns a named InfoBus. If no such InfoBus is found, then creates a new InfoBus by that name and returns it.

- `public String getName()`

  The function returns the string used as the unique identifier for this InfoBus.

- `public synchronized void join(InfoBusMember member)`
  ```
                    throws PropertyVetoException
  ```
  The function joins the member passed as the parameter to the InfoBus on which the method was called. The InfoBus calls the InfoBusMember's setInfoBus() method to set itself as the value for the member's InfoBus property.

- `public synchronized void leave(InfoBusMember member)`
  ```
                    throws ProperyVetoException
  ```
  Removes an InfoBusMember from the InfoBus. The member that wishes to remove itself from the InfoBus calls leave(). The InfoBus that has leave() method called calls the setInfoBus method with null passed as the member parameter on the InfoBusMember specified and removes itself as a listener on the member.

- `public void propertyChange(PropertyChangeEvent event)`

  The event passed as the parameter notifies about the InfoBus changes. The PropertyChangeEvent is constructed with the String InfoBus as its property name and the InfoBusMember as its source.

- `public synchronized void register(InfoBusMember member)`

    The function is used for registering the InfoBusMember on the InfoBus' list of active members and also causes the InfoBus to register itself as a PropertyChangeListener on the InfoBusMember's InfoBus property.

- `public synchronized void release()`

    Releases the artificial reference to an InfoBus instance set by calling the function get(). The function has to be called only after join and/or setInfoBus attempts using the InfoBus instance have completed. In case there are no registered members, event listeners, or data controllers for this InfoBus instance, this method allows this InfoBus instance to be garbage collected.

- `public synchronized void removeDataConsumer(`
    `            InfoBusDataConsumer consumer)`

    Removes the consumer passed as the parameter from the distribution list for InfoBusItemAvailableEvents and InfoBusItemRevokedEvents.

- `public synchronized void removeDataController(`
    `            InfoBusDataController controller)`

    Removes a controller from the list of InfoBusDataControllers registered on this InfoBus. If no such controller is registered, then nothing happens.

- `public synchronized void removeDataProducers(`
    `            InfoBusDataProducer producer)`

    Removes an InfoBusDataProducer from the distribution list for InfoBusItemRequestedEvents.

CLASS JAVAX.INFOBUS.INFOBUSEVENT

```
public class InfoBusEvent extends EventObject
```

This is a base class used commonly for events used in InfoBus communication. The InfoBusEvents are distributed via an InfoBus to InfoBusEventListeners registered on that Bus.

Methods

- ```
  public String getDataItemName()
  ```
  Returns a string that is used as the identifier for the data item that the InfoBusEvent concerns.

CLASS JAVAX.INFOBUS.INFOBUSITEMAVAILABLEEVENT

```
public class InfoBusItemAvailableEvent extends InfoBusEvent
```

This event is used for notifying the InfoBusDataConsumers that a named data item is available from an InfoBusDataProducer and will be returned on request.

Methods

- ```
  public Dataflavor[] getDataFlavors()
  ```
  This method provides a way for the consumer to consider the type of information being announced as available before requesting a data item. It returns a reference to an array of DataFlavor objects that describe the formats that the producer can provide, either in the data item itself or by the way of Transferable.getTransfer-Data ().
- ```
  public InfoBusDataProducer getSourceAsProducer()
  ```
  Returns the source of the event InfoBusItemAvailableEvent, which is always InfoBusDataProducer.
- ```
  public Object requestDataItem(
          InfoBusDataConsumer consumer,
          DataFlavor flavors[])
  ```
  Sends an event InfoBusItemRequestedEvent directly to the producer that announced the item's availability. This way is more efficient than broadcasting a request event. The flavor array specifies the flavor the consumer can use. The producer may choose to not return the data item if it cannot provide the data in one of the flavors requested.

CLASS JAVAX.INFOBUS.INFOBUSITEMREQUESTEDEVENT

```
public class InfoBusItemRequestedEvent extends InfoBusEvent
```

The event is sent for the data consumer to find a named data item it would like to receive. The producer can respond to this event by setting the data item field in this event with the requested data item object, using the setDataItemMethod.

Methods

- `public Dataflavor[] getDataFlavors()`
  The producers use this method to find out the flavors that the consumer prefers. If this method returns null, then the consumer did not specify any DataFlavor preferences when it requested the event.
- `public Object getDataItem()`
  The method extracts the data item that was provided in response to the request.
- `public InfoBusDataConsumer getSourceAsConsumer()`
  Returns the source of this requested event.
- `public void setDataItem(Object item)`
  Sets the item as the value for the data item field for the event. This method can be called only once when the data item field is null. An attempt made to replace a non-null data item will have no effect.

CLASS JAVAX.INFOBUS.INFOBUSITEMREVOKEDEVENT

```
public class InfoBusItemRevokedEvent extends InfoBusEvent
```

This event is sent for the data producer by the InfoBus to announce the revocation of a previously announced item. This event is used later then by controllers and consumers who may wish to update their lists with the updated status about the data item.

Methods

- `public InfoBusDataProducer getSourceAsProducer()`
  Returns the source as the return value of the InfoBusItemRe-vokedEvent, which is always an InfoBusDataProducer.

CLASS JAVAX.INFOBUS.INFOBUSMEMBERSUPPORT

```
public class InfoBusMemberSupport extends Object
            implements InfoBusMember
```

The class implements the methods of InfoBusMember interface. It encapsulates the InfoBus property, PropertyChangeSupport, and VetoableChangeSupport objects to ensure the property is bound and constrained.

Member Variables

- `Protected InfoBus m_infoBus`
- `Protected PropertyChangeSupport m_propSupport`
- `Property VetoableChangeSupport m_VetoSupport`
- `Protected InfoBusMember m_sourceRef`

Constructor

- `public InfoBusMemberSupport(InfoBusMember member)`
  Constructor for the class. The member passed as the parameter allows the parent of InfoBusMemberSupport to implement the InfoBusMember interface and have the parent instead of the InfoBusMemberSupport object specified in all Property-ChangeEvents and on the InfoBus itself. If the member is null, the InfoBusMemberSupport object is specified in those cases.

Methods

- `public void addInfoBusPropertyListener(`
  `        PropertyChangeListener pcl)`

  Adds a PropertyChangeListener that will be alerted whenever the InfoBusMember's setInfoBus method is called and not vetoed.

- `public void addInfoBusVetoableListener(`
  `        VetoableChangeListener vcl)`

  Adds a VetoableChangeListener to the list of listeners whenever the InfoBusMember's setInfoBus method is called.

- `public InfoBus getInfoBus()`

  Returns the InfoBus, which is currently assigned, to the InfoBus-MemberSupport's InfoBus property.

- `public synchronized void joinInfoBus(`
  `        Component component)`
  `        throws InfoBusMembershipException,`
  `        PropertyVetoException`

- `public synchronized void joinInfoBus(`
  `        String busname)`
  `        throws InfoBusMembershipException,`
  `        PropertyVetoException`

  Attempts to join the InfoBus depending on the parameter provided. If a component is passed as a parameter, then tries to obtain the default InfoBus and join it; else uses the Bus name provided to join that Bus.

- `public synchronized void leaveInfoBus()`
  `        throws InfoBusMembershipException,`
  `        PropertyVetoException`

  Invokes the leave method on the InfoBus to which this InfoBus-MemberSupport is attached. This method is called when the holder of the InfoBusMemberSupport is shutting down or finalizing to release unneeded resources.

- `public void removeInfoBusPropertyListener(`
  `        PropertyChangeListener pcl)`

  Removes a PropertyChangeListener from the list of listeners requesting notification of an InfoBus change.

- `public void removeInfoBusVetoableListener(`
  `        VetoableChangeListener vcl)`

Removes a VetoableChangeListener from the list of listeners that will be alerted whenever the InfoBusMember's setInfoBus method is called.

- `public synchronized void setInfoBus( InfoBus newInfoBus)`
        `throws PropertyVetoException`

Attempts to register with the InfoBus and set the InfoBus property. If it is successful, then sends notifications to all registered PropertyChangeListeners; else throws the PropertyVetoException if the attempt is denied.

CLASS JAVAX.INFOBUS.ROWSETCURSORMOVEDEVENT

```
public final class RowsetCursorMovedEvent
        extends DataItemChangeEvent
```

Indicates a change in a data item's value. If the data item is a collection, then this is used only when one or more existing items have been modified. Additions and deletions from the collection do not count as changes.

Constructor

- `public RowsetCursorMovedEvent(`
        `Object Source,`
        `Object changedItem,`
        `InfoBusPropertyMap propertyMap)`

The package also consists of seven exceptions. Following is the list of all available exceptions and their respective descriptions.

CLASS JAVAX.INFOBUS.COLUMNNOTFOUNDEXCEPTION

```
public class ColumnNotFoundException extends Exception
```

Thrown by a RowsetAccess object when a specified column does not exist.

Constructor

- `public ColumnNotFoundException(String s)`
  Creates a ColumnNotFoundException, with the string describing as the message details.

CLASS JAVAX.INFOBUS.DUPLICATECOLUMNEXCEPTION

```
public class DuplicateColumnException extends Exception
```

Thrown by a RowsetAccess object when more than one column exists matching a given name.

Constructor

- `public DuplicateColumnException(String s)`
  Creates a DuplicateColumnException, with the string describing as the message details.

CLASS JAVAX.INFOBUS.INFOBUSMEMBERSHIPEXCEPTION

```
public class InfoBusMembershipException extends Exception
```

Thrown if an inactive InfoBus is tried to be joined or if membership is not permitted for the joiner.

Constructor

- `public InfoBusMembershipException(String s)`
  Creates an InfoBusMembershipException, with the string describing as the message details.

CLASS JAVAX.INFOBUS.INVALIDDATAEXCEPTION

```
public class InvalidDataException extends Exception
```

Thrown by the data item if anyone attempting to change the contents of the data item has proposed a new value that is illegal.

Constructor

- `public InvalidDataexception(String s)`
  Creates an InvalidDataException, with the string describing as the message details.

CLASS JAVAX.INFOBUS.ROWSETVALIDATIONEXCEPTION

```
public class RowsetValidationException
            extends InvalidDataException
```

Thrown by the RowsetAccess DataItem when a method that modifies values fails.

Constructor

- `public RowsetValidationException(`
  `        String message,`
  `        RowsetAccess rowset,`
  `        InfoBusPropertyMap map)`
  Creates a new RowsetValidationException.

Methods

- `public RowsetAccess getRowset()`
  Returns the RowsetAccess object on which the validation exception was detected.

- `public Object getProperty(String propertyName)`
  Gets more information about the validation exception. The data provider overrides this method.

CLASS JAVAX.INFOBUS.STALEINFOBUSEXCEPTION

```
public class StaleInfoBusException extends RuntimeException
```

Exception is thrown if InfoBus instance involved is removed from the active list, thus making the InfoBus stale for the end user.

Constructor

- `Public StaleInfoBusException(String s)`
  Creates a new StaleInfoBusException.

CLASS JAVAX.INFOBUS.UNSUPPORTEDOPERATIONEXCEPTION

```
public class UnsupportedOperationException
            extends RuntimeException
```

Exception is thrown if the data item or the InfoBus participant does not support a method called.

Constructor

- `Public UnsupportedOperationException (String s)`
  Creates a new UnsupportedOperationException.

What's on
the CD-ROM?

The CD-ROM contains all the code examples that we presented in the book. In addition, it contains over 300 megabytes of third-party trial software:

IBM VisualAge for Java Entry for Windows version 1. This software enables you to create Java and JavaBeans applications easily.

MindQ's Java Tutorial. This tutorial software teaches you how to work with Java in a visually enriched environment.

IBM's VisualAge WebRunner Toolkit version 2.0. VisualAge WebRunner Toolkit works with Visual Age for Java software and helps you create JavaBeans and Servlets.

Inprise's VisiBroker for Java version 3.2. VisiBroker provides a customizable standards based infrastructure on which to build distributed applications.

IONA's OrbixWeb 3. OrbixWeb from IONA Technologies helps Java developers create flexible and scalable CORBA applications.

IONA's Orbix 2.3. Also from IONA, Orbix 2 helps you create CORBA applications for distributed environments.

WHAT IS THIRD-PARTY TRIAL SOFTWARE?

All the third-party software applications are offered on a trial basis. This means that you can use them only for a predetermined amount of time. Under no means can you duplicate or distribute them. These are commercial applications and are not freeware.

HARDWARE REQUIREMENTS

The software included (except for the book code examples) on the CD are Windows specific. You must have a machine that has the following:

- Windows 95 or NT
- Pentium 100 or better
- 100MB space (minimum)
- 32 RAM (minimum)

If you are looking to use the software for other platforms, please visit the Web sites of the representative software vendors (noted in the readme.htm file in the root directory of the CD).

INSTALLING THE SOFTWARE

- The book examples are located by chapter number under the directory called *Book_Ex* (i.e., chap01 directory contains the code for the examples in chapter 1).
- To install IBM VisualAge for Java, run the **setup.exe** file from the *IBM VAJ\SETUP* directory.
- To install MindQ Java Tutorial, double click on **setup.exe** located in the directory *IBM VAJ/Mindq*.
- Instructions for installing IBM Web Runner are located in the **ReadMe.html** file found in the *IBM Web Runner* directory.
- To install IONA OrbixWeb, execute the **ow30prof.exe** program found in the *orbixweb\WIN32* directory.
- To install IONA Orbix2, execute the **setup.exe** file found in *the \orbix 2\ORBIX* directory.

USING THE SOFTWARE

When you install each piece of software, you will notice that there is a readme file that will give you detailed explanations for how to use the software. For more information on any of the software, please visit the Web sites of the representative software vendors. The URLs are located in the readme.htm file in the root directory of the CD-ROM.

USER ASSISTANCE AND INFORMATION

The software accompanying this book is being provided as is without warranty or support of any kind. Should you require basic installation assistance, or if your media is defective, please call our product support number at (212) 850-6194 weekdays between 9 A.M. and 4 P.M. Eastern Standard Time. Or, we can be reached via e-mail at: **wprtusw@wiley.com**.

To place additional orders or to request information about other Wiley products, please call (800) 879-4539.

Index

Orbix® Evaluation
License Agreement

READ THE TERMS OF THIS ORBIX EVALUATION LICENSE AGREEMENT (THE "AGREEMENT") CAREFULLY BEFORE INSTALLING THE SOFTWARE CONTAINED IN THE PROGRAM DISKETTES, TAPES AND/OR COMPACT DISCS IN THIS PACKAGE. THE ORBIX SOFTWARE (THE "SOFTWARE") AND THE ACCOMPANYING DOCUMENTATION (THE "RELATED MATERIALS") IN THIS PACKAGE (COLLECTIVELY, THE "PRODUCT") ARE PROTECTED BY UNITED STATES, IRISH AND INTERNATIONAL COPYRIGHT LAWS, AND THE COPYRIGHTS AND OTHER INTELLECTUAL PROPERTY RIGHTS ARE OWNED BY IONA TECHNOLOGIES PLC. OF 8-10 LOWER PEMBROKE ST., DUBLIN 2, IRELAND ("IONA"). THE PRODUCT IS COPYRIGHTED AND LICENSED (NOT SOLD). BY INSTALLING THE SOFTWARE, YOU (THE "CUSTOMER") ARE ACCEPTING AND AGREEING TO THE TERMS OF THIS AGREEMENT. IF YOU ARE NOT WILLING TO BE BOUND BY THE TERMS OF THIS AGREEMENT, YOU SHOULD PROMPTLY RETURN THE PRODUCT (IN ITS ORIGINAL PACKAGE) WITH YOUR DATED RECEIPT WITHIN FOURTEEN DAYS, AND YOU WILL RECEIVE A REFUND OF THE AMOUNT YOU PAID.

1. OWNERSHIP

   The Software (including any header files and demonstration code that may be included) and Related Materials, and all associated copyrights and other intellectual property rights, are the property of IONA or its licensers. Customer acquires no title, right or interest in the Software or Related Materials other than the license granted herein by IONA and the title to the media upon which the Software is delivered.

2. PROPRIETARY NOTICES

Customer shall not remove any trademark, tradename, copyright notice or other proprietary notice from the Software or Related Materials, and shall be responsible for the conservation of the same on all copies of the Software and Related Materials received under this Agreement and on any back-up copy of the Software created in accordance with this Agreement. Customer may not reproduce any portion of the Software or Related Materials, except as permitted by this Agreement.

3. LICENSE

(a)   Subject to the terms and conditions of this Agreement, and payment of the appropriate license fees, IONA hereby grants to Customer a nonexclusive, nontransferable, internal, limited license to evaluate the Software and Related Materials at Customer's premises only. The Software and Related Materials are provided for evaluation purposes only; NO PRODUCT DEVELOPMENT WORK IS AUTHORIZED UNDER THIS AGREEMENT, whether such developed software is used internally or distributed to end users. (b) The source code of the Software (other than included header files and demonstration code) and design documentation are confidential and proprietary information and trade secrets of IONA, its suppliers and/or licensers, are never considered part of the Software, and are neither delivered to Customer nor under any circumstances licensed to Customer hereunder.

4. COPY RESTRICTIONS AND OTHER RESTRICTIONS

(a) Customer may make copies of the Software in machine-readable, object code form, as permitted by applicable law, solely for backup or archival purposes, provided that such copies of the Software shall include all applicable copyright, trademark and other proprietary notices of IONA in accordance with Section 2 above. Customer may not copy any of the Related Materials. Customer may obtain additional copies of any Related Materials from IONA or an authorized IONA distributor upon payment of the prices in effect at the time of ordering. (b) Customer will not display or disclose the Product to third parties, rent, lease, loan, sublicense, modify, adapt, translate, reverse engineer, disassemble or decompile the Product or any portion thereof, or create derivative works of the Product even for purposes of interoperability or error correction. In the event that Customer wishes information relating to the Software for purposes of achieving interoperability with independently created computer software, Customer may make a written request to IONA for such information. Customer shall promptly report to IONA any actual or suspected violation of this section and shall take further steps as may reasonably be requested by IONA to prevent or remedy any such violation.

5. **U.S. GOVERNMENT END-USERS**

    The Software and the Related Materials are "commercial items" as that term is defined in 48 C.F.R. 2.101 (October 1995) consisting of "commercial computer software" and "commercial computer software documentation" as such terms are used in 48 C.F.R. 12.212 (September 1995). Consistent with 48 C.F.R. 12.212 and 48 C.F.R. 227.7202-1, 227.7202-3 and 227.7202-4 (June 1995), if the licensee hereunder is the U.S. Government or any agency or department thereof, the Software and the Related Materials are licensed hereunder (i) only as a commercial item, and (ii) with only those rights as are granted to all other end users pursuant to the terms and conditions of this Agreement.

6. **SUPPORT**

    Support services for the Software are available from IONA for the term of this Agreement and may be requested by Customer by means of Electronic Mail (E-Mail) or Facsimile. As an alternative, queries may be made in writing to IONA at the address set forth above. Customer acknowledges and agrees that any comments and/or suggestions relating to the Software and/or Related Documentation made to IONA shall in no way convey any ownership of or rights over any IONA products or future products.

7. **DURATION**

    This Agreement is effective from the date this package of Software is opened by Customer (or, if unpackaged, the date this Software is installed by Customer) and shall remain in force for sixty (60) days unless and to the extent that any other period is specified by IONA in writing and unless earlier terminated as provided for herein.

8. **LIMITED WARRANTY**

    (a) IONA warrants that the medium on which the Software is recorded is free from defects in materials or workmanship under normal use and service for a period of sixty (60) days from the date Customer has obtained the Software. If Customer discovers any physical defects in the medium on which the Software is recorded, IONA will replace such medium at no charge to Customer, provided that Customer returns the item to be replaced with proof of payment to IONA during the sixty (60) day period after Customer has obtained the Software. This warranty gives Customer specific legal rights. Customer may also have rights which vary from jurisdiction to jurisdiction. THIS RIGHT OF REPLACEMENT IS CUSTOMER'S EXCLUSIVE REMEDY AND IONA'S ONLY LIABILITY FOR ANY DEFECTS IN THE MEDIUM. (b) IONA SPECIFICALLY DISCLAIMS ANY WARRANTY THAT THE FUNCTIONS CONTAINED IN THE SOFTWARE OR THE RESULTS OF USE WILL MEET CUSTOMER'S REQUIREMENTS, OR THAT THE OPERATION OF THE SOFTWARE WILL BE UNINTERRUPTED OR ERROR FREE. EXCEPT AS EXPRESSLY SET FORTH ABOVE, THE PRODUCT IS PROVIDED TO CUSTOMER "AS IS" WITHOUT WARRANTY OF ANY KIND, EITHER EXPRESS OR IMPLIED, STATUTORY OR OTHERWISE, INCLUDING, BUT NOT LIMITED TO THE IMPLIED WARRANTIES OF MERCHANTABILITY, FITNESS FOR A PARTICULAR PURPOSE AND NON-INFRINGEMENT. THE ENTIRE RISK AS TO THE SUITABILITY, QUALITY AND PERFORMANCE OF THE PRODUCT IS WITH CUSTOMER AND NOT WITH IONA. SOME JURISDICTIONS DO NOT ALLOW THE EXCLUSION OF IMPLIED WARRANTIES, SO SUCH EXCLUSION MAY NOT APPLY TO YOU.

9. LIMITED LIABILITY

IN NO EVENT SHALL IONA, ITS SUPPLIERS OR LICENSORS BE LIABLE FOR ANY INDIRECT, INCIDENTAL, CONSEQUENTIAL, SPECIAL, PUNITIVE OR EXEMPLARY DAMAGES (INCLUDING, BUT NOT LIMITED TO, DAMAGES FOR LOSS OF BUSINESS PROFITS, BUSINESS INTERRUPTION, LOSS OF BUSINESS INFORMATION, DATA, GOODWILL OR OTHER PECUNIARY LOSS) ARISING OUT OF THE USE OR INABILITY TO USE THE SOFTWARE, EVEN IF FORESEEABLE OR IF IONA HAS BEEN ADVISED OF THE POSSIBILITY OF SUCH DAMAGES. IN NO EVENT SHALL IONA BE RESPONSIBLE OR HELD LIABLE FOR ANY DAMAGES RESULTING FROM PHYSICAL DAMAGE TO TANGIBLE PROPERTY OR DEATH OR INJURY OF ANY PERSON WHETHER ARISING FROM IONAÆS NEGLIGENCE OR OTHERWISE. BECAUSE SOME JURISDICTIONS DO NOT ALLOW CERTAIN OF THE ABOVE EXCLUSIONS OR LIMITATIONS OF

LIABILITY, THE ABOVE LIMITATIONS MAY NOT APPLY TO YOU. IN THE EVENT THAT IONA IS HELD LIABLE UNDER THIS AGREEMENT, IONA'S, ITS SUPPLIERS' AND LICENSORS' LIABILITY SHALL BE LIMITED TO THE PRICE PAID BY THE CUSTOMER FOR THE PRODUCT SUPPLIED.

10. ASSIGNMENT

This Agreement and any rights granted hereunder may not be assigned, sub-licensed or otherwise transferred by Customer to any third party without the prior written consent of IONA. IONA may assign or transfer its rights and obligations under this Agreement at any time without notice to or the consent of Customer.

11. TERMINATION

(a) This Agreement and the license granted hereunder may be terminated by IONA upon written notice to Customer in the event Customer breaches any of the provisions of this Agreement. (b) Upon termination of this Agreement and of the license granted hereunder, Customer shall cease any further use of the Software, and must return to IONA or destroy, as requested by IONA, all copies of the Software and Related Materials in any form in Customer's possession or control. (c) The provisions of Sections 1, 2, 8, 9, and 11 through 16 and the definitions of this Agreement shall survive the termination of this Agreement (for any reason). Customer must promptly pay to IONA any amounts payable by Customer and damages incurred by IONA.

12. AMENDMENT; WAIVER

No modification or waiver of any provision of this Agreement shall be binding on either party unless specifically agreed upon in a writing and signed by both parties hereto. Any failure or delay by IONA to exercise or enforce any of the rights or remedies granted hereunder will not operate as a waiver thereof. No waiver by IONA of any breach of this Agreement will operate as a waiver of any other or subsequent breach.

13. SEVERABILITY

If any provision of this Agreement is found invalid or unenforceable, that provision will be reformed, construed and enforced to the maximum extent permissible, and the other provisions of this Agreement will remain in full force and effect.

14. LAW AND JURISDICTION

This Agreement shall be governed by and construed in accordance with the laws of Ireland, and the parties hereby irrevocably submit to the venue and jurisdiction of the courts of Ireland.

15. EXPORT PROHIBITION

Customer agrees that unless prior written authorization is obtained from the relevant governmental authority, it will not export, re-export, or transship, directly or indirectly, the Product or any technical data disclosed or provided to Customer, or the direct product of such technical data to or from any other country on as to which there is an applicable embargo or other trade restriction imposed by the US or other Government. US or other Government has placed an embargo or other restriction against the shipment of products or types of products, which is in effect during the term of this Agreement.

16. ENTIRE AGREEMENT

Customer has read this Agreement and agrees to be bound by its terms, and further agrees that, unless the parties have entered into a signed development license agreement relating to the subject matter hereof (a "Signed Agreement"), this Agreement (and the Orbix Runtime License Agreement, if applicable) constitutes the complete and entire agreement of the parties and supersedes all previous communications, oral or written, and all other communications between them relating to the subject matter hereof. If, however, the parties have entered into a Signed Agreement, to the extent of any inconsistency, such Signed Agreement shall take precedence over the terms of this Agreement. No representations or statements of any kind made by either party, which are not expressly stated herein, shall be binding on such party.

Inprise Corporation TRIAL EDITION SOFTWARE

LICENSE STATEMENT

YOUR USE OF THE TRIAL EDITION SOFTWARE DISTRIBUTED WITH THIS LICENSE IS SUBJECT TO ALL OF THE TERMS AND CONDITIONS OF THIS LICENSE STATEMNT. IF YOU DO NOT AGREE TO ALL OF THE TERMS AND CONDITIONS OF THIS STATEMENT, DO NOT USE THE SOFTWARE.

1. This Software is protected by copyright law and international coyright treaty. Therefore, you must treat this Software just like a book, except that you may copy it onto a computer to be used and you may make archive copies of the Software for the sole purpose of backing up our Software and protecting your investment from loss. Your use of this software is limited to evaluation and trial use purposes only.

   FURTHER, THIS SOFTWARE CONTAINS A TIME-OUT FEATURE THAT DISABLES ITS OPERATION AFTER A CERTAIN PERIOD OF TIME. A TEXT FILE DELIVERED WITH THE SOFTWARE WILL STATE THE TIME PERIOD AND/OR SPECIFIC DATE ("EVALUATION PERIOD") ON WHICH THE SOFTWARE WILL EXPIRE. Though Inprise does not offer technical support for the Software, we welcome your feedback.

   If the Software is an Inprise development tool, you can write and compile applications for your own personal use on the computer on which you have installed the software, but you do not have a right to distribute or otherwise share those applications or any files of the Software which may be required to support those applications. APPLICATIONS

THAT YOU CREATE MAY REQUIRE THE SOFTWARE IN ORDER TO RUN. UPON EXPIRATION OF THE EVALUATION PERIOD, THOSE APPLICATIONS WILL NO LONGER RUN. You should therefore take precautions to avoid any loss of data that might result.

2. INPRISE MAKES NO REPRESENTATIONS ABOUIT THE SUITABILITY OF THIS SOFTWARE OR ABOUT ANY CONTENT OR INFORMATION MADE ACCESSIBLE BY THE SOFTWARE, FOR ANY PURPOSE. THE SOFTWARE IS PROVIDED 'AS IS' WITHOUT EXPRESS OR IMPLIED WARRANTIES, INCLUDING WARRANTIES OF MERCHANTABILITY AND FITNESS FOR A PARTICULAR PURPOSE OR NONINFRINGEMENT. THIS SOFTWARE IS PROVIDED GRATUITOUSLY AND, ACCORDINGLY, INPRISE SHALL NOT BE LIABLE UNDER ANY THEORY FOR ANY DAMAGES SUFFERED BY YOU OR ANY USER OF THE SOFTWARE. INPRISE WILL NOT SUPPORT THIS SOFTWARE AND IS UNDER NO OBLIGATION TO ISSUE UPDATES TO THIS SOFTWARE.

3. While Inprise intents to distribute (or may have already distributed) a commercial release of the Software, Inprise reserves the right at any time to not release a commercial release of the Software or, if released, to alter prices, features, specifications, capabilities, functions, licensing terms, release dates, general availablity or other characteristics of the commercial release.

4. Title, ownership rights, and intellectual property rights in and to the Software shall remain in Inprise and/or its suppliers. You agree to abide by the copyright law and all other applicable laws of the United States including, but not limited to, export control laws. You acknowledge that the Software in source code form remains a confidential trade secret of Inprise and/or it suppliers and therefore you agree not to modify the Software or attempt to decipher, decompile, disassemble or reverse engineer the Software, except to the extent applicable laws specifically prohibit such restriction.

5. Upon expiration of the Evaluation Period, you agree to destroy or erase the Softwre, and to not re-install a new copy of the Software. This statement shall be governed by and construed in acccordance

with the laws of the State of California and, as to matters affecting copyrights, trademarks and patents, by U.S. federal law. This statement sets forth the entire agreement between you and Inprise.

6. Use, duplication or disclosure by the Government is subject to restrictions set forth in subparagraphs (a) through (d) of the Commercial Computer-Restricted Rights clause at FAR 52.227-19 when applicable, or in subparagraph (c) (1) (ii) of the Rights in Technical Data and Computer Software clause at DFARS 252.227-7013, and in similar clauses in the NASA AR Supplement. Contractor/manufacturer is Inprise Corporation, 100 Enterprise Way, Scotts Valley, CA 95066.

7. You may not download or otherwise export or reexport the Software or any underlying information or technology except in full compliance with all United States and other applicable laws and regulations. In particular, but without limitation, none of the Software or underlying information or technology may be downloaded or otherwise exported or reexported (I) into (or to a national or resident of) Cuba, Haiti, Iraq, Libya, Yugoslavia, North Korea, Iran, or Syria or (ii) to anyone on the US Treasury Department's list of Specially Designated Nationals or the US Conmmerce Department's Table of Deny Orders. By downloading the Software, you are agreeing to the foregoing and you are representing and warranting that you are not located in, under control of, or a national or resident of any such country or on any such list.

8. INPRISE OR ITS SUPPLIERS SHALL NOT BE LIABLE FOR (a) INCIDENTAL, CONSEQUENTIAL, SPECIAL OR INDIRECT DAMAGES OF ANY SORT, WHETHER ARISING IN TORT, CONTRACT OR OTHERWISE, EVEN IF INPRISE HAS BEEN INFORMED OF THE POSSIBILITY OF SUCH DAMAGES, OR (b) FOR ANY CLAIM BY ANY OTHER PARTY. THIS LIMITATION OF LIABILITY SHALL NOT APPLY TO LIABILITY FOR DEATH OR PERSONAL INJURY TO THE EXTENT APPLICABLE LAW PROHIBILITS SUCH LIMITATION. FURTHERMORE, SOME STATES DO NOT ALLOW THE EXCLUSION OR LIMITATION OF INCIDENTAL OR CONSEQUENTIAL DAMAGES, SO THIS LIMITATION AND EXCLUSION MAY NOT APPLY TO YOU.

9. HIGH RISK ACTIVITIES. This Software is not fault-tolerant and is not designed, manufactured or intended for use or resale as on-line control equipment in hazardous environments requiring fail-safe navigation or communication systems, air traffic control, direct life support machines, or weapons systems, in which the failure of the Software could lead directly to death, personal injury, or severe physical or environmental damage ("High Risk Activities"). Inprise and its suppliers specifically disclaim any express or implied warranty of fitness for High Risk Activities.

To use this CD-ROM, your system must meet the following requirements:

Platform/Processor/Operating System.   IBM-compatible system running Windows 95/NT or better, with a Pentium 100 or better

RAM.   32 MB RAM (minimum)

Hard Drive Space.   100 MB hard drive space to install all of the trial software

Peripherals.   CD-ROM drive; Web browser installed to navigate the CD-ROM